This book argues that community can exist at the international level, that security politics is profoundly shaped by it, and that those states dwelling within an international community might develop a pacific disposition. By investigating the relationship between international community and the possibility for peaceful change, this book revisits the concept first pioneered by Karl Deutsch: "security communities." Leading scholars examine security communities in various historical and regional contexts: in places where they exist, where they are emerging, and where they are hardly detectable. Building on constructivist theory, the volume is an important contribution to international relations theory and security studies, attempting to understand the conjunction of transnational forces, state power and international organizations that can produce a security community.

Emanuel Adler is an Associate Professor at the Hebrew University of Jerusalem. He previously taught at the University of Wisconsin, the University of California at Berkeley, and the University of California at Davis. He is the author of *The Power of Ideology* (1987) and *Progress in Postwar International Relations* (1991).

Michael Barnett is a Professor at the University of Wisconsin, Madison, and has also taught at Macalester College, Wellesley College and the Hebrew University of Jerusalem. He is author of *Confronting the Costs of War: Military Power, State, and Society in Egypt and Israel* (1992), and *Dialogues in Arab Politics: Negotiations in Regional Order* (1998).

CAMBRIDGE STUDIES IN INTERNATIONAL RELATIONS: 62

Security Communities

Cambridge Studies in International Relations is a joint initiative of
Cambridge University Press and the British International Studies
Association (BISA). The series will include a wide range of material,
from undergraduate textbooks and surveys to research-based
monographs and collaborative volumes. The aim of the series is to
publish the best new scholarship in International Studies from
Europe, North America, and the rest of the world.

For a list of books in the series, see end of book.

Security Communities

edited by

Emanuel Adler

Department of International Relations
Hebrew University of Jerusalem

and

Michael Barnett

Department of Political Science
University of Wisconsin–Madison

CAMBRIDGE
UNIVERSITY PRESS

PUBLISHED BY THE PRESS SYNDICATE OF THE UNIVERSITY OF CAMBRIDGE
The Pitt Building, Trumpington Street, Cambridge CB2 1RP, United Kingdom

CAMBRIDGE UNIVERSITY PRESS
The Edinburgh Building, Cambridge CB2 2RU, United Kingdom
   http://www.cup.cam.ac.uk
40 West 20th Street, New York, NY 10011–4211, USA   http://www.cup.org
10 Stamford Road, Oakleigh, Melbourne 3166, Australia

© Cambridge University Press 1998

First published 1998

Printed in the United Kingdom at the University Press, Cambridge

Typeset in Palatino $10/12\frac{1}{2}$ pt [CE]

A catalogue record for this book is available from the British Library

ISBN 0 521 63051 7 hardback
ISBN 0 521 63953 0 paperback

Contents

Contents

Notes on contributors

Emanuel Adler is Associate Professor of International Relations at Hebrew University of Jerusalem. He received his Ph.D. from the University of California at Berkeley, previously taught at the University of Wisconsin, the University of California-Berkeley, at the University of California-Davis, and was a Fellow at the Center for Science and International Affairs, Harvard University. He is the author of numerous articles and books on international relations theory and international cooperation, including *The Power of Ideology* (1987); co-editor of *Progress in Postwar International Relations* (1991).

Michael Barnett is Professor of Political Science at the University of Wisconsin-Madison. He is the author of *Confronting the Costs of War: Military Power, State, and Society in Egypt and Israel* (1992), *Dialogues in Arab Politics: Negotiations in Regional Order* (1998), and articles on the United Nations and the Middle East. He has been a Council on Foreign Relations International Affairs Fellow and a MacArthur/SSRC International Peace and Security Fellow.

Amitav Acharya is Associate Professor in the Department of Political Science at York University, Toronto, and Research Fellow of the Centre for International and Strategic Studies at York and the University of Toronto–York University Joint Centre for Asia Pacific Studies. Previously he was a lecturer in the Department of Political Science, National University of Singapore and a Fellow of the Institute of Southeast Asian Studies, Singapore. His recent publications include *A New Regional Order in Southeast Asia: ASEAN in the Post Cold War Era*, (1993) and an edited volume (with Richard Stubbs), *New Challenges for ASEAN: Emerging Policy Issues* (1995).

F. Gregory Gause, III is Associate Professor of Political Science at the University of Vermont. He is the author of *Oil Monarchies: Domestic and Security Challenges in the Arab Gulf States* (1994) and *Saudi–Yemeni Relations: Domestic Structures and Foreign Influence* (1990), as well as numerous scholarly articles in journals and edited volumes.

Guadalupe Gonzalez is Professor of Political Science at the Centro de Investigacion y Docencia Economicas in Mexico City and is a doctoral candidate at the University of California–San Diego. She is the author of *The Drug Connection in US–American Relations* (1989) and various articles on US–Mexican relations. Her recent interests involve domestic sources of US–Mexican cooperation on drug control policy.

Stephan Haggard is Professor in the Graduate School of International Relations and Pacific Studies at the University of California, San Diego. He is the author of *Pathways from the Periphery: The Politics of Growth in the Newly Industrializing Countries* (1990), *The Developing Countries and the Politics of Global Integration* (1995), and co-author with Robert Kaufman of *The Political Economy of Democratic Transitions* (1995).

Richard A. Higgott is Professor of International Political Economy in the Department of Politics and International Studies at the University of Warwick, Coventry, England, and editor of *The Pacific Review.*

Andrew Hurrell is University Lecturer in International Relations and Fellow of Nuffield College. His major interests include international relations theory and the international relations of Latin America, with particular reference to the foreign policy of Brazil, regional integration, regional security issues, and US–Latin American relations. Publications include (co-editor with Benedict Kingsbury) *The International Politics of the Environment* (1992) and (co-editor with Louise Fawcett) *Regionalism in World Politics* (1995).

Kim Richard Nossal is Professor in the Department of Political Science at McMaster University, Hamilton, Ontario, Canada. From 1992 to 1997 he was editor of *International Journal*, the quarterly of the Canadian Institute of International Affairs. His books include *The Pattern of World Politics* (1988); *The Politics of Canadian Foreign Policy* (1987), now in its 3rd edition; *Rain Dancing: Sanctions in Canadian and*

Australian Foreign Policy (1994); *The Beijing Massacre: Australian Responses* (1993); and with Andrew Cooper and Richard Higgott, *Relocating Middle Powers: Australia and Canada in a Changing World Order* (1993).

Bruce Russett is Dean Acheson Professor of Political Science and Director of United Nations Studies at Yale University. He also edits the *Journal of Conflict Resolution*, and is past-president of the International Studies Association and the Peace Science Society (International). He has held visiting professorships at the Free University of Brussels, Tel Aviv University, and the University of Tokyo. His most recent books are *Grasping the Democratic Peace* and *The Once and Future Security Council*.

Sean M. Shore is a Ph.D. candidate at the University of Wisconsin-Madison, completing his dissertation on the development of stable peace in North America. His research interests include international relations theory, and the domestic sources of foreign policy.

Charles Tilly, after teaching at Delaware, Harvard, Toronto, Michigan, and the New School, now teaches social science at Columbia University. He works chiefly on social change and political processes with special reference to Western Europe and North America.

Ole Wæver is Senior Research Fellow at the Centre for Peace and Conflict Research at the University of Copenhagen, a lecturer at the Institute of Political Science, and a member of several policy advisory bodies in Denmark. His most recent books are *Concepts of Security* (1997), and *Security: A New Framework for Analysis* (1997). He was a MacArthur/SSRC International Peace and Security Fellow.

Acknowledgements

Several years have passed since we first talked about a project that would reconsider Karl Deutsch's venerable concept of security communities. This project, like all attempts to construct communities, intellectual, security, and otherwise, has gone through many different phases and received tremendous assistance and support from colleagues and institutions. We have accumulated quite a few debts along the way, and one of the real pleasures is to be able to thank those who have generously offered their criticisms and advice. In addition to the contributors to the volume, the project has benefited from timely and thoughtful comments from Hayward Alker, Michael Antolik, Richard Bilder, Ken Booth, Beverly Crawford, Daniel Deudney, Raymond Duvall, Richard Eichenberg, Ernst Haas, Ian Johnstone, Arie M. Kacowicz, Ethan Kapstein, Peter Katzenstein, Yuen Foong Khong, Keith Krause, Charles Kupchan, Leon Lindberg, Rob McCalla, Andy Moravcsik, James Morley, Donald Puchala, John Ruggie, Shmuel Sandler, Anne-Marie Slaughter, Richard Van Wagenen, Alexander Wendt, and Crawford Young. We also would like to thank Jeff Lewis for skillful assistance in the early stages of the project.

Finally, we acknowledge our debt to the original pioneers of the concept of security community: Karl Deutsch, Sidney Burrell, Robert Kann, Maurice Lee, Martin Lichterman, Raymond Lindgren, Francis Loewenheim, and, the scholar who coined the very concept, Richard Van Wagenen. At the very moment that the Cold War heated up, these scholars dared to imagine a world that might look different. They were ahead of their time, and we are finally catching up.

This project has been supported by two very generous organizations. The first workshop occurred in Madison, Wisconsin in March,

1994 and was funded by the Global Studies Program at the University of Wisconsin-Madison. We owe a special thanks to David Trubek and Jim Riker for their efforts. The second workshop was funded by the Carnegie Council on Ethics and International Affairs. Joel Rosenthal and Matt Mattern provided divine intervention for the project and were gracious hosts of our second meeting, which occurred in New York City at Merrill House in December, 1995. Their efforts were much appreciated and made possible the completion of this volume.

Emanuel Adler would like to thank the Davis Institute of International Relations at the Hebrew University of Jerusalem for financial support. Michael Barnett would like to thank the MacArthur Foundation/Social Science Research Council International Peace and Security Fellowship for its financial support. The names of the editors appear in alphabetical order for the book's title and the first two chapters, and in reverse order for the concluding chapter. This is to indicate the truly joint nature of their collaboration.

This volume is dedicated to our children, Shirli, Nadav, and Jonathan Adler, and Maya and Hannah Barnett.

Part I
Introduction and theoretical overview

1 Security communities in theoretical perspective

Emanuel Adler and Michael Barnett

Scholars of international relations are generally uncomfortable evoking the language of community to understand international politics. The idea that actors can share values, norms, and symbols that provide a social identity, and engage in various interactions in myriad spheres that reflect long-term interest, diffuse reciprocity, and trust, strikes fear and incredulity in their hearts. This discomfort and disbelief is particularly pronounced when they are asked to consider how international community might imprint international security. Although states might engage in the occasional act of security cooperation, anarchy ultimately and decisively causes them to seek advantage over their neighbors, and to act in a self-interested and self-help manner. The relevant political community, according to most scholars, is bounded by the territorial state, and there is little possibility of community outside of it.

This volume thinks the unthinkable: that community exists at the international level, that security politics is profoundly shaped by it, and that those states dwelling within an international community might develop a pacific disposition. In staking out this position we summon a concept made prominent by Karl Deutsch nearly forty years ago: "security communities."[1] Deutsch observed a pluralistic security community whenever states become integrated to the point that they have a sense of community, which, in turn, creates the assurance that they will settle their differences short of war. In short, Deutsch claimed that those states that dwell in a security community had created not simply a stable order but, in fact, a stable peace.

Deutsch's observations of forty years ago seem particularly relevant at the present moment because of changes in global politics and international relations theory. Ever since the end of the Cold War, policymakers have been offering various statements on and blueprints for engineering a more peaceful and stable international order. Perhaps this is to be expected; the ends of wars have almost always invited a flurry of commentary on the world that is being left behind and hopeful speculation on the world that should be created in its place. But what is unexpected is that many state officials are pointing to social forces and state interventions nearly identical to those remarked by Deutsch – the development of shared understandings, transnational values and transaction flows to encourage community-building – to conceptualize the possibility of peace. Many seasoned policymakers and hardened defense officials are marrying security to community in new and unanticipated ways: they identify the existence of common values as the wellspring for close security cooperation, and, conversely, anticipate that security cooperation will deepen those shared values and transnational linkages. Security is becoming a condition and quality of these communities; who is inside, and who is outside, matters most.

By marrying security and community, moreover, states are revising the conventional meanings of security and power. Some states are revising the concept of power to include the ability of a community to defend its values and expectations of proper behavior against an external threat and to attract new states with ideas that convey a sense of national security and material progress. Thus, as the meaning and purpose of power begins to shift, so, too, does the meaning and purpose of security. Whereas once security meant military security, now states are identifying "new" security issues that revolve around economic, environmental, and social welfare concerns and have ceased to concern themselves with military threats from others within the community. There is emerging a transnational community of *Deutschian* policy-makers, if you will, who are challenging the once nearly hegemonic position of realist-inspired policy-makers and offering an alternative understanding of what is possible in global politics and a map to get there.[2]

Scholars, too, seem to have finally caught up to Deutsch's vision. Looking into the possible, some are departing significantly from realist-based models to understand the present and future security debates; looking into the past, others have noted that the realist paradigm is better realized in theory than in practice, that states are not as war-prone as believed, and that many security arrangements once assumed to derive from balancing behavior in fact depart

4

significantly from realist imagery.[3] Accordingly, Deutsch's suggestion that states can overcome the security dilemmas and recurring fear assumed by realist theories is less shocking than it once was, and his understanding that the causal mechanisms for this outcome could be found in the development of social networks and the quickening of transnational forces is consistent with the return by some international relations theorists to sociological models. The concept of community represents a direct challenge to the models of security politics that have dominated the discipline for the past several decades, and demands that we take seriously both sociological theorizing and the social character of global politics. Simply put, the issue is not whether there is such a thing as an international community, but rather: when does it matter, where does it matter, and how does it matter?

Our nostalgia for security communities, therefore, is driven by changes occurring in, and theories of, international politics; both represent damaging blows to a realist paradigm that has dominated how policymakers and scholars alike think about international politics. Yet our nostalgia does not drive us toward romanticism. Notwithstanding the tremendous admiration we have for Deutsch's scholarly and political vision, his conceptualization of security communities was fraught with theoretical, methodological, and conceptual difficulties. Therefore, our resuscitation of Deutsch's concept of security communities after decades of neglect and criticism is intended both to draw attention to the concept's importance for understanding contemporary events and to suggest refinements of his initial formulation in order to generate a viable research program.

This volume aspires to demonstrate the empirical and theoretical viability of a research agenda founded on the concept of security communities. Deutsch distinguished between amalgamated and pluralistic security communities: while both have dependable expectations of peaceful change, the former exists when states formally unify, the latter when states retain their sovereignty. Our concern is with pluralistic security communities because it is this form that is theoretically and empirically closest to the developments that are currently unfolding in international politics and international relations theory. This volume sets forth a framework for approaching the study of security communities and then explores that framework in places where a security community is generally understood to exist, in places where scholars have identified trace elements, and even in some places where few would think to look. The theoretical and empirical contributions have the collective goal of: better identifying the conditions under which security communities are likely to emerge; focusing on the relationship between transnational forces and interactions, state power, and security politics in ways that depart from traditional realist readings of security politics; harnessing the conceptual architecture of a security community to offer an alternative look at regional interactions and their relationship to security practices; and using the rich case material to identify future directions for the security communities research agenda. In short, this volume represents not the final word but rather the first sustained effort to lay firm foundations for the study of security communities.

In this introductory chapter we do three things. First, we briefly discuss the origins of the concept of security community and situate that concept within the corpus of Karl Deutsch's intellectual thought. We then concisely survey different theoretical approaches to the conceptualization of a "stable peace." Various theories of international relations offer an explanation for the absence of war between states; most of these perspectives rely on the language of force or the establishment of institutions to maintain a stable peace. The Deutschian contribution is to highlight that states can become embedded in a set of social relations that are understood as a community, and that the fabric of this community can generate stable expectations of peaceful change. We conclude by providing an overview of the contents of this volume.

Origins of a concept

The concept of security community was always more celebrated than investigated. Initially proposed in the early 1950s by Richard Van Wagenen,[4] it was not until the pioneering 1957 study by Karl Deutsch and associates that the concept of security communities received its first full theoretical and empirical treatment. In their study, a security community was defined as a group of people that had become integrated to the point that there is a "real assurance that the members of that community will not fight each other physically, but will settle their disputes in some other way." Security communities, they observed, come in two varieties. An amalgamated security community exists whenever there is the "formal merger of two or more previously independent units into a single larger unit, with some type of common government after amalgamation."[5] Deutsch offers the

United States as an instance. Alternatively, a pluralistic security community "retains the legal independence of separate governments." These states within a pluralistic security community possess a compatibility of core values derived from common institutions, and mutual responsiveness – a matter of mutual identity and loyalty, a sense of "we-ness," and are integrated to the point that they entertain "dependable expectations of peaceful change."[6] It is a matter of sociological curiosity that in their quest for "social laws" that rule the relationship between integration and peace, Deutsch and his colleagues stumbled upon "half-baked" integrative processes that offered "a more promising approach to the elimination of war over large areas."[7]

At the heart of Deutsch's "pluralistic," "cybernetic," or "transactionalist" approach was the assumption that *communication* is the cement of social groups in general and political communities in particular. "Communication alone enables a group to think together, to see together, and to act together."[8] Moreover, communication processes and transaction flows between peoples become not only "facilities for attention" but factories of shared identification. Through transactions such as trade, migration, tourism, cultural and educational exchanges, and the use of physical communication facilities, a social fabric is built not only among elites but also the masses, instilling in them a sense of community, which becomes

> a matter of mutual sympathy and loyalties; of "we feeling," trust, and mutual consideration; of partial identification in terms of self-images and interests; of mutually successful predictions of behavior ... in short, a matter of a perpetual dynamic process of mutual attention, communication, perception of needs, and responsiveness in the process of decision making.[9]

To measure this "sense of community," Deutsch and his associates quantified transaction flows, with particular emphasis on their volume, within and among nation-states. A relative growth in transaction flows between societies, when contrasted to flows within them, was thought to be a crucial test for determining whether new "human communities" might be emerging.

Deutsch's "transactionalist" perspective, which takes seriously the possibility of community, offers an alternative understanding of international politics. Deutsch hypothesized that many of the same processes that led to national integration and nationalism in domestic politics might be equally relevant for international politics and inter-

7

national community development. This simple move was actually quite radical, placing him at odds with how international relations theory generally evaluates the international system. Whereas most international relations theories use material forces, the language of power, and a very thin conception of society to understand interstate outcomes, the Deutschian perspective relies on shared knowledge, ideational forces, and a dense normative environment. Yet Deutsch is not arguing that all interstate interactions can be characterized as transpiring within the same international environment. After all, states are embedded in different environmental contexts, and some interactions occur within a thick social environment and others in a world that approximates that envisioned by neo-realism. Therefore, it is important to problematize what most international relations theories assume: that the context of interstate interaction can be situated within one model of the international environment.[10]

Deutsch attempts to connect the development of international community to a transformation of security politics. Specifically, he locates the dynamics for peaceful change as the result of a transformation at the international and the individual level. At the international level, community formation is transforming the very character of the states system – some states are integrated to the point that peaceful change becomes taken for granted. By making this move, Deutsch challenges international relations theory's general reliance on atomistic models of interstate behavior, and forwards the central role of transnational forces in transforming the behavior, if not the very identities, of states. At the level of the individual, community formation leaves its mark on the development of a "we-feeling," trust, and mutual responsiveness, suggesting that transnational forces have altered the identities of peoples. The transmission belt of values, in other words, is located at the interstate and transnational levels. By daring to contemplate the possibility of community, Deutsch reminds us of how a sociological spirit can enrich our understanding of international politics and international security.

Despite its potential theoretical and practical importance, the concept of security community never generated a robust research agenda.[11] Deutsch's conceptualization of security communities contained various theoretical, conceptual, and methodological problems that undoubtedly scared off future applications. Deutsch looked to transactions as the source of new identifications, but his emphasis on quantitative measures overlooked the social relations that are bound up with and generated by those transactions. His commitment to behavioralism, in these and other ways, overwhelmed the demand for a more interpretive approach at every turn. And because his model was generally inattentive to international organizations and to social groups or classes, decision-makers, business elites, and the mixture of self-interest and self-image that motivates their behaviors, he was inattentive to the complex and causal way in which state power and practices, international organizations, transactions, and social learning processes can generate new forms of mutual identification and security relations.[12]

Another reason why the security community project failed to generate a following way was because scholars began adopting new theories and concerning themselves with new research puzzles that shifted the ground away from it. Increasingly scholars interested in ideas of regional integration and international cooperation used the vehicles of international interdependence, and, later, international regimes. Moreover, any talk of a community of states, not to mention a security community, seemed hopelessly romantic and vividly discordant against the backdrop of the Cold War and the prospect of nuclear war. Quickly distancing themselves from the sociological spirit of these studies, the discipline became enamored with structural realism, rational choice methods, and other approaches to political life that excluded identities and interests as phenomena requiring explanation. Deutsch's study was often cited but rarely emulated.

Between the "logic of anarchy" and the "logic of community"

It is a sign of the times that sociological theorizing and Deutsch's concept of security communities have become fashionable once again. That this is so can be attributed not only to the end of the Cold War but also to developments in international relations theory that are exploring the role of identity, norms, and the social basis of global politics. The manner of this sociological resurgence and return to the concept of security communities, however, suggests not simply "old wine in new bottles" but rather new theoretical developments that conceivably enable scholars to overcome some of the conceptual and methodological difficulties that undermined Deutsch's arrested research program of thirty years ago. Chapter 2 draws on these

theoretical developments to offer a reformulated conceptual apparatus for the study of security communities. Our immediate task is to
provide a brief survey of this emerging sociological disposition and its
relationship to Deutsch's focus on peaceful change.

Theories of international relations that explain the absence of war
can be categorized according to whether they see structure as comprised of material forces alone or of material and normative forces:

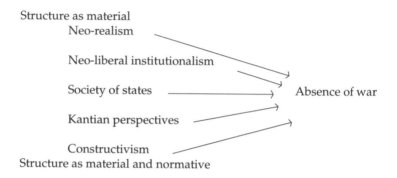

Structure as material
    Neo-realism

       Neo-liberal institutionalism

       Society of states   Absence of war

       Kantian perspectives

       Constructivism
Structure as material and normative

Viewed visually, international relations theories can be arrayed on a
continuum depending on how "social" they conceive the international
environment as being. On one end is realism, which assumes that the
structure of international politics is defined by the distribution of
power and thus a highly asocial environment, and observes a series of
discrete, exchange relations among atomistic actors. On the other end is
constructivism's recognition that international reality is a social construction driven by collective understandings, including norms, that
emerge from social interaction. Constructivism, therefore, holds the
view that international actors are embedded in a structure that is both
normative and material (that is, contains both rules and resources), and
allows for the possibility that under the proper conditions actors can
generate shared identities and norms that are tied to a stable peace.
Below we briefly consider their position *vis-à-vis* the possibility of the
absence of war in general and stable peace in particular.

Neo-realist and realist theories stress the notion that while war does
not take place all the time, like rain, it is always expected. If war does
not occur, it is because balances-of-power, alliances, hegemonies, and
deterrence are able to prevent it, though only temporarily.[13] Stephen
Walt explicitly rejects the proposition that states might overcome the
fears and dynamics associated with anarchy, and argues that it is

unclear how a shared "civic identity" will inhibit conflict. Groups sharing similar traits and values are hardly immune to discord: indeed, "family quarrels" are often especially bitter and difficult to resolve. "Shared identity" is a weak reed on which to rest a forecast in any case, given the malleability of changing loyalties and the speed with which they can change.[14]

By beginning with the assumption of anarchy and that states are driven by self-interest as defined by military security, neo-realists hold that the absence of war can be only temporary and solely attributable to material considerations.[15]

Neo-liberal institutionalism and the "English school" focus on how states construct institutions to encourage cooperation and to further their mutual interest in survival, respectively.[16] Those neo-liberal institutionalists who cut their teeth on integration dynamics in general and Europe in particular have once again picked up many of the themes once explored by Deutsch and other early integrationists.[17] Although neo-liberal institutionalists are focusing on many of the same variables discussed by Deutsch, their general commitment to how self-interested actors construct institutions to enhance cooperation prevents them from considering fully how: a community might be forged through shared identities rather than through pre-given interests and binding contracts alone; or, interstate and transnational interactions can alter state identities and interests. While neo-liberal institutionalism shares with neo-realism the assumption of anarchy, it is more interested in how self-interested states construct a thin version of society through the guise of institutions and regulative norms in order to promote their interests.

Although Hedley Bull, the dean of the English School, once portrayed security communities as "pregnant with implications of a general international relations,"[18] the English School generally focused not on peaceful change but rather on the norms of society of states, which includes sovereignty and admits balancing behavior and conflicts, that create an "anarchical society." Still, some who follow the English school have recently been flirting with the concept of security communities; specifically, they have resurrected the concept to imagine "islands" of international society that achieve the status of "mature anarchy"[19] or "zones of peace"[20] due to their high interaction capacity and dense networks of common rules and institutions. In short, they are interested in how the society of states (or, more specific, certain states) might "upgrade" its norms from the recognition of each other's right to survival (which does permit the occasional war) to the normative prohibition against, and the empirical decline of, war. In many respects, these scholars are moving fairly close to Deutsch's position, though still weighting their equation toward interstate interactions and away from transnational forces.[21]

The burgeoning literature on the "pacific thesis" – that democratic states do not wage war among each other – revives classic liberalism and Kantian Republicanism, and attempts to trace how international trade and domestic politics, respectively, affects foreign policy orientation.[22] As one leading interpreter of the Kantian perspective observed:

> to use or threaten to use force is not usually normatively acceptable behavior in disputes among democracies ... Relations between democracies therefore fit into the category of ... "security community" ... in which states not only do not fight each other, they do not expect to fight each other, or significantly prepare to fight each other.[23]

Frequenting their arguments are a combination of both rationalist and normative claims concerning the incentives and restraints on state leaders by their societies and the international system. However, they limit their analyses to democracies who are assumed to possess certain essentialized qualities and therefore omit from their purview the possibilities that a stable peace might also emerge among non-democracies.

Constructivist scholars have been most prominent in resurrecting Deutsch's concept of security community: urging that international relations scholarship recognize the social character of global politics; forwarding the need to consider the importance of state identities and the sources of state interests; suggesting that the purposes for which power is deployed and is regarded as socially legitimate may be changing; and positing that the cultural similarities among states might be shaped by institutional agents. Consequently, constructivist scholarship is well-suited to consider how social processes and an international community might transform security politics.[24]

This is not the place to detail the constructivist ontology, epistemology, and methods. Here it will suffice to say that constructivism, which should be clearly distinguished from non-scientific post-structuralist approaches, takes the social world to be emergent and constituted both by knowledge and material factors. Far from denying a reality to the material world, constructivists claim that how the material world shapes, changes, and affects human interaction, and is affected by it, depends on prior and changing epistemic and normative interpretations of the material world.[25] In doing so, they have been actively forwarding a theoretical agenda that holds out the possibility for the transformation of global politics as a consequence of changes in domestic, transnational, and interstate forces, and offers an alternative look at security politics and practices.

This abbreviated survey suggests that there are many possible explanations for the absence of war. Neo-realism relies on the language of force and deterrence. Neo-liberal institutionalism, though sharing with neo-realism many key assumptions, takes a more optimistic view because of its attention to the conditions under which states might establish a stable set of norms and institutions to further their shared interests. In this way, neo-liberal institutionalism and the English School share some key traits, though the willingness of some scholars to contemplate the presence of a global society that runs beneath or beside an international society introduces the possibility of community and a more sociological flavor. The Democratic Peace literature has by definition coupled the absence of war to a particular type of state and thus has narrowed considerably the Deutschian framework. The concept of security communities posits the possible relationship between the growth of a community and pacific relations, and offers a more exacting and demanding explanation of a stable peace, but also more fully opens up the sociological bottle.

The Deutschian challenge and promise is to conceptualize international politics as holding out the possibility of international community and to consider how it might imprint international security. By doing so it raises a number of defining issues concerning how we think about, approach, and study international relations theory and security politics. First and perhaps most controversially, it dares to contemplate the possibility of international community. While much of international relations theory has a difficult time doing so because of the assumption that the boundaries of community are both filled and limited by the borders of the state, as Charles Tilly reminds us in this volume, world politics have always had differing forms of transnational networks that can be reasonably understood as international communities.[26] To recognize this possibility, however, requires a willingness not only to look beyond the state for forms of political community and association (after all, realist thought assumes a political community but presumes that it is exhausted by the state's territorial borders) but also to adopt a sociological spirit.

Secondly, the study of security communities demands an examination of the relationship between transnational forces, state power, and security politics in novel ways. The growing transnational literature has been examining how and under what conditions transnational forces shape interstate practices and international politics, but heretofore has generally shied away from the "meatier" side of international politics, that is, security.[27] To make the connection between growing transnational networks and transformations in security practices, however, requires taking state power seriously. While various duties and domains might be slowly pried from the hands of the state in this era of diminishing sovereignty and downsizing, the provision of external security rest securely in its grasp. The issue at hand, therefore, is to focus on state power without overshadowing the presence of transnational forces that might encourage states to adopt a different security architecture.

Thirdly, the Deutschian focus on transactions brings us squarely back to processes and interactions: interactions between societies and interactions between states.[28] Although much of international relations theory focuses on structure to understand enduring patterns, Deutsch focused on processes and interactions that emerged between states and societies to understand historical change. Transactions and interactions, he suggested, generate reciprocity, new forms of trust, the discovery of new interests, and even collective identities. The essays in this volume illustrate how the study of security communities must focus on how strategic and patterned interactions between states and societies can represent the wellspring of new normative structures, identities, and interests that are more collective and less particularistic.

Fourthly, the study of security communities has implications for our theories of international politics as it demands a willingness to overcome the stale and artificial realist–idealist divide. By examining the dynamic relationship between state power, international organizations and institutions, and changes in security practices, the study of security communities offers a blend of *idealism* – which recognized state interests but also envisioned the possibility of progress and a promise for institutions in helping states overcome their worst tendencies – and *realism*, whose main proponents saw the worst but continued to write about the conditions under which there might be peaceful change and new forms of political organization. Theories of international politics, therefore, can and should occupy a pragmatic middle ground between the view that identities and international practices cannot change, and the view that everything is possible. They should be able to blend power, interests, and pessimism with norms, a dynamic view of international politics, and moderate optimism about the possibility of structural change that enhances human interests across borders.[29]

Such considerations, in our view, are consistent with and contribute to the constructivist research program – though we want to emphasize that not everyone in the volume would place themselves in this camp. States are still attentive to their interests and their power. But what state interests are or become, and the meaning and purpose of power, take shape within – and are constituted by – a normative structure that emerges and evolves due to the actions and interactions of state and non-state actors. The "problem of order" in international affairs, therefore, might be better addressed by situating norms alongside the realist presumption of force. Said otherwise, by exploring the relationship between structure, social interactions, and the possible transformation of that structure that leaves its mark on security practices, the security community research program can be seen as an effort to enrich, and provide further evidence of the potential insights of, the constructivist approach to international relations.

Understanding security communities

This volume aspires to demonstrate the conceptual dexterity of the concept of security community, to use this concept to investigate the historical experiences of different regions and different time periods, and to use these historical cases to reflect on and further refine the security community research agenda. Therefore, the volume attempts to cover as much territory – geographic, historical, and conceptual – as possible. But not everything could be included in one volume.

The case selection was motivated by three defining criteria. First, we desired to assemble a fairly representative geographical sample, one that moved the scope of the study of security communities away from its traditional Northern Atlantic focus and toward non-Western regions. Said otherwise, the concept of security community has been tied to the pioneering locale, and we desired to discover whether this concept "travels"[30] and how other historical regions demonstrate

alternative patterns and dynamics that can contribute to and compli-
cate our knowledge of security communities. To that end, there are
chapters on: Southeast Asia, which is frequently identified as a
possible security community in a non-democratic context; South
America, whose remarkable century-long record of rather pacific
interstate relations predates the European security community and
broadens our understanding of the normative and material factors
involved in the development of security communities; US–Mexican
relations, which suggests the possibility of a security community in a
highly asymmetrical setting; and the Gulf Arab states, which is better
understood as a paragon of realism than as an instance of community,
but nevertheless identifies some conditions that might foster the
development of a security community. In general, our desire is to
contribute to the fields of international relations theory and security
studies by demonstrating how the concept of security community
helps us to understand the security politics in different regions. To
achieve that goal requires not an exhaustive region-by-region search
but rather a regional and historical sampling.

Secondly, we desired to get a sample of regions that conceivably
were at different phases in the development of a security community.
We include some regions that are uncontested security communities –
Europe and North America; others that are perhaps at half-way points
– the Association of South East Asian Nations (ASEAN); and still
others that show some signs but are generally understood as laboratories for realism – the Gulf Cooperation Council (GCC). By examining different regions in terms of their phase in the development of a
security community, we can begin to compare the unfolding of a
security community on developmental grounds. In doing so, there is
no assumption that there is a single pathway or series of phases that
states must hurdle to construct a security community. But it makes
good methodological sense at the early stages of a research program
to proceed abductively and with some well-defined benchmarks to
generate some tentative comparisons. In short, this volume looks for a
geographical representation and a conceptual sampling.

Thirdly, by forwarding the cases of the Organisation for Security
and Cooperation in Europe (OSCE) and the United Nations, we
begin to consider how international organizations might contribute
to the development of regional and global security communities.
States are not the only actors in international politics, and international organizations are increasingly active in asserting their own

which main aimly to develop transnational linkages, to form regionalized identities, and to advance the cause of peace. Other regional organizations that are discussed in this volume, including the European Union, NATO, and ASEAN also further our understanding in this regard. But the OSCE and the UN are particularly noteworthy because their officials are quite explicit and self-conscious about their desire to nurture a transnational community because of its security implications. Our hope is that this volume provides something of an intellectual inspiration for other scholars to use the concept of security communities for regions and dimensions that we do not cover.

In chapter 2 Adler and Barnett outline the conceptual foundations of a security community. To begin to meet the Deutschian challenge and fulfill its promise requires better specifying the conditions under which the development of a transnational community might translate into pacific relations. We detect many more proclamations of security communities in recent years than we think are warranted, and part of the task is to separate the wheat from the chaff and to better assess empirically and theoretically when and under what conditions security communities are likely to emerge. To this end we proceed in three parts. We begin with an examination of a host of concepts, including international community and dependable expectations of peaceful change, that are central to the security community research enterprise. This conceptual stock-taking and reformulation is intended to overcome some of the problems of Deutsch's original design. We then present a framework for the study of the emergence of security communities that is analytically organized around three "tiers": (1) precipitating conditions; (2) process variables (transactions, organizations, and social learning) and structural variables (power and knowledge); and (3) mutual trust and collective identity. The positive and dynamic interaction between process variables and structural variables undergirds the development of trust and collective identity formation, which, in turn, drives dependable expectation of peaceful change. Afterwards we present a heuristic model of three phases in the development of a security community – "nascent," "ascendant" and "mature" and their corresponding indicators. This framework guides and provides a critical benchmark for the essays in this volume.

Ole Wæver opens the empirical studies with an analysis of the "classic" security community: Western Europe. Wæver contends that

Western Europe became a security community as a consequence of "desecuritization," a progressive marginalization of mutual security concerns in favor of other issues. He captures this transformation through the concept of a "speech act" – that security refers to the enunciation of something as security – and examines how the development of collective identity and community came through a process of discursive self-formation. Indeed, Western Europe has become a post-sovereign, neo-imperial entity, made of a European Union core and several concentric political circles around it. Thus, what began as an effort to exclude war in Western Europe, ended up as a "multi-perspectival"[31] entity. But Wæver suggests that a security community that can be constructed can also be deconstructed. He points to two bits of evidence: there are emergent processes of resecuritization that are a consequence of Europeans transforming integration into a matter of security and, consequently, disintegration a matter of insecurity; because the security community was socially constructed from the state outward, different states incorporated different and potentially contradictory constitutive meanings of "Europe" into their own national identities.

In chapter 4 Emanuel Adler examines the OSCE's security community-building functions and highlights how its activities and practices are working to spread new norms and establish collective transnational identities and mutual trust. Although the OSCE region, from Vancouver to Vladivostok, is not a security community, Adler contends that the OSCE's legacy resides in its innovative norms and trust-building practices. These norms and practices helped to bring the Cold War to a peaceful conclusion, and since the end of the Cold War they constitute a new model of "comprehensive," "indivisible," and "cooperative" security that grounds dependable expectations of peaceful change on "mutual accountability," shared identity, and mutual trust. An important feature of these developments is what Adler calls "seminar diplomacy," which integrate academic expertise and diplomatic discourse. Seminar diplomacy has become one of the OSCE's main instruments for transnational dialogue, and a principal mechanism for teaching norms and practices of cooperative security that allow state elites and civil societies to identify with each other and construct common understandings. It is noteworthy that other European and non-European organizations have begun to emulate the OSCE's practices and institutional reforms in order to foster cooperative security, trust, and common understandings.

The states of the Gulf Cooperation Council, argue Michael Barnett and F. Gregory Gause III in chapter 5, would never be mistaken for a security community. But the concept of security community sheds some light on the GCC, and the GCC illuminates some subterranean processes associated with security communities. First, given the similarities among the member states and their common security agenda, more progress in community-building could have been expected. Among the various reasons why cooperation failed to deepen is because these states could not create common expectations concerning non-interference in each other's domestic politics. Secondly, what began as an organization that denied its security function soon turned into a multifaceted entity that was an agent and result of many of the processes and developments that are associated with a security community. Specifically, while at the level of interstate cooperation the history of the GCC is less than glorious, at the level of transnational cooperation and transactions there developed a bustling and increasing traffic that, they argue, is traceable to the existence of the organization. At the level of the regime these countries made some modest moves toward a deepening of interstate cooperation, but seemingly always blocked if not undone by mistrust and suspicion. At the level of societies and transnationalism, however, there have been considerable developments that suggest sustained and deepened cooperation and mutual identification that are detectable in the emergence of a "khalijiin" (literally, "residents of the Gulf") identity. Barnett and Gause cannot predict whether and how this increasingly salient Gulf identity will translate into interstate behavior and dependable expectations of peaceful change, but they do suggest that an important condition for a security community has been fostered by the GCC.

In chapter 6 Amitav Acharya examines the Association of South East Asian Nations. That the members of ASEAN have managed to settle their disputes without the resort to violence for the last three decades has encouraged various scholars of the region to proclaim it a security community. Acharya finds that this claim is unwarranted; nevertheless, he concludes that the solid foundations for a security community have been built. But the case of ASEAN raises some additional concerns regarding the study of security communities. Perhaps most pressing is the presumption that security communities are possible only among liberal states. But the ASEAN states, Acharya notes, have been able to undertake a community-building project without liberalism; therefore, he interrogates whether liberalism is a necessary condition for security communities. Moreover, there is a growing ASEAN identity that represents a potential source of collective identity. The ASEAN case also points to the importance of domestic rather than systemic security concerns, and shows how this internal security dynamic led to a particular set of ASEAN practices. To this end, region-building was a highly self-conscious exercise determined not only to increase economic and political transactions but also to encourage elite socialization in order to manage conflict. Acharya then identifies the various factors that have contributed to collective identity formation, including the importance of conflict resolution as an identity-conferring practice.

Is South America a security community? South America has had relatively few wars over the last century, and such accomplishments have led many to speculate whether and why it is a security community. In chapter 7 Andrew Hurrell evaluates this claim and focuses on the relations between South America's principal powers, Brazil and Argentina, spanning three historical periods over the last three decades. Hurrell begins by noting the dramatic shift in relations over the last decade, from rivalry to institutionalized security and economic cooperation. On the security front this cooperation involves, for example, arms control and confidence-building measures; on the economic front it involves, for example, an attempt to integrate the economies of Argentina, Brazil, Paraguay and Uruguay. While structural constraints and power-based decisions played a role, to understand the development of new identities and interests that were instrumental in producing this shift requires a constructivist approach.

This is so for four reasons. First, most protracted conflicts between Argentina and Brazil took place against a background of shared understandings and established legal and diplomatic institutions that placed a brake on conflict spirals. Secondly, the process of democratization during the second and third periods led Argentina and Brazil to modify their understandings of power, autonomy, and independence in ways that facilitated regional cooperation and imprinted their identities. Thirdly, a shift toward market liberalism in the Southern Cone in the 1980s was accompanied by a collective understanding that only by means of regional association would South America be able to confront the challenges posed by economic globalization and technological change. This realization was also accompanied by a growing appreciation that regional cooperation and integration may be the key to control nationalism and militarism and, therefore, to maintain domestic peace. Finally, cooperation was also fostered by the emergence of new regional habits of cooperation, such as summit meetings of Heads of State, and the bundling of new security-producing practices to a Latin American identity and democratic practices.

Hurrell believes that stable expectations of non-use of force, non-fortified borders, and institutionalized habits of dialogue between the military establishments of Argentina and Brazil indicate that a security community may already exist between these two states. Moreover, a security community seems to be embedded in an increasingly dense process of economic integration and in the idea of a "club of states" to which only some governments are allowed to belong, and cooperative security becomes the symbol of democratic identity and the end of old rivalries. However, Hurrell cautions that Argentina and Brazil still face many constraints and that, so far, there is little evidence of the kind of "mutual responsiveness" that Deutsch referred to in the past. Although Hurrell considers that Chile, Paraguay, and Uruguay are prospective members of the Argentine–Brazilian security community, he also claims that the rest of Latin America is still too anchored in traditional power politics to be understood as a security community.

In contrast to the other essays that study a region or a dyad, in chapter 8 Richard Higgott and Kim Richard Nossal demonstrate how the focus on a single state, Australia, can illuminate some important features of a security community. Specifically, they highlight Australia's potentially dual identities that derive from the Anglo-American world of Australia's past and the Asia-Pacific world of Australia's economic future. Higgott and Nossal argue that Australia is shifting its economic and political interests from the old to the new world, and, therefore, from one security community – the alliance between Australia, New Zealand, and the United States – to another, more nascent, and more ambiguous, community in Asia. As a consequence of Australia's identity and policy shift, and due to the belief of Australia's elites that "community" exists in the Asia-Pacific region, policy-makers, and most enthusiastically, Gareth Evans, began to attach an increasing importance to multilateralism, regionalism, and "cooperative security" practices. Yet they also find that Australian elites have difficulty including a security dimension in this relocation;

the Asian states are equally hard-pressed to see Australia as a *bona fide* Asian state and easily amendable to an "Asian Way." Higgott and Nossal conclude that Australia is presently "condemned" to continue in this uncertain condition and that it is unclear whether it will be able to find a home in an Asia-Pacific security community.

In chapter 9 Guadalupe Gonzalez and Stephan Haggard support Deutsch's classic assertion that the United States and Mexico became a security community in the early 1940s. At the same time, this community has been chronically weak because the relationship is not supported by trust and a shared identity; in this respect it does not meet the definition of a security community outlined by Adler and Barnett in chapter 2. According to Gonzalez and Haggard, no security community can emerge between two asymmetrical powers, such as the United States and Mexico, unless it is based on structural convergence – the extent to which the weaker party adopts policies that are conducive to the stronger party. A historical analysis of the United States–Mexican relationship across three different periods demonstrates, however, that convergence showed no linear trend across time or issues. First, and most fundamentally, the relationship suffered from perceptions by the United States that Mexico is political unstable and thus unreliable. Secondly, the frequent unwillingness and capacity of Mexico to protect the property rights and economic interests of the United States further undermined the relationship. Thirdly, "cross-border externalities" (negative but unintentional consequences that arise from proximity) between the United States and Mexico, such as drug-flows, environmental problems, and immigration, have decreased the level of mutual trust. Finally, despite Mexico's new economic aperture and more cosmopolitan foreign policy, the asymmetry in bilateral relationship, the vulnerability associated with proximity, high interdependence, and domestic political constraints have all helped to maintain a low level of trust.

NAFTA did little to change this situation. To be sure, NAFTA led to: Mexico's increasing commitment to free trade with the United States and Canada; the creation of a dense network of consultative and dispute-settlement institutions; and the increasingly cooperative ties between subnational governments, private organizations and sectors. Yet NAFTA has no provisions for macroeconomic policy cooperation, did not improve the two countries' segmented cooperation over drug-trafficking and illegal immigration, and has had no appreciative effect on its increasingly militarized border. Gonzalez and Haggard conclude that although force appears to have been ruled out as a means of settling disputes, the main reason that the United States–Mexican relationship has not sparked the level of trust that is consistent with a security community is that Mexico has not achieved something resembling a modern democratic political form. But, they argue, cooperative relations need not be institutionalized to produce desirable levels of mutual trust; in fact, the historical record suggests that United States–Mexican relations were less conflictual when they were less institutionalized.

In chapter 10 Sean Shore begins his study of US–Canadian relations in a way that would make a realist smile: he notes the power politics that drove the relationship and informed their security practices. But because of various historical circumstances and geopolitical developments – and not because of a sense of community – the US–Canadian border became demilitarized. This demilitarized border then became part of the mythology of their relations, the future symbol of their shared collective identity. In other words, only after a radical change in security relations did there develop a collective identity and a denser network of economic, political, and cultural relations, reversing the presumed logic under which a security community develops. Shore's analysis of U.S.-Canadian relations offers an excellent example of how demilitarization and the development of stable peace because of structural-realist reasons came prior to the development of shared identity. But once the myth of the "longest unfortified border" took hold, there developed a bustling transnationalism and mutual identification that completed the development of a security community.

In chapter 11 Bruce Russett finds that the United Nations articulates what he calls a neo-Kantian perspective, one that now interweaves a narrative concerning the relationship between democracy, interdependence, and pacific relations. Such a perspective was part of the tradition of the United Nations and many other post-World War II organizations, but it has become particularly pronounced following the end of the Cold War. This neo-Kantian perspective is a tribute not only to the shifting fortunes of geopolitics but also to the civil servants, most notably the former Secretary-General Boutros-Ghali, who articulate a causal relationship between economic interdependence, democracy, and peace. To that extent, UN officials are self-consciously attempting to build democracies, promote economic interdependence, and encourage region-building because of their supposed relationship to pacific relations. Russett further argues, however, that if the UN is successfully to perform this function then it must overcome its institutional weaknesses and reform the various organs so that they obtain greater legitimacy and authority. Only with a modicum of institutional legitimacy will the UN be able to compel states to follow and adopt the values that it espouses.

In chapter 12 Charles Tilly provides a sociological and historical backdrop to the subject of security communities by briefly unpacking the question of community, the issue of how communities come into existence, and how communities provide for the security of their members. Drawing from the network literature, he provides a sophisticated defense of the use of the concept of community, a concept long thought *passé* in sociological theory. In doing so, he is able to imagine different types of transboundary communities that have existed over history and can be understood as having created a stable peace.

In the concluding chapter, Barnett and Adler weave the conceptual framework with the various contributions to tease out some general propositions concerning the study of security community, to identify some shortcomings, and to consider some future avenues of research. They conclude by reflecting on how the recognition that security communities are socially constructed offers some guidance for thinking about governing anarchy in theory and practice.

Notes

1 *Political Community and the North Atlantic Area* (Princeton: Princeton University Press, 1957).
2 Richard K. Ashley, "The Geopolitics of Geopolitical Space: Toward a Critical Social Theory of International Politics," *Alternatives* 12, 14 (1987), pp. 403–434.
3 Emanuel Adler, "Europe's New Security Order: A Pluralistic Security Community," in Beverly Crawford, ed., *The Future of European Security* (Berkeley: University of California, 1992), pp. 287–326; Emanuel Adler, "Seasons of Peace: Progress in Postwar International Security," in E. Adler and B. Crawford, eds., *Progress in Postwar International Relations* (New York: Columbia University Press, 1991), pp. 133–134; Peter Katzenstein, ed., *The Culture of National Security: Norms and Identity in World Politics* (Columbia: Columbia University Press, 1996); Patrick Morgan, "Multilateralism and Security: Prospects in Europe," in J. Ruggie, ed., *Multilateralism Matters* (New York: Columbia University Press, 1993), pp. 327–364; Steve Weber, "Shaping the Postwar Balance of Power: Multilateralism in NATO," in J. Ruggie, ed., *Multilateralism Matters*, pp. 233–292; and Paul

Schroeder, "The New World Order: A Historical Perspective," *The Washington Quarterly* 17 (1994), pp. 25–43.

4 Donald J. Puchala, *International Politics Today* (New York: Dodd, Mead, 1971), p. 165.

5 Deutsch et al., *Political Community*, p. 6.

6 Deutsch et al., *Political Community*, p. 5. See also by Deutsch: *Nationalism and Social Communication* (Cambridge, MA: MIT Press, 1953); *Political Community at the International Level: Problems of Measurement and Definition* (New York: Doubleday, 1954); *Politics and Government* (Boston: Houghton-Mifflin, 1970); and his essays in Philip E. Jacob and James V. Toscano, eds., *The Integration of Political Communities* (Philadelphia: Lippincott, 1964), "Communication Theory and Political Integration," pp. 46–74, "Transaction Flows as Indicators of Political Cohesion," pp. 75–97, "The Price of Integration," pp. 143–178, and "Integration and the Social System," pp. 179–208.

7 Deutsch et al., *Political Community*, pp. 30–31. Ernst Haas similarly argues that "modern nation-states" can be thought of "as communities whose basic consensus is restricted to agreement on the *procedure* for maintaining order and settling disputes among groups, for carrying out well-understood functions." *Beyond the Nation-State* (Stanford: Stanford University Press, 1964), p. 39.

8 Norbert Wiener as cited in Karl W. Deutsch, *The Nerves of Government* (New York: The Free Press, 1966), p. 77.

9 Deutsch et al., *Political Community*, p. 36.

10 This is consistent with Robert Powell's observation that whether states are or are not relative gains seekers is an effect of the structure. "Anarchy in International Relations Theory: The Neorealist-NeoLiberal Debate," *International Organization* 48 (Spring 1994), pp. 337-38. Also see David Lake, "Anarchy, Hierarchy, and the Variety of International Relations," *International Organization* 50, 1 (Winter, 1996), pp. 1–33.

11 The closest approximations of the security community approach were represented by the regional and integration studies of the period, which elevated the importance of values, learning, and socialization, how separate political communities interacted, merged, and unified. As exemplified in Joseph Nye's *Peace in Parts: Integration and Conflict in Regional Organization* (Boston: Little, Brown, 1971), there was an emerging sense that self-identified and selected regions might organize their relations in such a way to promote their self-interests and a sense of collective interest, and even perhaps collective identity. See, also, Ernst B. Haas, *The Uniting of Europe* (Stanford: Stanford University Press, 1958); and Leon Lindberg and Stuart Scheingold, eds., "Regional Integration: Theory and Research," special issue of *International Organization* 24, 4 (Autumn 1970). These literatures, too, eventually yielded to a barrage of damaging blows. Karl Deutsch himself drew the conclusion that European integration had effectively stopped by 1958. See "Integration and Arms Control in the

European Political Environment: A Summary Report," *American Political Science Review* 60 (June 1966), pp. 354–365.

12 For fuller critiques of the original formulation, see Emanuel Adler and Michael Barnett, "Pluralistic Security Communities: Past, Present, Future." *Working Paper on Regional Security,* No. 1 (Global Studies Research Program, University of Wisconsin, 1994); and Emanuel Adler and Michael Barnett, "Security Communities in Comparative and Historical Perspective," paper presented at a conference sponsored by the Carnegie Conference on Ethics and International Affairs, December 1–2, 1995. Also see Arend Lijphart, "Karl W. Deutsch and the New Paradigm in International Relations," in Richard L. Merritt and Bruce M. Russett, eds., *From National Development to Global Community: Essays in Honor of Karl W. Deutsch* (London: George Allen and Unwin, 1981), p. 246; and Donald J. Puchala, "Integration Theory and the Study of International Relations," in ibid., p. 157.

13 See Kenneth Waltz, *Theory of International Politics* (Reading, MA: Addison-Wesley, 1979); Barry Buzan, *People, States, and Fear,* 2nd edn (Boulder, CO: Lynne Reinner); and John J. Mearsheimer "The False Promise of International Institutions," *International Security,* 19 (Winter, 1994/95), pp. 5–49. See Richard Ned Lebow, "The Long Peace, the End of the Cold War, and the Failures of Realism," *International Organization,* 48, 2 (1994), pp. 252–259, for a good overview and criticism of the neo-realist focus on the role of force for understanding international stability and change. On the polarity debate, see Kenneth Waltz, "The Stability of the Bipolar World," *Daedelus* 93 (Summer 1964), pp. 881-909; and Emerson Niou and Peter Ordershook, "Stability in Anarchic International Systems," *American Political Science Review* 84 (December 1990), pp. 1207–34. On hegemonies, see Robert Gilpin, *War and Change in World Politics* (New York: Cambridge University Press, 1981). On balances of power, see Kenneth Waltz, *Theory of International Politics,* ch. 6.

14 "Commentary: Is there a Logic of the West?" *World Policy Journal* 11, 1 (1994), p. 118.

15 Realism should be understood as being much more sophisticated and theoretically supple than is presupposed by many neo-realist interpreters; this is particularly so as the original realist formulations were much more willing to entertain the possibility of a stable peace and the role of international institutions and norms for shaping the behavior of states. Some realists have stressed the notion that diplomatic prudence may momentarily achieve a truce. Hans J. Morgenthau, *Politics among Nations,* 4th edn (New York: Knopf, 1968). Reinhold Niebuhr saw the creation of a world community realized through daily practices and actions rather than through lofty ideals, and imagined that it would come into existence when there was mutual loyalty and trust rather than mutual dependence. *The World Crisis and American Responsibility* (New York: Association Press, 1950), pp. 80–86. And E. H. Carr opened and closed his pathbreaking *The*

Twenty Years' Crisis: 1919–1939 (NY: Harper Books, 1964) with strong statements concerning the possibility of peaceful change.

16 The outstanding works are, respectively, Stephen Krasner, ed., *International Regimes* (Ithaca: Cornell University Press, 1983), and Hedley Bull, *The Anarchical Society* (New York: Columbia University Press, 1977).

17 For example, see Richard N. Rosecrance, "Trading States in a New Concert of Europe," in Helga Haftendorn and Christian Tuschhoff, eds., *America and Europe in an Era of Change* (Boulder; CO: Westview Press, 1993), pp. 127–146.

18 Hedley Bull, "The Theory of International Politics, 1919-1969," in Brian Porter, ed., *The Aberystwyth Papers: International Politics, 1919-1969* (London: Oxford University Press, 1972), pp. 42–43.

19 Barry Buzan, "From International System to International Society: Structural Realism and Regime Theory Meet the English School," *International Organization* 47 (Summer 1993), pp. 327–352.

20 Arie Kacowicz, *Zones of Peace in the Third World: South America and West Africa in a Comparative Perspective* (Albany, New York: State University of New York Press, forthcoming).

21 However, some commentators of the English School contend that it makes the ontological claim that a "global society," which can be roughly equated with an international community, is one of the three "levels" of global politics alongside systemic and societal forces. See Richard Little, "Neorealism and the English School: A Methodological, Ontological, and Theoretical Assessment," *European Journal of International Relations* 1, 1 (1995), pp. 9–37; Chris Brown, "International Theory and International Society: The Viability of the Middle Way?" *Review of International Studies* 21 (April, 1995), pp. 183–96; and Chris Brown, "International Political Theory and the Idea of World Community," in Ken Booth and Steven Smith, eds., *International Relations Theory Today* (University Park, PA: Pennsylvania State Press, 1995), pp. 90–109.

22 Michael W. Doyle, "Kant, Liberal Legacies, and Foreign Affairs," *Philosophy and Public Affairs* 12 (Spring 1983), pp. 205–235; and 12 (Summer 1983), pp. 323–353; Bruce Russett, *Grasping the Democratic Peace* (Princeton: Princeton University Press, 1993); Zeev Maoz and Bruce M. Russett, "Normative and Structural Causes of Democratic Peace, 1946-86," *American Political Science Review* 87 (1993), pp. 624-638; John M. Owen, "How Liberalism Produces Democratic Peace," *International Security* 19 (1994), pp. 87-125; James L. Ray, "Wars Between Democracies: Rare or Nonexistent?," *International Interactions* 18 (1993), pp. 251–276.

23 Russett, *Grasping the Democratic Peace*, p. 42.

24 See Alex Wendt, "Anarchy is What States Make of It: The Social Construction of Power Politics," *International Organization* 46 (Spring 1992), pp. 391–425; Alex Wendt, "Collective Identity Formation and the International State," *American Political Science Review* 88 (June 1994), pp. 384–396; Emanuel Adler, "Cognitive Evolution: A Dynamic Approach for the

Study of International Relations and Their Progress", in Adler and Crawford, eds., *Progress in Postwar International Relations*; Ernst B. Haas, *When Knowledge is Power* (Berkeley: University of California Press, 1990); John Ruggie, "Territoriality and Beyond: Problematizing Modernity in International Relations," *International Organization* 47 (Winter 1993), pp. 161, 174; and Peter Katzenstein, ed., *Culture of National Security: Norms and Identity in World Politics* (NY: Columbia University Press, 1996).

25 For overviews, see Emanuel Adler, "Seizing the Middle Ground: Constructivism and World Politics," *European Journal of International Relations* 3, 3 (1997), pp. 319–363; Emanuel Adler, "Cognitive Evolution"; Wendt "Collective Identity Formation," pp. 384–396; Alex Wendt, "Constructing International Politics," *International Security* 20, 1 (Summer, 1995), pp. 71–81; and Ronald Jepperson, Alexander Wendt, and Peter Katzenstein, "Norms, Identity, and Culture in National Security," in P. Katzenstein, ed., *Culture of National Security* (NY: Columbia University Press, 1996), pp. 33–77. A highly accessible yet philosophically sophisticated introduction to social constructionism is John Searle's *The Construction of Social Reality* (NY: Free Press, 1995).

26 On this point, see Andrew Linklater, "The Problem of Community in International Relations Theory," *Alternatives* 2, 2 (Spring 1990), pp. 135–153, and Andrew Hurrell, "International Society and the Study of Regimes: A Reflective Approach," in Volker Rittberger, ed., *Regime Theory and International Relations* (Oxford: Clarendon Press, 1993), pp. 61–65.

27 See, for instance, Thomas Risse-Kappen, ed., *Bringing Transnational Relations Back In* (NY: Cambridge University Press, 1995).

28 For a comparable plea, see Fred Halliday, "State and Society in International Relations: A Second Agenda," *Millennium* 16 (1987), pp. 215–230.

29 Adler, "Cognitive Evolution," p. 75.

30 Giovanni Sartori, "Concept Misinformation in Comparative Politics," *American Political Science Review*, 64 (December, 1970), pp. 1033–1053.

31 Ruggie, "Territoriality and Beyond."

2   A framework for the study of security communities

Emanuel Adler and Michael Barnett

Security communities never generated much of a research program. Foundering on various theoretical, conceptual, and methodological brakers, the concept of security communities remained largely admired from afar. This chapter aspires to fulfill the initial promise of the security communities agenda by offering a reconstructed architecture. The presented framework benefits from the best of Deutsch's original conceptualization and corrects for its shortcomings by borrowing from four decades of substantial insights from sociological and international relations theory and various empirical studies that were informed by the concept of security communities.

This chapter is organized in the following way. The first section begins by offering a conceptual vocabulary for the study of security community. One of the virtues of the study of security communities is also one of its vices: it raises a host of important but potentially intractable concepts such as community, dependable expectations of peaceful change, governance, institutions, and on and on. Therefore, this section begins to provide a conceptual and definitional map. The second section presents a framework for studying the emergence of security communities that is analytically organized around three "tiers." The first tier consists of precipitating factors that encourage states to orient themselves in each other's direction and coordinate their policies. The second tier consists of the "structural" elements of power and ideas, and the "process" elements of transactions, international organizations, and social learning. The dynamic, positive, and reciprocal relationship between these variables leads to the third tier: the development of trust and collective identity formation. The sequenced and causal relationship between these three tiers is responsible for the production of dependable expectation of peaceful change. Section III takes another step toward a viable research program by offering a heuristic model of three phases in the development of a security community – "nascent," "ascendant" and "mature" and their corresponding indicators. This architecture attempts to reinvigorate the security communities agenda and guides the empirical studies of this volume.

A conceptual vocabulary

We are concerned with pluralistic and not amalgamated security communities. We define a pluralistic security community as a transnational region comprised of sovereign states whose people maintain dependable expectations of peaceful change. Pluralistic security communities can be categorized according to their depth of trust, the nature and degree of institutionalization of their governance system, and whether they reside in a formal anarchy or are on the verge of transforming it. These categories provide the basis for distinguishing between two ideal types, loosely and tightly coupled pluralistic security communities.[1]

Loosely-coupled security communities observe the minimal definitional properties and no more: a transnational region comprised of sovereign states whose people maintain dependable expectations of peaceful change. Owing to their shared structure of meanings and identity, members of loosely coupled security communities expect no bellicose activities from other members and, therefore, consistently practice self-restraint. Tightly coupled security communities, however, are more demanding in two respects. First, they have a "mutual aid" society in which they construct collective system arrangements. Secondly, they possess a system of rule that lies somewhere between a sovereign state and a regional, centralized, government; that is, it is something of a post-sovereign system, endowed with common supranational, transnational, and national institutions and some form of a collective security system.[2] This system of rule, while reminiscent of medieval heteronomy due to its "pooled" sovereignty, is a relatively novel development in global politics. In general, we (like Deutsch) are interested in the transnational and interstate interactions that can produce a transnational community with a governance structure that is linked to dependable expectations of peaceful change.

The distinctive feature of a security community is that a stable peace is tied to the existence of a transnational community. But what defines a community? There are probably as many definitions of political communities as there are actual communities. This conceptual looseness only feeds into the traditional skepticism of scholars of international politics when asked to consider whether global politics has any characteristics that resemble a community. After all, states usually maintain that their actions are performed in the interest of the wider community when, in fact, they derive from much more selfish concerns. But their well-founded cynicism has diminished in recent years as they increasingly acknowledge that there is a social basis to global politics, and that this social basis might have characteristics that resemble a community.[3] Sociologists, too, who can be credited with attempting to give the concept more rigor and then distancing themselves from its somewhat imprecise and confusing applications, have become more interested in identifying the conditions under which groups of actors form relations that can be theoretically and empirically catalogued as communities.[4] Charles Tilly's contribution speaks to these themes and draws from network analysis to argue for a more empirically and conceptually tractable view of community.

A community is defined by three characteristics.[5] First, members of a community have shared identities, values, and meanings. "Common meanings are the basis of community," writes Charles Taylor. "Intersubjective meaning gives a people a common language to talk about social reality and a common understanding of certain norms, but only with common meanings does this common reference world contain significant common actions, celebrations, and feelings. These are objects in the world everybody shares. This is what makes community."[6] Secondly, those in a community have many-sided and direct relations; interaction occurs not indirectly and in only specific and isolated domains, but rather through some form of face-to-face encounter and relations in numerous settings. Thirdly, communities exhibit a reciprocity that expresses some degree of long-term interest and perhaps even altruism; long-term interest derives from knowledge of those with whom one is interacting, and altruism can be understood as a sense of obligation and responsibility.

These last two points highlight how interest-based behavior continues to exist among members of the community. Ferdinand Tonnies's famous distinction between association and community – where the former admits self-interest and the latter denies it – has created the unfortunate impression that actors within communities do not have or act on their interests.[7] Although actors will come to identify with each other and derive many of their interests and beliefs from the social fabric of the group, they also will continue to harbor distinct interests, interests can generate competitive behavior, and competition can lead to conflict. Perhaps a better way of capturing the distinction between association and community is not whether there is or is not self-interested behavior but rather: the degree of diffuse reciprocity, where associations are distinguished by immediate reciprocity and communities have diffuse reciprocity; and the extent to which the actor's interests are interchangeable with those of the group. Therefore, while states within a security community are likely to exhibit rivalry and other interactive interactions associated with mixed-motive games, they no longer fear the use of violence as a means of statecraft and to settle their disputes.

These three defining qualities of a community can exist at the local, the domestic, or the international level. Simply stated, there is no *a priori* reason why they should be limited to the territorial state; a point succinctly and theoretically made by Tilly in this volume.[8] To be sure, there are good historical reasons why these qualities are more likely to reside at the domestic level; obviously networks, interactions, and face-to-face encounters have generally been limited to relatively short distances. But, again, this is a contingent claim and allows for the possibility that these elements may emerge at the international level under the right conditions. Such conditions, argue many social scientists, might be already present because technological developments and economic forces have radically transformed the international environment and made possible different forms of communication and identification previously unavailable, unimagined, and sometimes undesired. Indeed, some sociologists have argued that recent technological developments can facilitate the development of a sense of community among people "who are not physically co-present."[9] Note that classical realists made the radical distinction between the "community" that exists on the inside versus the "anarchy" that exists on the outside based on their observations regarding the formal organization of international and domestic politics. But the qualities that the classical realists used to demarcate the existence of a community at the domestic level could conceivably exist at the international level. Indeed, founding realists like E. H. Carr and Reinhold Niebuhr entertained this very possibility and imagined the conditions under which a sense of community might emerge in global politics.[10]

Recognizing that communities develop around networks, interactions, and face-to-face encounters that are not dependent on inhabiting the same geographic space reconceptualizes the very idea of regions. Most scholars, Deutsch included, have understandable difficulty identifying precisely where one region ends and another begins; yet they tend to define regions on the basis of geography because of the assumption that proximity generates common interests that derive from a common culture, economic circumstances, and security concerns. But individuals can organize and define themselves based on markers that are not necessarily tied to space, suggesting something of an "imagined region," or a "cognitive region."[11] The end of the Cold War, the collapse of the Soviet Union, NATO enlargement eastward, and the debate over "where is Europe?" dramatically highlights that regions are socially constructed and are susceptible to redefinition. The notion of the "family of democracies" suggests that democracies can be grouped as a region. The Organization of American States (OAS) Santiago Declaration of June 1991 essentially separates the organization's democratic states from others, and nearly claims that this represents a separate region. Security communities, in this reading, might emerge between noncontiguous states. The US–Israeli relationship can be conceptualized as a security community, and Australia is a member of the Western security community even though it resides thousands of miles from the "core" members; both cases suggest how a shared identity need not be tied to contiguous space.[12] In general, look for communities where actors have shared identities, values, and meanings, many-sided relations, and long-term reciprocity – and allow for the possibility that those characteristics can exist at the international level and even among non-contiguous states.

Different communities will establish different mechanisms to handle and regulate conflict within the group.[13] Some communities will develop dependable expectations of peaceful change – but many will not. In other words, while all political communities will contain norms to regulate their security and to foster order, there is no reason to assume (as Deutsch did) that they will generate the assurance of nonviolent dispute settlement. "'Communities,' as anthropologists well know, contain conflict; this may not make them any less "communities" to those who live in terms of them."[14] Some communities, in fact, might be thought of as "war communities." In this regard, the conflict mechanisms that emerge might very well be an expressive component of the individual's identity. To be a member of the community of democratic states in the contemporary era, for instance, requires certain war-avoidance practices. In general, what distinguishes a security community from other kinds of communities is that its members entertain dependable expectations of peaceful change.

This outcome – dependable expectations of peaceful change – can be best analyzed in its two companion elements. First, dependable expectations can be explained by different theories of social interaction. Stable expectations can result from either: (a) actors with pre-given interests and preferences, i.e., rationalist theories that are modeled after market behavior such as neo-realism and neo-liberal institutionalism; or (b) actors with shared identities, whose very identities and interests are shaped by their environment, i.e., sociological and interpretive theories such as those offered by Deutsch and by constructivists. As discussed in chapter 1, different theoretical approaches generate different explanations for the absence of war. But where rationalist and sociological theories can equally contemplate a condition of "non-war" that derives from the instrumental decisions designed to advance their immediate security and economic interests, only sociological theories allow for the possibility that interstate interactions can transform the identities and interests of states and induce dependable expectations of peaceful change. In other words, the "thickness" of the social environment does more than merely describe, it also explains the emergence of dependable expectations among people who, while organized around states, nevertheless come to share a transnational space. In general, while peaceful change might be explained through the language of power politics and the calculation of expected material benefits to be derived from a course of action, the sociological approach adopted here isolates knowledge, learning, and the existence of norms that emerge from both interstate practices and, more fundamentally, transnational forces.

Peaceful change can be best defined as neither the expectation of nor the preparation for organized violence as a means to settle interstate disputes. A reasonable assumption, therefore, is that states do not undertake – indeed, do not consider – security actions that can be interpreted by others within the community as militarily threatening. Therefore, security communities can exist in the absence of well-developed strategic ties or a formal alliance, but in any case there are tacit and/or formal normative prohibitions against states settling their disputes through military means.[15] How long must the community resolve its conflicts short of war before one can proclaim the existence of a security community? Do states have to exist within a pacific setting for ten years? twenty years? pass through two traumatic crises without waging war or suggesting the hint of war? Deutsch answered these questions in the following manner: "Integration is a matter of fact, not of time. If people on both sides do not fear war and do not prepare for it, it matters little how long it took them to reach this stage. But once integration has been reached, the length of time over which it persists may contribute to its consolidation."[16] Integration, which Deutsch included as one of the definitional properties of security community's "dependable expectations of peaceful change," exists at nearly any moment that both sides do not fear war or prepare for it. By answering in this manner, Deutsch was attempting to find a middle ground between two positions: that a security community that comes and goes with the night will be of little interest to most scholars, and might, in fact, be nothing more than an alliance; and that it makes little theoretical sense to erect some arbitrary passage of time to proclaim a security community. We can do no better than Deutsch other than to note that evidence of a security community should be sought not only in behavior that suggests the renunciation of military violence but also in the existence of deeply entrenched habits of the peaceful resolution of conflicts.

We may conceive the habits and practices of the peaceful resolution of conflicts, and the shared norms on which they are based, as a crude governance structure. Governance can be best defined as activities backed by shared goals and intersubjective meanings that "may or may not derive from legally and formally prescribed responsibilities and that do not necessarily rely on police powers to overcome defiance and attain compliance."[17] Deutsch, however, expected that political communities will have some degree of cohesion and coherence among a population that is generated not only from self-enforcement mechanisms from below but also by enforcement mechanisms from above. This distinction strikes us as crucial; indeed, a security community that depends heavily on enforcement mechanisms is probably not a security community. Security communities can count for compliance on the acceptance of collectively-held norms, however, because some of these norms are not only regulative, designed to overcome the collective action problems associated with interdependent choice, but also constitutive, a direct reflection of the actor's identity and self understanding.[18]

This suggests, moreover, that security communities will rely for their governance structures not only on an understanding of their member states' behavior in the international sphere but also on a reading of their domestic behavior and arrangements. In other words, a security community's governance structure will depend both on the state's external identity and associated behavior and its domestic characteristics and practices.[19] Deutsch and other early explorers of security communities focused on the interstate practices and transnational forces that created the assurance that states would not settle their differences through war. Yet equally important is that states govern their domestic behavior in ways that are consistent with the community.

Any discussion of a governance structure, particularly in the context where states have created a stable peace, raises obvious questions regarding the meaning of sovereignty and authority. While states comprising a security community are still sovereign in a formal-legalistic sense, their sovereignty, authority, and legitimacy is contingent on the security community in two respects. First, while a security community does not erode the state's legitimacy or replace the state, the more tightly coupled a security community is the more the state's role will be transformed. In other words, if in a pre-social environment the state's role is limited to and understood as "protector of the national good," the emergence of a transnational civic community will expand the role of the state as it becomes an agent that furthers the various wants of the community: security, economic welfare, human rights, a clean environment, and so on.

Secondly, the conditions under which the state is viewed as part of the community and given certain rights, obligations, and duties, depend on its ability to abide by the region's normative structure.[20] Because members of a community receive their very legitimacy and authority to act from the community, they frequently share their authority in certain spheres with the larger community. Hence, states in a tightly coupled arrangement, while retaining their juridical sovereign status toward the outside world, can be seen as *agents* of the transnational community. "This means that states can express their agency insofar as they meet and reproduce the epistemic and

36

normative expectations of the community. States remain 'free agents,' acting on the basis of their own preferences, as long as these preferences are cognitively framed by the shared understandings of the community."[21] Therefore, while people remain nationals of their respective states, they also become "citizens" of the community. These considerations are more relevant for tightly coupled than for loosely coupled security communities. In both cases, though, the emergence of a security community admits a governance structure that encourages states and their peoples to expect peaceful change.

States can become embedded in a set of social relations that can be properly understood as a community. Sometimes a community of states will establish pacific relations, sometimes a community will not. But those that do have formed a security community. Security communities are relatively rare developments, though their very existence has been made conceptually invisible because of the dominance of realist theories of international security. The obvious challenge is to isolate the conditions under which the development of a community produces dependable expectations of peaceful change.

The conceptual foundations of security communities

To answer this challenge we proceed in a highly stylized manner, building deductively from past research and inductively on recent empirical studies that attempt to delineate the factors contributing to peaceful change. Specifically, our framework is organized around three tiers. The first tier concerns the precipitating conditions. The second tier examines the positive, dynamic, and reciprocal relationship between the structure of the region, defined by material power and knowledge, and social processes, defined by organizations, transactions, and social learning. These dynamics create the conditions for the third tier: mutual trust and collective identity formation. This model can be diagrammed as in figure 2.1 on page 38.

Tier One

Because of exogenous or endogenous factors states begin to orient themselves in each other's direction and desire to coordinate their

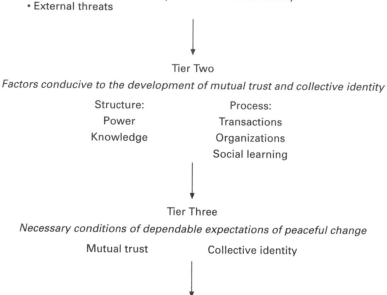

Tier One

Precipitating conditions

• Change in technology, demography, economics, the environment
• Development of new interpretations of social reality
• External threats

Tier Two

Factors conducive to the development of mutual trust and collective identity

Structure: Process:

Power   Transactions

Knowledge   Organizations

                             Social learning

Tier Three

Necessary conditions of dependable expectations of peaceful change

Mutual trust   Collective identity

Dependable expectations of peaceful change

Figure 2.1   The development of security communities

relations. Technological developments, an external threat that causes states to form alliances, the desire to reduce mutual fear through security coordination, new interpretations of social reality, transformations in economic, demographic and migration patterns, changes in the natural environment, these and other developments can propel states to look in each other's direction and attempt to coordinate their policies to their mutual advantage. There is no expectation that these initial encounters and acts of cooperation produce trust or mutual identification; but because they are premised on the promise of more pleasant and more numerous interactions, they provide the necessary conditions for these very possibilities. In general, states have an incentive to promote face-to-face interactions, dialogue, and policy coordination for any number of reasons; such developments can, at the least, allow states to achieve pareto superior outcomes, and, at the most, provide the context for the development of new social bonds. The more general implication is that security communities are likely to exhibit equafinality: common endpoints can have very disparate beginnings.

Tier Two

Perhaps the defining feature of this tier is that states and their peoples have become involved in a series of social interactions that have begun to transform the environment in which they are embedded. The task, then, is to isolate the structural context in which states are embedded and that shape their interactions, and how these interactions begin to transform their "possible roles and possible worlds."[22] To simplify matters and to present the materials in ways that are consistent with past international relations scholarship, we divide this tier into the "structural" categories of power and knowledge and the "process" categories of transactions, international organizations and institutions, and social learning. The dynamic, positive, and reciprocal relationship between these variables provides the conditions under which a collective identity and mutual trust can form, without which there could not be dependable expectations of peaceful change.

Structure. Power and knowledge are the structural girders for the development of a security community.[23] Past theoretical work and empirical studies suggest that power is central for understanding their development. According to Deutsch, "larger, stronger, more politically, administratively, economically, and educationally advanced political units were found to form the cores of strength around which in most cases the integrative process developed."[24] We also hypothesize that power plays a major role in the development and maintenance of security communities. Power conventionally understood can be an important factor in the development of a security community by virtue of a core state's ability to nudge and occasionally coerce others to maintain a collective stance. Yet power can be alternatively understood as the authority to determine shared meaning that constitutes the "we-feeling" and practices of states and the conditions which confer, defer, or deny access to the community and the benefits it bestows on its members. In other words, power can be a magnet; a community formed around a group of strong powers creates the expectations that weaker states that join the community will be able to enjoy the security and potentially other benefits that are associated with that community. Thus, those powerful states who belong to the core of strength do not create security *per se*; rather, because of the positive images of security or material progress that are associated with powerful and successful states, security communities develop around them. For instance, the former Eastern bloc states have not waited for the "Club of Europe" to extend invitations, they have invited themselves.

Knowledge also constitutes part of the international structure, and in this instance we are interested in cognitive structures, that is, shared meanings and understandings. In other words, part of what constitutes and constrains state action is the knowledge that represents categories of practical action and legitimate activity. In recent years international relations theorists have become interested in how such shared meanings are created out of practice and social interactions, but to simplify matters here we are interested in those cognitive structures that facilitate practices that are tied to the development of mutual trust and identity, and analytically tied to conflict and conflict resolution.[25] Deutsch offered little guidance on this issue because he descriptively established the connection between liberal democracy and market values and the formation of the North Atlantic community, and failed to consider whether there might be other ideas that are compatible with the development of peaceful change. In other words, part of the structural backdrop of Deutsch's study concerns the fact that these North Atlantic states shared certain ideas concerning the meaning of markets and democracy that were implicitly tied to a system of practices that facilitated transactions and, eventually, trust.

At the present moment if scholars of international politics are likely to identify one set of political ideas and meanings that are related to a security community it is liberalism and democracy.[26] To demonstrate that liberalism is a necessary condition for the formation of security communities, however, requires demonstrating how liberal ideas are more prone than are other ideas for the promotion of a collective identity, mutual trust, and peaceful change.[27] More simply, what is it about the quality of the ideas themselves – rather than the mere fact that they are shared – that leads people who reside in different territorial spaces to feel secure from organized violence in a liberal security community?

Two related hypotheses might account for connection between liberalism and security communities. First, liberal ideas are more prone to create a shared transnational civic culture, whose concepts of the role of government, tolerance, the duty of citizens, and the rule of law may shape the transnational identity of individuals of the community. Secondly, liberal ideas may be better able to promote strong civil societies – and the networks of organized processes between them – through the interpenetration of societies and the exchange of people, goods, and ideas. Yet other intersubjective ideas may also account for the formation of security communities. For example, a shared developmentalist ideology, perhaps similar to that pursued by Southeast Asian states, may promote not only transnational exchanges and policy coordination, but, more fundamentally, a shared project – characterized by increasing amount of transactions and the development of common institutions; in doing so, such exchange and this shared project might conceivably promote collective purposes around which emerge a shared identity and, thereafter, dependable expectations of peaceful change. In general, the causal connection between a particular set of ideas and the development of security communities must be theoretically and empirically demonstrated rather than simply asserted.

Process. The process categories involve transactions, international organizations and institutions, and social learning. A transaction can be defined as a "bounded communication between one actor and another."[28] A transaction, therefore, admits various types of exchanges, including symbolic, economic, material, political, technological, and so on. The more intensive and extensive transactions are related to the concept of "dynamic density," "the quantity, velocity, and diversity of transactions that go on within society."[29] According to Emile Durkheim, dynamic density is able to create and transform social facts. In this respect, social facts do not depend on material resources alone, but also on collective experience and human consensus. Thus, a qualitative and quantitative growth of transactions reshapes collective experience and alters social facts.

International organizations and institutions contribute directly and indirectly to the development of security communities. Following Oran Young, we differentiate between social institutions and formal organizations by defining social institutions as "social practices consisting of easily recognized roles coupled with clusters of rules or conventions governing the relations among the occupants of these roles," and organizations as "material entities possessing physical locations, offices, personnel, equipment, and budgets."[30] Although social institutions might have a concrete organizational expression, it is important not to conflate the two.

Institutions and organizations can be categorized as part of process. At first blush this move may seem puzzling. After all, a key constructivist point is that norms, rules and institutional contexts constitute actors and constrain choices; and international relations theory conventionally treats international institutions as constraints on state actions. But institutions and organizations may be depicted either as structures or as processes. As Alexander Wendt observes,

> Although theories of structure explain how structures regulate and/ or constitute practices and interactions, and as such are essentially static even if they reveal transformative possibilities within a structure, [t]heories of process explain how practices and interactions reproduce and/or transform structures, and as such are essentially dynamic even if what they explain is reproduction rather than transformation.[31]

Because we are interested in the development of security community, which involves a consideration of the conditions under which and the media that makes possible the transformation of social relations, we are attentive to and attempt to isolate the actors that are not only constituted by that structure but also might transform it.

The interest in examining how international organizations and institutions indirectly promote other factors that contribute to, and directly promote, mutual trust, shared identity elevates four issues. First, security and non-security organizations can contribute to the development of trust. At the most intuitive level, they facilitate and encourage transactions and trust by: establishing norms of behavior, monitoring mechanisms, and sanctions to enforce those norms.[32] But to the the extent that economic institutions contribute to an overall development of trust, they can have a security-related function and be instrumental to the development of a security community. The role of economic organizations and institutions as furthering this pacific propensity is one of the enduring principles of neo-functionalism and a hallmark of Deutsch's framework. In general, a key concern here is with how organizations and institutions encourage transactions and the development of trust.

Secondly, international organizations make possible state action by virtue of their trust-building properties. But their trust-building properties extend beyond their monitoring capacities, for they also can encourage actors to discover their preferences, to reconceptualize who they are, and to reimagine their social bonds. Organizations, in this important respect, are sites of socialization and learning, places where political actors learn and perhaps even "teach" others what their interpretations of the situation and normative understandings are. Because identities are created and reproduced on the basis of knowledge that people have of themselves and others, learning processes that occur within and are promoted by institutions can lead actors to develop positive reciprocal expectations and thus identify with each other.

Thirdly, international organizations may be conducive to the formation of mutual trust and collective identities, because of their often underestimated capacity to "engineer" the very conditions – for example, cultural homogeneity, a belief in a common fate, and norms of unilateral self-restraint[33] – that assist in their development. International organizations, for instance, may be able to foster the creation of a regional "culture" around commonly held attributes, such as, for example, democracy, developmentalism, and human rights. And they may be able to promote regional projects that instill belief in a common fate, such as, for example, a common currency; and/or generate and enhance norms and practices of self-restraint, such as, for example, mediation.

Behind every innovative institution stand creative and farsighted political elites. Political elites that are connected to international organizations use them to promote new possibilities. Deutsch's relative lack of attention to institutional agents, and, indeed, to political elites and even charismatic individuals, was a crucial shortcoming that we wish to correct. As John Hall argues, while "the creation of new social identities by intellectuals – that is, their capacity to link people across space so as to form a new community – is necessarily a rare historical phenomenon," it is one that scholars of international relations need to take seriously. [34] While communication between peoples, learning processes, and the thickening of the social environment plays a crucial role in the evolution of political communities, these are but propensities until agents transform them into political reality through institutional and political power.

Such matters highlight the critical role of social learning, which can be described as an active process of redefinition or reinterpretation of reality – what people consider real, possible and desirable – on the basis of new causal and normative knowledge.[35] In this respect, social learning is more than "adaptation" or "simple learning," that is, when political actors choose more effective means of achieving ends as a response to changes in the international environment.[36] Social learning represents the capacity and motivation of social actors to manage and even transform reality by changing their beliefs of the material and social world and their identities. In this critical respect, it explains why norms and other cognitive and cultural categories that are tied to a collective identity, interests, and practices, are transmitted from individual to individual and nation to nation, are internalized by individuals and are institutionalized in the halls of governments and in society. While social learning can occur at the mass level, and such changes are critical when discussing collective identities, our bias is to look to policymakers and other political, economic, and intellectual elites that are most critical for the development of new forms of social and political organization that are tied to the development of a security community.

Social learning plays a critical role in the emergence of security communities, and is facilitated by transactions that typically occur in organizational settings, and core powers. First, during their transactions and social exchanges, people communicate to each other their self-understandings, perceptions of reality, and their normative expectations.[37] As a result, there can occur changes in individual and collective understandings and values. To the extent that they promote shared normative and epistemic criteria and provide a fertile ground for the transmission of practices, transactions are essential feature for the development of collective learning and collective identities.

Secondly, learning often occurs within institutionalized settings. Institutions promote the diffusion of meanings from country to country, may play an active role in the cultural and political selection of similar normative and epistemic understandings in different countries, and may help to transmit shared understanding from generation to generation.

Thirdly, social learning may not be sufficient for the development of a security community unless this learning is connected to functional processes that are traceable to a general improvement in the state's overall condition. This is why core powers are so important to the process. States that possess superior material power, international legitimacy, and have adopted norms and practices that are conducive to peaceful change tend to confer increased material and moral authority to the norms and practices they diffuse and, thus, may also induce their political adoption and institutionalization. Indeed, while this process entails power projection and even hegemony,[38] it cannot come to fruition without active socialization and social learning. Said otherwise, social learning frequently occurs through a communicative exchange in the context of power asymmetries. That said, even those asymmetrical relationships can involve a situation where "teachers" and "students" negotiate a new regional collective identity around consensual norms and mutual understandings.

In general, social learning explains why transactions and institutional actions can encourage the development of mutual trust and collective identity. By promoting the development of shared definitions of security, proper domestic and international action, and regional boundaries, social learning encourages political actors to see each other as trustworthy. And it also leads people to identify with those who were once on the other side of cognitive divides.

The structural and process conditions are necessary for the development of mutual trust and collective transnational identities. Understanding how these variables effect the development of mutual trust and the creation, transformation, and reproduction of collective identities, requires, however, that we take full cognisance of their dynamic and reciprocal interactions. Trust, for instance, may be promoted by institutions that significantly increase the number and quality of transactions, which, in turn, further the diffusion of norms. And the emergence of collective identities may be prompted by learning processes that occur within institutionalized settings, and subsequently lead to changes in cognitive structures. In any event, the processes that develop are critical for the development of a security community.

Tier Three

The dynamic and positive relationships among the variables we described above are the wellsprings of both mutual trust and collective identity, which, in turn, are the proximate necessary conditions for the development of dependable expectations of peaceful change. Trust and identity are reciprocal and reinforcing: the development of trust can strengthen mutual identification, and there is a general tendency to trust on the basis of mutual identification. That said, because a minimal measure of mutual trust is needed for a collective identity to develop, trust logically comes prior to identity. Once some measure of trust develops, however, a collective identity is likely to reinforce and increase the depth of trust.

Trust can best be understood as believing despite uncertainty. Barbara Mistzal nicely captures this essential feature of trust in the following way:

> Trust always involves an element of risk resulting from our inability to monitor others' behavior, from our inability to have complete knowledge about other peoples' motivations and, generally, from the contingency of social reality. Consequently one's behavior is influenced by one's beliefs about the likelihood of others behaving or not behaving in a certain way rather than solely by a cognitive understanding or by a firm and certain calculation.[39]

Trust is a social phenomenon and dependent on the assessment that another actor will behave in ways that are consistent with normative expectations. Often times trust is facilitated by third-party mechanisms, as discussed in the previous section, but the social construction of trust shifts our attention to the beliefs that we have about others, beliefs that, in turn, are based on years of experiences and encounters.

When international relations theorists turn their attention to trust they generally elevate how anarchy makes trust highly elusive if not impossible. This is one reason why states establish international organizations and other means to monitor the behavior of others – "trust, but verify" as Ronald Reagan famously quipped. But the development of a security community – the very existence of dependable expectations of peaceful change – suggests that states no longer rely on concrete international organizations to maintain trust but do so through knowledge and beliefs about the other. For instance, democratic nuclear powers do not feel threatened by each other's nuclear weapons; even when in 1965 France withdrew from the NATO integrated command and insisted on maintaining an independent nuclear force, other NATO allies did not interpret this as a military threat against their physical survival. But these same countries are quite concerned when Iraq or Iran are feared as developing a nuclear weapons program. Identification of friend or foe, the social basis of trust, is a judgement based on years of experiences and encounters that shapes the cultural definition of the threat. Uncertainty, in such matters, is generated not by technological capabilities or its absence but by knowledge founded on mutual identification and trust.

Although there are many definitions of identity, most begin with the understanding of oneself in relationship to others.[40] Identities, in short, are not only personal or psychological, but are social, defined by the actor's interaction with and relationship to others; therefore, all political identities are contingent, dependent on the actor's interaction with others and place within an institutional context. This relational perspective informs the view that national and state identities are formed in relationship to other nations and states – that the identities of political actors are tied to their relationship to those outside the boundaries of the community and the territory, respectively.[41] To be sure, not all transactions will produce a collective identity; after all, interactions are also responsible for creating an "other" and defining threats. Therefore, we must consider not only the quantity but also the quality of the transactions in order to gauge the conditions and prospects for collective identity.

We have already described the critical factors leading to the creation of transnational collective identities. Keep in mind that collective identities entail that people not only identify (positively) with other people's fate but, also, identify themselves, and those other people, as a group in relation to other groups.[42] Such identities are likely to be reinforced by symbols and myths that serve to define the group and its boundaries. The distinction between loosely coupled and tightly coupled security communities acquires special significance. In the former case, it is mainly a social identity that generates a positive identification between peoples of members states. For instance, the category of democrat defines the group "by systematically including them with some, and excluding them from other related categories. They state at the same time what a person is and is not."[43] It follows, then, that when members of a loosely coupled security community assume a particular social category they are able to answer, in part, the question "who am I?" (and who I am not) and have a fairly proximate understanding of "what makes them tick." "This knowledge does not merely constrain the state. In a positive sense, it empowers it to act in the world and contributes to the development of mutual responsiveness."[44]

The closer we get to tightly coupled security communities, however, the shorter is the collective cognitive distance between its members, and the more the community acquires a corporate identity. In these communities, the identities of the people who exist within them no longer derives from the international environment (if they ever did) or from the self-contained nation (if it ever existed) but rather from the community's identity and norms as well. Indeed, even the meaning, purpose, and role of the state derives from the community. The state's interests, and the identity of its people, can be exchangeable with those of the community, and the foreign policy of the state takes on a whole new meaning and purpose. The discourse of the state and the language of legitimation, moreover, also should reflect that the relevant community is no longer coterminous with the state's territorial boundaries but rather with the region. With the emergence of tightly coupled security communities, therefore, state officials will increasingly refer to the boundaries of an expanded definition of community.

In sum, we envision a dynamic and positive relationship between core powers and cognitive structures on the one hand, and transactions, institutions and organizations, and social learning on the other. The positive and dynamic interaction between these variables undergirds the development of trust and the process of collective identity formation, which, in turn, drives dependable expectation of peaceful change.

Toward a research program

The Deutschian promise is a framework for understanding how the development and existence of a community leaves its imprint on interstate relations in general and security politics in particular. In this section we aspire to take another step toward translating that promise into a viable research program. We do so by making three moves. First, we present three stylized phases in the development of a security community – "nascent," "ascendent" and "mature," and further distinguish mature security communities according to loosely and tightly coupled variants. These phases are intended as heuristic devices rather than as uncomfortable teleological exercises. Secondly, we offer a corresponding set of indicators that are sensitive to the different phases of the security community. In doing so, we are attempting to overcome two drawbacks associated with Deutsch's operationalization of security communities: (1) the concept was resistant to precise operationalization because it was fuzzy and ill-defined;[45] and, (2) while Deutsch's behavioral methodology was able to capture increased transboundary movements that suggested greater interdependence, it could not detect a greater sense of cohesion and community based on mutual responsiveness, value orientation, and identity.[46] The current challenge is to devise indicators that overcome these shortcomings by being sensitive to different phases of a security community that can also tap into whether there is growing collective identity. Thirdly, we contemplate the disintegration of security communities.

The development of security communities

Our understanding of the development of security communities can be broadly termed as social constructivist and path-dependent. The notion that security communities are socially constructed means that they have a history and, therefore, exhibit an evolutionary pattern that follows the direction of "the arrow of time" (birth, growth, maturity, etc). But because security communities evolve from path dependent processes, their origins and paths will vary considerably. "Path-dependent patterns are characterized by self-reinforcing positive feed-back. Initial choices, often small and random, determine future historical trajectories. Once a particular path is chosen, it precludes others, even if these alternatives might, in the long run, have proven to be more efficient or adaptive."[47] Initial choices persist because individuals and social groups come to identify and benefit from past decisions, and because the cost of change become more significant over time.

Our constructivist and path-dependent approaches require, then, that we trace backwards the institutionalization of dependable expectations of peaceful change, from when they merely are imagined to exist to the processes that led to their development. We are neither so pretentious nor foolhardy, however, as to believe that we can offer *a* theory of community development or security communities. We suspect that to do so would duplicate the dead end of the first formulation of the state formation literature that had such pretensions. Our objective at this stage is modestly ambitious: to offer one conceptualization of the mechanisms and conditions by which security communities develop to provide the basis for further research. We want to be very clear here. The proposed pathway does not exhaust all possibilities; it derives from Deutsch's observations, prior theorizing on community-building and security communities, and recent empirical studies that have built on Deutsch's insights. The other contributions to this volume speak loudly to variations.

Phase I: Nascent. In this initial phase, governments do not explicitly seek to create a security community. Instead, they begin to consider how they might coordinate their relations in order to: increase their mutual security; lower the transaction costs associated with their exchanges; and/or encourage further exchanges and interactions. Accordingly, we expect to see various diplomatic, bilateral, multi-lateral exchanges, something akin to "search" missions, that are designed to determine the level and extent of cooperation that might be achieved. In order to deepen and extend their interactions, to foster cooperation, and to verify in the absence of trust, states will frequently establish "third-parties," that is, organizations and institutions that can observe whether the participating states are honoring their contracts and obligations.

As discussed earlier, there are undoubtedly many possible "trigger" mechanisms that initiate this initial search and the desire to create institutions or organizations to order and foster their relations. One is a mutual security threat. Deutsch posited that war or a common threat is a sufficient or necessary condition for generating an interest in a security community. In this instance, a security organization is vir-tually indistinguishable from a strategic alliance, and there is no expectation that people of these states will have a shared identity or knowledge of the other (at least in a prosocial and other-regarding sense). What matters is that they recognize or discover that they have joint interests that require collective action, and can mutually benefit from some modest coordination of security policies. The resulting acts of security cooperation, therefore, are likely to include greater specifi-cation of those actions that are and are not considered threatening, policies that are designed to overcome collective action problems associated with interdependent choice, and the development of se-curity programs that are intended to serve their mutual interests. Yet states frequently develop close security ties not only to provide for collective defense against a common threat, but also to: deepen the institutional and transnational linkages that bind these states together; capitalize on particular visions of a better material progress (economic, environmental, health, human rights, etc.); and, to promote ideas about "cooperative security," that is, the notion that the security of states – defined in terms of the interdependence of military, economic, environmental, and human rights issues – is interdependent.[48] This highlights that a broad effect of, if not the very intent behind, security organizations is the general nourishing of mutual trust.

The existence of or the desire to capitalize on an international division of labor or gains from trade also can encourage the development of international organizations and institutions. This is, of course, a standing argument of neo-liberal institutionalism. We anticipate, however, that there will be a relationship between the establishment of international economic associations that are designed to encourage economic interchange and the presence of international arrangements that are intended to produce order and security. The relationship between economic and security organizations is most obvious in the corporate body of the state, which is charged with enforcing property rights and maintains a monopoly of the means of coercion. Transboundary economic relations are similarly dependent on a stable international order.

Cultural, political, social, and ideological homogeneity can lead to greater interaction and association, and the development of new organizations and institutions. It may even create the desire, and the very expectation that it is possible, to develop a security community. People sharing cultural and social attributes across national borders frequently voice an interest in developing not simply a defensive strategic posture but rather an institutional form that is intended to give muscle to already existing expressions of mutual obligation. "One of the most deep-seated sentiments in favor of a stronger Atlantic political association is the view that, because our Atlantic neighbors seem to think, act, and look so much the way we do they are the countries with which we could most agreeably and successfully enter into a political marriage."[49] Arab nationalism held that Arab states should deepen their security and political ties not only because of an external threat but also to nurture and develop a political community; consequently, they proposed, albeit unsuccessfully, various organizations and mechanisms that were intended to deepen the political community.[50] That a common future might be as important as a shared threat in producing the desire for a security community is also evident in the various debates over the post-cold war security architecture.

In general, the trigger mechanisms for a security community are likely to have material and normative bases. Other material and normative factors can include, for instance: rapid shifts in the distribution of military power; cataclysmic events that produce changes in material structures, mindsets and sensibilities, and new ways of thinking about organizing political life; and, transnational, domestic, or international processes that generate common interests. In other words, a security community "gets out of the gate" because of either push or pull factors that cause states to reconsider how to organize their relations.[51]

Transnational and interstate interactions are accompanied and encouraged by the development of social institutions and organizations for a variety of reasons, though most relevant here is to facilitate trust. Although trust might be encouraged through political and economic agreements and symbolic events that increase the assurance and knowledge of the "other," organizations traditionally play a critical role. And while organizations that oversee functional areas other than security can also contribute to the development of trust (after all, this was a principal insight of the neo-functionalist literature), security organizations are particularly symbolic and prominent. In this regard, we are particularly attentive to the development of multilateral security organizations, for they reflect a belief that security is interdependent and should be overseen by a collective body. The ability of multilateral security organizations to alleviate security fears among members of the group can be detected in changes in patterns of military spending, deployment, and planning.

In general, interstate and transnational interactions can produce and are facilitated by international organizations and institutions that: contain norms and provide mechanisms that make states accountable to each other; institutionalize immediate (if not diffuse) reciprocity; identify common interests (or even identities) among a selected population; and produce charters and agendas, and convene meetings and seminars, that reflect the attempt to create a binding set of interests and a collective future. "Third-parties" can become region-builders.[52]

We posit that the existence of powerful states that are able to project a sense of purpose, offer an idea of progress, and/or provide leadership around core issues can facilitate and stabilize this phase.[53] The existence of core states or a coalition of states will be necessary for providing leadership, side payments, and perhaps protection to other members of the group. This reiterates an earlier point: that the development of a security community is not antagonistic to the language of power; indeed, it is dependent on it. What is important, however, is that power is not simply coercive but also conveys a sense of purpose and, potentially, a vision of the future.

52

In sum, we expect a dynamic and positive relationship between the transactions that occur between and among states and their societies, the emergence of social institutions and organizations that are designed to lower transaction costs, and the possibility of mutual trust. A core state or coalition of states is a likely facilitator and stabilizer of this phase, for only such a state or group of states can be expected to provide the leadership, protection, material benefits, and sense of purpose that is frequently required.

Phase II: Ascendant. This phase is defined by: increasingly dense networks; new institutions and organizations that reflect either tighter military coordination and cooperation and/or decreased fear that the other represents a threat; cognitive structures that promote "seeing" and acting together and, therefore, the deepening of the level of mutual trust, and the emergence of collective identities that begin to encourage dependable expectations of peaceful change. At the level of interactions, the multiple channels that existed in the nascent phase are extended and intensified, and states and their societies are increasingly embedded in a dense network of relations collectively portrayed as "friendly." An increase in dynamic density, moreover, might be encouraged and facilitated by the existence of common ideas of material progress and security that increasingly converge around a key, shared, expectation: that material progress and security, broadly defined, can be best guaranteed only among members of the region.[54]

Increased interactions, moreover, encourage the development of new social institutions and organizational forms that reflect diffuse reciprocity, shared interests, and perhaps even a collective identity (if not already present). Indeed, attempts to encourage greater regional interaction and acceptance for certain "ways of life" are frequently promoted by governments, security and other intergovernmental organizations, nongovernmental organizations, epistemic communities, social movements, and even by imaginative individuals who, placed in institutional positions of power, are able to turn their personal ideas into institutional ideas.

The widening networks and intensified relations between and among societies, states, and organizations institutionalize cognitive structures and deepen mutual trust and responsiveness. Trust continues to develop in and through various interactions and organizational contexts. Although evidence of mutual trust can be discerned in a variety of institutional and organizational forms that reflect diffuse reciprocity and so on, key indicators reside in the security sphere; specifically, growing evidence of trust in military matters can be found in those instances when military procurement decisions reflect interdependent military postures, and states begin to share intelligence information. Other indicators of a step-wise increase in mutual trust can be detected when organizations that were originally designed for verification and monitoring are increasingly dismantled or become less important for maintaining cooperation; therefore, there should be a change in bureaucratic structures that emerged in the nascent phase.

In large measure, the trust-building process is also driven by social learning. Learning increases the knowledge that individuals in states have not just about each others' purposes and intentions but also of each others' interpretations of society, politics, economics, and culture; to the extent that these interpretations are increasingly shared and disseminated across national borders, the stage has been laid for the development of a regional collective identity. One way of evaluating and ascertaining whether two actors have a collective identity is through narratives.[55]

> Human identities are considered to be evolving constructions: they emerge out of continual social interactions in the course of life. Self-narratives are developed stories that must be told in specific historical terms, using a particular language, reference to a particular stock of working historical conventions and a particular pattern of dominant beliefs and values.[56]

Because actors locate themselves within a storyline, an actor's identity is lived history and establishes a storyline from the past through the present and some imagined future.[57] To the extent that actors locate themselves within a shared or congruent storyline they can be said to have a collective identity.

In sum, this phase is defined by an intensive and extensive pattern of networks between states that is likely to be produced and be a product of various international institutions and organizations. Although functional organizations might help to encourage mutual trust, we look to changes in the organization and production of security for both the primary mechanisms by which this trust is produced and for its evidence. We expect that a core state or a coalition of states remain important for stabilizing and encouraging the further development of the security community (and for the same reasons cited in our discussion of the ascendant phase). By and large, because it is now harder for states and their peoples to imagine settling their differences through violence, we expect that states have altered how it is they organize their security and define the threat.

Phase III: Mature. The more these expectations are institutionalized in both domestic and supranational settings, the more war in the region becomes improbable. At this point, regional actors share an identity and, therefore, entertain dependable expectations of peaceful change and a security community now comes into existence. A threshold has now been crossed; it becomes increasingly difficult for the members of this "region" to think only in instrumental ways and prepare for war among each other. At this point we want to distinguish between the loosely and the tightly-coupled variants. In the former, minimalist, version: states identify positively with one another and proclaim a similar "way of life"; there are multiple and diverse mechanisms and patterns of interaction that reinforce and reproduce the security community; there is an informal governance system based on shared meanings and a collective identity; and while there remains conflicting interests, disagreements, and asymmetric bargaining, there is the expectation that states will practice self-restraint.

Evidence of the emergence of a security community can be found in various indicators that reflect a high degree of trust, a shared identity and future, low or no probability that conflicts will lead to military encounters, and the differentiation between those within from those outside the security community.

> *Multilateralism.* Decision-making procedures, conflict resolution, and processes of conflict adjudication are likely to be more consensual than in other types of interstate relations.[58] This type of architecture reflects the high degree of trust present in the relationship and that common interests are handled through common and consensual mechanisms that automatically incorporate the interests of all members.
>
> *Unfortified borders.*[59] Although still present, border checks and patrols are undertaken to secure the state against threats other than an organized military invasion.

Changes in military planning. "Worst-case" scenarios assumptions do not include those within the community. Although there might be some concern about the degree of cooperation and contribution to a joint military campaign, those within the community are not counted as potential enemies during any military engagement.

Common definition of the threat. This depends on the identification of core "personality" features of those within the security community. Self-identification frequently has a corresponding "other" that represents the threat to the community.

Discourse and the language of community. The state's normative discourse and actions reflect community standards. Thus, the discourse is likely to reflect the norms of the specific community, and refers to how its norms differ from those outside the community.

In a tightly coupled security community, mutual-aid becomes a matter of habit and, thus, national identity is expressed through the merging of efforts. The institutional context for the exercise of power changes; the right to use force shifts from the units to the collectivity of sovereign states and becomes legitimate only against external threats or against community members that defect from the core norms of the community. Power balances, nuclear deterrence, and threats of retaliation retain meaningful and functional roles, but only in terms of the defense of the community against "outsiders." In case of an external threat or attack, the security community may respond as a collective security system or even as an integrated military defense organization.

The indicators that demonstrate the existence of loosely coupled security community also apply to tightly coupled security communities, but, to distinguish between the two variants the following indicators apply only to the latter:

Cooperative and collective security. Movement from reciprocal arms control and confidence building to "cooperative security," with regard to security problems arising within the community, and to collective security, with regard to threats arising outside the community.

A high level of military integration. Although a security community does not require that there be military integration, it is quite likely that shared identities and a high degree of trust will produce a desire for the pooling of military resources; this will be particularly true if there was military cooperation in earlier phases of the emerging security community. We expect that if there was no military cooperation in earlier phases, then the emergence of a common threat at this stage would produce the desire for it. This indicator reflects not only high trust but also that security is viewed as interdependent.

Policy coordination against "internal" threats. There is greater policy coordination among those within the security community to "patrol" and stand vigilant against common definitions of the internal threat. (Although most working within the security community tradition point to the existence of external threats, many (territorially-based) communities also derive their identity from internal threats to the community.)

Free movements of populations. Allowing the citizens of other states free movement into and out of the state reflects that there is less differentiation between "us" and "them." For instance, visas are no longer required and routine movements are no longer restricted between different states because they are no longer seen as a potential threat.

Internationalization of authority. Shared and coordinated practices, and public policies, can further the creation of an informal system of rule. However, authority may also become internationalized, or, alternatively, states may attempt to co-ordinate and harmonize their domestic laws; as law becomes internationalized, so too will enforcement mechanisms.

A "Multiperspectival" Polity. Rule is shared at the national, transnational, and supranational levels.[60]

Disintegration

One of the startling tragedies of the post-Cold War period is the implosion of many political communities. Individuals, nationalities, and ethnic groups that co-existed, at some level, in relative peace, have quickly, and sometimes savagely taken revenge and retribution on their neighbors. The post-Cold War period is not the first instance of political communities disintegrating and clashing, for such tragic outbursts frequently occur after the decline of empires and other systemic shocks; and an important theme of Third World studies is the intrusion of external forces into the local community, leaving conflict, alienation, and anomie in its wake. In short, political communities can be disrupted from within and without. Because compatibility of core values and a collective identity are necessary for the development of security communities – and values and identities are not static but are susceptible to change[61] – the same forces that "build up" security communities can "tear them down." Therefore, many of the same social processes that encourage and serve to reproduce the security community are also associated with its decline. Most important, of course, is the loss of mutual trust. Needless to say, war among members of the community represents compelling evidence that a security community has ceased to exist.

Conclusion

This chapter advanced a framework for the study of security communities. By thinking the unthinkable – that community exists at the international level, that security politics is profoundly shaped by it, and that those states dwelling within an international community might develop a pacific disposition – we have attempted to show how the concept of security community can re-invigorate our understanding of global change, security politics, and international relations theory.

Equally provocative is that state officials of those regions that are not currently a security community are advocating various mechanisms that resemble the early phases of a security community, are using the language of transnational values, community and cognitive interdependence to conceptualize the foundations of a peace system, are sometimes drawing on and importing the institutional mechanisms devised in and lessons learned from other regions, and are explicitly attempting to fashion and foster the architecture for a security community.

In this respect, security communities may become not merely "half-baked" integration processes on the road to amalgamation, but somewhat permanent international (and transnational) actors whose boundaries are determined by shared understandings rather than geography. If so, pluralistic security communities may be a radically new form of regional governance, far more complex than historical counterparts. Its chances of survival, institutionalization, and expansion, however, may be enhanced by the fact that this type of governance system lies between, on the one hand, the anarchical arrangement of sovereign states – and national identities, and, on the other, a system of rule endowed with strong norms, institutions, transnational civic traditions, and trust – and transnational identities. The implication of these "half-baked" communities for the study of peace is profound: quasi-Kantian peaceful change without its teleological, deterministic, and universal elements might be presently evolving.[62] If so, peaceful change need not rely on the transcendence of the nation-state or the elimination of existing cultural and ethnic loyalties and identities; what matters is the creation of regions of social cognitive and normative bonds that can encourage peoples to identify, and to expect their security and welfare to be intimately intertwined, with those that exist on the same side of spatial and cognitive borders.

It follows, then, that studying security communities suggests not just a rethinking of regional or even global security issues, but rather a paradigm shift in international relations theory. This shift, as Donald Puchala once argued, involves the intellectual conjecture that violent conflict can be mitigated and even eliminated by the development of mutual identification among peoples and not through conventional practices such as balancing and collective security schemes.[63] The possibility that peaceful change might be established through the institutionalization of mutual identification, transnational values, intersubjective understandings, and shared identities, is most conducive to a constructivist approach. Realist and neo-liberal institutionalist approaches, by bracketing the very phenomenon we are interested in studying, are ill-equipped to entertain the possibility of community. A constructivist approach, which recognizes the importance of knowledge for transforming international structures and security politics, is best suited to taking seriously how international community can shape security politics and create the conditions for a stable peace.

Notes

1 We thank John Ruggie for this suggestion. See his *Winning the Peace* (NY: Columbia University Press, 1996), pp. 81–82, for a similar discussion.

2 John G. Ruggie, "Territoriality and Beyond: Problematizing Modernity in

International Relations," *International Organization* 47 (Winter 1993), p. 172.

3 See Barry Buzan, "From International System to International Society: Structural Realism and Regime Theory Meet the English School," *International Organization* 47 (Summer 1993), pp. 327–352, for a consideration of the concept of community as it applies to international relations.

4 The sociological and anthropological literatures on communities are enormous. For initial formulations, see the classic distinction between association and community by Ferdinand Tonnies, *Community and Association* (London: Routledge and Kegan Paul, 1955); Max Weber, *Economy and Society* (Berkeley: University of California Press, 1978), pp. 901–904; R. M. MacIver, *Community: A Sociological Study* (London: Macmillan Press, 1917); Robert Park, *Human Communities* (NY: Free Press, 1952); and Albert Hunter, *Symbolic Communities: The Persistence and Change of Chicago's Local Communities* (Chicago: University of Chicago Press, 1974). For more recent considerations, see Peter Hamilton, "Editor's Forward," in Anthony P. Cohen, *The Symbolic Construction of Community* (New York: Tavistock, 1985), p. 9; Dennis Poplin, *Communities: A Survey of Theories and Methods of Research*, 2nd edn. (New York: MacMillan Publishing, 1979); Margaret Stacey, "The Myth of Community Studies," *British Journal of Sociology* 20 (June, 1969), pp. 134–147; and Reinhard Bendix, "Definitions of Community in Western Civilization," in his *Unsettled Affinities* (New Jersey: Transaction Press, 1993), ch. 3. For the application of network analysis to identify the existence of communities, see Barry Wellman, Peter Carrington, and Alan Hall, "Networks as Personal Communities," in B. Wellman and S.D. Berkowitz, eds., *Social Structures: A Network Approach* (New York: Cambridge University Press, 1988); and David Knoke, *Political Networks: The Structural Perspective* (New York: Cambridge University Press, 1990).

5 Michael Taylor, *Community, Anarchy, and Liberty* (New York; Cambridge University Press, 1982), pp. 25–33; and Charles Tilly, this volume.

6 Charles Taylor, "Interpretation and the Sciences of Man," in Paul Rabinow and William Sullivan, eds., *Interpretative Social Science: A Reader* (Berkeley: University of California Press, 1979), p. 51.

7 This is the classic distinction offered by Tonnies between *Gemeinschaft* and *Gesellschaft*: whereas the former refers to an organic community involving bonds generated by tradition and culture, the latter sees society as a more contractual arrangement that emerges from self-interested behavior. Tonnies, *Community and Association*.

8 Also see Wellman, Carrington, and Hall, "Networks as Personal Communities."

9 Ira J. Cohen, "Structuration Theory and Social *Praxis*," in Anthony Giddens and Jonathan Turner, eds., *Social Theory Today* (Stanford: Stanford University Press, 1987), p. 298.

10 Reinhold Niebuhr, *The World Crisis and American Responsibility* (New York:

Association Press, 1950), pp. 80–86; and E. H. Carr, *The Twenty Years' Crisis: 1919–1939* (New York: Harper Torchbooks, 1964), especially ch. 13 and conclusion.

11 Emanuel Adler, "Imagined (Security) Communities: Cognitive Regions in International Relations," *Millennium* 26, 2 (1997), pp. 49–277.

12 For the US–Israeli case, see Michael Barnett, "Identity and Alliances in the Middle East," in Peter Katzenstein, ed., *The Culture of National Security: Norms and Identity in World Politics* (New York: Columbia University Press, 1996), pp. 400–447; see Higgott and Nossal in this volume for the Australian case.

13 Simmel, *Conflict and the Web of Group-Affiliations* (New York: Free Press, 1964), ch. 2; Marc Howard Ross, *Conflict in Cultures* (New Haven: Yale University Press, 1993).

14 Stacia Zabusky, *Launching Europe* (Princeton: Princeton University Press, 1995), p. 40

15 Deutsch confused the matter by suggesting that peaceful change means avoiding "*large-scale* physical force" (*Political Community*, p. 5). That states might engage in "small-scale" physical force or periodically threaten the use of force stretches most understandings of a pluralistic security community. Yet he has a point: a dyad within the community might go to war without necessarily leading the researcher to declare the end of the community; after all, murders occur within communities without necessarily defining their end.

16 Ibid., p. 6.

17 James Rosenau, "Governance, Order, and Change in World Politics," in J. Rosenau and Ernst-Otto Czempiel, eds., *Governance Without Government: Order and Change in World Politics* (New York: Cambridge University Press, 1992), p. 4.

18 See Martin Hollis, *The Cunning of Reason* (New York: Cambridge University Press, 1988), pp. 137–141, for the distinction between regulative and constitutive norms.

19 Barnett, "Identity and Alliances in the Middle East," p. 412.

20 Thomas Franck, *The Power of Legitimacy Among Nations* (New York: Oxford University Press, 1990), p. 196; Adler, "Imagined (Security) Communities," pp. 266–268.

21 Adler, "Imagined (Security) Communities," p. 266.

22 Jerome Bruner, *Actual Minds, Possible Worlds* (Cambridge, MA: Harvard University Press, 1986).

23 This is consistent with other theories of social structure that define them as comprised of rules and resources. See William Sewell, "A Theory of Structure: Duality, Agency, and Transformation," *American Journal of Sociology* 98 (July, 1992), pp. 1–29.

24 *Political Community*, p. 38.

25 On the development of shared meanings in international relations, see Ernst B. Haas, *When Knowledge is Power* (Berkeley: University of California

Press, 1990), and Peter M. Haas, ed., Special Issue of *International Organization* on Epistemic Communities, 46 (Winter 1992).

26 This, of course, is the central claim of the expansive "Democratic Peace" argument. See Michael W. Doyle, "Kant, Liberal Legacies, and Foreign Affairs," *Philosophy and Public Affairs* 12 (Spring 1983), pp. 205–235; and 12 (Summer 1983), pp. 323–353; Bruce Russett, *Grasping the Democratic Peace* (Princeton: Princeton University Press, 1993); Zeev Maoz and Bruce M. Russett, "Normative and Structural Causes of Democratic Peace, 1946–86," *American Political Science Review* 87 (1993), pp. 624–638; John M. Owen, "How Liberalism Produces Democratic Peace," *International Security* 19 (1994), pp. 87–125; James L. Ray, "Wars Between Democracies: Rare or Nonexistent?," *International Interactions* 18 (1993), pp. 251–276.

27 Colin Kahl, "Constructing a Separate Peace: Constructivism, Collective Identity, and the Democratic Peace" (unpublished manuscript, Columbia University).

28 Charles Tilly, "Durable Inequality," Center for Studies of Social Change, Working Paper Series, No. 224, New School for Social Research, p. 20.

29 John G. Ruggie, "Continuity and Transformation in the World Polity: Toward a Neorealist Synthesis," *World Politics* 35 (January 1983), p. 148. The concept derives from Emile Durkheim, *The Division of Labor in Society* (New York: Free Press, 1984).

30 Oran Young, *International Cooperation* (Ithaca: Cornell University Press, 1989), p. 32.

31 Alexander Wendt, *A Social Theory of International Politics* (Cambridge: Cambridge University Press, forthcoming), p. 328.

32 See Richard Burt and Marc Knez, "Kinds of Third-Party Effects on Trust," *Rationality and Society* 7, 3 (July 1995), pp. 255–292, for a discussion of organizations and trust.

33 Wendt, *A Social Theory of International Politics*, ch. 7.

34 "Ideas and the Social Sciences," in J. Goldstein and R. Keohane, eds, *Ideas and Foreign Policy* (Ithaca: Cornell University Press, 1993), p. 51. Iver Neumann similarly claims that identity is inextricably linked to a "region-building approach," where the existence of a regional identity is preceded by region-builders who imagine spatial and chronological identities and, who can talk and write these regions into existence. "A Region-Building Approach to Northern Europe," *Review of International Studies* 20 (1994), pp. 53–74.

35 Emanuel Adler, "Cognitive Evolution: A Dynamic Approach for the Study of International Relations and Their Progress," in Emanuel Adler and Beverly Crawford, eds., *Progress in Postwar International Relations* (New York: Columbia University Press, 1991), p. 52. Social learning, in this view can be likened to "cognitive evolution": "the process of innovation, domestic and international diffusion, political selection and effective institutionalization that creates the intersubjective understanding on which the interests, practices and behavior of government are based."

Emanuel Adler, "Seizing the Middle Ground: Constructivism in World Politics," *European Journal of International Relations* 3, 3 (1997), p. 339.

36 For adaptation, see Haas, *When Knowledge is Power*. For simple learning, see Joseph S. Nye, Jr., "Nuclear Learning and US–Soviet Security Regimes," *International Organization* 41 (Summer 1987). Also see Jack Levy, "Learning and Foreign Policy: Sweeping a Conceptual Minefield," *International Organization* 48 (Spring 1994), p. 290.

37 Erving Goffman, *Relations in Public* (New York: Basic Books, 1971).

38 G. John Ikenberry and Charles A. Kupchan, "Socialization and Hegemonic Power," *International Organization* 44 (Summer 1990), pp. 283–315.

39 Barbara Mistzal, *Trust in Modern Societies* (Cambridge: Polity Press, 1996), p. 19. Also see Burt and Knez, "Kinds of Third-Party Effects on Trust," p. 256.

40 Henry Tajfel defines a social identity as "that part of an individual's self-concept which derives from his knowledge of his membership in a social group (or groups) together with the value and emotional significance attached to that membership." Henry Tajfel, *Differentiation Between Social Groups: Studies in the Social Psychology of Intergroup Relations* (London: Academic Press, 1978), p. 63. Alex Wendt, in turn, distinguishes between "corporate identities," in our case the individual identity of political actors, and "social identities," identities that political actors generate through interactions with other actors and that, therefore, also take into account their perspective. See Alex Wendt, "Collective Identity Formation and the International State," *American Political Science Review* 88 (June 1994), p. 385.

41 For discussions of national and state identities that build on this definition, see Lloyd Dittmer and Samuel Kim, "In Search of a Theory of National Identity," in Samuel Kim and Lloyd Dittmer, eds., *China's Quest for National Identity* (Ithaca: Cornell University Press, 1993), pp. 1–31; Anthony Smith, *National Identity* (Reno: University of Nevada Press, 1991); and Wendt "Collective Identity Formation."

42 Bert Klandermans, "The Social Construction of Protest and Multiorganizational Fields," in Aldon D. Morris and Carol McClurg Mueller, eds., *Frontiers in Social Movement Theory* (New Haven: Yale University Press, 1992), p. 81.

43 John C. Turner, "Towards A Cognitive Redefinition of the Social Group," in Henri Tajfel, ed., *Social Identity and Intergroup Relations* (Cambridge: Cambridge University Press, 1982), p. 18.

44 Adler, "Imagined (Security) Communities," p. 264.

45 Joseph S. Nye, "Comparative Regional Integration: Concept and Measurement," *International Organization* 22 (Fall 1968), p. 873.

46 Philip E. Jacob and Henry Teune, "The Integrative Process: Guidelines for Analysis of the Bases of Political Community," in Philip E. Jacob and James V. Toscano, eds., *The Integration of Political Communities* (Philadelphia: Lippincott, 1964), pp. 26–29.

47 Stephen Krasner, "Sovereignty: An Institutional Perspective", *Comparative Political Studies* 21, 1 (1988), p. 83. Also see Stephen Jay Gould, *Wonderful Life: The Burgess Shale and the Nature of History* (New York: W. W. Norton, 1989).

48 See Janne E. Nolan, ed., *Global Engagement: Cooperation and Security in the 21st Century* (Washington, DC: The Brookings Institution, 1994).

49 H. Field Haviland, "Building a Political Community," *International Organization* 17 (Summer 1963), p. 735.

50 Michael Barnett, *Dialogues in Arab Politics: Negotiations in Regional Order* (New York: Columbia University Press, 1998).

51 This is akin to the concept of complex interdependence, in which there are multiple channels connecting societies and an absence of hierarchy among issues. Robert Keohane and Joseph Nye, *Power and Interdependence* (Boston: Little, Brown, 1977), pp. 24–25.

52 Neumann, "A Region-Building Approach to Northern Europe," pp. 54–74.

53 This is consistent with James Caporaso's concept of "k-groups." See "International Relations Theory and Multilateralism: The Search for Foundations," in John G. Ruggie, ed., *Multilateralism Matters* (New York: Columbia University Press, 1993), pp. 58–59.

54 Adler and Crawford, eds., *Progress in Postwar International Relations*.

55 On narrative analysis, see: Donald Polkinghorne, *Narrative Knowing and the Human Sciences* (Albany: SUNY Press, 1986); W. J. T. Mitchell, ed., *On Narrative* (Chicago: University of Chicago Press, 1980); Hayden White, *Metahistory* (Baltimore: Johns Hopkins University Press, 1973); William Sewell, "Introduction: Narratives and Social Identities," *Social Science History* 16, 4 (Winter, 1991), pp. 479–88; Jerome Bruner, "The Narrative Construction of Reality," *Critical Inquiry* 18, 1 (1991) pp. 1–21; Alex Callinicos, *Theories and Narratives* (Durham: Duke University Press, 1995), ch. 2; and Paul Riceour, *Time and Narrative*, 3 vols. (Chicago: University of Chicago Press, 1984, 1985, 1988).

56 Karl Schiebe, "Self-Narratives and Adventure," in Theodore Sarbin, ed., *Narrative Psychology: The Storied Nature of Human Conduct* (New York: Praeger Press, 1986), p. 131.

57 Also see Polkinghorne, *Narrative Knowing*, and Mitchell, ed., *On Narrative*.

58 See John G. Ruggie, "Multilateralism: The Anatomy of an Institution," in Ruggie, ed., *Multilateralism Matters*, pp. 3–47; and Thomas Risse-Kappen, *Cooperation Among Democracies: Norms, Transnational Relations, and the European Influence on US Foreign Policy* (Princeton: Princeton University Press, 1995).

59 Deutsch et al., *Political Community*, pp. 34–35.

60 Ruggie, "Territoriality and Beyond," pp. 172–174.

61 Van Wagenen, "The Concept of Community and the Future of the United Nations," *International Organization* 19, 3 (Summer, 1965), pp. 818–819.

62 Emanuel Adler, "Europe's New Security Order: A Pluralistic Security

Community," in Beverly Crawford, ed., *The Future of European Security* (Berkeley: IAS, University of California, 1992), p. 289.

63 Donald J. Puchala, "Integration Theory and the Study of International Relations," in Richard L. Merritt and Bruce M. Russett, eds., *From National Development to Global Community: Essays in Honor of Karl W. Deutsch* (London: Allen and Unwin, 1981), p. 151.

Part II

Studies in security communities

3   Insecurity, security, and asecurity in the West European non-war community
Ole Wæver

> When we use the term "integration or amalgamation" in this book, we are taking a short form to express an alternative between integration (by the route of either pluralism or amalgamation) and amalgamation short of integration. We have done this because unification movements in the past have often aimed at both of these goals, with some of the supporters of the movements preferring one or the other goal at different times. To encourage this profitable ambiguity, leaders of such movements have often used broader symbols such as "union", which could cover both possibilities and could be made to mean different things to different men.
>
> Deutsch et al., *Political Community*, 1957[1]

Western Europe is a security community. In contrast to the expectations of most contemporary theorists of security communities, this has not been achieved by erecting common security structures or institutions, but primarily through a process of "desecuritization", a progressive marginalization of mutual security concerns in favor of other issues. This chapter's main section traces how Western Europe has gone from insecurity (1940s and 1950s), over security (1960s) and desecuritization (1970s to the mid 1980s) to reach a situation in the 1990s of re-securitization. Mutual military fears are still absent at the level of state-to-state, but more issues are today cast in security terms, economy, environment and migration. Classical political security concerns appear but are mostly conceived for "Europe" not individual states. Re-securitization raises the specter of a possible unravelling of the West European security community, because when something is constituted as a security issue this enables more extreme action. Since Deutsch defines security community in terms of the absence of war, it really is a non-war-community, and security problems can continue to unfold within it. Radical security problems are likely to be the biggest risks for the security community because they drive states to override rules.

With the return of "security" concerns within Western Europe, it is important to investigate how solid the security community is. The third section of the chapter thus examines the way "Europe" as collective identity is articulated with the particular nation/state identities. It argues that "Europe" has attained a significant firmness because national narratives depend on it. Although nation/state identities remain in some sense primary, they have been transformed in ways that make "Europe" politically real and a source of stability.

The two main sections of the chapter use unconventional analytical methods – a study of the historical evolution of the use of the security speech act and a discourse analysis of the articulation of nation, state and European identity – because it is argued that straightforward approaches to the West European security community are not feasible. Paradoxically, the "nice" case is hard because too many theories are compatible with the emergence of stable peace in Western Europe.

Most often, in the other cases of this book, the question is *whether* some region is a security community, or what it would take to make it one. Europe is the region most often accepted as a security community (maybe with the exception of sub-regions like Scandinavia and US–Canada). Therefore, the questions here are rather: (1) How do we prove it? Is it really a security community, or does it only look like one? Is peace carried by community logic or some other mechanism – balance of power, interdependence, alliance logic? (2) What decides its stability and will it last? (3) What can we possibly learn from this region, from the experience of this security community?

The first section presents some logical, conceptual and empirical difficulties, and drawing on the Scandinavian case, advances four warnings. These are used to formulate researchable questions and point out two theoretical core approaches to carry the analysis further. First a refocussed concept of security is used in the second section to assess the role of military and non-military security concerns respectively through a historical survey of the West European case.[2] The third section investigates the stability of the West European security community and the nature of a common European identity through an exploration of how "Europe" has become embedded in the meaning of state and nation for key countries. At the end of this section it is suggested that the way security is provided in the Europe of the mid 1990s reveals an emerging regional polity rather than simply a set of universalized norms keeping separate states in place. This raises the theoretically troubling perspective that the European security community is not strictly a pluralistic security community, but an in-between form bordering on amalgamation. Finally, it is asked whether the emergence of a West European security community relates to some deeper change in the international system. Can we delineate causes, not of the original origins of the community, but causes of the ensuing identity-based stabilization of it? The conclusion summarizes the analysis and reflects on the benefits of using the concept of security community for these investigations.

Four warnings, a mini-case and two ways out

The difficulties of a simple case and the long road to researchable questions

Four problems preclude a simple, historical and causal excavation of the formation of the West European security community:

- The origins seem terribly "over-determined," and therefore we need to separate between on the one hand the question of explaining origins and on the other factors influencing its sustainability.
- What is called in the literature a "security community" is really a non-war community, and therefore if we accept a concept of security wider than non-war there can be (non-military) security problems and security dynamics in a "security community."
- It is important, but often difficult in practice to avoid identifying a security community with security institutions. More abstractly: security and insecurity are not exhaustive options, and more attention needs to be given to a-security. Usually, those who do not feel insecure, do not self-consciously feel (or work on being) secure; they are more likely to be engaged in other matters. For practitioners, to concentrate on non-security matters might be a sound security strategy.
- "Community" in security community should not primarily be conceived in terms of "identity" of one member with the next. Instead, one should stress the socially constructed nature of

the community and thus its cognitive or semiotic rather than its soci(ologic)al nature. Rather than tracing the causal relationship between factors external to each other (identity of individuals ⇒ security order), we look at the identity *of* the community as security factor.

Each of these four problems will be outlined in greater detail in the third part of section 1. They can, however, usefully be introduced by pre-viewing a smaller case before the real one:

A Scandinavian intervention

Scandinavia – or as we prefer to say in the region "Norden" – is probably *the* standard example of an uncontested security community. Some doubt that Western Europe is one, but few would question USA–Canada or the Nordic case, and of these two the latter avoids the possible counter-arguments of quasi-imperial hegemony explanations. Yet, the Nordic case is not much researched, probably because it has been seen as too easy or self-evident: Of course, Sweden and Denmark do not fight each other. This is a perfect illustration of the existence of a security community: no one can *imagine* a war between these countries any more! The self-evidence imputed to the case is, however, false. Historically, it was not obvious that the Nordic countries should form a security community. It emerged against a historical record of incessant and often ferocious warfare. "During the past five centuries, there have been some fifty international or civil wars in the Nordic area. The frequency of intra-Nordic wars declined drastically only in the nineteenth century."[3]

That Scandinavia is indeed a security community can be shown by the existence of what Håkan Wiberg calls "a series of non-wars in the twentieth century; that is, there have been several conflicts about issues that would typically lead to war, but these were peacefully resolved":[4] Norwegian secession from Sweden in 1905, the Åland Islands issue 1918–21, Svalbard, Icelandic independence, and Norwegian–Danish contest for Greenland. "The significance of these non-wars should be underscored, since issues related to secession, territory, and sovereignty normally have a strong tendency to cause military action."[5]

This strong security community contains several peculiarities. It is not strongly institutionalized, and in particular there has been a marked and for the Cold War period deliberate absence of *security* institutions; the security community was not intentional, not formulated as security project, but emerged inadvertently; it does not reflect exceptionally dense societal transactions; and it is not based on economic foundations.[6] In addition to the geopolitical factor of long periods of low strategic interest, and a certain level of interaction, most of the explanation hangs on ideological factors such as a shared Protestant culture, joint romantic myths of ancient origins, nordism of the nineteenth century, neutrality and pacifism. Shared identity was, however, not opposed to nationalism. In the case of the Nordics, nationalism was combined with a second nationalism: Nordism (or Scandinavism).[7] For a short time this larger/pan identity was a challenger for the nations – suggesting an alternative state-formation and thus a parallel to other pan-nationalisms of the nineteenth century such as pan-Germanism and pan-Slavism – but it came later to serve as a kind of second-order nationalism imbedded in the particular national identities as a part of what it meant to be Swedish, Norwegian etc. While often reinforcing nationalism against non-Nordics, internally it exacts some degree of mutual affiliation, a feeling of being "broderfolk" (sister nations).[8] Chronologically, Nordic identity could not have caused the security community; it rather emerged together with or partly as an effect of non-war, but became one of its main pillars of stability. Origins are a different story.

Håkan Wiberg, in the best study of the formation of the Nordic security community, emphasizes the role of historical coincidence, with *fortuna* in this case materialized in the figure of Tsar Alexander I. In connection with the Napoleonic wars and the Vienna Congress, Finland was transferred from Sweden to Russia, Norway from Denmark to Sweden.

Both nations obtained more autonomy and got into an arrangement which they could more easily get out of a century later, which helped to forestall bitter struggles of national liberation. If Norway had been Danish and Finland Swedish at the time of their national liberations, they would have had to liberate themselves from countries they had been part of for centuries and where they were seen as essential parts of the realm. This would have been much tougher than being accepted as defecting from countries they had been under for less than 100 years.[9]

The Nordic system is "tightly coupled" only in a few areas such as free movement ("passport union"). Generally, Nordic cooperation is

unable to overcome any major conflict with nationally defined interests due to an unwillingness to enter into anything approaching
diffuse reciprocity.[10] Much adjustment takes place in a very undra-
matic bureaucrat-phones-bureaucrat manner,[11] but there has been a
lack of will to "invest" in the relationship through foregoing short-
term gains.[12] Achievements are mainly in the realm of coordination
games, and thus compatible with immediate self-interest. Weakest are
security cooperation and internationalization of authority.

This successful security community deviates from the stage-model
explored in this book: it is not achieved through institutions, it is not a
security effort, it has little to do with actual density of transactions,
there is not much sacrifice of narrow self-interest, and not an increasing attachment to a new identity that weakens the old state/nation
identities. The case might be explained away because Scandinavia is a
sub-region within a larger region and therefore not responsible for its
own peace. Possibly the study of security communities should focus
on those regions that constitute security complexes (which means the
scale of security interaction where actors form clusters where they are
necessary for understanding each others' security[13]). Maybe the
anomalies will then disappear. The study of Europe – this chapter –
will answer this.[14]

Four problems with Western Europe

Historical difficulties of the simple case

The first problem is simply too many possible explanations. The
emergence of a post-World War II West European security community
is compatible with a number of competing theories. There is no
puzzle, and for instance few realists will be tempted to turn to
alternative theories if they see no anomalies on the basis of balance of
power and alliance theory. (Realists are more likely to debate amongst
themselves about the respective merits of bipolarity and nuclear
weapons.[15]) The democracies-don't-fight-each-other theory could do
the full job as well, and so could, for instance, transactionalist or
transnationalist explanations in terms of peoples' exchanges, communication and interdependence. Much changed in Western Europe
after World War II, and therefore in terms of correlations, too many
explanations are tenable.

However, even if there is some truth to, say, the realist argument, this could be the coincidence factor (the equivalent to Alexander I in the Nordic case). In a perspective assuming path dependence, correlation-like origins are not the final word. Situations can obtain different supporting conditions and causes later on. We must study the social construction of the security community and investigate whether it has over time achieved sources of stability different from its sources of origin.

Pure power structuralists such as John Mearsheimer[16] note that the pillars of stability have now been removed and predict a return to Europe of the inter-war period. Similarly, Hedley Bull argued already during the Cold War that "Even the idea that Western European nations constitute a 'security-community' or area of peace is mere wishful thinking, if it means that war between them could not happen again, and not simply that it has not happened in recent decades and would not make sense."[17] The recent habit of cooperation among the nation-states of Western Europe – after a history of "endemic mutual conflict" – "has been under the shadow of the American presence and the threat from the East."[18]

However, other theories could equally explain the long peace (so we cannot know that bipolarity was *the* cause). Moreover, original causes can be supplemented by additional forces that eventually replace these as pillars of stability. Andrew Hurrell has recently argued that

> one can adopt a phased or "stage-theory" to understanding regionalism. Although theoretically somewhat unsatisfying, it is historically often very plausible. Thus, it might be argued that the early phases of regional cooperation may be the result of the existence of a common enemy or powerful hegemonic power; but that, having been thrown together, different logics begin to develop: the functionalist or problem-solving logic stressed by institutionalists, or the logic of community highlighted by the constructivists. Thus, neorealists may be right to stress the importance of the geopolitical context in the early stages of European unity, and yet wrong in ignoring the degree to which both informal integration and successful institutionalization altered the dynamics of European international relations over the ensuing forty years.[19]

Thus, a study of "security communities" should not focus on origins but try to grasp the clashing social forces that uphold and undermine "expectations of non-war," especially those made up of identity and community.

Security vs. war avoidance

Deutsch conceives of a security community only as a *non-war* community and his concept of security is thus at odds with most ongoing efforts to redefine and broaden it. Thinking about security community is often misled by this apparently trivial linguistic feature and reasons as if the existence of a security community ruled out all security dynamics and for instance had eliminated the security dilemma from the region.[20] If one had used the term "non-war community" these arguments would have been made less easily, despite the fact that the theorists in principle know that non-war community is exactly what Deutsch's "security community" means. This article will follow convention and use the term "security community" for "stable expectations of non-war", but keep open the possibility of non-military security dynamics operating in the West European security community. This turns a complication into an analytical instrument for grasping the dynamics of the community.

As noted above, the stability of a security community should be investigated as a question separate from its causal origins. It then becomes all the more important to grasp the forces threatening such a social formation. Security dynamics are particularly likely to play a key role in unravelling the community. When the security community is not based on hard causal connections to specific factors, it is clear that a security community can never be definitive – it remains precariously balanced on a constellation of a large number of factors.[21] Even a "democratic peace" might unravel due to the de-democratizing effects of war-expectations and arguments about a country's international position, as e.g. in Weimar Germany.[22] Seeing Europe as "probably a security community but not solidly anchored" points towards a focus on such potentially unravelling factors. Policies driven by security are able to unravel democratic peace and non-war communities.

The role of asecurity and unintended peace

As illustrated by the Nordic case, we should not decide *a priori* that a security community is closely linked to either formal institutions or self-conscious security efforts. Scandinavia is probably a case of unintended peace. There was not a powerful program for securing peace among the Nordic countries. Transactions, institutions and community feelings were generated by other aspirations and as a side effect contributed to the creation and consolidation of a security community.

Two different but related distinctions are involved. The first is the distinction between institutions and institutionalization (formal organizations and a general social shaping).[23] The second is the distinction between activities motivated *by security* versus those that have security as a side effect while motivated by other concerns. In some cases security might be furthered exactly by the downgrading of security concerns. It has been a much-criticized part of integration theory – functionalist as well as neo-functionalist – that it wanted to direct attention away from security issues. This has often been presented as naive, especially when it was given a too manipulative formulation – a formulation which implied too strongly that the integration threorists were manipulating actors who did not understand what was done to them. But the very idea, that *desecuritization* might be important for cooperation, is worth taking seriously, cf. the Nordic case.

The identity of identity and the stability of "Us"

Often "identity" is conceptualized in terms of how *alike* people (or other units) are in a given area. Deutsch's concept of the compatibility of core values could lead in this direction. At most this can be an important causal factor – one among many – that influences the distinctive object of interest: the strength of community feeling. Even with the strongest communities, nations, identity operates through a second-order reflection: we agree to assume that we share an identity. As explained by Ernest Gellner, national identity appears on the historical scene when it is no longer possible to make functional reference to one's location in the stratification of society; capitalism and industrialism need mobility and circulation in a much wider sphere, but also to have this space defined: "So culture, which had once resembled the air men breathed, and of which they were seldom aware, suddenly becomes perceptible and significant ... So – let culture be worshipped directly in its own name. That is nationalism."[24] What distinguishes (national) identity is not similarity or actual connectedness but the self-conscious *idea* of a community. In line with this book's *constructivist* redefinition of security communities: the community works when the actors choose to act *as if* there is a community.[25]

A common identity means that the category of the collective is part of the self-conception of individuals. It can always only be a *part of* and therefore its stability depends on how well it is articulated with other identity components. "We's" can not be studied as "me and my identity". An identity has to be seen in relation to other identities, not only the famous "Other" of self–other arguments, but also other "we's," because each self is constructed with the help of a complex constellation of collective identifications – identifications that have to be articulated with each other.

A distinct analytical field of discursive identity emerges where different collective categories are defined in relation to each other (a layer quite different from actual "similarity" or connectedness). By this approach we avoid the sterile debate over the relative power of loyalty to Europe versus loyalty to nation/state (where the latter is still likely to win out and thus make "Europe" seem irrelevant[26]). More interestingly, one can ask how the concept of Europe is stabilized by its inner connections to other – maybe more powerful – we's, by being implied in the redefinition of each nation/state identity.[27]

A research agenda and approach

Due to these four problems, it is not possible to go directly for the causal question of "what produced the security community?". Nor can one study the "community" in security community the traditional way through analysis of values or culture. Innovative strategies are necessary in order to get around the conceptual traps to researchable questions. Two theoretical pillars will be: (1) a re-sharpened concept of security, and (2) discourse analysis of state/nation/Europe (because stability is determined by how the mutual/inner relationships of the different we-identities are connected from the actors' perspective). The main analysis in the paper is built on these two main pillars – the second and third sections. The interpretation is then extended to questions about the security mechanisms in the emerging polity and the role of long-term change in "dynamic density", and draw on two additional theoretical traditions: English School and liberal transformationalist IR.

A security history of Western Europe after 1945

Twenty-five years ago, the urge to have done with our violent past left us no choice but to advance towards a common goal. What was decided on then is still just as vital; and now it is part of the everyday reality of our lives. Jean Monnet, *Memoirs*, 1976[28]

When a group of states is put into a quasi-permanent alliance – as was the case in Western Europe after the Second World War – where they must expect to be "on the same side" in a possible war, this does not make them a security community according to the Deutschian definition. The "dependent variable" ("dependable expectations of 'peaceful change'") is fullfilled, but it is a criterion that these expectations are assured *by* a sense of community (ignoring the further complication that "sense of community" is by Deutsch defined back circularly in terms of the dependable expectations of non-war; this has been remedied in the Adler/Barnett version). As spelled out in the introductory chapter of this book, the revised definition of security community is as *the species of non-wars that rests on identity and community.* Irrespective of how we weigh the various factors causing the *emergence* of the community, we have to track its social construction, its possible later base in something other than geopolitical rationality.

To determine whether the states are held together by fears of an external threat or by identity and community factors within, we will chronicle the evolution of "security" (in the wider sense). Non-war was assured, but what happened "underneath this" to security thinking in the region? Since non-military security dynamics are among the most likely sources for an unravelling of a security community, this will furthermore explore the stability of the community.

The concept of security

To study as an *empirical* question what is securitized in specific instances, "security" cannot be fixed *a priori* in its definition. The concept has to be open, clearly specified as a specific *form* of politics, but open for varying formulations and extensions by different actors. Furthermore, it needs to be an in-between concept of security between the narrow (always state, only military) and the wide (everything people worry about).

The meaning of a concept is in its usage. Not something we can define analytically according to what would be "best" or most "logical". This is not the same as asking what people (consciously) think it means. *What are the rules that implicitly define when and where the concept of security can be used meaningfully?* Security is a practice, a specific way to frame an issue. Security discourse is characterized by dramatizing an issue as having absolute priority. Something is presented as an existential threat: if we do not tackle this, everything else will be irrelevant (because we will not be here, or not be free to deal with future challenges in our own way). By labelling this a security issue, the actor has claimed a right to handle it with extraordinary means, to break the normal political rules of the game (e.g. in the form of secrecy, levying taxes or conscripts, limitations on otherwise inviolable rights).[29]

It follows from the always implied act, that security is about survival. Something is presented as existentially threatened, and on this basis it is argued that "we" must use extra-ordinary means to handle the threat. In the case of traditional state security: by saying "security", a state representative moves the issue into a specific area and demands a right for using the necessary means to block a threatening development.[30] The necessity of an existential quality ('survival') follows from the function of security discourse as *lifting* issues to an urgency and necessity above normal politics. To attempt to take an issue out of the normal weighing of issues against others demands both that it is generally accepted that the threatened has to survive, and that there is a possible point of no return where it can suddenly be too late, and it is therefore *necessary* to act in time – and therefore legitimate to over-rule normal procedures.

Because rules and procedures *otherwise* binding can be voided by the security argument, the labelling of issues as security problems contain the risk of unravelling patterns of mutual adjustment. The rules pushed aside can be internal – classically in the case of secrecy – or external – as when violation of GATT/WTO rules is legitimized by national security. Studying the use of "security" will therefore be informative for the purpose of tracing the security community. If security is legitimized with the community as referent object this assists in consolidating the community, and if it is done within the community it contains risks of triggering political escalations within which the community might unravel. Many different actors can use the security move, but typically there are a relatively limited number of possible "referent objects", i.e. those whom you can make reference to, and say "X is threatened, therefore we have to ..." Not all collectivities or principles have a widely accepted demand for survival.[31]

The idea of securitization immediately changes security/insecurity from being an exhaustive set of options (the more security, the less insecurity and vice versa) to being only two out of three basic categories. In the case of *desecuritization*, we have neither security nor insecurity. To talk of a situation as characterized by security means that a threat is articulated but that sufficient counter-measures are felt to be available – in contrast to insecurity with a threat and insufficient defence. If the situation is taken out of the realm of security conceptualization, the situation might inelegantly be described as one of "a-security." Since a security community is defined by the *impossibility of imagining* violence, it is at least as likely to be built on a-security as on security, because in the case of security, one imagines the violence but also believes one has a counter-measure.

A full documentation of the interpretations that follow would require a book-length examination at the level of textual analysis of a wide sample of central documents throughout the whole post-World War II period. This chapter provides a more impressionistic account, based on a number of general historical works on the period.[32]

The 1940s and 1950s

The five main issues securitized on a large scale and with general social resonance were as follows:

(1) The Soviet threat. Obviously, this was the issue securitized most dramatically, consistently and with the greatest social affect. It legitimized a wide array of activities and contributed to defining the identity of what was first of all a Western or North Atlantic community. With the strong, binary logic of the East–West conflict, European identity was naturally secondary and instrumental in relation to that of *the West*. This was also a product of the general admiration in Western Europe of the great American model society, but undoubtedly "the West" was strengthened by corrresponding to the general construction of "us" and "them"; if they were the Soviet Bloc, the communists, we were "the West". There is no need here to tell the story of the peaks and troughs of this threat construction over the Berlin blockade of 1948, fears strengthened by the outbreak in 1950 of the Korean war, limited détente 1953–55, etc.

(2) An internal political threat, the Communists. If the communists were simply a domestic political force, it was problematic to present this in public as a threat leading to security action. Its possible security

articulation therefore depended on its conjunction with the Soviet threat (whether the "real" hierarchy of fears in the elite was really the opposite need not concern us here). Beyond pointing back to threat no.1, it also linked on to threat no.3, because the major policy response to the alleged domestic threat was to insist on economic success, and thereby to infuse economic performance with a security rationale.

(3) *The economy* could be presented as a security argument, as a matter of survival in the years immediately after the Second World War when it was uncertain whether Europe would recover.[33] But the spectacular and lengthy boom which took place in West European economies relatively soon after the war meant that a form of concern sufficiently dramatic to warrant the security label probably subsided around the end of the 1940s.[34] Since it took longer to overcome the various imbalances created by the boom itself, Alan Milward argues, there were a number of difficult and dangerous situations specific to individual countries. For instance, French concerns about the time needed to establish competitiveness motivated much of its European and thus security, policy. In Germany, in particular historical experience fostered fears of the economy as something that could "break down," with inflation as the early symptons. The same attitude contributes to present-day policy (e.g. resistance against giving up the D-Mark).

(4) *The German question.* With the prospect of Germany returning to the scene, the answer dominant both within Germany and among American and European countries was one of *Einbindung* into NATO as well as (what became) the EU. Most important in this context were the considerations of France – to which we return below. The constant wavering in French attitudes between keeping Germany down and integrating (with) Germany for most of the period usually favored integration, but it was clear that a major motive for this was the German problem and arguments about why it was unwise to try the first strategy or the lack of a real possibility heretofore, i.e. a security argument.

(5) With *Europe*, rather than simply Germany, as referent, one saw a more general historical argument: Europe had to make a choice to *change course from wars to integration*. Jean Monnet in his memoirs presents his reflections in the period around the end of the war: "If, as I believed, the Provisional Government proved capable of preventing anarchy or a Communist takeover [NB: threats no. 2 and 3; OW], there would soon be a tendency to return to the old order. In that case, the greatest danger would be that of rebuilding a Europe made up of

sovereign States, each exposed to the facile temptations of protectionism." And then he quoted a note he had written in 1943:

> There will be no peace in Europe if States re-establish themselves on the basis of national sovereignty, with all that this implies by way of prestige policies and economic protectionism. *If the countries of Europe once more protect themselves against each other*, it will once more be necessary to build up vast armies [...] Europe will be reborn yet again under *the shadow of fear*.[35]

The threat is mutual security policy as such. It is not a question of assuring a good, stable security system, but of avoiding security concerns being directed at each other at all, by somehow circumventing this traditional logic, directing energies elsewhere. This interpretation does not arise only if one – idealistically, some would say – asks from the perspective of "Europe", because Monnet concludes his note by stating "The solution to the European problem is all-important to the life of France."[36] The argument about Europe having to learn the lesson of the war was central to thinking within the resistance movements of the war.[37] The idea of Europe presented in such circles after the war was not one of restoration, of recapturing the good traditions of Europe; it was rather an argument about a necessary break with European traditions, especially the tradition of organizing on the basis of sovereign states. (More will be said below on this rupture argument.)

Most remarkable about this list[38] is that there is not much of "this European country fears that one". Of course, there was a certain resentment against Germany and a corresponding German worry about its future. Of this type of classical state-to-state security fear, the most important instance is probably French long-time concern about Germany. Milward has asked and answered like this:

> How did France, starting from so weak a position in 1945 and pursuing an unrealizable set of foreign policy objectives, arrive at such a satisfactory long-term political and economic solution? The answer must be, not that the French policy-making machine was in any way superior to that in Britain, which largely failed to achieve its own objectives in the reconstruction of Europe, but that the German threat to French national security simply would not go away and, because it was always there, forced French policy-formulation to consider a more distant horizon. In the constant effort of lifting the eyes to that horizon a longer-term solution was eventually found.[39]

Thus, even this concern was partly displaced to another level, but mutual security concerns remained a conscious motivation for policy.

Together with the other five fears, the elements of state-to-state concerns produced a general situation where insecurity was wide-spread.

Several of these security arguments were in various mixes involved in the establishment of the "Western" organizations, OEEC (later OECD), NATO, the Council of Europe, the European Coal and Steel Community, the failed attempt at a European Defence Community, revival of the Brussels treaty, German accession into it and NATO, and then in 1957, the treaty of Rome establishing the EEC and Euratom.

In this first period, European integration worked relatively well. Conflicts concentrated on the differences in approach between the Six and the rest, led by Britain, that became in 1960 EFTA. Conflicts of approach among the six did not break out clearly until the early 1960s with Charles de Gaulle as catalyst and focal figure. Therefore, the image of European integration could be colored by odd mixtures of the discourse of federalists on supranational institutions and functionalist arguments about practical cooperation.[40] Early integration theory was born under these conditions.[41]

Reaching the second half of the 1950s, "Western Europe had largely recovered from the difficulties of the immediate post-war years, and the perceived threat from internal communist subversion or imminent Soviet invasion was receding. The sense of being beleaguered therefore declined, although a defensive and highly suspicious attitude remained."[42] "Moreover, after the upheavals of 1956, it was evident that the post-war order on the continent was not likely to change as a result of war or violent revolution".[43]

1960-1985: neo-functionalism and Gaullism

During this period, security rhetoric was generally much less drastic. Feelings of urgent threat receded and security arguments became increasingly a ritual for securing a *continued* upholding of the deterrence order. From insecurity – seeing a "security problem" with a lack of counter-measures – debate moved towards a picture of "security" as an important field of constant effort, one that actually provides security. The East–West conflict was a problem *with* a "solution", and the whole arrangement became institutionalized. The East–West situation was one of "security" rather than "insecurity".

The crises in Berlin and Cuba were turning points. With the Berlin Wall in 1961 and Cuba 1962, it seemed more and more impossible that one side or the other would make large gains by means of military operations, or military-based political manipulation or bluffing. It became increasingly clear that in the non-military area it was always possible for the regime to control things – if not in any other way then with the help of some friends with tanks – and military threats could be fenced off because of the general nuclear condition. Quoting the late Franz Josef Strauss, "In the present European situation there is no possibility of changes through war, but neither through revolution or civil war."[44] In the European post-war constellation there seemed to be no change possible without some degree of consent of the power-holders. Change had to be a negotiated process of pressure and acceptance, stabilization and de-stabilization, crystallizing in debates over degrees and forms of détente.[45] For this reason, most of the drama was taken out of security. Opposition parties could try to denounce the détente policy of the government for exposing our side to some kind of abuse from the other. But it became increasingly difficult to imagine a major military move with a political purpose. The fear of war as such and of the fall-out from the miliary systems (nuclear testing) peaked in the early 1960s too (nuclear disarmament movements).

The 1960s might be seen as a period of explorations and probings, culminating in the gradual change of Germany policies – not least West German policies towards the East and in relation to German unity – towards the formal recognitions of the post-war order in 1969–74. Pierre Hassner has described the period from 1961 to 1968 as a period of selective détente where hopes persisted that one might use détente for fooling allies out of the grip of the other side, where Paris/Prague 1968 created the definite shift towards "status quo détente".[46]

Only in specialist circles did intense security concerns continue. Within the logic of deterrence strategy, security problems continued to emerge – missile gaps, windows of opportunity – and necessary counter-measures were debated.[47] Some security specialists interpreted eurocommunism as a dangerous plot in the East–West struggle. Such concerns became institutionalized and professionalized, and although they did not operate in the public as ostentatious security arguments, they continued to have policy effects. While the public sphere experienced a general desecuritization, strategic studies (security experts) reached its high point. This shows how securitization can be institutionalized through professionalization, thereby upholding the prioritizing function of the security speech act without a need for constant public drama.[48]

Simultaneously, the process of integration moved into a period of desecuritization. Where the peace argument had been foremost in the early period, later work came to concentrate on practical progress in the various issue areas. The ruling neo-functionalists were, of course, aware of an original security motivation behind the project, but the strategy to realize this was through desecuritization. The European states amongst themselves moved towards a state of *asecurity*, where the very question of what kind of security arrangement one relied on became absurd. The West European states did not think in terms of security/insecurity, but tried to think about something else. This was to create some of the problems of the 1980s and especially 1990s where it was suddenly difficult especially in the new member countries (such as Britain and Denmark) to explain that security was central to the rationale of European integration because it played so little a role at the time of their accession (1972).

Wasn't the resulting semi-automatic process of integration then seen as a threat? A possible candidate for security action could be de Gaulle's policy of the first half of the 1960s culminating in the EC's "constitutional crisis" of 1965–66 (France's empty chair and eventually the Luxembourg compromises). A first thought could well be that this is a security move on behalf of state sovereignty. That is partly the way it has been constructed in hindsight, for example, the Stanley Hoffmann high/low politics argument that states are not *allowing* supranationality to run further than so far, then they re-assert authority.[49] Security mobilization on behalf of a threatened state was, however, not de Gaulle's style. It would have been far too defensive and weak to say: EC integration is a threat to state sovereignty. Much more offensively he said: this is the wrong way to construct Europe, we have to do it my way. If he used an argument about a threat, it was rather Europe that was the referent object, Europe that was to be defended. With a British-influenced and technocratic-unpolitical Europe, there would be too much American dominance (through NATO), and thus really no "Europe". In order to create "une Europe européenne", it had to be political in a sense which only the states (and France in particular) could perform, whereas the Commission, useful as it might be as a technical organ could not constitute a political power.[50] For Europe's sake: if the others were not willing to proceed in the areas of security, defence and foreign policy, France had better keep its freedom of action.[51] The main slogan was now "the independence of France." Only at the most intense moments of the crisis of the empty chair did the French President (and other French politicians) use rhetorics with the grand historical sweep about the technocratic and supranational EC posing a threat to French democracy and sovereignty.[52] A security argument about the threat from integration is not systematic and widespread in any sense equivalent to the 1990s.

The net effect of the crisis and resolution was to reinforce a process of moderate and controlled integration; and thereby also reinforce the low politics "strategy." There was in the whole crisis paradoxically a sign of strength for integration: EC integration had proceeded so far that states could not allow bureaucrats to run it. Even de Gaulle did not want to stop it but only ensure that we the states(men) had check on it, which concretely meant to move power from Commission to Council and ensure the veto on vital matters. On the one hand this meant that the political side was strengthened by the statesmen appearing more on the scene; on the other, it removed the prospect of a swift and easy state-making of the EC and thereby consolidated the image of a mainly technical cooperation. The period was one of desecuritization.

Towards the end of the 1970s, Europe experienced a rhetoric that could be seen as verging on security argumentations: the fear of "euro-sclerosis" at times took on an existential quality, where Europe was seen as decisively falling behind in the global competition. This argument did, however, not become the basis for major action until the next period.

Revival of European integration – before and after the revolution (1985–1992)

From the mid 1980s and into the 1990s, integration accelerated in terms of a spread to new issue areas, new rounds of enlargement and a resurfacing of supranational potentials subdued since the Luxembourg compromise. Again, security arguments played a role. In the mid-1980s around the time of the Single European Act (SEA) and the beginning of the internal market ('1992') project, two security arguments were at play:

- Military security played a role in the form of a fear of East–West confrontation and thereafter of the opposite, of uncontrolled détente, i.e. fear of US–Soviet condominium. Both swings in the US-Soviet relationship under Reagan were interpreted as necessitating an independent security voice. This period generally witnessed strong securitization attempts in the area of military matters: the peace movements who asserted an existential threat from nuclear weapons, an establishment arguing an urgent Soviet threat and European politicians claiming a need for a more distinct European role.

• Probably more important for European integration was the impression of global economic competition which Europe was seen as losing so decisively that this became a security argument. This was a major motive in the SEA and internal market process.[53]

After 1989, new elements were added to the security discourse of Europe: environmental security, migrants, ethnic conflict, organized crime, terrorism. The diversity of securitization increased, but it was difficult to see what general patterns emerged from these new security problems – except complexity as such and increasingly an atmosphere of "insecurity" in contrast to the a-security of especially the 1970s. Increasingly, two specific security arguments came to organize the scene and they will be the focus of the next sub-section.

In relation to the post-1989 situation, we need to address an issue raised more generally in relation to security communities: the role of military transparency and confidence building. Military transparency today exists in Europe at an unusually high level. This is a product of decades of cooperation in NATO. There are attempts to extend this through NACC (North Atlantic Cooperation Council), PfP (Partnership for Peace), EAPC (Euro-Atlantic Partnership Council) and actual NATO enlargement, all based on NATO. Some more clearly "East–West" defined cooperation exists in the CSCE, now OSCE, however at a completely different level from what has been achieved among the NATO countries. Because NATO was an Organization, not only a paper alliance, and developed integrated command structures, joint exercises, and numerous exchange systems, the whole military institution and profession became internationalized in a historically unique way. A major transformation has taken place: sociologically, the military is no longer the core nationalist and militarist interest group it used to be in previous centuries (and still is to some extent in e.g. Latin America). The military has a quite internationalist self-perception and thus a culture of openness and transparency has emerged that does not have to be imposed through constant confidence-building treaties.[54] Whereas the general institutionalist interpretation of European security is problematic because international institutions might prove dependent on the international power structure, the de-nationalization of the military operates at a different sociological micro-level, and is therefore not vulnerable to this objection.

Integration/fragmentation and the emerging European security identity after 1992

The two most clearly articulated long-range scenarios for European security are interlocked in a strange way where each is the other's main argument. An integrated Europe is presented by some as the only way to avoid a return to a war-ridden, balance of power driven Europe. Conversely, the process of integration is seen as the main threat by substantial groups in several member states, who argue for the defence of national identity or state sovereignty against a threatening European super-state.[55]

Fear of integration. In contrast to the 1960s, anti-EU discourse of the 1990s has been framed with reference less to sovereignty and more to defending (national) identity – rarely from state elites, mostly anti-establishment groups. *Raison d'Etat* is less dangerous to the EU than *raison de nation*. This is an important instance of the increasing diversity of referent objects of security in Europe.

Integration and fragmentation trigger each other. It was widely assumed after 1989 that the only viable way to counter and contain fragmentation in Eastern Europe was to strengthen European integration. This in turn generated opposition and resistance among peoples (such as Danes and Britons) in Western Europe, and this in turn leads to new initiatives for integration with a hard core, which again ... etc. In a meta-stability of contradictory possibilities, these two become the dominant images of what could be Europe's future, integration or fragmentation – or in Francis Beer and Jeffrey Kopstein's expression "Europe-Maastricht" and "Europe-Sarajevo".[56]

Fear of fragmentation. European integration increasingly rests on the security argument that Europe needs integration in order to avoid fragmentation. Europe has for most of its modern history been a balance of power system where a number of great powers compete for influence and allies. The Cold War was an exception, interrupting this internal power balancing (and wars following from it) as external powers "overlaid" the European system. Without this overlay, Europe after the Cold War faced the basic choice of whether to return to traditional power balancing or to create enough concentration of power to achieve a centered development (as e.g. North America – and a long list of historical cases from other regions). In this argument, it is obviously *Europe* which is at stake – and at stake in some fateful manner. Which direction shall European history take? In one (integration) there is room for much more "Europe" than in the other (fragmentation). The choice is fateful because it is difficult to change directions when developments have proceeded beyond a certain point down either of these roads. This is a security argument attached to Europe as such, and appeals to "European security" increasingly build on this argument.[57]

After World War II, the European idea was to a large extent shaped as a revolt against Europe's own past. Only to a limited extent was the European project promoted as a return to a lost time of greatness; much more so as the possibility that Europeans learn from their past and set new aims[58]. The Europe discourse of the 1990s contains a mixture of this future-oriented logic and elements of more nostalgic, euro-national celebration of uniquely European traditions. Exactly in the field of security there is a strong emphasis on the self-negating, self-transforming argument in relation to Europe itself. Europe's "Other", the enemy image, is today not to a very large extent "Islamic fundamentalism," "the Russians" or anything similar – rather Europe's Other is Europe's own past which should not be allowed to become its future.[59]

After the displays of fear of integration in 1992, Brussels backed down from heavy-handed cultural nation-building. European identity is phrased as a predominantly political identity, while ethno-national cultural identity remains with the nation states (and regions). Instead of building identity from within through homogenization,[60] it is increasingly done on the outside – by achieving an "identity" in the eyes of others. Europe can exist only if it has a "defense identity" and is a recognized actor on the international arena.[61] Europe as project, as history, is at a crossroads and security is at play as the question of integration vs. fragmentation. *Integration* is made an aim in itself because the alternative is fragmentation, a self-propelling process that by definition will destroy "Europe" as a project. Whether "Europe" exists or not appears as an either–or question, and a question with security dimensions. The question of integration thus gains a grammatical form that brings it closer to security logic. *If* first fragmentation sets in, it will be a self-reinforcing force that rules out for a long time any possibility of "Europe". Integration is thus the referent point for a security rhetorics of "Europe", and it takes on the existential quality characteristic of security, because integration/fragmentation is a question not of how Europe will be, but whether Europe will be. This particular security argument is one of the clearest cases today of security *in the name of Europe,* and it is close to the core question in the present context of "we-feeling" and identity *in the security field.*

Stages in the emergence of the security community

The phases can be summarized in this way. First, *insecurity* (not only military but various forms of non-military insecurity) and security became a main motive for integration. The second phase was one of first *security* and on this basis *desecuritization* leading towards a-security. Thirdly, there has been some *resecuritization* – but not with the state(s) as referent object, and in the fourth and current phase this crystallizes at two other levels: Europe (integration in order to avoid fragmentation) and nations (defending themselves against integration).

These four phases do not completely parallel the three-phase model explored in this book. The first phase *was* marked by institution building and motivated by both mutual and common external security concerns. However, security integration went very far very quickly, and mainly for external security reasons (NATO). The middle period was not spent gradually getting used to close involvement in security or building trust to allow further integration. War amongst the members was almost unthinkable all the time anyway because of the East–West context. National identity is not of decreasing importance throughout the period. To the contrary, nationalism was banished in the immediate post-World War II years because of the war, whereas it has become more legitimate in the 1990s. This, however, does not always question the security community. Most of the deviations thus relate to the "premature" integration of security and the non-confrontation between nation and region.

The first could be due to the peculiarities of the case, where in Europe the preeminent security organization has been NATO which was there from the beginning, already before the security community and probably part of the reasons for its formation. The second important organization, the EU, has been the main format for the continued non-war community and probably for its cultivation of the real "security community" features in terms of identity and the non-imaginability of war, but this has happened for most of the period in the form of desecuritization! Therefore, the EU has secured the security community not by upgrading joint security activities but on the contrary by doing other things. While there are thus peculiarities of the case that could explain the deviance from the three-phase model, the reformulated theory of security communities has the problem that its basic conception does not operate with security *organizations* as necessary feature, and therefore their inclusion in the phases can only be as a heuristic device.

The European case, however, exposes a more general and theoretically more interesting problem with the phases: a too linear conjunction of "we-identity", formal institutions, polity and peace. Do we necessarily get more peace only in parallel with more organization and more identity? Such links are characteristic of the modern nation-state, but in a longer historical perspective, polities have exhibited radical disjunctures. For instance, the idea that a ruler should speak the same language as the peasants that were his subjects did not occur to a medieval or even early-modern king – as anthropologist Anne Knudsen has remarked: what should they be talking about?[62] Social life was stratified transnationally and horizontally, only with the combination of the modern state and romanticism did one get the ideal of the nation as one big family, and suddenly identity became powerful in politics. The identity-politics fusion is not an ahistorical necessity. The complexity of the emerging European situation with overlapping authorities reminds us of the need to stay free of sovereignty infused inside/outside logic and the domestic analogy. It might seem strange to place this a criticism at the door of the security community literature, which exactly tried to overcome the domestic/international dichotomy,[63] but as R. B. J. Walker has kept reminding the IR discipline: these concepts are not easy to escape, they are so foundational to our whole political vocabulary that they easily slip into the attempts to transcend traditionalism. Our concepts of democracy, security, community and identity are deeply marked by the modern principle of sovereignty, and if we try to think about new forms of security that might begin to transcend the sovereignty-based codes, we need to be extremely wary about sovereignty creeping back in through surprising passageways.[64] Without explicit state-centrism, it can show up in our new concepts as well. For instance, in assumptions of correlation between peace, organizations and communal identity.

Although Europe has not obeyed the three-phase model, this section has shown that it clearly went through distinct phases. A period of desecuritization, the ideal condition for a security community, has been replaced by reemerging but decentralized securitization, potentially a less stable situation. The obvious next question is therefore exactly where we are and where we are likely to be going.

Imagining Europe and identifying us

The struggle for Europe begins with a struggle inside each nation.
Etienne Tassin[65]

This section will focus on the question of the solidity of the security community that emerged as outlined in the previous section. The definition of security community is peace that is stable *because of* community and identity. We therefore investigate how community/identity is stabilized and stabilizing.

Europe

Europe became an increasingly powerful political symbol during the 1980s, but different actors gave the concept quite different meanings.[66] Different discourses compete internationally about defining the term, but since politicians still have to legitimize their policy first of all domestically, they are mostly constrained by what can make political sense according to the domestic rules of political discourse. When "Europe" becomes more important, this then means first of all that this concept becomes more central within national systems of meaning. "Europe" is shaped by the different traditions of political thought, but each of them has Europe more centrally tied into the networks than before.

Is Europe then a community? Without a shared conception does it fulfil the criteria for security community, that non-war is based on identity and community? Yes. Europe takes increasingly important positions *in* the different discourses, and among the most important pillars of stability in Europe today are the various parallel, interconnected identity definitions of state-nation-Europe. To assume that the identity of a region has to be a big over-riding we – we "Europeans" –

is to reify the nation-state model. The region is rather a constellation of we's. Maybe Europe is not even that much of a we, but a way, a how, where there is more and more of a European flavor to being French, German, and so on. Since concepts of state and nation are strong organizing ideas for foreign policy, a consistent European definition of these will make for a social anchoring of the security community. As Michael Barnett has noticed in relation to the Arab world: "scholarship on Arab nationalism has an either/or quality: the Arab nation either takes precedence over all other identities or it is meaningless; either Arab nationalism necessitates political unification or it is without force."[67] Similarly, "Europe" should be seen neither as a project replacing the nation/state nor as irrelevant. It is an additional layer of identification. Since this is vulnerable to re-mobilization of the better established state/nation identities, it is important to study how the state/nations themselves have been transformed, and the European level integrated *into* the meaning of state/nation. Because – as often pointed out by constructivists – a re-assertion of national "self-interest" will be less problematic when the self has changed to a less narrow form. In this case, in a direction, where the national "self" contains a narrative with Europe as required component.

The identity pillars of European integration and security

The discursive role of "Europe" is not captured by contrasting Europe to the national identities, but by studying how e.g. the meaning of "French" interests is redefined by an inclusion of "Europe". EU/rope is essential to the dominant narration of what "France" is and where it is heading in the future. If Europe were removed (integration collapsed), the meaning of France would have to be radically re-articulated. Identity is narrative,[68] and there are only so many basic stories to be told about what France is about.

Especially for a major power, the overall foreign policy line must be explainable as to where this leaves "us": what kind of future for "France"/"Germany"/"Russia" in what kind of Europe? This is not a static challenge in the sense that there is one fixed idea of say France. But there are some basic core meanings (the state-nation) that can only be related to Europe in a limited number of ways. Therefore, several different Europe policies are meaningful in a French political context – but not just *any* Europe policy. Several policies that would seem perfectly logical from a Finnish perspective – or from the perspective of some abstract theory of "state interests" – would be very difficult to present in the French political language.

Good statesmanship will try to find ways to articulate the nation/ state that result in Europe policies that also leave room for the other major nation/states (and their Europes). Immediately after the fall of the Berlin Wall, Germany – who had potentially much to win, but also a lot to lose if others turned against it – was especially active in building the French and the Russian Europe (and the Americans by playing with and not again unification secured a place for the Atlantic Europe) and thus we arrived at the relatively successful "grand bargain" of 1990.[69] Europe to the French meant strengthening of a France-like EU, to the Russians it meant securing some all-European framework that defined Russia as within Europe, and to the Germans Europe meant allowing interactions, societies and economies to re-connect across old divisions.

In 1990 it was possible to give Europe a direction of development where all of the Europe projects could unfold simultaneously. They are competitors, but not incompatible – and thereby all major powers were able to imagine themselves in the Europe promised. Henry Kissinger once introduced the important concept of a power's *vision of itself*:

> [Security] is not a mechanical problem [...] an exact balance is impossible [...] because while powers may appear to outsiders as factors in a security arrangement, they appear domestically as expressions of a historical existence. No power will submit to a settlement, however well-balanced and however "secure", which seems totally to deny its vision of itself.[70]

The European post-Wall order was stable because it fullfilled the dual criteria of two kinds of compatibility: first, that it is possible in each of the major countries to construct a narrative of state, nation and Europe that makes sense in relation to the national tradition of political thought, and secondly, when we in this way get Europe in the plural, that these different Europes are politically compatible, that it is possible for a French integration project, German border-pene-trating networks and Russian all-European structures to unfold at the same time. Then it is unproblematic that e.g. the German version of creating a "vision of itself" – with a low political profile, an emphasis upon economy, and the downgrading of borders – is seen as mildly ridiculous in France.

The main question for the future of Europe, for stability and peaceful change, is now not directly the relations among the major powers, but the *inner* struggles over national identity/Europe projects in France, Germany and Russia. In each country strong competitors have emerged to the project that functioned in the comprehensive *quid pro quo* of 1990.

To judge how stable this constellation is, one has to enter into the different constructions as they look, as it were, from the inside. This is of course a quite demanding task, and we will here take only a brief look at two of the most important countries, France and Germany.[71] This leads amongst other things to the somewhat surprising conclusion that Europe does not first of all have a German problem, but a French problem.

Germany after the Cold War has witnessed an increasing presence of alternative lines, of more nationalist suggestions for a more German, less European policy, but basically the very Europe oriented version of what Germany is, where Germany is going, and thereby what German "interests" are, have kept its solid hold on the political elite. New voices like notably a "neo-statist" position of "a nation-state has to act like a nation-state, a power has to conduct power politics" has not achieved much influence, but this is first of all because the elite has been able to keep up its story about where Germany is going, one based on European integration. This only works if there is some relatively successful European integration to point to. The two leading political combattants (SPD and CDU/CSU as well as the leading challenger, "D-Mark nationalism") all share a conception of the German state and nation tied to a vision of an integrating Europe.[72] Only if the EU breaks down will the situation change radically – then all of these three drop out, and the only serious candidate is the neo-statist position of "we have to act as a great power because we are one."

In the case of France, it is even more clear what the basic logical options are. There is a very distinct French concept of the state-nation saying first of all that state and nation are mutually defining (and then furthermore hinting at the *patrie* and at an external role for the state). This state-nation can relate to Europe in three ways: (1) externally with Europe as the scene on which France acts, (2) through a doubling where Europe is created as a larger France which takes on the tasks and ideals of France because France has become too small to project its universal values itself (Mitterrand), and (3) to execute the typical French state-nation operation on Europe as such, i.e. to create a Europe that is French in its form, but not with a distinct France in it. What is remarkable about French politics – in contrast to German – is that the three main competing rationales for French foreign (and domestic) politics represent the different basic structural options. Whereas François Mitterrand ten years ago had a solid consensus around his position of the doubling of France as EU, and therefore transferring state-qualities to Europe, there have been increasing problems and challenges, and especially in the 1992 Maastricht referendum and less in the 1995 Presidential election, ideas of more strict Gaullist derivation were present as the main challenger (much stronger than the federalist alternative represented by Valery Giscard d'Estaing). Jacques Chirac is ruling on the basis of a coalition that mixes Mitterrand continuation with strong elements of French independence, for instance with state-based alliance politics both with and against Germany. Various internal as well as external problems have made the "Mitterrand line" more and more difficult to present convincingly, and therefore a meaning vacuum threatens in France. Up to the EU's 1996–97 Inter Governmental Conference, France which normally represents "the vision thing" found it unusually difficult to come with any concept for Europe.

Because France experiences increasing tensions both on the internal side – making the new Europeanized France compatible with basic traditions of French statehood (discussions on banalization, regionalization etc.) – and on the external side (are we binding Germany or rather binding ourself?), there is increasing room for alternative stories. If implemented they would demand radical change on either side – in France, in Europe or both. It is increasingly questioned whether the existing France and the evolving Europe are immediately compatible, or whether a new compatibility must be created by statesmanship in either the internal or external arena.[73]

Those who assume that "talk is cheap" will say, you can always come up with a narrative for France to suit any policy. If, in contrast, one believes there is structure to language and that a large part of politics is about structuring the national conceptual landscape, options are not so abundant. For France there are the three basic structural routes, and each of these can be given different concrete policy formulations. But there are many policies (for instance most of the roles allocated to France in American plans for Europe) that are completely unrealistic. Even if the actual resources of France make most of the grand visions hard to carry through, it is more likely that the winning line will be either a self-defeating grand policy or eventually the far-reaching federalism that at least takes a French political *form,* rather than an un-heroic, Anglified policy without any vision for France and for Europe.

The inner stability of a cooperative, parallel realization of the different Europes has already been broken on the Russian side, and it is more and more likely that Russia will slide out of the bargain to a mixture of confrontation and cooperation. In Germany an alternative story is available, but it is not able to break the hold of the dominant one – nor is there any need for this, because the dominant one continues to produce a convincing vision for Germany's future. France is the weak point of the European scene – the Europe oriented self-interpretation of France is challenged. If France turns away from this line, Germany's overall concept of Europe *and thereby of itself* will loose its rationale. Then the alternative narratives in Germany will suddenly have the chance of filling a vacuum, and German "interests" and "orientations" could change drastically. This interaction of domestic struggles over the meaning of state, nation and Europe, is where the direction of developments will be decided. The regional identity "Europe" clearly has become more important and today plays a key role *in* self-conceptions. Its meaning is not settled once and for all, but of the concepts of state and nation that compete, most are thoroughly Europeanized.

Security provision in the Europe of the mid-1990s – beyond the pluralistic/amalgamated dichotomy

Most of the discussion above has been about European integration rather than European security. Does keeping the different "Europes" together generate security? Who and what is able to alleviate and (equally important) forestall security concerns and conflicts in Europe? By answering this, we also answer another of the questions asked of all chapters, that of boundary and expansion of the community.

At first sight – of Bosnia – some could conclude that the gloomy Mearscheimer predictions of "back to the future" have been vindicated. However, developments in Europe went wrong the wrong way. Yes, there are conflicts in Europe, but no, they are not driven by nor

have they triggered balance-of-power behavior, competitive interventions and rivalling alliances among the powers of Europe. The
basic pattern in Europe is not one of a number of centers competing
(the "normal" one), nor is it simply one of abstract "cooperation" or
collective security – it is too asymmetrical for that. It is one where the
many centers have been replaced by *the* center, by a pattern of
concentric circles around the EU center (or sometimes the EU/NATO
center).

Since 1989, European politics has unfolded not between the centers
but around *one* center. A surprisingly large section of European
controversies of recent last years can be translated into issues of center-
periphery, distance, questions of getting in to achieve influence versus
keeping distance for the sake of independence. The overarching
image is of one center and concentric circles, a completely different
mental geography from the usual one of several competing centers.

The EU as a crucial security "institution" decides which of the two
European patterns will unfold: integration or fragmentation. The EU
is important for European security at three levels. It has (1) the
primary function of keeping the core intact, ensuring there *is* one
center rather than several in Western Europe; (2) silent disciplining
power on "the near abroad"; the magnetism working already in East-
Central Europe; (3) a potential role as direct intervenor in specific
conflicts. These three functions follow a quasi-geographical distribution as concentric circles. The first is about the core itself, the
second is about the close outsiders, and the third about those
peripheral actors that still in some sense circle around this center.[74]

The first is primary (because without it there would be no "we" to
deal with the others, only separate powers), the second is the most
interesting, and the third the most precarious. The second about East
Central Europe is a lot about enlargement, but even more about the
prospect of enlargement. The "Eastern" countries act according to
anticipated Western judgements because of the prospect of membership. That is the reason why the EU rarely gives a no to an application
for membership (only Morocco, not Turkey, no country in the East),
but always a "yes but"! This works even more strongly probably as a
discipline than actual membership (cf. Greece!).[75] Thus, it could seem
that this mechanism would fade away as enlargement is realized.
Europe, however, has the form of a number of layers or concentric
circles, and the countries that were in the yes-but-but position move
up to yes-but while a new group enters yes-but-but. Thus the pattern

– the magnet and its field of forces – stays the same, only the status of specific members change. This mechanism reveals something about the boundary of EU-ordered Europe: that it does not exist. The EU operates by giving the continent a center, by shifting the basic mechanics from politics among competing centers (balance of power) towards a center–periphery model, and therefore the task for the EU is to keep all relevant actors oriented towards Europe. Its power fades off gradually as does the short-term prospects for membership, but the EU has absolutely no interest in drawing a border and saying "no" and "you are out". So, despite the wish of various post-structuralists and critical theorists to catch the EU and the West "Othering" various neighbors – islamic Middle East, Russia or the Balkans – the dominant trend in European security rhetoric is that the Other is Europe's own past (fragmentation), and those further away from the center are not defined as anti-Europe, only as less Europe. Europe has no clear border – it fades away as you move out over the Russian plains. Europe's Eastern border has historically been compli-cated and contested.

The nature of the non-border is, however, rarely noticed in academic writings where one does not take the odd, emerging order of concentric circles seriously because it does not fit into established categories. In debates on European security, this the most important form of security provision, is generally forgotten. We could call it regional unipolarity, quasi-empire or integration in concentric circles. The EU itself is not usually mentioned as a security organization, only its derived activities in the form of the WEU or the common foreign and security policy. But integration itself has far greater security importance. In a historical perspective we have the precedence of "empires", and the EU could be seen as yet another instance of the best-tried method of peace provision in history: that a region does not have a balance of power among competing powers, but a clear though far from all-dominant center whose power extends radially with fading force, as a number of quasi-independent political units operate around the center with increasing independence as the distance to the center increases. This creates difficulties for IR-theory because it is not sovereignty-based.

This analogy reminds us that European security is not simply a collection of equal states that are somehow showing an increasing reliance on "norms." The constellation is far more differentiated than that. It is a centered formation (which is the reason why it works), and some are closer to the centre than others. If one talks in terms of the separate "member states," this can be phrased as relations of power and dependence, but if one views the whole as a formation, it is a polity somewhere in-between anarchy and hierarchy.[76] It is a world of functional differentiation beyond "like units" because Europe consists either of the Union as replacement of the states nor only of states (with an international organization); both the EU as a political unit in itself and the member states are units, of different kinds. This emerging polity might explain some of the peculiarities met above, e.g. that there is a certain political identity (and a we-feeling among the elite), but much less cultural identity (and we-feeling among the people). This is different from the modern nation state – but not from empires and various other historical polities.

Surprisingly, it is a problem for the theory of security communities to handle such in-between forms. Strangely, Deutsch is still caught in a dichotomy such as domestic/international, inside/outside and hierarchy/anarchy – here called amalgamated/pluralistic security communities. However, in the Deutsch quote placed at the beginning of this chapter it is stated that the *rhetoric* of union builders is often an intentional ambiguity between amalgamation and plurality. Should we not then as constructivists expect that these actors might construct something that moved in the in-between?

Precisely those security mechanisms that kept the continent stable after the Cold War have an empire-like concentric circle quality that is difficult to grasp on the basis of the logics of sovereignty. I am not saying that developments in Europe have undermined or overruled sovereignty – for many purposes the states are still sovereign, and the grammar of international society based on sovereignty explains much. For other purposes another lens is more helpful, and the same region comes into view as a centered formation, a polity of its own which is distinctly post-sovereign.

Conclusion

Security after sovereignty: reconnecting to deep causality

It was argued in the first section why a straightforward causal analysis was unfeasible, and the focus has been on the institutionalization of the security community. Because the theory of security communities is about non-war that rests on identity/community, we have shown in the second section *that* security came to rest on identity rather than external threat, and in the third section *how* this functions (through articulation of state, nation and Europe). However, we now have to ask *why* this has been possible. What were the conditions in Western Europe that allowed for such an evolution? Many other regions have temporarily been stabilized from the outside without a security community emerging.

The explanation for the beginnings of the community could well be geopolitical, realist, i.e. the Cold War, balance of power and alliance. The middle period of the 1960s and 1970s produced a more self-evident non-expectation of war amongst the states largely through de-securitization, i.e. by the states redefining their relationship in non-security terms, not by an explicit security order. Still, in this period, Western Europe was shielded by the geopolitics of the Cold War, and the relative importance of alliance logic and desecuritization can not be measured. With the end of the Cold War, the puzzle stands out distinctly: how is the security community stabilized now, what is it based on? An explanation of this needs to reach for deeper, almost world historical, factors relating to the general transformation of societies and politics in Europe.

Whether one talks of "dynamic density" (Durkheim/Ruggie) or "transactions" (Deutsch), Western Europe is among the most closely connected regions of the world. It is difficult to establish strict causal connections from such deep processes to security strategies, but it seems intuitively plausible that behind this whole transformation from balance of power security to security community, there could somehow be a link from deeper systemic or world historical changes. This would be the ultimate of the underlying conditions discussed in the introductory chapter. This important theme is often subdued because it is the clearest echo of interwar liberalism/utopianism, and therefore triggers the standard IR ritual of the "realist-or-idealist?" blackmail. Nowadays, however, we see innovative ways of carefully articulating some of these themes anew, in terms of dynamic density/interaction capacity (Ruggie/Buzan)[77] or liberal states (Moravscik, Slaughter)[78], zones of peace/zones of turmoil analysis[79] and more narrowly, but part of the trend: the "democratic peace."

Europe is not technologically ahead of all other parts of the world, so the dynamic density explanation is not about a direct link between technology and political forms. It has to be put in an IR context, it has to be seen spatially in relation to distance and size. When a *region* is made up of states at this technological level of development, able to penetrate each other in so many ways – militarily to culturally – this has implications for possible interaction. As argued by John Ruggie in his analysis of transformations, changes in the material environment do not directly speak political solutions. They can alter "the matrix of constraints and opportunities for social actors, giving rise to different situations of strategic action among them."[80] To take new political forms, however, still involves an act of epistemic invention (as happened 400 years ago with the concept of sovereignty).[81]

Dynamic density as large-scale explanation for the European security community refers to the combination of level of interaction capacity and geographical closeness in the region. This has pushed politics beyond the sovereign format, towards a yet unlabelled unicentric, multi-layered formation. Here security community became possible, and when allowed to unfold on its own without Cold-War overlay, it emerges as a centered, concentric circles system.

This, however, raises a great paradox in relation to much of the liberal security literature. Moving beyond the sovereign state, some of the premises for their "security" disappear. In classical liberalism, ideally state and security should be linked *very* closely: the state should not do much else than security, and security should be confined to the military affairs of the state and thus space opened up for civil society by the desecuritization of all other matters.[82] Due to the democratic ideal, liberals often are much more dependent on state-centrism, than realists who can actually be more flexible and allow whatever powers that be. Because of its deep commitment to the domestic sphere, liberalism exhibits a more profound state-centrism than realism.[83]

Such concepts as security community and even more clearly collective security presuppose (at least in their original formulations) that only states are security objects – otherwise security problems would start to pop up in many other places. One could hardly make formalized guarantee systems like collective security, without having a system of a definite number of clearly defined like units. It is difficult to have your security cake and eat it too, i.e. to draw on a liberal-statist concept of security where security is reduced to the state and military matters and simultaneously move into post-sovereign political space. If a security community has emerged in Europe through the formation of a centered, non-sovereign polity, this at first reinforces several liberal and/or progressive security theories, but at the same time it questions a lot of the premises of progressive security analysis inspired as it mostly is by liberal-statist ideals.

Constructing security and community

In Western Europe, *security* was gradually squeezed out as a strong concern among the states, and Western Europe thus became a security community (or "asecurity community"), although it started as a probably structurally determined *non-war* community. Its development from non-war community into full security community stabilized the behavioral fact of "dependable expectations of 'peaceful change'." The Deutschian formulation of what he called "security community" but what really was a non-war community, pointed to an interesting occurrence – a constellation where states don't expect to use war as a means in their quarrels – but gave no clear causal foundation for this, and therefore it remained a frail occurrence, not a stable order. With the evolution from "non-war community" to "military as well as non-military security community," however, Western Europe achieved a much more solid basis because this excluded the most threatening mechanism for an unravelling: non-military security fear and security action.

Most of the remaining security concerns were in post-sovereign patterns pushed towards referents other than state-to-state relations. Hard-core security concerns have become aggregated (or rather sublimated) as a "European" problem (fragmentation), whereby the argument becomes part of European identity: in order to avoid a replay of the dark side of European history, we have to secure sufficient unification. Although security concerns have returned, they have mostly been kept away from the nation-state as referent object, and thereby the security community is not radically threatened.

This exclusion of state driven security through a particular articulation of "Europe" and stabilized through its gradual inclusion *in* the definition of nation/state has made Europe relatively solid (without taking the form of a replacement of the nation states).

Although Deutsch's concept of security community has been accused of being Euro-centric,[84] it is actually difficult to apply to present-day Europe. As indicated by Kal Holsti, this might be due to the problematic, residual element of "the theoretical assumption of unit similarity,"[85] i.e. the belief in states as the main and as like units. Not only do other parts of the world exhibit strong variations in the stateness of states, but there are in Europe, where the states most approach the ideal type of "strong states',[86] processes of multi-level politics that point to a much more complex picture. Deutsch's conception still carries some elements of domestic analogy and sovereignty-infused inside/outside logic when it conceives of security communities as made up of simply "states" (individuals and societal transactions are important, but states are states) and when it models the security community with its correlations of identity, politics and security on the modern state. This does not correspond to the nature of the EU as an emerging neither-state-nor-international-organization polity, and it does not reflect the looming post-sovereign complexity in the form of trans-regions and criss-crossing identities. Euro-centrism becomes incompatible with comprehending Europe.

The approach in this book is generally constructivist – a reconstructured, constructivist Deutschianism. In the present chapter it has been necessary to give constructivism a twist that differs from most "mainstream constructivism" (Wendt, Katzenstein, Adler & Barnett).[87] This chapter has placed less emphasis on the system-level (or region-level) construction of rules and shared understanding that conditions action for the various units. It has more of its focus on how each unit has to construct its own world. In the words of Erik Ringmar, "A theory of the construction of identities and interests is radically incomplete as long as it views individuals and collective entities only from the perspective of the system."[88] States are redefined not only "as states" but also each in their own "subjectivity". This might be a more extorting approach, but in some sense more true to the basic constructivist premise that we can't start from some world "as it really is", but only from worlds as they are created.[89]

Also, *we* analysts can then create new worlds, new stories. About security communities, for instance. "Security community" proved to be a fertile organizing question in that it produced a re-thinking of European politics in the complex field where the historic novelty of non-war meets a transformation of security from state monopoly to multiple units. This revealed that the regional construction has gone through a complex process from an early phase where it was build on arguments related to war-avoidance over state-based de-securitization (neo-functionalist integration) to post-sovereign non-military re-securitization (the integration/fragmentation argument). Without war, security becomes much more complex, and the identities built on this kind of security pose challenges not only to security analysis but generally to international relations theory, unprepared as it still largely is for structured thinking about post-sovereign politics.

Notes

I am grateful to Barry Buzan, Lene Hansen, Pertti Joenniemi, Charles Kupchan, Robert Latham, Paul Roe, Mike Williams, participants in the December 1995 workshop in New York, two anonymous CUP reviewers, and in particular the editors for useful comments on earlier drafts.

1 Karl W. Deutsch, Sidney A. Burrell, Robert A. Kann, Maurice Lee, Jr., Martin Lichterman, Raymond E. Lindgren, Francis L. Loewenheim and Richard W. van Wagenen, *Political Community and the North Atlantic Area: International Organization in the Light of Historical Experience*, (Princeton, NJ: Princeton University Press, 1957), p. 7.
2 The term West European is used in – especially the first part of – the chapter because the community grew out of a formation in Western Europe. The extent to which this Western Europe grown community can and will expand to become all-European is addressed in section 4. The discussion will therefore occassionally be in terms of "Europe", partly because the security community is growing, partly because the West European self-conception and rhetoric often was about "Europe".
3 Håkan Wiberg, "Scandinavia," in Richard Dean Burns ed, *Encyclopedia of Arms Control and Disarmament – Volume 1* (New York: Charles Scribner's Sons 1993), pp. 209–226, quotation from p. 211.
4 Ibid., p. 210.
5 Ibid., p. 211.
6 Ibid., pp. 211f. Peter Wallensteen, Unto Vesa and Raimo Väyrynen in *The Nordic System: Structure and Change, 1920–1970* (Tampere: TAPRI Research Report No.6/Uppsala: Department of Peace and Conflict Research, Report No. 4, 1973) rebut standard explanations typified by Reinhold Niebuhr in terms of "natural" affinity or geopolitical determination.
7 Norden is not a language community, but the three core countries (Sweden, Denmark, Norway) form a community of mutual (alleged) comprehension with the old elite of the two others (Finland, Iceland) also understanding those three.
8 Cf. eg. two anthologies published by the Nordic Council during a new wave of interest in the 1990s in Nordic identity: Svenolof Karlsson, ed., *En okänd själ – på jakt efter det nordiska* [An unknown soul – searching for the nordic], 1991 and Anders Linde-Laursen and Jan Olof Nilsson, eds., *Nationella identiteter i Norden – ett fullbordat projekt* [National identites in Norden – a completed project], 1991. See also the monumental work edited by Kirsten Hastrup, *Den nordiske verden* [The Nordic world], vols. 1–2 (Copenhagen: Gyldendal 1992); and special issue of *Den Jyske Histor-*

iker 69–70 (1994) on "De Nordiske Fællesskaber" [The Nordic Communities].

9 Wiberg, "Scandinavia," pp. 210 and 212.

10 Johnny Laursen, "Fra nordisk fællesmarked til Helsingfors Konvention – nordisk økonomisk samarbejde, 1945–62" in *Den Jyske Historiker*, pp. 179–200.

11 Cf. e.g. Nils Andrén, "Nordic Integration: Aspects and Problems" *Cooperation and Conflict* 2, 1 (1967); Martin Sæter, "The Nordic Countries and European Integration. The Nordic, the West European and the All-European Stages," in T. Tiilikainen and Ib Damgaard Petersen, eds., *The Nordic Countries and the EC* (Copenhagen: Political Studies Press 1993), pp. 8–22; Håkan Wiberg, "The Nordic Countries: A Special Kind of System?" *Current Research on Peace and Violence* 1, 2 (1986), pp. 2–12; Carl-Einar Stålvant, "Nordic Cooperation," in William Wallace, ed., *The Dynamics of European Integration* (London, New York: Pinter Publishers for RIIA, 1990), pp. 125–140.

12 Cf. Jervis's definition of security regimes and Keohane's of diffuse reciprocity: Robert Jervis, "Security Regimes", *International Organization*, 36, 2 (1982), pp. 357–378; Robert O. Keohane, "Reciprocity in International Relations", *International Organization*, 40, 1 (1986), pp. 1–27.

13 Barry Buzan, *People, States and Fear: An Agenda for International Security Studies in the Post-Cold War Period*, 2nd edn (Brighton: Harvester Wheatsheaf, 1991) ch. 5.

14 Pertti Joenniemi has explored the Nordic case further with the use of some of the concepts from the present chapter: "Norden: A Community of Asecurity?", forthcoming in Tuomas Forsberg (ed.), *Finnish Foreign Policy Yearbook* (Helsinki, 1998).

15 Cf. discussion between Gaddis and Hassner in Øyvind Østerud, ed., *Studies of War and Peace* (Oslo: Universitetsforlaget, 1986; John J. Mearsheimer, "Back to the Future: Instability in Europe after the Cold War", *International Security* 15, 1 (Summer 1990), pp. 5–56; plus exchange in subsequent issues of *International Security*, Keohane and Hoffmann in vol. 15, no. 2 and Risse-Kappen and Russett in vol. 15, no. 3; "The False Promise of International Institutions," *International Security*, 19, 3 (Winter 1994/95), pp. 5–49 with comments by Keohane and Martin, Kupchan and Kupchan, Ruggie, Wendt and Mearsheimer in vol. 20, no. 1 (Summer 1995). Kenneth N. Waltz, "The Emerging Structure of International Politics", *International Security* 18, 2 (1993), pp. 44–79.

16 Mearsheimer, "Back to the Future."

17 P. 163 in Hedley Bull, "Civilian Power Europe: A Contradiction in Terms?" in Loukas Tsoukalis, ed., *The European Community: Past, Present & Future* (Oxford: Basil Blackwell, 1983), pp. 149–164.

18 Ibid.

19 Andrew Hurrell, "Explaining the Resurgence of Regionalism in World

Politics," *Review of International Studies* 21, 4 (1995), pp. 331–358; quoting from p. 358.

20 Adler and Barnett for instance assert in chapter 2 that "these regions [where security community exists] are noteworthy for overcoming the security dilemmas...".

21 This is argued in abstract terms – related to the argument that in the social world there are *no* causal relations that can be defined in terms of simple necessary and sufficient conditions – by Heikki Patomäki, *Critical Realism and World Politics: An Explication of a Critical Theoretical and Possibilistic Methodology for the Study of World Politics* (Turku: Department of Political Science, Studies on Political Science No. 12, 1992), pp. 331–365. For more specific arguments in relation to European security and the Deutschian definition, see Heinz Gärtner, "Eine gesamteuropäische Sicherheitsstruktur?" in *Österreichische Zeitschrift für Politikwissenschaft* 4 (1990), pp. 365–378, esp. pp. 368f; and Ole Wæver, "Power, Principles and Perspectivism: Understanding Peaceful Change in Post-Cold War Europe" in Heikki Patomäki, ed., *Peaceful Change in World Politics* (Tampere: TAPRI 1995), pp. 208–282.

22 Sometimes the correlation of democracy and war might hold due to causation the opposite way of what is normally claimed: democratic because not (on the way to) war (i.e. the statistics was not ruined by democracies fighting democracies because before they reached the war, at least one party had stopped being a democracy). Therefore, the democracy thesis cannot be an excuse for ending all concern about security dynamics and security systems and just concentrate on exporting democracy.

23 John G. Ruggie, "Collective Goods and Future International Cooperation," *The American Political Science Review* 66, 3 (1972), pp. 874–93, "International Responses to Technology: Concepts and Trends" *International Organization* 29, 3 (1975), pp. 557–583.

24 Ernest Gellner, "Nationalism and the Two Forms of Cohesion in Complex Societies," Radcliffe-Brown lecture in social anthropology, read 3 February 1982 (The British Academy, 1983), pp. 175f.

25 Cf. the argument presented in parts of the "democratic peace" debate, that what really matters is whether one views the other state as being a "democracy like us". Who are seen like this has changed drastically across time and does not always correspond to the analytical definitions that are applied a-historically today. Thomas Risse-Kappen, "Democratic Peace – Warlike Democracies? A Social Constructivist Interpretation of the Liberal Argument," in *European Journal of International Relations* 1, 4 (1995), pp. 491–518; Ido Oren, "Research Project Summary – Historizing the Democratic Peace: The Evolution of the American Perception of Imperial Germany," paper for SSRC/MacArthur Foundation Fellows" Conference, Washington DC, May 20–25 1995; Oren, "The Subjectivity of the "Demo-

cratic" Peace: Changing U.S. Perceptions of Imperial Germany," *International Security* 20, 2 (Fall 1995), pp. 147–184.

26 Anthony Smith, for instance, has argued that European identity is unlikely, because Europe does not have a sufficient arsenal of common myths and symbols; "National Identity and the Idea of European Unity," *International Affairs* 68, 1 (Jan. 1992), pp. 55–76.

27 Most constructivists have concentrated on how the meaning of statehood or nationhood (or sovereignty as such and identity as such) has changed. However, it is also a question how the different state/nations in *different* ways have "Europe" integrated into their we's. This case has been made at the level of abstract theory, where Erik Ringmar has criticised Alexander Wendt's influential constructivism for being

> "fundamentally one-sided: the problem of identity formation is constantly seen from the perspective of the system and never as a problem each state and each statesman has to grapple with. He can tell us why a certain identity is recognized, but not *what that identity is* [. . .] His structural bias constantly sets limits to his investigation: just as the structure of the international system cannot make a state act, it cannot make someone have a particular identity. Just as the structure cannot explain historical changes, it cannot by itself explain changes in identities. What Wendt needs, but cannot provide with the help of the theoretical perspective he has made his, is an account of how states *interpret* the structures of international politics and how they *use* them in interaction with others."

Erik Ringmar, "Alexander Wendt: A Social Scientist Struggling with History" in Iver B. Neumann and Ole Wæver, *eds.*, *The Future of International Relations: Masters in the Making?* (London: Routledge, 1997), pp. 269–289.

28 Jean Monnet, *Memoirs* (Garden City, NY: Doubleday & Company 1978 [French original: 1976]), p. 521.

29 This approach is outlined in Ole Wæver, "Securitization and Desecuritization" in Ronnie D. Lipchutz, ed., *On Security*, (New York: Columbia University Press 1995), pp. 46–86; Barry Buzan, Ole Wæver and Jaap de Wilde, *Security: A Framework for Analysis* (Boulder, CO: Lynne Rienner, 1997).

30 In practice, it is not necessary that the *word* security is spoken. There can be occasions where the word is used without this particular logic is at play, and situations where security is metaphorically at play without being pronounced. We are dealing with a specific logic which usually appear under the name security, and this logic constitutes the core meaning of the concept security, a meaning which has been found through the study of actual discourse with the use of the *word* security, but in the further investigation, it is the specificity of the rhetorical structure which is the criterion – not the occurrence of a particular word.

31 Environmental issues are for instance increasingly addressed in the form characteristic of security. Environmental activists claim that we face irreparable disasters: if we do not give absolute priority to this, it will soon be too late, and exactly therefore, *we* (Greenpeace, Earth First, etc) have a right to use extra-ordinary means, to depart from the usual political rules of the game. Because this is a security question. There is a "point of no return," and *we* have to make sure it is not crossed – therefore our issue can not enter the usual balancing of interests in relation to other concerns. Over time, it changes what and who holds a widely accepted claim to survival, and thereby – controlled by the audience's acceptance of security claims – different referents achieve this particular social power.

32 For how to do such empirical studies of security discourse and documentation for the most recent period, see Buzan et al., *Security*, ch. 8.

33 Melvyn P. Leffler, *A Preponderance of Power: National Security, the Truman Administration, and the Cold War* (Stanford, CA: Stanford, University Press, 1992), pp. 148–64.

34 Alan S. Milward, *The Reconstruction of Western Europe 1945–51* (London: Routledge 1984), p. 501. Leffler (*Preponderance of Power*, pp. 159ff) has contested this interpretation partly by emphasizing the links between concerns about economy and communists, both in a security perspective. West European governments were constrained by the political situation not allowing them to adopt economic policies that would strengthened the communists. Still, Leffler would probably accept that at least by 1952, the economy as such would no longer be securitized; cf. *Preponderance of Power*, pp. 314–323.

35 Monnet, *Memoirs*, pp. 221–222, emphasis added.

36 Ibid.

37 Walter Lipgens, *Europa-Föderationspläne der Widerstandsbewegungen 1940–45* (Munich: Schriften des Forschungsinstitutes der deutschen Gesellschaft für Auswärtige Politik No. 26, 1968); Pierre Gerbert, *La Construction de l'Europe* (Paris: Imprimerie nationale, 1983), pp. 48–57; Pim den Boer, Peter Bugge and Ole Wæver, *The History of the Idea of Europe*, ed. Jan van der Dussen and Kevin Wilson (Milton Keynes: Open University 1993, re-issued by Routledge, 1995), pp. 152f.

38 In addition to the four main cases, Suez and Algeria posed threats to the *empires*, and thus to some extent to the "vision of itself" of these states. The humiliation of Suez, however, helped European integration along by showing the limits of European independent power in a US-defined order.

39 Milward, *The Reconstruction*, p. 501.

40 Cf. e.g. Derek W. Urwin, *The Community of Europe: A History of European Integration Since 1945* (London and New York: Longman, 1991), pp. 104 and 110.

41 Amitai Etzioni, "A Paradigm for the Study of Political Unification" *World Politics*, 15, 1 (October 1962), pp. 44–74; *Political Unification: A Comparative Study of Leaders and Forces* (New York: Holt, Rinehart and Winston, 1965);

The Active Society (New York: The Free Press, 1968), "The Dialectics of Supranational Unification," *American Political Science Review*, 46, 4 (Dec. 1962), pp. 927–935; and "The Epigenesis of Political Communities at the International Level" in James Rosenau ed. *International Politics and Foreign Policy*, 2nd edn (New York: The Free Press, 1969). Karl W. Deutsch, *Political Community at the International Level: Problems of Definition and Measurement* (Garden City, NY: Doubleday 1954); "Towards Western European Integration: An Interim Assessment," *Journal of International Affairs*, 16, 1, (1962), pp. 89–101. Ernst B. Haas, *The Uniting of Europe: Political, Social and Economic Forces 1950–1957* (Stanford: Stanford University Press, 1958); "The Challenge of Regionalism," *International Organization*, 12, 4 (Autumn 1958); and *Beyond the Nation-State: Functionalism and International Organization* (Stanford: Stanford University Press, 1964).

42 Adrian Hyde-Price, *European Security Beyond the Cold War: Four Scenarios for the Year 2010* (London: Sage/RIIA 1991), p. 32.

43 Ibid.

44 Rudolf Horst Brocke, *Deutschlandpolitische Positionen der Bundestagsparteien – Synopse* (Erlangen: Deutsche Gesellschaft für zeitgeschichtliche Fragen, 1985), pp. 66f and 79f.

45 Ole Wæver, "Conceptions of Détente and Change: Some Non military Aspects of Security Thinking in the FRG," in O. Wæver, P. Lemaitre and E. Tromer, eds, *European Polyphony: Beyond East–West Confrontation* (London: Macmillan, 1989), pp. 186–224.

46 Pierre Hassner, "The Politics of Western Europe and East–West Relations," in Nils Andrén and Karl Birnbaum, eds., *Beyond Détente: Prospects for East–West Cooperation and Security in Europe* (Leyden: A. W. Sijthoff, 1976), pp. 15–37.

47 Barry Buzan and Ole Wæver, "Liberalism and Security: Contradictions of the Liberal Leviathan," forthcoming.

48 Cf. Buzan et al., *Security: A New Framework for Analysis*, pp. 27–29.

49 Stanley Hoffmann, "Obstinate or Obsolete? The Fate of the Nation State and the Case of Western Europe," *Dædalus* 95, 3 (1966), pp. 862–915.

50 Gerbet, *La Construction de l'Europe*, pp. 273ff.

51 Ibid., pp. 318ff and Martin Sæter, "De Gaulle's Europapolitikk" (in Norwegian) in *Internasjonal Politikk*, 48, 3 (1990), pp. 392–402.

52 Gerbet, *La Construction de l'Europe*, pp. 325f. What actually happened, was possibly much less dramatic. Alfred Grosser in his 375 page-book on "the alliance" (on intra-Western relations) handles the whole crisis in four lines where he presents it almost only as a tactical maneuver to ensure a better bargain on agricultural politics; Grosser, *The Western Alliance: European–American Relations since 1945* (London: Macmillan 1980; French original 1978), cf. also Urwin, *The Community of Europe*, pp. 110ff.

53 Wayne Sandholtz and John Zysman, "1992: Recasting the European Bargain", *World Politics*, 42, 1 (October 1989), pp. 1–30.

54 Comparing the West to Asia, one is struck by the importance of NATO

(and EU) being constructed as multilateral institutions, not simply bilateral alliances. In East Asia, in particular, where there are no equivalents to either EU, NATO or OSCE, the situation of the states after the Cold War resembles a Mearsheimerian "back to the future" scenario of power balancing and each-state-for-itself (except that this is not actually East Asia's past which consisted rather of empires which might point to different patterns if Asia moves "back to the future'). European security is at present deeply marked by the structures and institutions formed during the Cold War period. John G. Ruggie, "Multilateralism: The Anatomy of an Institution" *International Organization*, 46, 3 (1992), pp. 561–198; "The False Premise of Realism," *International Security*, 20, 1 (Summer 1995), pp. 62–70, and "Peace in Our Time? Causality, Social Facts, and Narrative Knowing," in the Proceedings of the 1995 Annual Meetings of the American Society of International Law: *Structures of World Order* (ASIL 1995), pp. 93–100; Steve Weber, "Shaping the Postwar Balance of Power: Multilateralism in NATO," in Ruggie, ed., *Multilateralism Matters*, pp. 233–292; John S. Duffield, "Explaining the Long Peace in Europe: The Contributions of Regional Security Regimes," *Review of International Studies*, 20, 4 (1994), pp. 369–88; Robert O. Keohane and Lisa L. Martin, "The Promise of Institutionalist Theory," *International Security*, 20, 1 (1995), pp. 39–51; Celeste A. Wallander and Robert O. Keohane "Toward an Institutionalist Theory of Alliances", paper presented at the Annual Meeting of the International Studies Association, Chicago, Illinois, February 22–25, 1995.

55 It is possible to argue exactly these two scenarios on the basis of some version of neo-realism that, in contrast to Mearsheimer's predictions, focus on the regional level: Barry Buzan, Morten Kelstrup, Pierre Lemaitre, Elzbieta Tromer and Ole Wæver, *The European Security Order Recast: Scenarios for the Post-Cold War Era* (London: Pinter Publishers 1990); Barry Buzan and Ole Wæver "Framing Nordic Security: Scenarios for European Security in the 1990s and beyond," in Jan Øberg, ed., *Nordic Security in the 1990s: Options in the Changing Europe* (London: Pinter Publishers, 1992), pp. 85–104; Wæver, "Europe: Stability and Responsibility," in *Internationales Umfeld, Sicherheitsinteressen und nationale Planung der Bundesrepublik. Teil C: Unterstützende Einzelanalysen. Band 5. II.A Europäische Sicherheitskultur. II.B Optionen für kollektive Verteidigung im Kontext sicherheitspolitischer Entwicklungen Dritter* (Ebenhausen: Stiftung Wissenschaft und Politik, SWP – S 383/5, 1993), pp. 31–72.

For the present purpose it is less relevant whether integration and fragmentation are social constructions alone or whether they are also founded in some kind of structural priority. (On the relationship between these two dimensions, see Ole Wæver, "The Politics of International Structure," ms in preparation.)

56 Francis A. Beer and Jeffrey S. Kopstein, "Between Maastricht and Sarajevo: European Identities, Narratives, Myths," paper for the 2nd pan-

European Conference on International Relations, ECPR, Paris, September, 13–16, 1995.

57 This argument, of course, echoes classical Hobbesian "discourses of danger," the classical "shock therapy" of getting acceptance for unification or institutions through a terrifying presentation of *anarchy*; cf. David Campbell, *Writing Security: United States Foreign Policy and the Politics of Identity*, (Minneapolis: University of Minnesota Press 1992), ch. 3; William E. Connolly, *Political Theory and Modernity* (Oxford: Basil Blackwell 1988), ch. 2. My argument for the security nature of the argument for integration is spelled out in "European Security Identities," *Journal of Common Market Studies*, 34, 1 (1996), pp. 103–32 and in ch. 8 of Barry Buzan, Ole Wæver and Jaap de Wilde, *Security: A New Framework for Analysis* (Boulder, CO: Lynne Rienner, 1997).

58 Pim den Boer, Peter Bugge and Ole Wæver, *The History of the Idea of Europe* (Milton Keynes: The Open University, 1993; London: Routledge, 1995), pp. 151–3, 174.

59 Jean Baudrillard, *The Illusion of the End* (translation of *L'Illusion de la fin: ou La greve des evenenments*, Galilee, 1992), trans. Chris Turner (Stanford, CA: Stanford University Press, 1994), pp. 02f, Jacques Derrida, *The Other Heading: Reflections on Today's Europe* (Bloomington, IN: Indiana University Press, 1992 [1991]); Helle Rytkønen, "Securing European Identity – Identifying Danger" paper presented at the annual conference of International Studies Association, Chicago, February 1995.

60 A good case can be made against a cultural essentialism like the one used in the nineteenth century to build our existing nations, i.e. against arguing that we Europeans really belong together because we are so alike, share a history and a culture, and we therefore should unify politically. Cf. Derrida, *The Other Heading*, Jürgen Habermas, "Citizenship and National Identity: Some Reflections on the Future of Europe," *Praxis International*, 12, 1 (1992), pp. 1–19; den Boer et al., *The History*; Gerard Delanty, "The Limits and Possibilities of a European Identity: A Critique of Cultural Essentialism," *Philosophy and Social Criticism* 21, 4 (1995), pp. 15–36.

61 Marlene Wind ("Eksisterer Europa? Reflektioner over forsvar, identitet og borgerdyd i et nyt Europa," in Christen Sørensen, ed., *Europa Nation-Union – efter Minsk og Maastricht* (København: Fremad, 1992), pp. 23–81, here p. 24) quotes an article by Francois Goguel from *Le Figaro* of April 4, 1991 entitled "Europe does not Exist" (reflecting on the feeble appearance of the EU in the Gulf War), and e.g. French historian François Furet writes: "Europe now stands at a crossroads, where only by uniting may it still parry its decline. If it cannot accomplish this, the twenty-first century may well take shape without it" (p. 89 in "Europe after Utopianism," *Journal of Democracy* 6, 1 [January 1995], pp. 79–89).

62 Various lectures; a related argument – though not the phrase – is found in Anne Knudsen, *Europæiske Identiteter* (Copenhagen: Christian Ejlers, 1989).

63 Even if it is in some sense correct that "Deutsch made no theoretical distinction between intra- and inter-state relations" (Wolf-Dieter Eberwein, "The Future of International Warfare: Toward a Global Security Community", *International Political Science Review* 16, 4 [October 1995], pp. 341–60) in that he posed the same question of peace and war to both domestic and international situations and made the question of a possible difference empirical in stead of aximomatic (cf. Ole Wæver, "Identity, Integration and Security: Solving the Sovereignty Puzzle in E.U. Studies," *Journal of International Affairs*, 48, 2 (Winter 1995), pp. 389–431, especially pp. 391–393.), he did distinguish between pluralistic security communities (international) and amalgamated security communities (domestic). Likewise, if the phases assume parallelism in the emergence of identity, community, security and authority, this means to reify a characteristic of the modern state not valid for all polities. (Eberwein draws on the argument in Arend Lijphart, "Karl W. Deutsch and the New Paradigm in International Relations," in R. L. Merritt and B. M. Russett, eds., *From National Development to Global Community* [London: George Allen & Unwin, 1981], pp. 233–251 – see also Lijphart, "International Relations Theory: Great Debates and Lesser Debates," *International Social Science Journal*, 26, 1 [1974], pp. 11–21.)

64 R. B. J. Walker, *Inside/Outside: International Relations as Political Theory* (Cambridge: Cambridge University Press, 1993). On domestic analogy, see Hedley Bull, *The Anarchical Society: A Study of Order in World Politics* (London: Macmillan, 1977); Hidemi Suganami, *The Domestic Analogy and World Order Proposals* (Cambridge: Cambridge University Press, 1989) and Richard Ashley, "The Powers of Anarchy: Theory, Sovereignty, and the Domestication of Global Life," in James Der Derian, ed., *International Theory: Critical Investigations* (London: Macmillan, 1995), pp. 94–128.

65 Etienne Tassin, "Europe: A Political Community?" in Chantal Mouffe, ed., *Dimensions of Radical Democracy: Pluralism, Citizenship, Community* (London: Verso, 1992), p. 189.

66 Ole Wæver, *Hele Europa: Projekter. Kontraster* [All of Europe: Projects. Contrasts] (Copenhagen: SNU, 1989); "Three Competing Europes: German, French, Russian," *International Affairs* 66, 3 (1990), pp. 477–493.

67 Michael N. Barnett, "Sovereignty, Nationalism and Regional Order in the Arab States System," *International Organization*, 49, 3 (1995), pp. 479–510, quote on p. 509.

68 Paul Ricoeur, "Reflections on a New Ethos for Europe," *Philosophy & Social Criticism* 21, 5–6 (1995), pp. 3–14.

69 Wæver, "Three Competing Europes." More extensively on France and Germany in O. Wæver, U. Holm and H. Larsen, *The Struggle for "Europe": French and German Concepts of State, Nation and European Union* (forthcoming).

70 Henry A. Kissinger, *A World Restored: Castlereagh, Metternich and the*

114

Restoration of Peace, 1812–1822 (Boston: Houghton Mifflin Company, 1957), p. 146.

71 Studies of specific states and their foreign policies are starting to emerge along lines more or less similar to the here outlined: France: Holm, *Det Franske Europe* [The French Europe], (Århus: Århus Universitetsforlag, 1992); Holm, "The French Garden is not what it used to be," in Knud-Erik Jørgensen, ed., *Reflective Approaches to European Governance* (London: Macmillan, 1997), pp. 128–145; Wæver et al., *The Struggle*; Germany: Wæver et al., *The Struggle* and Wæver "Hvordan det hele alligevel kan gå galt ...," in Henning Gottlieb and Frede P. Jensen, eds., *Tyskland i Europa* (Copenhagen: SNU, 1995), pp. 297–336; Russia: Iver B. Neumann, *Russia and the Idea of Europe* (London: Routledge, 1996); Turkey: Işıl Kazan, "*Omvendt Osmannisme og Khanaternes Kemalisme,*" MA thesis, Copenhagen 1994; and Işıl Kazan and Ole Wæver, "Tyrkiet mellem Europa og europæisering", *Internasjonal Politikk* 52, 1 (1994); Finland: Pertti Joenniemi, "Euro-Suomi: rajalla, rajojen, välissä vai rajaton?" in Pertti Joenniemi, Risto Alapuro and Kyösti Pekonen, *Suomesta Euro-Suomen: Keitä me olemme ja mihin matkalla* (Tampere: Occasional Papers of Tampere Peace Research Institute, No. 53, 1993), pp.13–48; UK: Henrik Larsen, *Discourse Analysis and Foreign Policy: British and French policy towards Europe* (London: Routledge, 1998) and Thomas Diez, "Reading the EU: Discursive Nodal Points in the British Debate on European Integration", unpublished ms 1996; Egypt and India: Sanjoy Banerjee "National Identity and Foreign Policy," unpublished; Slovenia: Lene Hansen, "Nation Building on the Balkan Border," *Alternatives* 21, 4 (1996), pp. 473–496; Greece: Helle Stauersböll, MA in preparation; the Nordic Countries: Lene Hansen and Ole Wæver, eds., *Between Nations and Europe: The political construction of "Norden" in Finland, Norway, Sweden and Denmark* (London: Routledge, forthcoming).

72 Most of the foreign attention and worries about German orientation concern struggles among two versions of the same conception of the state, nation and relation to Europe (the same position at "the second tier" in a three tiered structuralist analysis; Wæver et al., *The Struggle*): between on the one side semi-pacifist Greens and social democrats who want a continuation of total abstentionism and on the other the present government which also emphasizes integration as the rationale for Germany, but is interested in gradually taking on more "normal tasks." The most visible challenger outside this branch is economic nationalism wanting to defend the D-mark. It too builds on European integration, only it claims that integration is so robust that Germany can actually be more selfish without risking dramatic effects on the EU as such.

73 For the theoretical framework behind this reasoning, see Ole Wæver, "Resisting the Temptation of Post Foreign Policy Analysis," in Walter Carlsnaes and Steve Smith, eds., *European Foreign Policy: The EC and Changing Perspectives in Europe* (ECPR/Sage 1994), pp. 238–273. The

empirical interpretation of France is based on Ulla Holm, *Det franske Europe*.

74 This brings to mind Deutsch's argument about "cores of strength." However, he was most explicit about this phenomenon in relation to amalgamated security communities, and did not spell out for pluralistic security communities, how a community *functions* when it has a core of strength. In most later treatments this idea was forgotten, and security communities idealized as much more equal and "democratic". Cf. Thomas Petersen, *Asymmetrical Federalization: Germany, France and the Creation of the Union* (London: Cassell, forthcoming).

75 Cf. Hans Mouritzen, "The Two Musterknaben and the Naughty Boy: Sweden, Finland, and Denmark in the Process of European Integration", *Cooperation and Conflict*, 28, 4 (1993), pp. 373–402; "The Nordic Model as a Foreign Policy Instrument: Its Rise and Fall", *Journal of Peace Research*, 32, 1, pp. 9–23; Hans Mouritzen, Ole Wæver and Håkan Wiberg, *European Integration and National Adaptations* (New York: Nova Science Publishers, 1996).

76 There are theoretical perspectives able to see this – new reflections on polities (Yale H. Ferguson and Richard W. Mansbach, *Polities: Authority, Identities and Change* (Columbia, SC: University of Southern Carolina Press, 1996); Philippe C. Schmitter, "Examining the Present Euro-Polity with the Help of Past Theories" and "Imagining the Future of the Euro-Polity with the Help of New Concepts," in Gary Marks, Fritz W. Scharpf, Philippe C. Schmitter and Wolfgang Streeck, *Governance in the European Union* ([London: Sage, 1996]), the English School (with its studies of suzerainty and empires; Martin Wight, *Systems of States* [Leicester University Press 1977]; Adam Watson, *The Evolution of International Society* [London: Routledge, 1993]; Ole Wæver, "Europe's Three Empires: A Watsonian Interpretation of Post-Wall European Security," in Rick Fawn and Jeremy Larkins, eds., *International Society After the Cold War: Anarchy and Order Reconsidered*, [London: Macmillan in association with Millennium: Journal of International Studies, 1996], pp. 220–60), governance (at least in its German brand; Markus Jachtenfuchs and Beate Kohler-Koch, eds., *Europäische Integration* [Opladen: Leske + Budrich 1996]; Markus Jachtenfuchs, "Theoretical Perspectives on European Governance", *European Law Journal*, 1, 2 [July 1995], pp. 115–133; Markus Jachtenfuchs and Beate Kohler-Koch, "The Transformation of Governance in the European Union," Mannheimer Zentrum für Europäische Sozialforschung, *Working Papers* ABIII/Nr.11; presented at the 2nd pan-European IR conference, Paris, September, 1995) and not least the writings of Deudney on the early American "negarchy" (Daniel Deudney, "The Philadelphian System: Sovereignty, Arms Control and Balance of Power in the American States-Union, ca. 1787–1861," *International Organization* 49, 2 [Spring 1995], pp. 191–228).

77 John G. Ruggie, "Continuity and Transformation in the World Polity:

Toward a Neo-Realist Synthesis," *World Politics*, 36, 2 (1983); Barry Buzan, Richard Little and Charles Jones, *The Logic of Anarchy: Neorealism to Structural Realism* (New York: Columbia University Press, 1993).

78 Andrew Moravcsik, "Taking Preferences Seriously: A Liberal Theory of International Politics", *International Organization* 51, 4 (Autumn, 1997), 513–34 Anne-Marie Slaughter, "International Law in a World of Liberal States," *European Journal of International Law*, 6 (1995).
79 James M. Goldgeier and Michael McFaul, "A Tale of Two Worlds: Core and Periphery in the Post-Cold War Era," *International Organization*, 46, 2 (1992), pp. 467–492; Max Singer and Aaron Wildavsky, *The Real World Order: Zones of Peace/Zones of Turmoil* (Chatham , NJ: Chatham House, 1993). See also Robert O. Keohane, " 'Hobbes' Dilemma and Institutional Change in World Politics: Sovereignty in International Society," in Hans-Henrik Holm and Georg Sørensen, eds., *Whose World Order? Uneven Globalization and the End of the Cold War* (Boulder, CO: Westview Press, 1994), pp. 165–86.
80 Ruggie, "Territoriality and Beyond: Problematizing Modernity in International Relations", p. 154.
81 As further suggested by John Ruggie, "the institutional, juridical, and spatial complexes associated with the community may constitute nothing less than the emergence of the first truly postmodern international political form." Ruggie, "Territoriality," p. 140. The EU is a "multiperspectival polity, where the EU does not replace the separate powers, nor can it be seen as simply a result of their strategic interaction" (ibid., p. 172). It is an additional political will itself, as is also increasingly true of other centres – cf. the security differentiation between state and nation and also various other "regional" identities (sub-regional, trans-regional, euro-regions). Lothar Brock and Mathias Albert, "De-Bordering the State: New Spaces in International Relations", paper presented at the second pan-European conference on International Relations, Paris, September 13–16, 1995 (see also for more IR-theoretical reflections: Mathias Albert, *Fallen der (Welt-)Ordnung: Internationale Beziehungen und ihre Theorien zwischen Moderne und Postmoderne*, dissertation, Johann Wolfgang Goethe-Universität zu Frankfurt am Main, 1995); Pertti Joenniemi, ed., *Cooperation in the Baltic Sea Region* (New York: Taylor & Francis, 1993); Ole Wæver and Pertti Joenniemi, "Region in the Making: A Blueprint for Baltic Sea Politics," in Christian Wellmann, ed., *The Baltic Sea Region: Conflict or Cooperation? Region-Making, Security, Disarmament and Conversion. Proceedings of the TAPRI-PFK-Workshop*, Kiel, December 6–8, 1991, Kieler Schriften zur Friedensweisseschaft/Kiel Peace Research Series, vol. 1 (Münster/Hamburg: Lit Verlag, 1992), pp. 13–60; Iver B. Neumann, "A Region-Building Approach to Northern Europe," *Review of International Studies* 20, 1 (1994), pp. 53–74.
82 Michael W. Williams, presentation at the Centre for Peace and Conflict Research, Copenhagen, October 10, 1995; "Identity and Politics of Se-

curity," forthcoming *European Journal of International Relations;* "Hobbes and International Relations: A Reconsideration," in *International Organization* 50, 2 (Spring, 1996), pp. 213–236; Barry Buzan and Ole Wæver, "Liberalism and Security: Contradictions of the Liberal Leviathan," forthcoming.

83 Robert Latham, "Getting Out From Under: Rethinking Security Beyond Liberalism and the Level-of-Analysis Problem," *Millennium* 25, 1 (1996), pp. 77–110; quote from pp. 89–90.

84 Richard L. Merritt "Dangers of Our Time – Introduction," *International Political Science Review*, 16, 4 (October 1995), pp. 317–318 and K. J. Holsti, "War, Peace, and the State of the State," ibid., pp. 319–340, especially p. 320 and 324.

85 Holsti, "War," p. 324.

86 From Barry Buzan, *People, States, and Fear*, pp. 96–107.

87 Alexander Wendt, "The Agent-Structure Problem in International Relations Theory," *International Organization*, 41, 3 (1987), pp. 335–70; "Anarchy is what States Make of It: The Social Construction of Power Politics," *International Organization*, 46, 2 (1992), pp. 391–426; "Collective Identity Formation and the International State," *American Political Science Review*, 88, 2 (1994), pp. 384–396; Michael N. Barnett, "Institutions, Roles and Disorder: The Case of the Arab States System," *International Studies Quarterly*, 37 (September 1993), pp. 271–296; "Sovereignty, Nationalism and Regional Order in the Arab States System," *International Organization*, 49, 3 (1995), pp. 479–510; Emanuel Adler and Peter M. Haas, "Conclusion: Epistemic Communities, World Order, and the Creation of a Reflective Research Program," *International Organization*, 46 (Winter 1992), pp. 367–90; Peter J.Katzenstein, ed., *The Culture of National Security: Identity and Norms in World Politics* (New York: Columbia University Press, 1996).

88 Ringmar, "Alexander Wendt," p. 285.

89 There is thus no logical contradiction between the present analysis and the premises of constructivism. Rather it seems that constructivism has for contingent reasons started out working mostly at the systemic level, whereas this article has tried to show some of the benefits of the opposite direction.

4   Seeds of peaceful change: the OSCE's security community-building model

Emanuel Adler

> The essence of European security lies in the process of creating an inclusive community of democratic states. This is the special genius of the CSCE ... In this sense, free elections are as much a security measure as ceilings on tanks.
>
> James Goodby[1]

In this chapter, I introduce and analyze the concept of a "security community-building institution." I argue that collective identities, the "stuff" of which security communities are made, do not always evolve spontaneously; rather, as in the case of the expansion eastward of the Euro-Atlantic pluralistic security community, they are socially constructed by institutions. Although some international institutions – including the European Union (EU) and the North Atlantic Treaty Organization (NATO) – have, as a collateral outcome of their functional tasks, helped set up some of the building-blocks of security communities, none has gone as far as the Organization for Security and Cooperation in Europe (OSCE)[2] in transforming itself into an explicit and distinct security community-building institution. Regardless of its accomplishments, or lack thereof, we cannot understand what the OSCE has become or is trying to do unless we embed this understanding in the concept of *pluralistic security community*.

When taken together, the OSCE's innovative security community-building processes and practices suggest a new model of international security. According to this "association-exclusion"[3] – I prefer to call it *inside-out* – model, security is increasingly defined as *"comprehensive"* (it links classic security elements to economic, environmental, cultural, and human-rights factors), *"indivisible"* (one state's security is inseparable from that of other states), and *"cooperative"* (security is based on confidence and cooperation, the peaceful resolution of disputes, and the work of mutually reinforcing multilateral institutions).[4]

In fact, the *inside-out* model of regional security pursued by most of the multilateral institutions of the Euro-Atlantic pluralistic security community of North America and Western Europe (such as NATO, the Western European Union [WEU], the EU, and the Council of Europe [CoE]), with the aim of integrating former Communist countries into the West, is really a reflection of the institutionalization in the Euro-Atlantic space of a logic of international political community that the OSCE, armed with innovative security-community norm-setting activities and security practices, helped to pioneer. With the institutionalization of the North Atlantic Cooperation Council (NACC) in 1991, the Partnership for Peace (PfP) in 1994, and the Euro-Atlantic Partnership Council (EAPC) in 1997, NATO has gone the farthest in emulating OSCE and adopting community-building practices.

To some extent, the model is also beginning to imprint the emerging Mediterranean region (the EU-sponsored 1995 Mediterranean Plan), the Asia-Pacific region (the Association of South Eastern Asian Nations [ASEAN], and the Asia-Pacific Economic Cooperation [APEC]), Africa (the Conference on Security, Stability, Development, and Cooperation in Africa), and the Middle East (the multilateral Arab–Israeli peace talks). Indeed, we can view the diffusion of the OSCE's community-building practices to other multilateral institutions as one of its most important and lasting legacies to international security and peaceful change in Europe and elsewhere.

The causal relation between international institutions and security communities rests on agency, that is, the catalytic function of institutions to promote, induce, and socially construct community by means of community-building practices. In other words, institutional agency and community-building practices affect other necessary conditions of dependable expectations of peaceful change, including (a) cognitive and material structures, (b) transactions between states and societies, and (c) collective identity or "we-feeling."[5] They do this by providing purpose, meaning, and direction to security relations and by supplying a set of material and cognitive resources through which structures are constituted and reproduced. Moreover, institutional agency and community-building practices play an important role in transforming strategic practices, both behavioral and rhetorical, which, according to Alexander Wendt, also induce the development of collective identities.[6] Through political dialogue, the establishment of a liberal normative structure for the entire OSCE region, and constant pressure to implement normative commitments, the OSCE first imprinted the development of political community during the Cold War, when it contributed to the emergence of civil societies in the East, and then to the peaceful end of the Cold War.

Since the end of the Cold War, and in spite of the ethnic conflicts now ranging in the OSCE region and the fact that two steps forward have sometimes been followed by one step backward (though the opposite has also been true), OSCE practices have been helping to increase the interdependence and transactions between East and West and to lay the foundation for a liberal transnational collective understanding in the area from Vancouver to Vladivostok. By means of *seminar diplomacy* – a relatively new tool for pursuing state interests, which integrates academic expertise and diplomatic discourse and practice – and other innovative means of cooperation, the OSCE and other post-Cold War European security institutions have been making significant political efforts to change the intersubjective knowledge through which identities are defined. Also, by stimulating cooperative behavior through a plethora of face-to-face interactions on a large variety of technical, practical, and normative subjects, these security community-building institutions are gradually strengthening civil society in former Communist countries and changing people's beliefs about who they are. "By teaching others and themselves to cooperate . . . actors are simultaneously learning to *identify* with each other – to see themselves as a 'we' bound by certain norms."[7]

When assessing and measuring the influence of OSCE's practices, we cannot simply look at this institution's regulative tasks or short-range activities, because what matters most is the long-range effectiveness of its practices and activities as constitutive of community identity and bonds. For example, when the OSCE sends a mission to Tajikistan or to Estonia, organizes a seminar on military doctrines or confidence-building measures (CBMs), or, as part of its CBM regime, requires states to open up their military activities for inspection, what matters most is not the short-range success of the mission, seminar, or inspection, but the construction of a foundation for community practice and behavior. Moreover, one needs to assess whether OSCE innovative practices and activities have contributed to the collective understanding of the OSCE as a "region" and to changing the way that peoples in this region collectively think about their security.

It follows that, when studying the relevance of security community-building institutions, we should not and cannot use only formal product indicators, such as the number of conflicts solved or pacified, the amount of economic welfare that can be directly traced back to institutional performance, or the number of human-rights violations registered in a year. Nor can we assess institutional impact only on the basis of behavioral indicators, such as interaction between political elites, the number of letters sent, or tourist visits within a given region. Rather, we should assess institutional performance by studying the direct impact that a regional institution has on the way diplomatic, military, and economic communities perceive and understand reality – for example, their security, welfare, rights, and duties – as measured by their domestic and international practices, political behavior, and discourse. We also need to consider the extent to which institutions promote the trickle-down of elite "we-feeling" to civil society. For example, the OSCE is widely associated with helping establish constituencies in civil society – with the assistance of non governmental organizations (NGOs) – creating networks around them, and articulating and sustaining policies for them.

Note what this chapter is *not* about. First, it is not about a security community in the entire OSCE space because, so far, there is none. Nor do I claim that the OSCE will ultimately succeed in establishing a pluralistic security community in the OSCE region. Secondly, this chapter is not about European security "architecture" nor about which of the various security institutions – NATO, the OSCE, or the WEU – should be entrusted with European security. Third, it is not about the OSCE's latest institutional developments nor about specific OSCE human rights or preventive diplomatic undertakings. Finally, although I mention OSCE's history briefly, the chapter is not primarily about its role in helping bring about the relatively peaceful end of the Cold War and the Soviet empire.

In the chapter's first section, I provide a short and general historical background of the OSCE and discuss its influence on European security during the Cold War and after. In the second section, I examine the OSCE's community-making functions and describe the main features of the OSCE model, with special attention to the attributes and innovative processes that have enabled the OSCE to affect European politics and security. I also show how the OSCE's practices have become devices for the construction of a shared identity and shared interests within the OSCE space. The third section introduces and describes the practice of seminar diplomacy. In the fourth section, I show that we also need to measure the OSCE's impact as a security community-building institution by the long-term influence it has already had on the goals, strategies, and practices of other European security institutions, such as the NACC, PfP, and WEU. In conclusion, I show that the workings of security community-building institutions support the constructivist argument that international institutions matter not just as media for the international coordination of policies, but also as agents of the social construction of regional security systems.

The OSCE: general background

Short history

The OSCE was constituted in August 1975 by the Helsinki Final Act, which was signed by thirty-five countries: Canada, the United States, and all European states (including the Soviet Union) except Albania. This act, as supplemented over the years by a series of follow-up conferences and experts' meetings, provides a normative framework for its member states based on adherence to multi-party democracy, the rule of law, human rights, and liberal economic systems.

The Helsinki Final Act created three broad areas of activity, known as "baskets." Basket One contains the ten basic principles of the OSCE, as well as the guidelines for a "cooperative security" system based on confidence-building measures, disarmament, and mechanisms for the peaceful resolution of disputes. Through the years it has added injunctions concerning human rights and international terrorism. Basket Two created the framework for economic, scientific, and environmental cooperation, stressing the elimination of restrictions to trade, industrial cooperation, and technology transfer. In Basket Three, dealing with the "human dimension," members committed themselves to cooperate on all sorts of humanitarian issues that encourage human contacts and enhance human freedoms.

The effectiveness of the OSCE processes has depended on the way in which these baskets were tied together in negotiating processes[8] – for example, the linking of human rights with military security and territorial guarantees, of economic with environmental issues, of environmental issues with human rights, and of security with the flow of goods, persons, and ideas.

The Belgrade follow-up meeting (1977–78), held in the shadow of rising superpower tensions, could do no more than provide continuity to the process. The second follow-up conference, held in Madrid (1980–83), was more successful, and prepared the ground for the 1986 Stockholm CBM agreements. The third follow-up conference, held in Vienna (1986–89), further expanded human-rights commitments and played an important role in promoting superpower arms control.

In November 1990, the OSCE formally acknowledged the end of the Cold War by adopting the "Charter of Paris."[9] It not only reaffirmed the values on which the OSCE was based, but also turned democracy, the rule of law, and human rights from what had previously been a regional code of conduct into the normative structure for a security community expected to evolve in an area extending from Vancouver to Vladivostok. The Charter of Paris also created a new set of formal institutions – such as the OSCE Secretariat and the Council of Foreign Ministers, the Conflict Prevention Center, and the Office of Free Elections (in January 1992 renamed the Office for Democratic Institutions and Human Rights [ODIHR]) – with the purpose of improving decision-making, enhancing the OSCE's monitoring capabilities, promoting the peaceful settlement of disputes before they become violent, and implementing the goal of extending the reach of democratic pluralism, the rule of law, human rights, and market systems to the East. Since 1991, a OSCE Parliamentary Assembly, created to foster cooperation between parliamentarians of member countries, has been monitoring elections in former Eastern Bloc countries.

Particularly noteworthy has been the beefing-up of the Human Dimension with intrusive CBM-like tools that require on-site inspection:

> The Human Dimension includes commitments for exchanging information and responding to requests for information on the condition of human rights in participating countries, for meeting bilaterally with participating states requesting such a meeting to examine the human rights situation in question and to bring this situation, if deemed necessary, to the attention of the other participating states. It also provides the right of states to bring information on what has occurred to the meetings of the Conference on the Human Dimension as well as the main CSCE review meetings.[10]

The OSCE has also developed a series of practices that allow it to react quickly without having to rely on formal meetings of all member states and, thus, on the consensus rule adopted in 1975. These institutionalized practices or "mechanisms" (as they came to be called) allow for the exchange of information and the convening of bilateral and multilateral meetings on human-rights violations (the Human Dimension Mechanism); the querying of other states about their military activities (Unusual Military Activities); the facilitation of the peaceful resolution of disputes by a group of third-party experts (the Valletta Dispute Settlement Mechanism, followed by the 1993 Convention on Conciliation and Arbitration);[11] provisions relating to early warning and preventive action (a High Commissioner on National Minorities [HCNM] and long-term missions); the holding of emergency meetings at a high political level (the Emergency Meeting Mechanism); and fact-finding, rapporteur, and sanctions-assistance missions.[12] Missions can be requested by states or can be sent at the initiative of the OSCE itself. A large number of the participants in these missions are drawn from lists of experts, many of them academics, specializing in international law and minorities.

In 1992, following the dissolution of the Soviet Union and Yugoslavia, the OSCE's membership rose to fifty-three and later to fifty-five. Follow-up meetings were held in Helsinki (1992), Budapest (1994), and Lisbon (1996). The first two meetings, in the shadow of the conflict in the former Yugoslavia, attempted to transform the old Cold War institution into a community-building device with monitoring capacity, including peacekeeping, and with some enforcement faculties, especially in the area of the peaceful resolution of disputes. Noteworthy are two institutions created at the Helsinki meeting: (1) the Forum for Security Cooperation (divided into three segments: (a) arms control, disarmament, and confidence-building measures; (b) security enhancement and cooperation; and (c) conflict management); and (2) the HCNM (mentioned above), who provides early warning, and, if deemed necessary, early action regarding tensions that involve national minorities. The HCNM, empowered to gather information and promote dialogue, investigates national minority-related problems through quiet diplomacy before they reach crisis proportions.[13] But the HCNM is not supposed to determine the legality of or compliance with actions against minorities, nor is he/she a mediator in any classical sense. Rather, acting independently of governments and minority groups, the HCNM alerts political institutions to impending disputes involving national minorities and can take preventive action to remedy the situation.[14] Although the HCNM's activities are directed mainly at conflict prevention, they also focus on human rights. At Helsinki, the OSCE also became a regional arrangement in the sense of Chapter VIII of the United Nations Charter.

At the Budapest follow-up meeting, the newly renamed OSCE settled into its present institutional structure, consisting mainly of Summits of Heads of Government (that meet every two years), a Ministerial Council (that meets once a year); a Senior Council (that meets at least twice a year and also convenes as the Economic Forum); a Permanent Council (that meets weekly for regular political consultations); the Forum for Security Cooperation; the HCNM; the ODIHR; the Court of Conciliation and Arbitration, and the OSCE Parliamentary Assembly. In addition, there is a Chairman-in-Office (CIO), who has overall responsibility for executive action during one calendar year; a Troika (made-up of the immediate past, present, and future CIOs), and a Secretariat General, under a Secretary General who provides administrative assistance to the CIO. At the Budapest meeting, the OSCE also approved a Code of Conduct on Politico-Military Aspects of Security[15] (which sets forth principles guiding the role of armed forces in democratic societies) and decided that the ODIHR, acting in an advisory capacity and in consultation with the CIO, will participate in discussions of the Senior and Permanent Councils to report on its activities and implementation issues. In addition, in March 1995, the Pact on Stability in Europe, a French initiative aimed at fostering good neighborly relations by applying preventive diplomacy to resolve minority and border problems, was placed under the aegis of the OSCE. Finally, the Lisbon follow-up meeting approved a "Common and Comprehensive Security Model for Europe for the Twenty-First Century," a politically binding document that outlines the future of the OSCE as a security community.

The OSCE's short-term track record

Two stages, Cold War and post-Cold War, best characterize the OSCE's security community-building process. During the Cold War, the OSCE's role was mainly to set domestic and international standards and norms for its members:

> It broadened the scope of accountability to include ... environmental issues, information, culture, economics, education, and human rights as well as more traditional military and security issues. It also served as a constant reminder to the East that a full normalization of relations would require fundamental internal reforms. It can also be

credited with reducing military tensions through confidence- and security-building measures, creating transparency in arms control and routinization in arms inspection."[16]

The innovation of cooperative security and human rights practices by the OSCE contributed not just to the recovery of East-West relations but also "to the emergence of a 'civil society' in various Eastern countries which prepared the ground for the revolutions of 1989."[17] Thus, it ended up having a subversive effect on the Soviet empire, promoting and speeding its demise by peaceful means. Indeed, the OSCE's notion that the manner in which a state treats its own citizens is a legitimate concern of the entire regional community[18] had revolutionary effects on millions of Soviet and East European citizens, who, with the active help of Helsinki Committees, such as Czechoslovakia's Charter 77, organized transnationally to secure their rights.

Their demands generated a crisis of legitimacy that impelled Soviet leaders to devise measures for restoring it, both at home and abroad. Gorbachev's reforms, rather than being aimed at destroying Communism, were intended to recover this legitimacy, without which the Soviet Union could not obtain foreign assistance to rebuild its ailing economy.[19] In the end, "Helsinki provided for peaceful change by chipping away Soviet and East European stonewalling on human rights. By focusing the efforts of Western governments and private citizens in both East and West, it helped set the stage for much of what is happening today."[20] But OSCE standards and mobilized Eastern civil societies did not just put pressure on the Soviet leaders; in some Eastern and Central European countries they also helped reproduce a liberal normative structure, on whose basis the new Eastern leaders formed a new identity for themselves and their states.[21] In addition, the Helsinki process was instrumental in legitimizing German unification, specially *vis-à-vis* Moscow,[22] which helped speed up the demise of the Soviet empire.

After the Cold War, the main task of the OSCE, building on past achievements, became securing the internalization of liberal norms by former Communist countries and devising the means of conflict prevention and normimplementation to guarantee the evolution toward security community-ascendance and, later, maturity. In other words, because of the end of the Cold War, cooperative security on the European continent became a real possibility; confidence-building measures and human rights activities became not only a means for providing a temporary solution to military instability or to gross human rights violations, but also a matter of shaping a common identity. Poland, the Czech Republic, Hungary, and the Baltic States approached Western human-rights standards; many other former Communist countries have made striking progress toward compliance with human-rights norms.[23] Also, even though "the new democratic structures are still fragile, and there can be doubt as to whether the commitment to democracy is truly genuine in all states ... it still remains highly significant that today no CSCE participating state proclaims an alternative model of political organization."[24]

In addition, important conventional arms-control agreements have been signed in the context of the OSCE, including the Treaty on Conventional Armed Forces in Europe (CFE), which limits non-nuclear ground and air forces between the Atlantic and the Urals; a similar agreement covering personnel; the Open Skies agreement; and extended agreements on confidence-building measures (1975, 1986, 1990, 1992, 1994). Equally notable is the fact that, due first to OSCE confidence-building and arms-control measures and, more recently, to NATO programs, such as the PfP, integration between the militaries of former rival blocs has become a real possibility. The fact that the military establishments of the two former Cold War alliances promote the integration of their military forces and are willing to take practical measures to achieve it attests to the fact that the overall integrative effort of the OSCE's practices aims at achieving a level of mutual trust that is consistent with a security community. For example, Estonia, Latvia, and Lithuania have initiated the formation of a joint Baltic battalion for eventual participation in NATO exercises and international peacekeeping operations.

The OSCE has also been involved in conflict prevention and resolution in various European contests through early warning, preventive diplomacy, and human-rights monitoring. Noteworthy are OSCE missions that, although limited in their ability to solve ongoing conflicts, "serve as a barometer measuring the degree of the participating States' concern over events in their region."[25] Thus, OSCE missions are able to "monitor developments, promote dialogue between the disputing parties, establish contact points for solving problems ... ensure close OSCE cooperation with local authorities [and] ensure that potentially explosive situations ... do not deteriorate into war."[26] As Marianne Hanson has argued, it is less important that these missions have not averted conflict in every instance – it would be naive to expect that they would – than that they represent an apparent willingness on the part of states to subject their actions and their constitutional arrangements to international scrutiny of this kind. What is notable about these missions is that, with one exception, no state has yet refused or terminated a mission.[27]

The OSCE plays important roles in the implementation of the Dayton peace agreement in Bosnia-Herzegovina: (1) supervising the preparation and conduct of elections (for example, it has elaborated a comprehensive voter education program); (2) monitoring human-rights violations, with the help of a special ombudsman; and (3) assisting with negotiations on CBMs (such as the exchange of military information and restrictions on military deployment in certain districts) and arms control (limits on tanks, armored vehicles, combat aircraft, and attack helicopters). While these activities in themselves can do little to uproot Bosnia-Herzegovina's deep ethnic conflict, they can contribute to the creation of a minimum sense of trust, the strengthening of civil societies shattered by war, and the propagation of conditions that can help reestablish peaceful coexistence in the region.[28] The OSCE has also been helping Albania's warring parties to settle their differences peacefully.

The HCNM has been particularly active in investigating the condition of Russian minorities in Estonia, Latvia, and Lithuania and, more recently, has investigated the condition of minorities in Albania, Crimean separatism in Ukraine, Slovakia's Hungarian minority, the situation of the Russian-speaking minority in Kazakhstan and Kyrgyzstan, and the problems of the Roma (Gypsy) population. Part of the HCNM's success so far has been due to his ability to take up minority problems at an early stage and establish confidence in quiet diplomacy. "This confidence has often been rewarded by governments accepting his recommendations (such as Albania and Macedonia reacting favorably to his proposals concerning respectively the Greek and Albanian minorities on their soil) and even requesting additional advice following earlier involvement (for example Estonia requiring his expert opinion on the country's law on aliens)."[29]

In addition, there is the ODIHR, whose three clusters of activities – (a) promoting the establishment of democratic institutions, (b) supporting free and fair elections,[30] and (c) fostering the development of a civil society in the former Communist societies – have had mixed results to date. ODIHR was most successful with regional seminars, organized in the context of the "Programme for Newly Admitted States," which clearly exemplify OSCE's function of teaching norms.[31] ODIHR's work in support of free elections has encountered a problem of competence because it has clashed with other institutions, such as the CoE. But ODIHR has played a major role in making OSCE decisions and procedures more accessible to NGOs and, even more important, in bringing NGO information on human-rights violations to the attention of the OSCE's governing institutions. By actively supporting NGOs, ODIHR follows in the footsteps of the CSCE during the Cold War as a key contributor to the creation and nurturing of an active civil society, which is a necessary condition for the construction of a pluralistic security community.[32]

On the darker side of developments in the OSCE region, of course, there are Bosnia, Chechnya, and other conflict-torn areas, where human rights violations, ethnic cleansing, and other atrocities became the norm. These conflicts raised serious questions not just about the ability of the OSCE to control ethnic conflicts in Europe, but also about the *inside-out* model itself. The Balkan quagmire has made it very clear that unless the OSCE develops effective means of preventive diplomacy, the new democracies will not be able to survive for long – and the OSCE will not be able to continue its community-building mission. While OSCE conflict-prevention and crisis-management practices have made some difference in a few areas, such as Nagorno-Karabakh and Kosovo, in Bosnia and Chechnya the OSCE was almost powerless to stop conflicts after they erupted.

Moreover, due mainly to domestic political developments, by the end of December 1993 Russia was preventing access by OSCE missions to Russian peace-keeping facilities in Moldova and Georgia and "proclaimed CSCE demands for monitoring of such operations in exchange for international support to be interference in legitimate Russian affairs."[33] Russia's obstruction of OSCE missions has raised serious doubts about the Russian inclination to cooperate with the OSCE when such cooperation clashes with its national and regional interests. True, Russia consented to co-chair the "Minsk Group" mediating a solution in Nagorno-Karabakh and a mission to

Chechnya, but the Russian military has been uncooperative, to say the least.

In addition, although CBM and arms control agreements have promoted the development of stable and higher expectations for treaty compliance and verification, some of the security mechanisms described above have been toothless or seen their bite dull over time. For example, while the Human Dimension Mechanism was widely used until the end of 1989 (approximately 150 times), its invocation has diminished to a trickle since the outbreak of ethnic conflicts in Europe in 1990. The OSCE has also been weak in affecting the nature, scope, and pace of economic interdependence in the OSCE region; other organizations, such as the EU, are better endowed to perform this task. On the other hand, the OSCE facilitated the development of shared norms that made possible economic interdependence and the enlargement of the EU toward Eastern Europe.

In the short-term sum, the balance of OSCE activities has been mixed. According to the 1995 US President's Report on OSCE activities, there were "considerable effects in the fields of security, restructuring and downsizing armed forces, acceding to arms control and reduction agreements, confidence-building measures, and non-proliferation treaties. Tough government economic decisions in several states are bearing fruits. Free and fair elections held in former Communist states resulted in legislatures which passed laws ensuring political and economic freedom."[34] Of twenty-three former Communist OSCE countries surveyed by the President's Report, fifteen (65 per cent) received good marks in democracy, fourteen (60 per cent) in the rule of law, and thirteen (56 per cent) in human rights. The list of countries did not include the Czech Republic, Hungary, and Poland, which have moved the farthest in adopting liberal values. On the other hand, according to the Report, "there is ample proof of the continuing existence of old, undemocratic attitudes and habits which reflect the great difficulty in changing deeply rooted totalitarian behavior and show that many countries still have a long way to go."[35]

Short-term gains and losses, however, are relatively insufficient indicators of whether the OSCE is laying the foundations for a security community in the long run. Hence the rest of this chapter will highlight OSCE practices and institutional efforts to construct a security community for the long haul.

The OSCE as a security community-building institution

The OSCE's community-building functions

The OSCE performs seven functions that contribute to the development of community. (1) It promotes political consultation and bilateral and multilateral agreements among its members. (2) It sets liberal standards – applicable both within each state and throughout the community – that are used to judge democratic and human rights performance, and monitors compliance with them. (3) It attempts to prevent violent conflict before it occurs. (4) It helps develop the practice of peaceful settlement of disputes within the OSCE space. (5) It builds mutual trust by promoting arms control agreements, military transparency, and cooperation. (6) It supports assistance to newly independent states and supports the building of democratic institutions and market-economic reforms. (7) It provides assistance to post-conflict reestablishment of institutions and the rule of law.

More generally, the OSCE is geared to shape new transnational identities based on liberal values. It serves as a conduit for the transmission of liberal values, norms, and practices to the East, thereby helping create new vested interests in a pan-European space.

The OSCE's security community-building model

The above functions can be understood only in light of six special characteristics of the OSCE security community-building model.

1. *Cooperative security.* This "demilitarized" concept of security "has resulted in imbuing security with political and human dimensions, and in basing security on confidence and cooperation, the elaboration of peaceful means of dispute settlement between states, the consolidation of justice and democracy in civil society, and the advancement of human freedom and rights, including national minority rights."[36] Cooperative security is also predicated on the interdependence of traditional security matters with economic and technological cooperation and on the joint advancement of environmental protection.

Thus, according to the classic notion of security, no adversary's weapon or political intention may be beyond the reach of another's state's concern. According to the OSCE's notion of cooperative security, however, *"no domestic institution or norm is beyond the jurisdic-*

tional reach of the CSCE ... Once human rights, the rule of law, and democratic pluralism are made the subject of international commitment, there is little left in terms of governmental institutions that is domestic."[37] Particularly striking in this regard (especially if "one considers that most conflicts in today's Europe arise as a result of the denial of rights of particular groups of people"[38]) are the various links that the OSCE establishes between human rights and regional security, such as between the mandate and activities of the HCNM and the OSCE crisis mechanisms, or the fact that the OSCE's field missions increasingly combine a human rights and conflict resolution and prevention component.

2. *Socialization and the teaching of norms.* Probably more than any other international organization today (with the exception, perhaps, of the CoE), the OSCE gives meaning to the practice of active socialization and the international teaching of norms. Like the CoE, the OSCE provides new members "with knowledge necessary for imitation, i.e., information and consultation about the workings of democracy, the rule of law, and the market economy."[39]

In contrast to the CoE, NATO, and the EU, however, the OSCE, hoping to affect and transform collective perceptions and identities, has from the outset incorporated all states that express a political will to live up to the standards and norms of the community. In other words, the OSCE has adopted the view that you must first let the largest possible number of people from different states *imagine* that they are part of a community; only then, when all have formally and instrumentally accepted the institution's shared normative structures and practices, do you socialize their elites and peoples by means of continual diplomatic interaction and a wide range of community-building practices. Thus, the rationale for the crucial 1992 decision to bring all the successor states of the Soviet Union into the OSCE was: "We know you are not 'us.' Let's pretend, however, that you are, so we may teach you to be 'us.' The far worse alternative – not to invite you to leave the 'outside' and become associated with us – is most likely to turn you into 'them' and against us."

On the other hand, the rationale for socialization followed by the CoE, NATO, and the EU has been: "It's not enough to behave like us; you have to be one of us." In other words, these institutions admit *selected* "applicants" only after they have learned and internalized common norms and institutionalized practices. The status of "partnership" or "association" instituted by NATO, the EU, and the CoE is intended to provide a probationary status to countries that wish to join the community. More than anything else, this probationary status is intended to enable community members to distinguish whether applicants are making instrumental choices or are adopting a shared liberal identity. In addition, their partnership in common economic and security enterprises is meant to play a major role in changing the applicants' identities to make them "more like us."

The OSCE's socialization strategy differs from that of NATO, the EU, and the CoE in another important way. The latter organizations

> expand on the sense of security which already exists among their members who share common levels of development and approach. The CSCE was based upon the assumption that its signatories do not share common approaches. It seeks to create security by expanding areas of consensus among differing points of view. This consensus is translated into action through the political will of its members to succeed in defining common goals.[40]

3. *Expectations of international legitimacy and the "accountability norm."* The OSCE strategy has been to create shared values and achieve mutual responsiveness by exploiting expectations of international legitimacy and by fundamentally transforming the region's constitutive norms. In other words, changing the identities and interests of former Communist countries entailed setting, promoting, and diffusing (a) the *expectation* that international legitimacy depends on the democratic nature of domestic regimes (peaceful change is predicated on the knowledge that member states and societies have of one other as liberal democracies, thus as "doves"); and (b) the *accountability norm*, according to which OSCE states are accountable to one another and to the OSCE community for what they do to their own citizens (trust and peaceful change are predicated on replacing the non-intervention norm with the mutual accountability norm).

4. *System of governance.* The OSCE's constitutive norms and associated institutions and practices may be conceived as a crude governance system, relying for compliance on a shared transnational liberal identity that creates and maintains public order within the OSCE region. Thomas Buergenthal caught the subtle but crucial essence of the OSCE when he asserted that OSCE instruments can be compared to those national constitutions that, without being legally binding or enforceable in the courts, serve as the normative source of the nation's public order.[41] An effective system of governance cannot be based solely on legitimation, however. This is why the OSCE has began to

develop scrutiny mechanisms, some of them unprecedentedly intrusive, such as the dispatching of OSCE missions to states suspected of violating human rights, without their consent.[42]

In part, this governance system draws its effectiveness from the ability of states "to link compliance with stated norms to important political, economic and military issues covered in the Helsinki document."[43] For example, during the Cold War, the West linked Eastern compliance with human-rights norms to progress in arms control; this allowed it to empower the social groups that eventually brought down the Soviet empire.[44] Linkage worked, however, because of what Hanson has called a "psychology of compliance," according to which "political leaders were ... subject to an intensive degree of moral censure if they failed to live up to their Helsinki commitments."[45]

5. *Cognitive Region and Agent States.* OSCE's discourse and community-building practices encourage people to imagine that, with regard to their security and well-being, borders run more or less where shared understandings and common identities end. Moreover, they promote the shared understanding that OSCE states should feel insecure not only when their authority is challenged or their existence is endangered, but also when the basic understandings that constitute the community are threatened.[46]

This collective perception of transnational identity gives a new meaning to the idea and practice of sovereignty within a pluralistic security community. In the current ascendant phase of the OSCE community, this meaning has yet to become even partially institutionalized; nevertheless, its implications for a *future* security community are far-reaching. Even if some new members still have a hard time understanding this, when states join the OSCE they do not just pledge to "coordinate" their policies in a given issue-area or to cooperate to solve any given ethnic conflict within the region. Rather, and primarily, they commit themselves to the notion that legitimacy is contingent on their ability to abide by the community's normative structure. In a mature, tightly coupled security community this means that states can express their agency insofar as they meet and reproduce the community's norms and understandings. States remain "free agents," acting on the basis of their own preferences, as long as these preferences are cognitively framed by their shared understandings.[47]

The OSCE approach to the treatment of national minorities clearly exemplifies the nascent notion of "agent-state." "Anyone whose human rights have been violated shall have access to remedies not only on the national level but on the international and regional levels as well ... Under the OSCE individuals and groups may turn to international bodies with information on human rights." And because "the OSCE recognizes and promotes the role of nongovernment groups as agents of international human rights order, such groups have direct access to the OSCE institutions." It is important to note, however, that "the state *itself*, the Copenhagen document recognized, is the critical mechanism in advancing human rights."[48] In other words, mutual accountability does not reduce state agency; if anything, it increases it for the sake of monitoring, and thus reproducing, community norms.

6. *OSCE practices as community-building devices.* The same cooperative security practices that offer a means of dealing with specific problems, such as early warning, conflict prevention, and the protection of human rights and minorities, "are designed to be part of a process of community building."[49] These practices, together with the normative structure embodied in OSCE documents, institutionalize a new way of collectively defining regional solutions around liberal ideas. They help constitute new vested interests in, and generate the material and institutional resources for, these solutions. In other words, the institutionalization in the OSCE space of cooperative security practices is intended to ground regional security on a collective transnational identity and, therefore, on dependable expectations of peaceful change.

For example, the Human Dimension apparatus is superficially intended only to monitor behavior, namely, the implementation of human rights provisions.[50] *In practice,* however, it also aims at reconstructing the identities and thus preferences of OSCE members. The Valletta Dispute Settlement Mechanism, though inadequate in its present form to guarantee the peaceful settlement of disputes, socializes OSCE members to norms of peaceful change. As part of the same effort, the OSCE has also "established a conciliation and arbitration court for those members that wish to subscribe to it [and it] has exercised the capacity to send observers, fact finders, and mediators to troubled spots."[51]

Equally important for community-building are the innovative practice of CBMs, now diffused around the world, which the OSCE created *ex nihilo* back in the early 1970s.[52] Originally thought to be merely a variant of arms control measures aimed at enhancing transparency so as to reduce the danger of surprise attack, CBMs have become a community-building mechanism based on the social construction of mutual trust. Because trust is closely related to the legitimacy of a government "and the way it treats its people,"[53] military cooperation and trust – and, more generally, peaceful change – are inseparable from the norms that constitute the community's public order. Thus the right to request information and make representations about human rights is the other side of the CBM coin.

The OSCE's institutional processes and attributes, frequently criticized for their lack of coherence and teeth, are in fact compatible with the task of community-building. For one thing, the fact that most of the OSCE's injunctions are politically rather than legally binding makes "adherence to stated intentions a test of political credibility rather than an invitation to search for legal loopholes";[54] this promotes mutual trust. Furthermore, politically binding instruments lead to changes in practices, political interests, and public policies, rather than in legal instruments. In other words, OSCE processes work less by constraining political behavior than by promoting public policies that are congruent with the region's norms.

Secondly, the informality of the Helsinki process, especially in its early stages, prevented the development of huge bureaucracies; instead, it has empowered individuals, NGOs, social movements, and other civil society actors to act on behalf of their rights. The informality generated the dense web of transnational relations throughout the region that is essential for the development of a transnational community.

Thirdly, the consensus rule, only recently modified to consensus-minus-one in the event of gross violations of OSCE norms, means that, once achieved, consensus "has higher moral credibility and greater political weight."[55] It also generates the need to persuade other members, thereby promoting socialization and learning processes. According to Marton Krasznai, a Hungarian ambassador to the OSCE, the consensus practice works because of the existence of "a unique political culture within the OSCE community."[56]

Fourthly, institutionalized learning also results from the OSCE's follow-up conferences, which review the effectiveness of previous documents, decisions, and measures. "This review of practices," maintains Alexis Heraclides, "was novel not only in the Helsinki process, but also in the history of diplomacy."[57] Due in part to follow-up conferences, a "wandering" OSCE community of diplomats and experts gradually developed; its members became the OSCE's staunchest advocates after they returned to their home countries and agencies. Moreover, the follow-up practice bred the need to define the notion of success and failure, promoting both self-correcting and goal-oriented behavior. A dynamic developed wherein the threat of a break-up at follow-up conferences motivated members to look for compromises and find solutions that might otherwise not have been forthcoming.

Fifthly, in contrast to balances of power, which "can exist and function regardless of whether or not the actors involved recognize it,"[58] security communities require institutions that instill this self-reflective recognition in its members. The OSCE, mainly through shared practices, is making its member states "more conscious of the larger relational context underlying their specific policy problem."[59] As one observer of the OSCE process has stated: "Negotiating in the CSCE is often slow, tiresome, at times even painful, and does not always lead to common positions. But the intensive process of dialogue has the virtue of deepening mutual recognition of other states' positions, which is a necessary presupposition for further steps in the direction of common understanding."[60]

Finally, the Helsinki process promoted seminar diplomacy. Now widespread in other security organizations, such as NATO's NACC and the PfP, seminar diplomacy institutionalizes the diplomatic practice of teaching norms and legitimizes expertise as the basis of agreements. More importantly, seminar diplomacy encourages the generation not only of causal understandings about specific technical issues, but also of a measure of we-feeling and mutual trust among seminar members. Due to its theoretical and practical importance, I will deal with seminar diplomacy separately.

Seminar diplomacy

By *seminar diplomacy* I mean not just the holding of seminars, which became a normal practice of OSCE institutions, but, more broadly, all types of multilateral diplomacy[61] (meetings of diplomats, practitioners, civil servants, and academic experts, the use of experts in diplomatic missions) aimed at promoting political dialogue and international cooperation (political, social, economic) and preventing or managing conflict by means of consensual technical or normative knowledge. From a security community perspective, seminar diplomacy is a vehicle to socially construct shared values and mutual responsiveness in a given region and the transnational identity of a region.[62]

Seminar diplomacy is not necessarily an OSCE invention, but the negotiations provided under the Helsinki Final Act gave the impetus to its development. The premise that European security should be based on cooperation in three functional baskets almost inevitably determined that the follow-ups would be carried out in multilateral meetings of experts in the functional areas of the various baskets.[63]

Although meetings of experts have been the rule since 1975 in areas like the peaceful settlement of disputes, human rights, national minorities, CBMs, the environment, science and technology, and economics, the most striking manifestation of seminar diplomacy by far has taken the shape of forums modeled after university seminars. First suggested and promoted by the United States,[64] a seminar is a socialization mechanism that, based on interaction and dialogue, promotes the development of common meanings, innovative ideas, and cooperative solutions. In other words, the rationale behind seminars is teaching the would-be members of the community the principles on which the community should be based, as well as teaching the means for effectively implementing these principles. From the beginning, the OSCE took a "pedagogical" approach, based on recommendations and technical support – related to the establishment of democratic and free market systems, the protection of minorities, or the development of confidence through mutually agreed restrictions on military maneuvers. In fact, one can argue that the OSCE became a venue and institutional home for epistemic community – like groups or a sort of "community of epistemic communities," which linked issues by means of epistemic and normative knowledge in innovative ways.[65]

Seminars are informal and break up into working groups; larger plenary sessions only open and conclude the seminars. Because what matters most is not the outcome but the pedagogical process, not all seminars produce final documents and reports. The expectation is that, in addition to their results' coming to the attention of the OSCE's policy-making units, delegates will later disseminate the ideas raised at the seminar in their respective political systems, thus spreading the seeds of shared understandings across national borders. This is why NGOs can and do play an important role in seminar diplomacy; they are an invaluable conduit of information from the OSCE seminar to civil societies, and from civil societies, through the seminars, to OSCE authorities and OSCE governments.

The Charter of Paris mandated two seminars, one on national minorities and the other on democratic institutions. Since the end of 1990, however, a plethora of seminars has been undertaken by OSCE institutions, especially the ODIHR. There have been seminars on Tolerance (November 1992, May 1995), Migration (April 1993), National Minorities (May 1993), Free Media (November 1993), Early Warning and Preventive Diplomacy (January 1994), Migrant Workers (March 1994), Local Democracy (May 1994), Roma (i.e., Gypsies) (September 1994), the Building Blocks of Civil Society (April 1995), and Private Sector Investment in the CIS Countries (September 1996). While these and other seminars should be evaluated in part by their ability to achieve specific goals in their respective topics, they can be interpreted as confidence-building measures aimed at developing trust and ties among peoples and elites of the OSCE states.

Like their senior partners, the follow-up meetings, seminars have been an invaluable tool for generating and evaluating the body of experience about implementing cooperative security. For example, the seminars on military doctrine in 1990 and 1991 played a significant role in creating patterns of military cooperation between the former blocs. "The open, non-confrontational dialogue between the highest-ranking representatives of the Eastern and Western military establishments was considered a substantial breakthrough in East–West dialogue. This experience was instrumental in promoting the idea of an open-ended dialogue on security matters that would not necessarily be aimed at negotiating concrete results."[66] The Economic Forum seminars, too, have been a useful tool for setting an economic agenda for the OSCE's main decision-making bodies. OSCE seminars are also a source of institutional innovation and a conduit of innovations to decision-making bodies. For example, the idea of a regional ombudsman, raised at the seminar on Case Studies on National Minorities, was later put to practice in Bosnia-Herzegovina. OSCE seminars also promote dialogue with non-OSCE states and the diffusion of cooperative security practices beyond the OSCE region. This is the case with OSCE seminars on the Mediterranean region, held together with non-OSCE Mediterranean states (Algeria, Egypt, Israel, Morocco, and Tunisia) in Cairo (September 1995) and Tel Aviv (June 1996).

Among the most successful seminars have been the so-called "regional seminars," organized in the context of the "Programme for

Newly Admitted States" of the former Soviet Union. Their success has been due to the fact that they are small, focus on the specific needs and conditions of the region where they take place, and are able to attract local participants who need exposure to OSCE principles and procedures. Referring to a regional seminar in Kyrgyzstan on the promotion of small and medium-sized business, the US Helsinki Commission concluded that not "only is international support for the process of transformation thus displayed, but exposure to international ideas and norms are expanded dramatically ... As a catalyst for discussion, a signal of international support, and a method of promoting CSCE aims, and through them long-term stability in the CSCE region, such activities promise to be among CSCE's best tools."[67]

Seminar diplomacy can be a source of institutional and technical innovation and of institutional learning. For example, technical suggestions raised at the OSCE seminar on early warning and preventive diplomacy in Warsaw (January 1994) were later reviewed by the Permanent Committee in Vienna.[68] The seminar raised questions about the implications of innovative institutional instruments for national bureaucratic structures and produced suggestions for institutional change. Conclusions were also drawn about NGO participation in early-warning activities and about the possible use of their sophisticated network of basic human-rights information.[69] Equally important is OSCE's use of seminar diplomacy to develop a viable "Common and Comprehensive Security Model for the Twenty-First Century."

Seminar diplomacy can also play a critical role in the diffusion of community norms and practices to new member countries. For example, the intensive discussions at the 1994 OSCE seminar on the Human Dimension, in Kazakhstan, were predicated not only on diplomatic courtesy or academic curiosity but took place, in the words of the Swedish foreign minister, Margaretha af Ugglas, to "draw the Central Asians into CSCE."[70] Furthermore, as attested by the Human Dimension Seminar on Tolerance (Warsaw, July 1992), the success of seminar diplomacy can in part be traced to the preference for practitioners and experts over traditional diplomats as delegates. In this case, experts on the role of educational and cultural institutions and the media in promoting tolerance shared their views with the OSCE's newest members, such as Uzbekistan and Kazakhstan, demonstrating that the seminar framework can be "a clearinghouse for assistance in democracy-building."[71]

One should not easily dismiss seminar diplomacy and the injection of expertise into political diplomatic processes as irrelevant to politics, however. Starting with the Helsinki Final Act, through rapporteur missions, and on to the drafting of normative standards and the development of CBMs that affected the practice and public policy of governments, the OSCE process and its innovative practices have been profoundly influenced by technical knowledge, expertise, and the seminar method. For example, scholars of international law played a prominent role in the negotiations leading to the 1990 Copenhagen agreement that set the rule of law as the constitutive norm of the OSCE community. Noteworthy is the case of a US delegate, Thomas Buergenthal – a world-renowned expert on international law – who ended up having a significant influence on the final text, not necessarily because he exercised American power but because (as he himself and others attested) some of the European delegates – also international lawyers – deferred to his opinions because they were his former students.[72]

Moreover, after the Cold War, seminar diplomacy may have acquired strategic relevance. When the strategic goal was deterring the enemy, nation-states used technological innovation, the deployment of new weapons, and classic arms-control diplomacy. However, when regional security became cooperative security, and bringing former enemies into the Euro-Atlantic community became one of the West's key strategic goals, nation-states began using community-making means, such as seminar diplomacy, which can reassure, create trust, build a common civic culture, transfer practical knowledge, and teach norms. On this point I cannot improve on what the deputy secretary-general of NATO, Sergio Balanzino, said at a recent RAND seminar:

> Some may view skeptically the importance of "soft" diplomacy. But I think it is wrong to underestimate the power of such dialogue and its potential to stimulate and develop constructive and deepening cooperation. In fact, all the major developments associated with the end of the Cold War, from German unity to NATO's deepening relationship with Russia, began with dialogue ... To understand how powerful dialogue can be as an instrument of change, you only have to look at the development of the CSCE, which began tentatively as a forum for discussion across a geographically and ideologically divided Europe. Now it is a fully fledged organization, building its own capacity for conflict prevention.[73]

The diffusion of OSCE practices to other European institutions

One of the most remarkable features of the OSCE security model is how extensively it has "travelled" throughout Europe. In other words, were the OSCE to cease to exist today, it still would continue to "live" on, embedded in the practices of other European multilateral institutions. In the following pages, I briefly describe the adoption of OSCE inside-out practices by NATO, the WEU, the EU, and the CoE.

NATO approached the post-Cold War demand of former East-Bloc countries for legitimation, a shared identity, and security by steering a course that would slowly begin to transform its institutions and practices from being exclusively geared to balancing the power of and deterring a competing alliance to maintaining the peace, like the OSCE, by cooperative security measures, and extending the Euro-Atlantic pluralistic security community eastward. It did so, however, without abandoning its traditional goals of collective defense and by developing new tasks to deal with the challenges of post-Cold War European security, as in Bosnia-Herzegovina.

In other words, NATO has become Janus-faced, looking at realist power politics while betting on idealism and a security community. By adopting OSCE's definition of cooperative security and many of its community-making practices and applying them to former Communist states, NATO is steering a two-track course between (a) basing security within the OSCE region on cooperation and dependable expectations of peaceful change and (b) keeping a strong defense capability as an insurance policy against Russia, should the latter turn against NATO. NATO enlargement to the East aims at fulfilling both goals.

To make the enlargement process more palatable to Russia, however, NATO has engaged the latter in a cooperative security dialogue, which includes military, political, economic, and environmental OSCE-like community-building activities. The purpose of this dialogue is to persuade Russia that NATO's enlargement strategy follows the logic of community. In other words, the aim is to show Russia that NATO's expansion to the East is not the threatening act of an alliance in a balance of power system but the stabilizing action of a security community attempting to extend its boundaries to include former enemies. Thus, when in July 1997, NATO formally decided to incorporate the Czech Republic, Hungary, and Poland into the Alliance, it first signed with Russia a Charter ("Founding Act on Mutual Relations, Cooperation and Security"), aimed at reassuring, increasing mutual trust, and developing mutual habits of conciliation and cooperation.[74]

Javier Solana, the current secretary-general of NATO, explained the rationale of NATO's multilateral diplomacy:

> Our strategy changed from one of preventing war to actively shaping peace. These changes are genuine, not just words in communiqués ... NATO has transformed itself both politically and militarily. That it could successfully go through all these changes is due to the fact that NATO is about much more than just collective defense. It is as much about developing trust, about establishing patterns of cooperation, about managing crises collectively, and about creating peaceful, stable relations among European and North American democracies.[75]

Two "inside-out" institutions, the NACC (replaced and upgraded by the EAPC in May 1997) and PfP, stand at the forefront of NATO's security community-building mission. The NACC was created at the NATO summit in Rome in November 1991. Comprising the foreign ministers and representatives from all sixteen NATO states, Eastern and Central European states, and all the Soviet successor states, including the Baltics (a total of thirty-eight countries), the NACC became an attempt by NATO to take the initiative of community-building from the OSCE, while adopting OSCE-like community-building practices. Thus, cooperation through the NACC included issues such as the development of democratic institutions, civilian–military relations, peacekeeping, conceptual approaches to arms control and disarmament, defense planning, scientific and environmental affairs, civil/military coordination of air-traffic management, and the conversion of defense production to civilian purposes (including joint meetings, military contacts and visits, and in joint seminars). These activities were channels for military-to-military liaison and for the social construction of a sense of community and common purpose among military representatives from NACC states. The NACC's successor, the EAPC, will increase the role partners play in joint decision-making and planning and will make the PfP more operational. Membership is open to all OSCE states able and willing to accept the EAPC basic principles.

This type of "East–West" interaction, which emphasizes dialogue, partnership, and cooperation, resembles power-political diplomacy neither in content nor in discourse. On defense and political issues, "cooperation partner countries" are invited to participate in joint institutions with NATO states, where they can learn the ins and outs of the alliance and the practices of its members. In October 1994, a NACC seminar was held on "peacekeeping and its relationship to crisis management"; its summary report was forwarded to NACC ministers. Based on the results of this seminar, the NACC's Political-Military Steering Committee/Ad Hoc Group on Cooperation in Peace-keeping (PMSC/AHG) developed a shared understanding of conceptual aspects of peace-keeping.[76] Another seminar on Legal Aspects of Peacekeeping (July 1995), which drew on the seminar on the NATO Status of Forces Agreement (April 1995), contributed to a third seminar, on the relationship between the military and civilian organizations in international peacekeeping operations (November 1995).[77] A recent (June 1996) NACC seminar, like its OSCE counterparts, looked into the Human Dimension perspectives of economic and defense issues.

The PfP was first established at the NATO Summit in January 1994, within the framework of the NACC. Its twenty-seven member states include Austria, Finland, Malta, Slovenia, Sweden, and Macedonia, which are not NACC members. PfP's distinctive advantages can be understood only as part of NATO's attempt to extend the security community eastward. First, the PfP's thrust is avoiding a new division of Europe, "unless Russian expansion is seen to require that step."[78] Secondly, through "deeper and more extensive working links between new PfP members and NATO governments," the PfP is supposed to be a catalyst for internal reforms in Eastern and Central Europe. Thirdly, "PfP prepares candidate NATO members to function effectively in NATO's integrated military command system." Fourthly, it is a mechanism to bring Eastern and Central European countries to NATO military standards, thus making it easier for NATO states to extend the Alliance's security guarantee to new members. In essence, the PfP is a process to teach Western rules, including multilateralism, to Eastern political and military establishments.[79]

As a means for promoting peace by developing cooperative military relations with Partner countries, and for preparing some of the former adversaries to join the West, the PfP has first to build mutual confidence, trust, and knowledge. This is done mainly by: (a) facilitating transparency in national defense planning and budgeting; (b) ensuring democratic control of defense forces; (c) developing cooperative military relations with NATO, for the purposes of joint planning, training, and exercises; (d) maintaining the capability and readiness to contribute to operations under the authority of the United Nations or the OSCE; and (e) developing, over the long term, forces better able to operate with those of the Alliance.[80]

NATO's detailed "Individual Partnership Programs," established with most members of the PfP, "range over subjects and activities such as seminars on radio-spectrum management, provision of NATO technical documentation on standardization, adapting airfields to NATO standards, and exercises in compatible command and control systems. Recently, the PfP's work program has moved from "peace-keeping exercises [and search and rescue and humanitarian opera-tions] to defense review planning," and to peace-keeping itself, for example, in Bosnia-Herzegovina.[81] As a means for fulfilling its mission, the PfP has made an extensive use of seminar diplomacy; for example, it convened seminars on implementation of conventional arms agreements (October 1995 and March 1996). To subscribe to the PfP, member states reaffirm their commitment to the Helsinki Final Act and subsequent OSCE documents.

Like NATO, the WEU, referred to by the treaty on European Union as an integral part of the development of the Union, has been using its structures and processes to integrate Eastern and Central European states into the Euro-Atlantic security community.[82] In June 1992, the WEU established a "Forum of Consultation" with eight such states. Two years later, nine Eastern and Central European states were granted the status of "associates," opening the possibility for them to participate in the WEU's humanitarian, peacekeeping, and crisis-management operations. At the 1995 meeting of the WEU Ministerial Council, twenty-seven member, associate, and observer countries adopted OSCE-like policies of comprehensive, indivisible, and coop-erative security. The main idea, of course, is to make associate states increasingly involved in the WEU's policy-making process before they join the organization. Like the OSCE and NATO, the WEU is increas-ingly using seminar diplomacy and attempting to establish a special relationship with Russia and Ukraine.

Seen from the perspective of the logic of community, the EU's long-term strategy of enlargement to the East is a fundamental link in the chain of extending the Euro-Atlantic security community to the East and of diffusing there the norms and values that led to the institutio-nalization of peaceful change in Western Europe. On this count, it is noteworthy that since 1990 the EU has signed so-called "association agreements" with Eastern European states – ten so far, including Estonia, Latvia, Lithuania, and Slovenia – placing them on probation before they can be accepted as full EU members. The Essen European Council of December 1994 adopted a specific pre-accession strategy for preparing eligible countries for admission to the EU. The EU has negotiated Partnership and Cooperation Agreements with Russia and the CIS, providing for political, economic, industrial, scientific, and cultural cooperation.[83] These agreements are not just about achieving instrumental gains – in this case, increasing trade – but, more importantly, are meant to test Eastern European intentions and institutions and help their institutions conform to Western standards and values. The EU decision of July 1997 to recommend the admittance of Poland, Hungary, Cyprus, Slovenia, the Czech Republic, and Estonia to the Union at a later date, is also intended, in part, to prepare countries for membership, speed up democratization and liberalization processes, and thus enhance the chances of moving the borders of the Euro-Atlantic security community eastward. EU enlargement activities are thus as much about "security" as they are about economic welfare.

The CoE, Europe's oldest (May 1949) institutional watchdog of human rights principles, pluralistic democracy, and the rule of law, formally grants legitimation to European countries that have recently internalized the above principles. The Council says to prospective members: "Become truly democratic and practice the rule of law and human rights, and you will get Western Europe's seal of approval, namely, membership in the Council of Europe." Although this approach differs from the OSCE practice of granting membership to former Communist states before they become truly democratic, other OSCE's established practices, "such as those relating to the collective rights of minorities, the connection between the protection of human rights and the maintenance of peace, and humanitarian interference itself, have gradually been assimilated by . . . the United Nations and the Council of Europe."[84] In 1993, the CoE followed in the OSCE's footsteps when it passed a resolution setting the Council the task of helping establish a region of democratic security in Europe, as a *sine qua non* for security and stability throughout the continent. In all, fourteen former Communist countries, including Russia and Ukraine, have joined the CoE. Other countries, including Belarus, Bosnia-Herzegovina, and Armenia have begun admission procedures.

Conclusion

For almost thirty years, the OSCE has played a pivotal role in promoting the development of a security community in the area stretching from Vancouver to Vladivostok. Between 1975 and 1990, the OSCE helped establish the standards and norms of a *nascent* security community. During this time, the OSCE also played an important role in bringing about the end of the Cold War, which prepared the stage for the security community's *ascendant* phase. Since 1990, this phase has included the development of an institutional structure and the encouragement of habits necessary for ensuring compliance with OSCE standards and norms. The OSCE also turned itself into the "most creative organization today in the field of preventive diplomacy"[85] and diffused its practices to other European organizations, which adopted some of the OSCE's security community-building practices.

The OSCE's most important effect on security-community development, however, has been in helping to change the way people in the OSCE region define security. By helping to devise, diffuse, and institutionalize the concept of comprehensive, indivisible, and cooperative security, the OSCE has set in motion a learning process that is inducing governments and military establishments to replace deterrence, let alone the use of military power, with reassurance and trust-building measures, as means of achieving security objectives. This redefinition of security has been necessary for the development of mutual trust and a growing sense of mutual identification in the OSCE region.

So far, however, dependable expectations of peaceful change are not prevalent in the entire OSCE region. First, many states that were invited to join the OSCE after the end of the Cold War have yet to internalize the norms and practices that can ensure the ascendance of the OSCE region into a mature security community. Secondly, the OSCE still must cope with the paradox that deepening the process of community-building depends, in part, on reaching and sustaining levels of shared understandings and trust that are not yet available in the entire region. Thirdly, because of ethnic conflicts, civil wars, and gross human rights violations that are still common in the region, and that will be so for the foreseeable future, regional peace will depend, in part, on collective security activities of NATO, the WEU, and/or individual European powers. Finally, to play a significant role in the future, the OSCE will need to streamline its organizational structure and processes and establish a better division of labor with other international organizations, such as NATO and the EU.

What does the OSCE experience, and that of other European security community-building institutions, teach us so far about international relations theory? Certainly not that balances of power, alliances, hegemonies, and deterrence are fading entirely from the international political landscape, including in areas where security communities have already developed, such as the European continent. In the future, the architects of security communities still must compete with and fight against strongly reified power-political practices and conflicting identities. On the other hand, the OSCE's marked influence in bringing the Cold War to a peaceful end and redefining the way in which Euro-Atlantic states and international organizations understand and practice security is enough to raise serious doubts about mainstream realist arguments and their dismissal of international institutions and their community-building functions.[86] While it is true that the OSCE was a direct outgrowth of the superpowers' global confrontation and, more specifically, of the Soviet interest in legitimizing its postwar borders and influence and of the American interest in pleasing its European allies, the OSCE became the breeding ground of norms and new practices of peaceful change and a "conveyor belt" for their diffusion, through the unique institutional process created by the Helsinki Act. In and through *practice*, the OSCE changed itself; so much so that, since the early 1980s, its strength was based mainly on the capacity to mobilize civil societies, NGOs, and groups of experts behind normative understandings and expectations of material and moral improvement.

But the workings of security community-building institutions, such as the OSCE, the EU, and NATO, also suggest that the neoliberal argument that international institutions matter only because they help states coordinate their exogenously developed interests – mainly by reducing "transaction costs" and by providing information to the parties[87] – may be limited only to areas possessing a very thin social environment, where the transformative potential of organizational life is small or nonexistent.

The OSCE played a meaningful role in changing the European security environment, but not by reducing "transaction costs" (for most of the history of the OSCE, the US saw the OSCE less as a benefit than as a necessary cost) or by providing information to the parties.

Rather, by helping to change the way security is understood in Europe, it also led to a transformation of the cognitive, institutional, and material context within which post-Cold War domestic and international politics takes place. It helped institutionalize a new way of cognitively framing international problems and solutions around ideas of human rights, and later of democratic governance and the rule of law, and created new interest in and capabilities for reducing human-rights violations, for helping minorities, and for solving bilateral conflicts by peaceful means. Moreover, its innovative practices in the area of human rights and confidence-building helped define the meaning of "cooperative security" now prevalent in Europe.

Likewise, the activities of the OSCE and other security community-building institutions demonstrate the limits of the literature's mainstream understanding of "multilateralism"– the coordination of behavior "among three or more states on the basis of generalized principles of conduct."[88] This "weak" type of multilateralism should be complemented with "strong" multilateralism, which refers to the institutionalization of security communities by means of multilateral debates, dialogue, persuasion, seminar diplomacy, and discursive legitimation, on the basis of collective knowledge. Collective knowledge helps structure international reality and, thus, constitutes transnational identities and interests. Because constructivist scholarship recognizes the importance of knowledge for transforming identities and security interests, it can do a better job than neoliberalism in explaining the activities of security community-building institutions.[89]

Thus, for example, institutions not only prescribe behavioral roles and constrain activity, they also constitute the identity of such agents and empower them to act on the basis of their institutional reality. Thus the creation of institutions, such as the OSCE, is not merely an act of rational choice. It is also an act of the construction of social reality that is grounded not only on the physical world, but also on normative and epistemic agreements. Furthermore, it is the source and medium of practices that give meaning and direction to social choice and action.

Furthermore, security community-building institutions help determine which shared understandings will be culturally and politically selected to become the practices and interests of governments. To begin with, security community-building institutions are innovators, in the sense that they create the evaluative, normative, and sometimes even causal frames of reference around which a security community is constructed. Also, these institutions may play a critical role in the diffusion and institutionalization of values, norms, and shared understandings. Finally, these institutions may play a role in the intra- and inter-state political processes that shape the political choices that make possible the development of security communities.[90]

More generally, strong multilateralism and the workings of security community-building institutions show that the "latent" functions of security community-building institutions may be as important as the "manifest" functions emphasized by neoliberals. Referring to international institutions, John Ruggie said that their

> activities may be as important as their products. If the *activities* succeed, they will have three consequences apart from their substantive accomplishments: to trigger the creation of constituencies where none exist ... to establish permanent networks around such constituencies; and to articulate, support and sustain a continuing policy role for these constituencies ... In other words, they potentially contribute to processes of institutionalization and thereby affect policy formation.[91]

The OSCE's track record goes a long way to support Ruggie's insight. Endowed with little organization, especially during its first fifteen years, and depending mainly on an ongoing process of follow-up conferences and self-correcting practices, the OSCE's source of political influence has been the ability to: (a) create constituencies, in the form of human-rights Helsinki groups and social movements, in most if not all of the CSCE member states; (b) utilize the power of these constituencies to pressure governments to reach political agreements; and (c) provide a new liberal identity to the leaders of the Helsinki groups, who, like Václav Havel, became the leaders of their countries after the peaceful revolutions of 1989. During the Cold War, these sources of influence played a catalytic role in turning process into product, that is, the delegitimation of the Soviet empire and the diffusion of liberal ideas to former Communist countries.

Moreover, institutions need not be formally or materially organized – although they usually are – in order to have important political effects. Conference and seminar diplomacy may be institutionalized but not formally organized. A recurrent set of intersubjective normative understandings may be expressed in political decisions, arrived at through international bargaining, and institutionalized in recurrent diplomatic conferences. Each conference learns from, builds on, and adds to its predecessor. Such an institution does not just assign new roles, order expectations, and help constrain members' behaviors. It also intervenes in the world to reproduce common understandings and identities. And, while the OSCE commitments are not enshrined in a legal document, they are almost the same as a treaty.[92]

In sum, security community-building institutions and practice amount to a serious effort to replace the Cold War cognitive and discursive structure with a new structure based on cooperative security understandings and expectations. First, these institutions, such as the OSCE, NACC and PfP, help mobilize material and normative resources for the development of a transnational liberal collective identity. Secondly, as exemplified by OSCE's human rights practices and seminar diplomacy, security community-building institutions and practices increase the quality and nature of transactions in the region and help constitute a regional intersubjective structure. Finally, strategic practices, such as the OSCE's CBMs and early warning, and the PfP's military-civil society activities, are helping materialize the knowledge foundation on the basis of which a "we feeling" is defined or redefined.

Notes

I would like to thank Michael Barnett, Beverly Crawford, Richard C. Eichenberg, Ernst B. Haas, Arie Kacowicz, Charles Kupchan, Jeff Lewis, Joel H. Rosenthal, and Ole Wæver for useful comments. I am also grateful to Jeff Lewis for research assistance. I thank the Carnegie Council on Ethics and International Affairs, the Davis Institute of International Relations at the Hebrew University of Jerusalem, and the German and European Studies Center at UC Berkeley, for financial help.

1 James E. Goodby, "The Diplomacy of Europe Whole and Free," in Samuel F. Wells, Jr., ed., *The Helsinki Process and the Future of Europe*, Woodrow Wilson Center Special Studies, no. 1 (Washington, DC: The Wilson Center Press, 1990), p. 59.
2 The OSCE was known until January 1995 as the Conference on Security and Cooperation in Europe (CSCE). To avoid confusion, all my references to this institution, other than in citations, will be to the OSCE. For some recent studies on the OSCE, see Stefan Lehne, *The CSCE in the 1990s: Common European House or Potemkin Village?* (Vienna: Braumuller, 1991); Michael Lucas, ed., *The CSCE in the 1990s: Constructing European Security and Cooperation* (Baden-Baden: Nomos, 1993); Vojtech Mastny, *The Helsinki Process and the Reintegration of Europe 1986–1991: Analysis and Documentation* (New York: New York University Press, 1992); Alexis Heraclides,

Security and Cooperation in Europe: The Human Dimension, 1972–1992 (London: Frank Cass, 1993); Arie Bloed, *The Conference on Security and Cooperation in Europe: Analysis and Basic Documents, 1972–1993* (Dordrecht: Kluwer Academic Pub., 1993); Victor-Ives Ghebali, *L'OSCE dans l'Europe post-communiste, 1990–1996: Vers une identité paneuropéenne de sécurité* (Brussels: Bruylant, 1996); and Diana Chigas, with Elizabeth McClintock and Christophe Kamp, "Preventive Diplomacy and the Organization for Security and Cooperation in Europe: Creating Incentives for Dialogue and Cooperation," in Abram Chayes and Antonia H. Chayes, eds., *Preventing Conflict in the Post-Communist World* (Washington, DC: The Brookings Institution, 1996), pp. 25–97.

3 According to Paul Schroeder, since the end of World War II, international order has increasingly come to depend on "associations" based on a normative consensus that "certain kinds of international conduct ... had to be ruled out as incompatible with their general security and welfare." Paul W. Schroeder, "The New World Order: A Historical Perspective," *The Washington Quarterly* 17 (1994), p. 30.

4   Our approach is one of cooperative security based on democracy, respect for human rights, fundamental freedom and the rule of law, market economy and social justice. It excludes any quest for domination. It implies mutual confidence and the peaceful settlement of disputes ... The OSCE plays a central role in achieving our goal of a common security space. Its fundamental elements – the comprehensiveness and indivisibility of security and the allegiance to shared values, commitments and norms of behavior – inspire our vision of empowering governments and individuals to build a better and more secure future ... Within the OSCE, no State, organization or grouping can have any superior responsibility for maintaining peace and stability in the OSCE region or regard any part of the OSCE region as its sphere of influence.

From the OSCE's "Lisbon Declaration on a Common and Comprehensive Security Model for Europe for the Twenty-First Century," *Lisbon Document 1996*, Ref.S/174/96, Lisbon, December 3, 1996 <http://www.osceprag.c2/news/ls96ew08.htm>.

5 Adler and Barnett, in this volume.

6 Alex Wendt, "Collective Identity Formation and the International State," *American Political Science Review* 88 (June 1994), pp. 384–396.

7 Ibid., p. 390.

8 Michael Lucas, "The Conference on Security and Cooperation in Europe and the Future of U.S. Foreign Policy," in Beverly Crawford and Peter W. Schulze, eds., *The New Europe Asserts Itself: A Changing Role in International Relations* (Berkeley: International and Area Studies, 1990), pp. 47–50.

9 Conference on Security and Cooperation in Europe, *Charter of Paris For a New Europe*, Paris, 1990.

10 Janie Leatherman, "The CSCE's (Im)possibilities for Preventive Diplo-

macy in the Context of Ethnic Conflict," *International Journal on Group Rights* 2 (1994), p. 42.

11 "The Berlin Emergency Mechanism is indirectly related to peaceful dispute settlement, since it authorized a certain degree of intervention by the CSCE without the consent of the states perpetrating violations of CSCE principles." Michael R. Lucas and Oliver Mietzch, "Peaceful Dispute Settlement and the CSCE," in Lucas, ed., *The CSCE in the 1990s*, p. 93.

12 See US Commission on Security and Cooperation in Europe, *Beyond Process: The CSCE's Institutional Development, 1990–1992*, Washington DC, December 1992. The U.S. Commission on Security and Cooperation in Europe (The Helsinki Commission) – a US government agency created in 1976 by Public Law 94–304 – monitors human rights' compliance within the OSCE region. For an analysis of the "Helsinki Commission," see William Korey, *The Promises We Keep: Human Rights, The Helsinki Process, and American Foreign Policy* (New York: St. Martin's Press, 1993).

13 US Commission on Security and Cooperation in Europe, "CSCE's High Commissioner on National Minorities," Washington DC, June 1993.

14 Chigas et al., "Preventive Diplomacy and the Organization for Security and Cooperation in Europe," pp. 51–63.

15 See Conference on Security and Cooperation in Europe, *The Challenges of Change: CSCE Helsinki Document 1992*, CSCE Secretariat, Prague, 1992; Conference on Security and Cooperation in Europe, *Towards A Genuine Partnership in a New Era: Budapest Document 1994*, CSCE Secretariat, Prague, December 12, 1994.

16 Walter A. Kemp, "The OSCE in a New Context: European Security Towards the Twenty-first Century," *RIIA Discussion Papers*, no. 64, The Royal Institute of International Affairs, 1996, p. 14.

17 Lehne, *The CSCE in the 1990s*, p. 5. "The understanding of the CSCE as a fruitful interaction between the official process and 'citizen activities' has been gradually emerging in CSCE documents and at a slower pace in practice." Ritva Gronick, "The CSCE and Non-Governmental Organizations," in Lucas, ed., *The CSCE in the 1990s*, pp. 227–248. See also Patricia Chilton, "Mechanisms of Change: Social Movements, Transnational Coalitions, and the Transformation Processes in Eastern Europe," *Democratization* 1 (Spring 1994), pp. 151–181, and Daniel Thomas, "Social Movements and International Institutions: A Preliminary Framework," paper presented at the Annual Meeting of the American Political Science Association, Washington DC, 1991.

18 Lehne, *The CSCE in the 1990s*, p. 2.

19 Thus, on the one hand, the CSCE provided the Soviet Union with a stage to display its "new thinking." On the other hand, "an active and positive role in the CSCE was a way of demonstrating Russia's good intention, and natural affinity with the West, in the initial pro-Western period." Heather Hurlburt, "Russia, the OSCE and European Security

Architecture," *Helsinki Monitor* 2 (1995) <http://www.fsk.ethz.ch/osce>. 1995.

20 US Commission on Security and Cooperation in Europe, "The Conference on Security and Cooperation in Europe: An Overview of the CSCE Process, Recent Meetings and Institutional Development," Staff Report, Washington, DC, May 1992, p. 35.

21 "The effects were also more cognitive than behavioral. The CSCE process fostered empathy and confidence and thus, in the long run, the participants were embedded in a common culture of conflict regulation and cooperative problem solving" (Frank Schimmelfenning, "The CSCE as a Model for the Third World? The Middle East and African Cases," in Lucas, ed., *The CSCE in the 1990s*, p. 328).

22 Ingo Peters, "The OSCE and German Policy: A Study in How Institutions Matter," paper presented at the 1997 Meeting of the International Studies Association, Toronto, March 18–23, p. 17.

23 US Commission on Security and Cooperation in Europe, "Human Rights and Democratization in Poland," Washington DC, January 1994, p. iii.

24 Lehne, *The CSCE in the 1990s*, p. 24.

25 US Commission on Security and Cooperation in Europe, "CSCE Missions," p. 3.

26 Kemp, "The OSCE in a New Context," p. 20. For example, OSCE missions have been sent to: (a) Kosovo, Sanjak, and Vojvodina; (b) Skopje; (c) Nagorno-Karabakh, as part of the OSCE-sponsored Minsk Group, entrusted with solving the conflict there; (d) Abkhazia and South Ossetia in Georgia, to assess the political and human-rights situation there; (e) Tajikistan and other Central Asian republics, to foster confidence-building, democracy, and human rights; (f) Latvia and Estonia, to promote integration between the communities there; (g) Moldova, where OSCE recommendations were accepted as the basis for future negotiations on the status of Trans-Dniester; (h) Ukraine, to deal with the problem of minorities in Crimea; (i) Grozny, to promote human rights and the political settlement of the Russian-Chechnyan conflict; and, more recently, (j) Bosnia-Herzegovina, as mandated by the November 1995 Dayton peace agreement.

27 Marianne Hanson, "Democratisation and Norm Creation in Europe," *Adelphi Papers* 284 (January 1994), p. 34.

28 The OSCE's conflict prevention programs fall under the category of "the dogs that did not bark" problem. In other words, "the CSCE suffers from the unrewarding lot of preventive diplomacy: the test of its success is a non-event, i.e. the non-occurrence of conflicts." North Atlantic Assembly, "The CSCE's Human Dimension: Principles, Mechanisms and Implementation." Draft Interim Report. Lord Lucas of Chilworth, Rapporteur, International Secretariat, CC/CSCE 94(4) November 1994. <gopher://marvin.nc3a.nato.int:70/11/Other_International/naa/pub/C-C/1994/al198cc.asc>. October 31, 1994.

29   Ibid.

30   Between October 1994 and October 1996, the ODIHR monitored thirty parliamentary, presidential, and local elections, for example in Tajikistan (presidential elections, November 1994); Georgia (parliamentary and presidential elections, November 1995); Russian Federation (presidential elections, June 1996); and Lithuania (parliamentary elections, October 1996). Office for Democratic Institutions and Human Rights, *From Budapest to Lisbon: Review of Activities of the ODIHR November 1994–November 1996* (Warsaw: October 1996), pp 15–17.

31   Martha Finnemore, "International Organizations as Teachers of Norms: The United Nations Educational, Scientific, and Cultural Organization and Science Policy," *International Organization* 47 (Autumn 1993), pp. 565–597.

32   It is noteworthy that the entire range of OSCE activities is remarkably cost-efficient: the total OSCE budget for 1996 was approximately $52.9 million, of which half was devoted to the action in Bosnia-Herzegovina. Organization for Security and Cooperation in Europe, *OSCE Handbook 1996*, Second Edition, OSCE Secretariat, Vienna, 1996, p. 15.

33   Hulburt, "Russia, the OSCE and European Security Architecture."

34   US Department of State, *The President's Thirty Third OSCE Report: Implementation of the Helsinki Final Act, April 1, 1994–March 31, 1995.* <http://dosfan.lib.uic..edu/dosfan.html>. 1995.

35   Ibid.

36   Janie Leatherman, "Conflict Transformation in the CSCE: Learning and Institutionalization," *Cooperation and Conflict* 28 (1993), p. 414.

37   Thomas Buergenthal, "The CSCE Rights System, *"The George Washington Journal of International Law* 25 (1991), p. 382. Emphasis added.

38   North Atlantic Assembly, "The CSCE Human Dimension."

39   Frank Schimmelfennig, "Idealistic Liberalism and International Community, " paper presented at the 1996 Annual Convention of the International Studies Association, San Diego, April 16–20, p. 24.

40   Conference on Security and Cooperation in Europe, Plenary Intervention by the American Representative, Ambassador John C. Kornblum, Helsinki Follow-Up Meeting, March 31, 1992, p. 3.

41   Buergenthal, "The CSCE Rights System," pp. 380–381.

42   Conference on Security and Cooperation in Europe, Document of the Moscow Meeting of the Conference on the Human Dimension of the CSCE, Moscow, 1991.

43   Hanson, "Democratisation and Norm Creation in Europe," p. 31.

44   See Korey, *The Promises We Keep,* esp. chapter 12.

45   Hanson, "Democratisation and Norm Creation in Europe," p. 32.

46   Thomas M. Franck, "The Emerging Right to Democratic Governance," *The American Journal of International Law* 86 (1992), pp. 46–91.

47   My reasoning here is structurationist: cognitive structures – like games whose moves are given their meanings by constitutive rules – constitute identities, interests, and behavior, and are also constituted by them. Thus

156

agents (states, or rather people acting on behalf of states) and structures (pluralistic security communities) socially co-construct one other. For structurationist theory see Anthony Giddens, *The Constitution of Society* (Berkeley: University of California Press, 1984).

48 David Jacobson, *Rights Across Borders: Immigration and the Decline of Citizenship* (Baltimore: The Johns Hopkins University Press, 1995), pp. 111–112.

49 Statement made by the Head of the US Delegation to the CSCE, Ambassador John Kornblum, at the CSCE Seminar on Early Warning and Conflict Prevention, Warsaw, January 20, 1994.

50 Lehne, *The CSCE in the 1990s*, p. 5.

51 Leonard S. Spector and Jonathan Dean, "Cooperative Security: Assessing the Tools of the Trade," in Janne E. Nolan, ed., *Global Engagement: Cooperation and Security in the 21st Century* (Washington DC: The Brookings Institution, 1994), p. 140.

52 According to John Borawski, who cites Rolf Berg, the term CBM first appeared in a December 16, 1955 UN General Assembly Resolution for the "Regulation, Limitation, and Balanced Reduction of all Armed Forces and All Armaments." John Borawski, *From the Atlantic to the Urals: Negotiating Arms Control at the Stockholm Conference* (New York: Pergamon-Brassey's, 1988), p. 32. It appears that CBMs were first suggested within the Helsinki process by Norway. Vojtech Mastny, Introduction: "The CSCE and Expansion of European Security," in Vojtech Mastny, *Helsinki, Human Rights, and European Security: Analysis and Documentation* (Durham: Duke University Press, 1986), p. 7.

53 Lehne, *The CSCE in the 1990s*, p. 15.

54 Mastny, *The Helsinki Process and the Reintegration of Europe*, p. 2.

55 Lehne, *The CSCE in the 1990s*, p. 73. The "consensus-minus-one" provision (1992) refers to the human dimension and not to all the commitments and principles of the OSCE. However, in practice, the provision has been used more widely. On paper, at least, there also exists a "consensus-minus-two" provision in the case of directed conciliation procedures, directing two disputants to seek conciliation irrespective of their will. Alexis Heraclides, *Helsinki-II and its Aftermath: The Making of the CSCE into an International Organization* (London: Pinter, 1993), pp. 179–80.

56 Marton Krasznai, "The OSCE and Dialogue Among Governments," Mediterranean Seminar, "The OSCE as a Platform for Dialogue and the Fostering of Norms of Behaviour, " Tel Aviv, June 2–4, 1996 (SEM.MED/TA/12), pp. 2–3.

57 Heraclides, *Security and Cooperation in Europe*, p. 51.

58 Barry Buzan, *People, States, and Fear*, 2nd edn (Brighton: Wheatsheaf, 1991), p. 191–192.

59 Ibid.

60 Niels Moller-Gulland, "The Forum for Security Cooperation and Related Security Issues," in Lucas, ed., *The CSCE in the 1990s*, p. 34.

61 On multilateralism see John G. Ruggie, ed., *Multilateralism Matters* (New York: Columbia University Press, 1993).

62 Conceptually, seminar diplomacy stands on similar but broader grounds than Herbert Kelman's social-psychological "Problem-Solving Workshop" approach for settling international conflicts (Herbert C. Kelman and Stephan P. Cohen, "The Problem-Solving Workshop: A Social-Psychological Contribution to the Resolution of International Conflicts," *Journal of Peace Research* 13 [1976], pp. 79–90), and its Middle-East application in the form of unofficial and non-structured "track-two" diplomacy (William D. Davidson and Joseph V. Montville, "Foreign Policy According to Freud," *Foreign Policy* 45 (Winter 1981–82), pp. 145–157. For an informative study of "track-two" diplomacy in the Middle East see Joel Peters, *Pathways to Peace: The Multilateral Arab-Israeli Peace Talks* (London: Royal Institute of International Affairs, 1996).

63 Conference on Security and Cooperation in Europe, *Helsinki Final Act*, Helsinki, 1975, p. 133.

64 US Commission on Security and Cooperation in Europe, "The CSCE Human Dimension Seminar on Tolerance," November 16–20, 1992. A Report, Washington DC, nd.

65 On epistemic communities, see Peter M. Haas, ed., "Knowledge, Power, and International Policy Coordination," *International Organization* 46 (Winter 1992).

66 Moller-Gulland, "The Forum for Security Cooperation," p. 35.

67 US Commission on Security and Cooperation in Europe, CSCE Support for Newly Admitted Participating States. "The Bishkek Seminar on Promoting Small and Medium-Sized Business," February 23–5, 1994, Washington DC, nd.

68 Erika Schlager, "CSCE Convenes Early Warning, Preventive Diplomacy Seminar," *CSCE Digest* 17, 1 (January 1994), p. 4.

69 Conference on Security and Cooperation in Europe, "Seminar on Early Warning and Preventive Diplomacy Warsaw," Jan. 19–21, 1994. Summary of the Moderator of Workshop, Ambassador Raumo Viemero, February 1, 1994.

70 US Commission on Security and Cooperation in Europe, CSCE Support for Newly-Admitted Participating States. "Seminar on the Human Dimension," Almaty, Kazakhstan, April 20–22, 1994, Washington DC, nd. Assessing the results of this seminar, a US Helsinki Commission report argued that "the most welcome dimension of the Almaty Seminar was the strong interest displayed in human rights, both among government officials struggling to mold international standards to governments in uncertain transition, and among a nascent but vocal NGO community in Kazakhstan and Kyrgyzstan . . . A further positive element of the Seminar was the interaction among Central Asian states, and the growth of indigenous debate on human dimension issues." Ibid.

71 Vinca Showalter, "CSCE Tolerance Seminar Breaks New Ground," *CSCE Digest* 15, 8 (November 1992), p. 3.

72 Interviews with Tom Buergenthal and Lynn Davidson, Washington DC, October 1993.

73 Keynote Address by the Deputy Secretary General of NATO, Sergio Balanzino, at a Rand Seminar, October 16, 1995.
    <gopher://marvin.nc3a.nato.int:70/11/natodata/PRESS/SPEECHES/95-/rand.asc>.

74 The Charter establishes a NATO-Russian Permanent Joint Council and broadens existing areas of military consultation and cooperation.

75 Speech by the Secretary General of NATO, Javier Solana, at the Russian Council on Foreign and Security Policy, March 20, 1996.
    <gopher://marvin.nc3a.nato.int:70/00/natodata/PRESS/SPEECHES/96-/russia.txt>.

76 North Atlantic Treaty Organization, Meeting of the North Atlantic Co-operation Council in Noordwijk Aan Zee, the Netherlands, 31 May, 1995. Report to Ministers by the Political Steering Committee/Ad Hoc Group on Cooperation in Peacekeeping, Press Release M-NACC 1(95)50
    <gopher://marvin.nc3a.nato.int:70/00/natodata/PRESS/NATOPRESS/PRESS-95/pr50e.asc>.

77 Ibid.

78 Joseph Lepgold, "The Next Step Toward a More Secure Europe," *The Journal of Strategic Studies* 17 (December 1994), p. 10.

79 Ibid., pp. 10–15.

80 Gebhardt von Moltke, "Building a Partnership for Peace," *NATO Review* 42 (June 1994), p. 4.

81 North Atlantic Assembly, "Projecting Stability in an Undivided Europe: Partnership for Peace and a Pact on Stability in Europe," Draft Interim Report, Maurice Blin Rapporteur, International Secretariat, 1995.
    <gopher://marvin.nc3a,nato.int:70/Other_International/naa/pub/PC/1995/am105pc.txt>.
    In order to fulfill its growing functions, PfP's budget increased by 27 per cent in 1995. North Atlantic Treaty Organization, Basic Fact Sheet on "Partnership for Peace," no. 9, March 1996.
    <gopher://marvin.nc3a.nato.int:70/00/natodata/FACTSHEETS/FACT/fs09.txt>.

82 The WEU, created in 1954, and reactivated thirty years later, is a ten-member security organization that, as a defense component of the EU and as a means to strengthen the European pillar of the Euro-Atlantic alliance, is rapidly finding its place in the European security architecture. The WEU not only endorsed the EU concept of a Common European Defence Policy; consistent with the principle of developing separable but not separate military capabilities for use by NATO or the WEU, it also adopted, in concert with NATO, the idea of Combined Joint Task Forces (CJTF).

83 Fraser Cameron, "The European Union and the OSCE: Future Roles and Challenges," *Helsinki Monitor* 2 (1995) <http://www.fsk.ethz.ch/osce>.

84 Ettore Greco, "The OSCE After the Budapest Summit: the Need for Specialization," *The International Spectator* 30 (April-June 1995), p. 6.

85 Chigas et al., "Preventive Diplomacy and the Organization for Security and Cooperation in Europe," p. 68.

86 John J. Mearsheimer, "The False Promise of International Institutions," *International Security* 20 (Summer 1995), pp. 5–49.

87   See, for example, Robert O. Keohane, *After Hegemony: Cooperation and Discord in the World Political Economy* (Princeton: Princeton University Press, 1984); and Stephen Krasner, ed., *International Regimes* (Ithaca: Cornell University Press, 1983).

88 John G. Ruggie, "Multilateralism: The Anatomy of an Institution," in Ruggie, *Multilateralism Matters*, p. 14.

89 Constructivism is "the view that the manner in which the material world shapes and is shaped by human action and interaction depends on dynamic normative and epistemic interpretations of the material world." Emanuel Adler, "Seizing the Middle Ground: Constructivism in World Politics," *European Journal of International Relations* 3, 3 (1997), p. 322. See also Alex Wendt, "Anarchy is What States Make of It: The Social Construction of Power Politics," *International Organization* 46 (Winter 1992), pp. 391–425.

90 Innovation, diffusion, political selection, and institutionalization are the four stages of an international learning process I call "cognitive evolution." See Emanuel Adler, "Cognitive Evolution," in Emanuel Adler and Beverly Crawford, eds., *Progress in Postwar International Relations* (New York: Columbia University Press, 1991), pp. 43–88. For a slightly different conceptualization of cognitive evolution see Ernst B. Haas, *When Knowledge is Power* (Berkeley: University of California Press, 1990).

91 John G. Ruggie, "On the Problem of 'The Global Problematique': What Roles for International Organizations?," *Alternatives* 5 (1979–1980), p. 538.

92 See Charles Lipson, "Why are Some International Agreements Informal?" *International Organization* 45 (Autumn 1991), pp. 495–538; Anthony Aust, "The Theory and Practice of Informal International Instruments," *International and Comparative Law Quarterly* 35 (1986), pp. 787–812; Franck, "The Emerging Right to Democratic Governance."

5 Caravans in opposite directions: society, state, and the development of community in the Gulf Cooperation Council

Michael Barnett and F. Gregory Gause III

The states that comprise the Gulf Cooperation Council – Oman, Bahrain, the United Arab Emirates, Kuwait, Qatar, and Saudi Arabia – are not a security community. Nor do we anticipate their becoming a security community in the near future. Indeed, for most of its history the Gulf Cooperation Council (GCC) demands a realist reading and little else.[1] The proximate causes of the formation of the GCC are to be found not in deep social structural factors pushing toward integration but in immediate regime security needs; specifically, the GCC was born in the circumstances of Iranian Revolution and the ongoing and escalating Iraq–Iran War, suggesting little more than a classic security alliance. The fifteen years since its birth also favor a strict and secular realism. As the Iran–Iraq War progressed the GCC states experimented with some modest, but for all practical purposes inconsequential, military cooperation. The end of the Iran–Iraq War abruptly halted such experimentation. The 1990–91 Gulf War produced a short-term upswing in group cohesion but the post-war period was characterized by increasing rivalries, a halt to any meaningful military coordination and a return of border disputes among the GCC states. The GCC's trajectory seems consistent with alliance formation – formed in response to specific security threats, enduring as those threats endure, and fraying as those threats recede. In general, statism and realism mark the history of the GCC states.

In this chapter we want to take an alternative look at the GCC states through the concept of security community. We do so not because we claim that there is a security community in existence or even soon in the making but rather because this concept highlights the following features. First, the GCC points to obstacles rather than facilitators toward community-building. That is, we are drawn to the case of the

GCC not because it represents a successful case but rather because it represents a "stalled" case. Given the similarities among the member states and their common external security agenda, more progress in community-building could have been expected. Many of the obstacles toward deepened cooperation are quite familiar – fear of hegemony, possessive sovereignty, and the like – but perhaps most intriguing is the failure of the regimes to create common expectations concerning non-interference in each other's domestic politics. Such disagreements, built around recent charges of domestic interference and meddling among the members, have contributed to reversing the progress toward security cooperation achieved in the 1980s and during the Gulf crisis. In a region where internal security threats pose as serious a challenge to regime stability as do external threats, cooperation and agreement (or lack thereof) on issues regarding domestic politics are as important as cooperation in interstate issues.

Secondly, the concept of security community focuses attention on some facets and features of the GCC that are generally overlooked. What began as an organization that denied its security function soon turned into a multifaceted entity that was both an agent and a result of many of the processes and developments that are associated with a security community. Specifically, we intend to highlight that while on the level of interstate cooperation the history of the GCC is less than glorious, at the level of transnational cooperation and transactions there developed a bustling and increasing traffic that, we argue, is traceable to the existence of the organization. In short, while Gulf leaders constructed the GCC for statist purposes, its very existence has encouraged, however unintentionally, greater mutual identification at the societal level. At the founding of the GCC there were few if any social institutions that brought together citizens of the six member states; there was certainly no discernible popular pressure for, or outpouring of popular support for, the foundation of the organization. However, over the past fifteen years indications have grown that increasing numbers of citizens of these states see themselves as having common interests and a common identity as "khalijiin" (literally, "residents of the Gulf"). This phenomenon is reflected in the growth of regional functional organizations and in the political vocabulary of Gulf citizens. By no means is such a "Gulf" identity universally accepted in the six states, but it is undeniable that "Gulf" discourse is much more common now than before and that increasing numbers of citizens identify their material interests and political identity as (at least partially) tied up with the GCC.

The story of the GCC is thus one of two caravans (or, for a nautical metaphor appropriate to the Gulf, dhows) traveling in opposite directions. At the level of the regime these countries made some modest moves toward a deepening of interstate cooperation, but seemingly always blocked if not undone by mistrust and suspicion. At the level of societies and transnationalism, however, there have been considerable developments that suggest sustained and deepened cooperation and mutual identification. We cannot predict whether and how this increasingly salient Gulf identity will translate into interstate behavior and dependable expectations of peaceful change, but we want to suggest that an important condition for a security community has been an unintended consequence of the GCC.

This chapter is organized in the following way. The first section provides a brief historical overview of the GCC states and the factors that contributed to the creation of the organization. The second section examines the development of the GCC through the 1980s, highlighting that what began as a symbolic organization became something more substantial at the level of interstate and transnational cooperation. The final section provides an overview of the GCC since the Gulf War. Although the GCC states responded collectively to the invasion of Kuwait in ways that suggest an increase in their inter-dependence and group cohesion, much of the post-Gulf War period suggest fragmentation at the level of the regimes but modest integration at the level of societies. We conclude by commenting on the two caravans of the GCC and how the case of the GCC highlights certain central features of the security community.

The founding of the organization

The six member states of the GCC, while having historical roots that date back centuries, are all products of the twentieth century. The modern Saudi state dates to 1901, when Abd al-Aziz Al Sa'ud (Ibn Saud) recaptured Riyadh from a rival Arabian dynasty and set out to rebuild the patrimony of his ancestors. Saudi Arabia reached its current territorial extent in 1932 when it ran up against British power to its north (the mandates of Iraq and Transjordan), south (the protectorate of South Arabia) and east. British protection of the smaller states of eastern Arabia had its roots in the nineteenth century policy of controlling the sea routes to India. By the 1920s the British had protectorate relations with the Sultan of Oman and the shaykhs of Kuwait, Bahrain, Qatar and the Trucial Emirates, which would become the United Arab Emirates. The British guaranteed their independence, drew their borders, and became increasingly involved in their domestic affairs as the century progressed. Kuwait became independent in 1961, the others in 1971 (Oman was formally independent throughout, but the British exercised effective control there as well).[2]

The GCC states share a number of common historical features that have helped to bring them together. Tribalism was an important element in state formation and remains a central social reality in all the states. Since the 1960s their political economies have all depended heavily upon the export of oil. Internationally they all were aligned with the West in the Cold War, with the smaller states retaining close ties to Great Britain and Saudi Arabia looking to the United States for political and military support and for the development of its oil industry. They have also been on the same side in regional disputes, threatened by Nasserist pan-Arabism in the 1950s and 1960s and by Iranian-supported Islamic revivalism in the 1980s.

Those real similarities, however, mask some salient differences that have been a source of resentment, suspicion, and hostility. Disputes and even armed conflicts have occurred among the six member states of the GCC episodically throughout the twentieth century. In the 1910s and 1920s Saudi forces routinely raided Kuwaiti territory, as Riyadh attempted to enforce a commercial blockade of Kuwait to divert regional trade to Saudi-controlled ports.[3] In the 1950s Saudi forces clashed with British-officered troops from Oman and the Trucial Emirates (now the UAE) over control of the Buraimi Oasis, and Saudi Arabia supported internal opponents of the Omani sultan.[4] Riyadh withheld diplomatic recognition of the UAE for four years after the latter's independence, until 1975, awaiting the settlement of border disputes. There remains a real if muted fear of Saudi dominance all along the Gulf littoral.

Differences also exist among the smaller states. The original British proposal for UAE independence had Qatar and Bahrain, also British-protected states, joining the new federation. However, both opted for independence rather than unity with their neighbors farther down the Gulf. Qatar and Bahrain have a long-standing and contentious dispute over a number of small islands. There is a substantial history of serious differences among the member states of the GCC. It was by no means "automatic" that they would come together.

Even at the "cultural" level there are differences among the six states. While all the GCC ruling families are Sunni Muslims, there are important Shi'i minorities in Kuwait, Saudi Arabia, Qatar and the UAE; the majority of Bahrain's native population is Shi'i. About 40 percent of Oman's native population subscribes to the Ibadi Kharijite sect of Islam. Moreover, the brand of Sunni Islam dominant in Saudi Arabia – the severe "Wahhabi" interpretation – is shared only by Qatar. Oman historically has directed its political and economic efforts toward the Indian Ocean, having little contact with the areas in the northern Gulf. The vast majority of the Saudi population, residing in the Kingdom's western coast and central areas near Riyadh, is far removed geographically from the Gulf. In general, there are various religious, tribal, and national identities that barely exist within a shared narrative.

Until the completion of decolonization in the early 1970s, regional security was largely the province of Great Britain. As independence neared, however, the Gulf states (alongside Egypt and others in the Arab world) began to forward different proposals for Gulf security. Most of the Gulf states were willing to continue to rely on the British and the Americans for a tacit security umbrella for pragmatic and political reasons. Still, through the mid-1970s the Gulf states continued to discuss but ultimately to discard different proposals for regional security and the possibility of a regional organization.

In the period between the Algiers Agreement of 1975 (which temporarily settled border disputes between Iran and Iraq) and the fall of the Shah's regime at the beginning of 1979, there were a number of consultations among Saudi Arabia, Iraq and Iran about security issues in the Gulf. Saudi leaders during this period also pressed the smaller Peninsula states to coordinate with Riyadh on defense and internal security matters. However, no formal security grouping was formed. Suspicions among Iran, Iraq and Saudi Arabia remained too strong, and the smaller states either could not (out of fear of Iranian or Iraqi reactions) or would not (out of fear of Saudi hegemony) acknowledge Riyadh as their leader.[5] Even among the Arab monarchies of the Peninsula, the strong integrative forces present were not sufficient to overcome *realpolitik* considerations keeping them apart.

The Iranian Revolution of 1978–79 worked to push the smaller shaykhdoms closer to the Saudis, but Iraqi ambitions prevented the consolidation of a Gulf monarchical grouping in the immediate post-revolutionary period. With the revolution in Iran and the ostracism of Egypt from Arab political circles after Camp David, Iraq had emerged as the dominant player in inter-Arab politics. Saddam Hussein, who had become president of Iraq in July 1979, tried to capitalize on Iraq's new leadership position by issuing in February 1980 an "Arab National Charter," calling on other Arab states to join Iraq in a framework of security and economic cooperation.[6] In these circumstances, excluding Iraq from an Arab Gulf organization would have invited serious reprisals. Including Iraq, a secular nationalist republic that up until 1975 had trumpeted its opposition to the "reactionary" Arab regimes on the Peninsula and had routinely made territorial claims on Kuwait, would have meant Baghdad's dominance of the organization. Neither choice was a palatable one for the Gulf monarchs. Only when Iraq became bogged down in its war with Iran, which began in September 1980, and dependent upon political, financial and logistical support from the Gulf monarchies did the Gulf states revisit the possibility of forming an exclusive association.

Creation of the GCC

On May 15, 1981 the leaders of Oman, Bahrain, the United Arab Emirates, Qatar, Saudi Arabia, and Kuwait met in Abu Dhabi, the capital of the United Arab Emirates, and signed the GCC charter.[7] We want to highlight four important features surrounding the establishment of the organization: the role identity played in determining who was worthy of membership; the fact that the GCC states downplayed the possibility of integration; the role of internal rather than external security threats as the stimulus to the creation of the GCC; and the attempt to produce security through symbolic means, including the inaugural attempt to offer a "Gulf identity."

First, membership was determined largely by their shared identity.[8] The final statement of the first meeting of the GCC expressed the sentiment that their common destiny, shared interests and values, and common economic and political systems produced a natural solidarity among Arabs of the Gulf region.[9] The GCC was open only to those Gulf States that shared similar characteristics, an expression of "the aspiration for identification with a psychologically satisfying political community."[10]

What were these common traits? To begin, all are monarchies that developed out of tribal political structures, differentiating them from their larger republican neighbors (Iraq, Iran and Yemen). Indeed, North Yemen was keen to join the new GCC, and lobbied publicly for its inclusion. From a simple balance of power perspective, permitting North Yemen to join the group would make sense. Its large population (about 10 million at the time) would have helped compensate strategically for the manpower shortages in the other states. Culturally, there were substantial similarities among their populations, most importantly in the social importance of tribalism. However, its republican character placed it outside the bounds of the community Gulf leaders intended to build.[11] All the GCC states are rich (though some are richer than others), with their wealth dependent upon the export of oil and petroleum products that concentrates much of national revenue in the hands of the state. And all of the rulers are Arab and Sunni Muslims, differentiating them from Iran.

There also are some striking similarities at the societal level. Tribalism still plays a major role in social identity, though the independent political power of the tribes has waned considerably. Tribal and family ties cut across the state borders; it is not unusual to have branches of the same extended family represented in three or four of the six GCC states. Modern consumer society has put down deep roots in the region in the past three decades of oil wealth, so the vast majority of citizens share middle-class consumption habits that are very similar to those in the West. The citizens even dress alike, with the men favoring the long, white, body-length garment called the *dishdashu* and the "traditional" head covering (*ghutra wa 'iqal*), differentiating them from most other Arabs and Iranians who adopted "Western" style dress.

In addition to feelings of solidarity, the GCC states also saw the other Arab states as something of a threat, and, therefore, hoped to isolate themselves from their Arab brethren.[12] Although all these states joined the Arab League upon independence (Saudi Arabia was a founding member) and waved at the GCC's role in furthering Arab aspirations, the Arab Gulf states were rather wary of and aloof from the rest of the Arab world and often followed their statements of fraternity with aggressive claims that they were a separate entity bounded by common interests, and, accordingly, shared little with the other Arab states.

The common identity of the Gulf Arab states, then, informed the criteria of exclusion and inclusion. All GCC states were quick to explain that the Gulf Arab states were "natural" allies, sharing key biographical features and historical characteristics. By accentuating and identifying the commonalities enveloping the Gulf Arab states, the GCC leaders were implicitly creating a boundary between themselves and others in the Arab world and Iran based on ideational features. In general, notwithstanding the constant pronouncements that the GCC was consistent with, and carried out the ideals embodied in, the League of Arab States, the GCC was quite resistant to extending membership to other Arab states.[13]

The announcement of the GCC was accompanied by as much stress on what it was not as on what it was. What is was not, claimed many of its members, was either a step toward political integration or a security organization. The GCC states stressed at the moment of creation that they had no intention of marching down the road of political integration or unification. The organization was intended to coordinate their political, economic, and cultural policies to their mutual advantage, not to lead to anything akin to political unification. Simply put, the GCC was about cooperation, not integration. King Fahd, for instance, said: "The aim of the GCC is to achieve practical cooperation among GCC members. At present it is premature for the GCC to become a political union or federation, and talk about this matter is also premature."[14] The GCC states went to great pains to insist that they were not absenting themselves from Arab politics and that the GCC would provide an important foundation for, if only as a positive role model of, inter-Arab cooperation.

That the GCC states would have to expend such diplomatic and political energy in this direction can only be properly understood once it is recognized that the idea of integration and unification in Arab politics was a longstanding, though increasingly marginalized, goal. Since the moment of inception of the Arab states system, Arab states have espoused the need to strengthen the Arab political community, which included a range of goals from far-reaching schemes such as political unification to much more minimalist efforts as political and foreign policy coordination. Within the context of Arab politics, the GCC was viewed as a *sub*regional organization because it comprised a subset of Arab states who were members of the Arab League. In fact, the Gulf states, always on the fringes of Arab nationalist sentiment, were among the most ardent opponents of unification. Indicative of this posture was that the GCC states were particularly opposed to pan-Arabism's demand for a greater Arab union; therefore, they were wary that close cooperation might trigger memories of and hopes for unification. This concern increased dramatically after the late 1960s when the Gulf Arab states became the Gulf Arab *oil* states – leading them to become highly suspicious of the economic motivations underlying any new expressions of fraternal devotion. In general, the Gulf States denied that the GCC had any intention of marching down the road of political unification and continually insisted that their objective was coordination and cooperation among sovereign states. It seemed that the GCC states discarded the idea of becoming a security community, at least the tight variant, from the outset.

The Gulf states also insisted that the GCC was not a security or military organization. Although the leaders adopted a charter for a commission to settle disputes among the members states, no body was set up to coordinate security issues, and security issues were hardly mentioned in the group's founding documents.[15] Emphasis was placed upon economic and cultural cooperation. The founding rhetoric stressed the "mutual bonds of special relations" that linked the member states and their people, not the common threats they faced. The objectives of the GCC, listed in Article 4 of the Charter, did not include military or security coordination. Four functional committees were established at the founding summit to coordinate: (a) economic and social planning; (b) financial, economic and trade issues, (c) industrial cooperation; and, (d) oil issues. In short, there was a hint that GCC might be more tempted by a loose rather than a tight security community.

There were good strategic reasons for downplaying any security role for the GCC. To some extent, this concentration on functional cooperation and masking of security issues in the GCC's establishment was meant to avoid exciting the opposition of Iran, Iraq, or any other Arab state to the new grouping. The leaders were at pains to underscore that the GCC was not being formed against anyone, as a regular military alliance would be. By stressing that the GCC aimed at avoiding entangling the region with outside powers and internationalizing the Iran–Iraq War, they sought to allay suspicions in Iran and the Arab world that the organization was a cover for an alliance with the United States. Therefore, while a superpower alliance would provide an immediate increase in external security – and both the Soviets and the Americans were actively courting the Gulf States – the GCC states rebuffed such overtures,[16] and uniformly and stridently asserted their regional independence and resistance to foreign intervention.[17] The emphasis on economics and culture was also an indication that the smaller states had not completely abandoned their worries about Saudi hegemony. Rhetoric about economic and cultural cooperation was simply less threatening to outsiders and to insiders.

Despite their public silence on the subject, the Gulf states' leaders were concerned about security threats, though these threats were more internal than strictly external. As Sunni states with substantial Shi'i minorities (and Bahrain with a Shi'i majority), most GCC members were more concerned with the threat posed by the model of the Iranian revolution than they were of an actual military invasion from Iran itself. If anything, the Revolution led to a serious degradation of Iranian military capabilities; the officer corps was decimated, the enlisted ranks were in disarray and, as a result of the US–Iranian confrontation over the embassy hostages, Iran had lost its major arms supplier and superpower ally.

Yet revolutionary Iran was a more threatening neighbor than the militarily more powerful Shah because the government of Ayatollah Khomeini openly called for the downfall of monarchical regimes throughout the Muslim world. The revolutionary message struck a chord among Shi'i citizens of the Gulf monarchies. There were disturbances in Bahraini, Kuwaiti and Saudi Shi'i communities within a year of Khomeini's coming to power.[18] Also, Sunni militants took over the Grand Mosque in Mecca, the holiest shrine in Islam, in November 1979 and called for revolt against the House of Saud. It took Saudi forces, with the aid of French counter-terrorist experts, two weeks to regain control of the Mosque.[19] The threat of externally-supported domestic upheaval led the smaller states to put aside their fears of Saudi hegemony and move closer to Riyad.

The Gulf states did not emphasize publicly internal security issues when forming the organization, but one purpose of the GCC was to provide Gulf citizens with a rhetorical and an institutional alternative identity (beyond their state identities) that would compete with Iran's Islamic revolutionary and Iraq's secular Arab nationalist platforms. Both the Iranian Revolution and the beginning of the Iran–Iraq War presented serious challenges to the GCC leaders' ability to define the political identity of their subjects. The revolutionary regime in Iran appealed to all Muslims, with particular success to Shi'i Muslims, to define their identity and give their loyalty to the Islamic community as the Iranian revolutionaries defined it. Iraq's initiation of the war, following on its campaign to expel Egypt from the Arab League after the Camp David accords, was accompanied by an explicit claim by Baghdad to be the leader of the Arab world. Saddam Hussein routinely reminded his listeners that Iraq was fighting Iran on behalf of the entire Arab nation, and his media called on all Arabs to support his efforts.[20] Both of these assertions of transnational political loyalties struck chords in the Gulf monarchies during the period 1979–81, with Shi'i demonstrations in support of the Iranian Revolution and enthusiastic support for Iraq among Arab nationalists (mostly Sunnis) in the media and intellectual circles.

The "Gulf" identity proposed by the GCC state leaders and promoted by the organization stressed historical, tribal and cultural factors that differentiated the citizens of the states from other Arabs, while not denying that Gulf Arabs are part of a larger Arab community. That "Gulf" identity, moreover, posited a version of Islam far from the revolutionary interpretation of Ayatollah Khomeini. The GCC, even if it could successfully integrate its military forces, could hardly provide a challenge to either Iraq or Iran on the battlefield. But it could provide a safe (for GCC rulers) political alternative for citizens' loyalties against the appeals of Baghdad and Teheran.

The "Gulf" identity that the GCC sought to foster, while based upon concrete social and historical realities, was a very new construction at the beginning of the 1980s. There is little evidence that citizens of the six states shared a conscious "Gulf" political identification at that time. There were certainly no popular movements advocating such a political platform. Grass roots political organizing – legal and illegal – in recent Gulf history occurred under Arab nationalist, Islamic, tribal and (less often) Marxist banners. In a survey aimed at eliciting opinions of political identity among citizens of five of the six GCC states (Oman excluded) conducted between 1979 and 1982, questions about a "Gulf" identity were not even included.[21] The only institutional expression of a "Gulf" identity limited to the six states before the establishment of the GCC was the Development Panel (*nadwa al-tanmiyya*), an informal group of intellectuals organized in 1979 to discuss the particular problems of economic and social development in oil-rich Gulf states. The Development Panel, later renamed the Development Forum (*muntada al-tanmiyya*), now consists of members from all six states (originally Oman was not represented, and one member was Iraqi). Since 1980 it has organized a yearly conference around a different theme of Gulf development.[22] The assertion of a "Gulf" identity implicit in the founding of the GCC was something new in the region, and clearly a political and instrumental creation meant to enhance the stability of the GCC regimes. Because the challenge posed to these regimes was to their social purpose and identity, they engaged in an instrumental use of identity in order to increase their security. At this stage, however, there was no anticipation of military coordination or integration among the various states; this is security as practiced through symbols.

The six, like-minded, Gulf states founded the GCC with a declaratory purpose of increasing their economic and cultural cooperation but with a close eye toward their security. The security threat that truly aminated them, however, was not a military invasion but rather domestic instability. This path toward security cooperation began not from an alliance to confront an external threat but rather against an internal threat. In the contest for the political allegiances and loyalties of their residents, the GCC states began to emphasize not the state flag but rather the "khaliji" identity as a way of placing a fence between themselves and Arab Iraq and Muslim Iran. Notwithstanding the instrumental, symbolic, and strategic origins of the GCC and the Gulf identity, such political creations would later have real, and somewhat unexpected and unintended, political consequences.

External threats and community building in the 1980s

Despite, first, the official founding rhetoric that downplayed security issues and, second, the attempt to enhance their security through symbols rather than through institutionalized military coordination, soon the GCC leaders found themselves cooperating on military and internal security issues in a manner that outpaced cooperation in all other areas and far exceeded their initial expectations. The stimulus behind such movements were a series of domestic disturbances that might have had external linkages. An abortive coup attempt in Bahrain in December 1981, ostensibly supported by the Iranian government, focused the Gulf leaders' attention on the GCC as a mechanism for security coordination. A string of bombings in Kuwait in December 1983, an attempt on the life of the Kuwaiti ruler in May 1985, and later acts of violence attributed to Kuwaiti Shi'is sympathetic with Iran, brought home the connections between external and internal security. Iranian pilgrims used the hajj, the yearly Muslim pilgrimage to Mecca, to demonstrate against the Saudi government, a combined challenge to Saudi domestic legitimacy and international standing. As Sultan Qabus of Oman commented:

> I firmly believe that the main threat facing the Gulf is the attempt to destabilize it from within – by exporting terrorism across the national borders. We should watch out for destabilization attempts, particularly because domestic instability can blow the door open to foreign intervention. I believe that this is the main hazard and we can take it into consideration despite the fact that ours is the most stable country in the area.[23]

The GCC states became increasingly alarmed by the prospect of domestic instability and the possibility that it was being sparked by Iran.

Security issues dominated the agenda of the emergency GCC foreign ministers and interior ministers meetings in February 1982, called in the wake of the Bahraini coup attempt. The severity with which the GCC leaders saw the threat was expressed by Secretary-General Abdullah Bishara, who said that "what happened in Bahrain was not directed against one part of this body but against the whole body." By the third GCC summit in November 1982, the leaders had before them a draft agreement for cooperation on internal security issues. The agreement stated that "preservation of the security and stability of the GCC countries is the joint responsibility of the GCC countries." It explicitly included commitments by each state to co-operate not only against criminals, but also against "opponents of regimes." However, Kuwait refused to sign the agreement, pleading that some of its clauses conflicted with Kuwaiti sovereignty;[24] specifically, there was substantial opposition to the agreement in the Kuwaiti parliament based on fears that it would facilitate Saudi interference in Kuwaiti domestic affairs. While the Kuwaiti refusal to adhere to the agreement was an indication that fears of Saudi dominance were stronger than feelings of Gulf community at the popular level, Kuwaiti security organs still cooperated informally with their Gulf counterparts on security issues.[25] Saudi Arabia also signed bilateral security agreements with Bahrain, Qatar and Oman in the wake of the coup attempt.[26]

The success of these early cooperative ventures on internal security issues, combined with Iranian battlefield successes in the Iran–Iraq War, generated the confidence and interest among the GCC states in undertaking more ambitious projects for military cooperation. Prior to the Bahrain coup attempt in 1981, the GCC Secretariat established a military committee as a forum for multilateral discussions, which, in turn, produced a concept paper on collective defense the following year.[27] Beginning in the early 1980s the GCC states conducted numerous multilateral military exercises. At the fifth GCC summit in November 1984 the states agreed to establish a joint GCC strike force under Saudi command, to be called the Peninsula Shield force. By late 1985 all GCC states had stationed small military contingents at the Saudi base in Hafr al-Batin, near the Kuwait border. In general, the GCC developed a series of elaborate and sustained measures designed to increase military coordination and cooperation: a rapid deployment force, the outline for a unified army, an early warning network, a series of joint maneuvers through the "Peninsula Shield" exercises, attempted coordination of military procurement to standardize equipment and training, and an integrated training academy.[28]

However impressive such developments appeared on paper, they remained, in fact, largely paper developments. The GCC Secretary-General admitted, given the small number of troops committed, that the Peninsula Shield force was largely symbolic. Ambitious plans for an integrated air defense system and cooperation in arms acquisitions were discussed but not realized during the 1980s.[29] There were various practical, logistical, and operational reasons precluding effective military integration and coordination,[30] but there were two principal stumbling blocks. The first was fear of Saudi hegemony. The smaller Gulf states had a longstanding fear that the Saudis would use their greater wealth and military power to their disadvantage. In short, hegemony in this context was not about projecting purpose but rather about displaying power. The second was possessive sovereignty. Notwithstanding the modest amounts of cooperation, these were rich, in some cases newly-independent countries that were extremely sensitive to possible infringements on their decision-making latitude and feared conceding too much authority to any international body. Cooperation in modest amounts was all well and good, but interdependence could easily translate into unwanted dependence.

Still, various features of this growth in security cooperation are worth noting. First, there was a direct linkage between internal and external security, with the modest successes in the former spilling over into the latter and then leading toward a more comprehensive view of security that included both internal and external features. As GCC Secretary-General Bishara stated:

> A security umbrella means linking internal security forces with military institutions responsible for external security as well as linking with political institutions. In other words, the Gulf countries should have political, security, and defense institutions with identical goals. These institutions should be so intertwined that they will generate a *psychological umbrella of assurance* and security.[31]

Secondly, the Gulf states were progressing toward military integration that far outpaced anything they had initially envisioned. As Bahraini Minister of Foreign Affairs Shaykh Muhammad Khalifa observed: "We feel we have started a never-ending effort, because every coordination action has unknown results."[32] The general impression is that the GCC states were taken by surprise by what they had accomplished, as they began to build on these modest experiments.

Thirdly, there is scattered evidence that these interactions and experiments were producing a growing sense of interdependence and shared interests among the regimes. The very decision to begin coordinating their military and security policies suggested a degree of interdependence previously unknown. The notion that they had shared interests, for instance, contributed to the desire to institutionalize GCC summit and ministerial meetings.[33] And while none of the states surrendered any important aspect of their independent decision-making power, by the 1980s a norm took hold that important foreign policy and security decisions needed to be at least ratified, if not discussed beforehand, in the GCC context. For example, after Kuwait invited foreign naval forces to protect its oil tankers in November 1986, the GCC approved the decision and all the GCC states cooperated with the United States to facilitate the reflagging, risking hostile reactions from Iran. The states used the GCC framework to take common positions on the Iran–Iraq War and to help mediate a border agreement between Oman and South Yemen. In general, these discussions led to a greater convergence of opinion over many principled and substantive issues.[34]

The institutionalization of cooperation also contributed to dispute resolution. Whereas in the past bilateral disputes tended to be worked out through *ad hoc* arrangements and/or with the possibility of war on the horizon, now the GCC states began to use the GCC as a forum for peaceful dispute settlement. For instance, the GCC helped to author the Saudi–Omani border agreement of 1990 (before the Iraqi invasion of Kuwait). A flare-up in the Qatari–Bahraini border dispute in 1986 was settled within a GCC framework, with the leaders of the two countries agreeing to return to the status quo ante.[35] On these scores, it appeared that the states of the GCC were developing a set of norms and procedures for dealing with internal disputes and coordinating policies toward external actors that took them beyond the parameters of a modest alliance and pushed them toward a more binding framework. While preceding the formation of the GCC the Gulf Arab states had expressed an interest in regional cooperation, such expressions were nearly always extinguished by longstanding regional rivalries, feuds, and conflicts over border demarcations. Although the latter continued, now such disputes never led to war, and there is reason to suspect that the developing security norms and institutional mechanisms were a major reason for this non-event.

The GCC's economic relations followed a similar pattern in the 1980s, though here it is important to point out that while at the outset the GCC states were touting economic over security cooperation they closed the decade with far fewer accomplishments in the former relative to the latter. The GCC heads of state adopted the Unified Economic Agreement in their summit of November 1981, calling for (among other things): (a) the formation of a GCC customs union and free trade zone; (b) the creation of a "collective negotiating force" to enhance the group's leverage in international economic negotiations; (c) free movement of capital and labor within the group; (d) coordinated industrial, development and oil policies; and (e) a common currency.[36] Of this far-reaching agenda, some important first steps were taken. The Gulf Investment Corporation was established in 1982, with capital from all the states, to fund joint projects. Common GCC standards, measures and procedures in a range of economic areas were set. Intra-GCC tariffs on a range of goods were eliminated (but since trade among the states amounts to a small percentage of their overall trade, the economic effect of this step was minimal).[37]

While these steps toward economic coordination and integration were not trivial, they fell far short of the sweeping promises made in the Unified Economic Agreement that had envisioned their implementation by the end of the 1980s. Emphasizing economic cooperation at the outset served the leaders' interest in deflecting criticism of the GCC from its security rivals. But the simple fact of the matter was that there is little complementarity among the Gulf states' economies since they all export oil and have similar (and limited) industrial profiles. Political factors also frustrate any attempted economic interdependence. Economic integration would heighten the dependence of the smaller states on Saudi Arabia, and could threaten protected economic interests in all the states. Therefore, actions on economic issues did not live up to the GCC's founding rhetoric. No steps were taken toward a common currency. Serious differences among the states prevented them from forming a customs union that could negotiate as a unit with the United States and the European Union. Cooperation on oil policy was informal and *ad hoc*, when it occurred at all. Individual states dragged their feet on adopting implementing legislation to bring into effect a number of the agreements made at the GCC level, most noticeably those permitting the free flow of capital and labor among the member states. By 1990, there were still severe restrictions on property ownership and investment by other GCC citizens in some of the states. Even proponents of GCC integration admitted these failings.[38]

While the GCC states did not become a single economic entity during the 1980s, as the ambitious Unified Economic Agreement indicated they would, the cooperation that did occur on economic issues reinforced the norm of collective decision-making that was developing on internal security and foreign policy questions. The GCC as a group began negotiations with the United States and the European Union on trade issues, and, because of those negotiations, had to begin working toward collective positions. The change here was more procedural than substantive, as common positions on difficult issues were frequently not reached, but it did represent a further institutionalization of collective decision-making at the inter-governmental level.

There was evidence that the shell of the GCC was providing the home for increased interstate contacts, consultations, and modest moves toward cooperation. The successful discussions and decisions on items of shared interests were having a snowball effect, gathering greater speed, leading to institutionalized norms of consultation and coordination, and offering a glimmer of greater trust. Although economic cooperation was far less impressive than security cooperation – if only because the former was expected and the latter was not – there is reason to conclude that there was some modest spillover between the two, with these streams feeding into a growing level of trust and willingness to experiment further in interstate cooperation.

Perhaps more provocatively, however, the establishment of the GCC created new opportunities for transnational interactions. GCC official rhetoric and action on economic integration had an important community-building effect where perhaps none was really intended or expected. Businessmen (and they are almost exclusively men in these countries) from across the six states began to see the need to cooperate among themselves to affect GCC economic regulations and influence GCC positions in international negotiations. In 1981 the Gulf Chambers of Commerce was founded, institutionalizing links among the state-level chambers. The importance of this step should not be exaggerated. For businessmen in each of the states the most important locus of decision-making remained their government, not the GCC. Riyadh, the GCC headquarters, did not become Brussels. Yet as economic interests began to be affected, however marginally, by decisions taken at the regional level, business elites began to think, at least somewhat, in regional terms. If identity is shaped, at least in part, by economic interests, then these trends in the 1980s supported the development at the societal level of a stronger "Gulf" identity.

At the popular level it is very difficult to tell the depth and breadth to which GCC and state efforts to promote a "Gulf" identity took root. A public opinion survey conducted in Kuwait in 1984 showed a relatively high level of knowledge about and interest in the GCC, and high levels of support for cooperation among the member states, but did not probe respondents views about a "Gulf community" and their own political identity.[39] Citizens of the six states certainly had more interactions with each other during that decade than in previous periods, as a result of improved transportation and the dropping of visa requirements among the GCC states. It became normal for Omanis to weekend in Dubai, and for Saudis to drive across the causeway to Bahrain to spend an evening. Whether those kinds of interactions fostered a sense of common identity cannot be known, but they do represent an increase in transactions between states and societies and provide at least the possibility of sustained group interaction.

Gulf intellectuals met together much more often during the 1980s than was the case previously, in meetings of the *muntada al-tanmiyya*, in the newly established national universities and in other fora. A "Gulf" discourse began to develop among them that dealt with the six states as an historical unit. The best expression of this discourse is a 1983 book by Kuwaiti historian Muhammad al-Rumaihi entitled *al-khalij laysa naftan* ("The Gulf is Not Oil").[40] While acknowledging the specific histories and social settings of each of the six states, Rumaihi presents a strong case that they share a common set of socio-economic and political problems that can only be addressed at a regional level. As important, Rumaihi was only one of many intellectuals and individuals who were beginning to think in regional terms. However, while some public figures and intellectuals were beginning to use the term "khaliji," there is little evidence that this Gulf identity was meaningful for more than a few of the inhabitants or was politically consequential.

In general, the establishment of the GCC provided the context and the opportunity for public officials, private businessmen and intellectuals to begin, first, to consider how their individual interests could be furthered through collective action, and, second, to think in regional terms. In the 1980s the two caravans of interstate and transnational politics were heading in the same direction of regional integration. The GCC states were now cooperating in new areas and ways previously unimagined, beginning to take seriously the possibility that they might be better off acting multilaterally than unilaterally; and to establish new normative arrangements that were intended to regulate their relations and to further cooperation. However commendable and impressive were these experiments in security cooperation, they did not manifest themselves in tangible and robust operational policies. But there was an important advance in the area of dispute settlement, as the GCC states began to use the institution to successfully handle border disputes and other areas of disagreement. And the populations of the GCC were beginning to interact and imagine themselves in new ways. It bears repeating that at the outset the GCC was to be a symbolic organization at best and not initially intended as a trust-building organization, but that its mere creation: (1) presented new opportunities and incentives for interstate cooperation and transnational exchanges; and, (2) enabled new forms of imaginings to pursue their individual interests. Within less than a decade the GCC had developed into one of the international system's more vibrant and multifaceted experiments in regional organizations, far surpassing anything previously accomplished in Arab politics and offering a multilateral ethic against their initial instincts.

The Gulf War and after

GCC cooperation faced its most serious test with the Iraqi invasion of Kuwait in August 1990. And it seemed to have risen to the challenge.

The speed and unanimity with which the Gulf states came together to support Kuwait and accept the American and other international forces that would expel Iraq from Kuwait were remarkable. The extent of that cooperation on the political level need not be rehearsed here. Suffice it to say that the GCC stood behind Kuwait from the outset. There were no indications, at any time during the crisis, that any GCC government was less than fully committed to the liberation of Kuwait, even if that required a coalition military attack on Iraq. If there were second thoughts or doubts among GCC leaders about the wisdom of Kuwait's conduct before the invasion or about the hand-ling of the crisis after August 2, 1990, those thoughts and doubts were kept private. The wholehearted commitment of the states of the lower Gulf (Qatar, UAE and Oman), whose security was not immediately threatened by the Iraqi occupation of Kuwait, bespeaks the belief that they envisioned their security as interdependent.

Group solidarity (and also its limits) was symbolically expressed by the role of Peninsula Shield, the joint GCC force, in the war. With each GCC state sending more forces toward the Kuwaiti border after the invasion, Gen. Khalid bin Sultan, the Saudi commander in the crisis, decided to assign most of the units in Peninsula Shield to the forces of their individual state. However, he did mix units from different GCC states in various task forces, assigning battalions of Omani, Emirati and Qatari forces and a Bahraini brigade to accompany Saudi brigades in the original defense plans after August 2.[41] The GCC forces cooperated under a single command, but maintained their national organization and officers. These were no minor achievements. Penin-sula Shield was not a unitary GCC force, but it did express tangibly the unified sense of threat the Gulf regimes perceived from Iraq.[42]

It must be stressed, moreover, that their political and military stand was not cost-free for the rulers of the Gulf states. All Arab–Islamic societies (and this was true of the GCC states) are highly sensitive to an explicit alliance with the USA, and fear that a too visible American presence might increase domestic instability. Indeed, many have experienced serious domestic problems in the wake of the Gulf War, most spectacularly the bombings of American facilities in Saudi Arabia in November 1995 and June 1996. Though these problems have deep local roots, recent manifestations of increased political activity in the Gulf states date to the immediate post-Gulf War period.[43] Despite the risks involved, the GCC navigated the Gulf crisis with an impressive showing of solidarity and commitment.

Post-war statism and rivalry

Yet perhaps the singular result of the Gulf War was not the promotion of regionalism but rather the retreat to statism. After a decade of rather surprisingly successful experimentation in security cooperation and a successful collective response to the challenge of the Gulf War, the Gulf states seemingly abandoned any sense of regionalism in favor of statism and particularlism. Why the unbridled statism? We suggest two related reasons. First, the shock of the Iraqi invasion meant that state security was understandably uppermost in the minds of the governments of the region. Whereas before the war the GCC states were willing to minimize their security preparations because there was no immediate threat of war, the Iraqi invasion meant that immediate security was a justified obsession. But this interest in state security is coupled with a decline in Arabism; Arabism had already been quite frail and, according to Jordanian journalist Fahd al-Fanek, Saddam's invasion represented the "last nail in the coffin."[44] The constraints on what Arab states were and were not allowed to do disappeared alongside any concept of "Arab national security." Whether the Gulf War was a cause or, in the view of former Jordanian Ambassador to the United Nations Adnan Abu Odeh, a convenient pretext, there was little doubt that Arab states were now thinking in statist rather than in regional terms.[45]

While the exact causes are debatable, there is little debate that the Gulf crisis brought out centrifugal tendencies and unilateral scrambles for security. The first post-Gulf War security arrangement was statism in regionalism's clothes. Under pressure from Egypt and Syria, the most important Arab members of the international coalition, the GCC states agreed in March 1991 to the "Damascus Declaration," a statement that could be read as calling for a permanent Egyptian and Syrian military presence in the Gulf states as part of an Arab deterrent force. Despite the numerous conversations and conferences designed to implement its principles, the Declaration soon became a dead letter because of Gulf state reluctance to implement the ambitious Egyptian and Syrian reading. As noted in Egypt's official daily *al-ʾAhram*, "We have to acknowledge the apprehensions of the people of the Gulf, or at least some of them, who fear an Arab presence in the Gulf, because the past is not very encouraging."[46] Larger Arab security umbrellas were no longer good enough for the Gulf rulers.

Indeed, for many the real importance – and the only surviving principle – of the Declaration was not its promise of further military cooperation but rather its insistence on sovereignty as the basis of inter-Arab politics and regional order. Coming on the heels of Iraq's denial of Kuwaiti sovereignty and claim that Gulf oil belonged to the Arabs, the GCC states held sovereignty and security as indistinguishable. GCC Secretary-General Bishara's interpretation of the Declaration was that it recognized the legitimacy of the Arab state's borders, the right of each state to arrange its own security, and the exclusive claim to its resources – that is, its sovereignty and exclusivity.[47] Sovereignty meant possessive sovereignty in this instance, a jealous and protective stance and a return to unilateralism after movement toward multilateralism.

Their insistence on the sanctity of borders and the centrality of state sovereignty during the Gulf crisis imprinted intra-GCC relations after the war. At the GCC summit of December 1990 the leaders requested that Sultan Qabus of Oman prepare a plan for an integrated Gulf defense system. At the next summit he presented an ambitious blueprint to expand the size of the Peninsula Shield force to 100,000, making it a truly integrated GCC army. The plan barely elicited any discussion, much less support, among his fellow rulers, who referred it back to a committee of military experts where it has languished since.[48] In lieu of deepening their own cooperation, the GCC states sought to bolster their security by signing bilateral defense agreements with the Great Powers. Kuwait negotiated such pacts with every permanent member of the U.N. Security Council. The other smaller states renewed or initiated agreements with the United States, Great Britain and/or France. Saudi Arabia was the only GCC member not to enter into a new, formal security arrangement with any Great Power after the Gulf War, largely to avoid criticism from Islamic groups within the Kingdom. However, it did deepen its security relationship with the United States, buying vast amounts of new weaponry and engaging in even closer consultations with Washington. It is noteworthy that none of the Great Powers sought to negotiate security issues with these states through the GCC (as the EU has done on trade issues), and that none requested that kind of multilateral context for security arrangements. In their voluminous arms purchases after the Gulf War, the GCC states showed no desire to come to common understandings about burden-sharing, avoidance of duplication, or inter-operability.

In general, while there has been some progress toward the establishment of an integrated air-defense system,[49] the general record on defense cooperation is dismal. Despite, or perhaps because of, their experiences during 1990–91, the Gulf monarchies have basically chosen a "go it alone" defense strategy. But if the Gulf War spurred not military integration but rather statism it was partly in response to the fact that Great Powers were ready, willing, and able to extend security guarantees. More to the point, none of the Western powers who were the preferred security option required or encouraged the Gulf states to devise multilateral formulas to foster their security. Third-parties can provide an incentive to group action and coordination, but they can also represent a deterrent.

Although military cooperation has stalled, some internal security cooperation continues – but on a bilateral rather than on a multilateral basis. According to opposition sources and news reports, both Kuwait and Saudi Arabia have assisted Bahraini authorities in their confrontation with domestic dissidents – the Saudis by sending forces to Bahrain and the Kuwaitis by arresting Bahraini opposition figures in Kuwait.[50] Multilateral GCC cooperation on internal security has been stymied by the resurgence of serious conflicts among the member states, conflicts that the GCC has not been able to resolve. For instance, both Kuwait and Oman opted not to adhere to a new internal security accord presented at the 1994 GCC summit.[51] It appears that every step toward internal security cooperation is a tortured one, laden with suspicions and doubts.

A more ominous and more serious setback for multilateralism was the re-emergence of territorial disputes and rivalries. After a decade hiatus, the GCC states began to settle their border disputes through sabre-rattling rather than peaceful adjudication. Qatar and Saudi Arabia had a minor border clash in 1992 in which two Qatari soldiers and one Saudi tribal shaykh were killed. Mediation by President Mubarak of Egypt (not, it should be noted, other GCC members) smoothed over the incident at the time.[52] In April 1996 Qatar and Saudi Arabia agreed to appoint a committee to demarcate their border,[53] but a final settlement of the issue has yet to be achieved. Qatar and Bahrain also revived border disputes. In July 1991 Qatar petitioned the International Court of Justice to rule on its dispute over the Hawar Islands with Bahrain. Bahrain rejected the Court's jurisdiction, urging Qatar to settle the issue within the GCC. Qatar has not openly rejected GCC mediation but has continued to pursue its claim at the Hague. As of July 1996 the matter was still before the Court, and was the occasion for frequent verbal sniping between Doha and Manama. Oman in 1993 raised objections at the UN to the Saudi–UAE border agreement, which it said encroached on Omani territory.[54] The persistence of border disputes is particularly bothersome, given that the GCC leaders in their summit of December 1994 declared 1995 to be the year in which all border issues among them would be resolved.

The bottom line here is that the residents of the region could easily imagine border disputes igniting into border wars. In the spring of 1994, Gause participated in a faculty seminar at Qatar University on US foreign policy in the Middle East. The first question directed to him by a Qatari academic was, "What would the position of the United States be if one GCC country attacked another?" It is difficult to imagine a full-scale war between GCC members. It is, however, not difficult to imagine serious tensions that could escalate to armed clashes. Simply put, there is little evidence of dependable expectations of peaceful change at the multilateral level.

Part of the reason for these continuing suspicions and clashes is because of meddling, involvement, and interference in each other's domestic politics. Perhaps the most glaring example concerns the recent developments in Qatar. An intra-family coup in the summer of 1995 deposed the Amir, Shaykh Khalifa al Thani, and brought to power his son, Shaykh Hamad. Hamad, who had effective control of Qatari politics for a number of years prior to the coup, was largely blamed in Riyadh for the Saudi–Qatari border troubles after the Gulf War, and was seen throughout the Gulf as the driving force behind Qatari efforts to establish closer relations with Iran, Iraq and Israel than his GCC partners favored. He embarrassed his fellow GCC leaders by very publicly boycotting the closing session of the December 1995 GCC summit, protesting the failure of his favored candidate to be chosen as secretary-general of the organization.[55]

At the end of December 1995 and the beginning of January 1996 his deposed father made a very public tour of the capitals of the other GCC states, claiming to be the legitimate ruler of Qatar and being received by the GCC heads of state. The former Amir then set up housekeeping in the UAE as a guest of the government. In February 1996 Qatar arrested around 100 people in an alleged coup plot planned by the deposed Amir. Qatari officials indirectly accused some of their neighbors of facilitating the plot, and called for an emergency GCC meeting to examine the issue. Their GCC partners, however, refused to agree to such a meeting, with one official of another GCC state saying that Qatar had to apologize for its accusations before such a meeting could be convened.[56] In reaction, Qatar refused to participate in the Peninsula Shield exercises of March 1996.[57] Qatari officials also signaled their GCC partners that they had other friends who would help them if the GCC would not. They told journalists that Iran had offered to send troops to Qatar to protect it, but that Qatar had refused with thanks, and that France was rushing a contingent of troops to the country, pushing forward a previously scheduled military training mission.[58] Qatar's relations with its GCC neighbors were eventually patched-up, at least for public consumption. However, this incident was a major setback for the GCC, an organization founded largely on a common interest in maintaining regime security.

The Qatari episode highlights the fact that, when it comes to regime security, some GCC states still see other GCC states as potential threats. The commonalities in state-society relations and regime types among the Gulf states are striking. These commonalities facilitate cooperation when outside forces call into question the legitimacy of monarchy or call for Gulf oil wealth to be shared with all the Arabs. When challenged by pan-Arabists inspired by Nasser's Egypt or Ba'thist Iraq or by Islamic republicans looking to Teheran for models, the GCC leaders have had no trouble circling the wagons. However, the history of dynastic conflict in the Arabian Peninsula has left a residue of suspicion among the ruling families about their intentions toward each other. Qataris and Bahrainis both know well that the al Khalifa family that rules Bahrain once ruled in Qatar. Saudi expansionist pressures during the first half of the 20th century are not forgotten. Some Kuwaitis and Bahrainis hold the Saudis at least partially responsible for the closings of their parliaments in the 1970s.[59] With the immediate threats of Iran and Iraq to both external and internal security reduced after the Gulf War, those inter-elite suspicions and jealousies reappeared on the agenda.

In general, if the GCC success in promoting greater trust and identification is based solely on interstate relations then there is little good news in the post-Gulf War period. The work of the GCC continues, with some progress being made in the long process of customs unification demanded by the EU before a comprehensive GCC–EU trade agreement can be reached.[60] But the hopes nurtured during the 1980s for steady progress toward Gulf integration on security and economic issues have not been realized. Particularly in security areas, earlier progress seems to have been undone by the Gulf War and the return of rivalries and suspicions. Although the mere existence of the GCC forces the regimes to at least entertain cooperation at the regional level, the last few years suggest statism and unilateralism rather than regionalism and multilateralism.

Postwar transnationalism and regional identity

If the regimes were now engaging in greater in-fighting and showing signs of greater divisions, their populations were actually registering greater mutual identification. Specifically, since the 1980s there has been a notable growth in the discourse about the "Gulf" identity. The Gulf crisis provided a strong boost for this development. Saddam Hussein, and many others in the Arab world, lumped the six states together in their propaganda attacks, using both Arab nationalist and Islamist vocabularies to question the legitimacy of the monarchical regimes. That propaganda had the opposite effect, at least in some quarters, of making more salient the common "Gulf" identity that the GCC had been trying to foster for a decade.

At the societal level, the Gulf crisis strengthened the nascent sense of a common "Gulf" identity among citizens of the GCC states. Kuwaitis, caught outside their country on August 2 or escaping the Iraqi forces, were taken in as guests in the other Gulf countries for the duration of the crisis. This hospitality had a profound and positive effect on Kuwaiti perceptions of their Gulf neighbors, whom many Kuwaitis had previously seen as somewhat backward and bumptious desert folk.[61] Kuwaiti intellectuals began to urge an accelerated schedule for Gulf integration, where before the crisis they resisted such proposals as veiled plans for Saudi hegemony.[62]

While the effects of the crisis were greatest on Kuwaitis, other Gulf citizens felt the sting of the hostility toward them in other quarters of the Arab world just as acutely. Being lumped together in one group ("khalijiin") by their critics tended to reinforce that nascent identity. This "us vs. them" feeling is clear in much of the writing by Gulf intellectuals immediately following the crisis.[63] The turn in intellectual circles was particularly telling, as Arab nationalist sentiment tended to be over-represented in that group in comparison with Gulf publics in the period before the crisis. The "group feeling" among Gulf citizens generated by the criticisms they heard from other Arabs during the crisis is clear in the comments by Abd al-Khaliq Abdalla, a political scientist from the UAE who participated in one of the first Arab academic conferences after the Gulf War. The conference, organized by the Center for Arab Unity Studies in Cairo, included few participants from the Gulf. In the concluding session, Abdalla told his fellow Arab intellectuals:

> I want to begin frankly, and I hope that your hearts are open to hearing this. I think that some Arabs have a strange perception of the Gulf and also a misunderstanding about the Arab people there. This understanding is dominant among Arab intellectuals especially and the Arab masses, unfortunately, also. It is greatly similar to the Western perception of this region and the Arab people in it. The basis of this perception is that there is nothing in the Gulf except oil ... There are people and intellectuals and individuals with dreams and ambitions who suffer daily and who are trying to make a better future as part of [the Arab-Islamic] community.[64]

This increased salience of the "Gulf" identity was manifested in a number of ways. The Union of Gulf Chambers of Commerce became much more outspoken after the Gulf War, with the state-level chambers joining together to urge their governments to attack economic problems like unemployment, deficit spending, privatization and the slow pace of trade negotiations with the EC.[65] Gulf businessmen were increasingly perceiving that they faced a common set of problems and needed to address them in common, across state borders. In May 1992 ninety Gulf intellectuals and businessmen established the *"Gulf National Forum"* (*al-Multaqa al-watani al-khaliji*) with the aim of encouraging cooperation among the GCC states, presenting itself as a "popular reserve" to support official moves toward integration.[66] With no encouragement from the governments, this group has had little impact on Gulf politics, but the timing of its establishment is an indication that the vocabulary of "Gulf" identity had begun to seep into popular consciousness. In November 1994, for the first time members of the parliaments and consultative councils of the six GCC states met formally to discuss regional issues.[67]

The increasing prominence of this kind of "Gulf" discourse was examined by a number of Gulf intellectuals in a series of articles under the title "A Symposium on Gulf Identity" published in *Shu'un Ijtima'iyya* (Journal of Social Affairs), the journal of the Sociological Association of the UAE, in the fall of 1992. Seven authors participated – three from the UAE, two from Saudi Arabia and one each from Kuwait and Bahrain. They differed markedly on whether there was in fact a distinct "Gulf" identity, with some contending that such an identity was forming, based on a common history and a common set of current political challenges, while others denied that there was anything that set Gulf Arabs apart at the identity level from other Muslim Arabs.[68] Yet all agreed with Ahmad Ali al-Haddad, the author of the first article in the collection, that "talk about a Gulf identity has increased markedly since the Gulf War."[69]

It is important not to exaggerate the extent to which a "Gulf" identity became widespread or displaced other identities at the popular level. In Islamic political discourse in the Gulf, the concept is completely absent. Even those authors in the above-mentioned symposium who thought there was a distinct Gulf identity were at pains to emphasize that such an identity was in the earliest stages of development[70] and that it neither negated nor displaced larger Arab and Muslim identities.[71] The political agendas in the six GCC states are still largely focused on issues at the state level, not the regional level. But the very fact that there has been so much discussion, pro and con, about a "Gulf" identity in the years after the Gulf War is an indication that the idea of a Gulf community, something beyond a grouping of states in a regional organization, has taken root.

Another indicator that the citizens of the GCC are beginning to conceive of themselves in regional rather than strictly statist terms recently occurred in the protest at the possibility of normalization of relations with Israel. A Kuwaiti-based organization called "The Popular Conference to Oppose Normalization with the Zionist Entity in the Gulf" is attempting to mobilize support among citizens of all the GCC states. It is instructive that the Kuwaitis organizers, though motivated by their objections to their own state's policies, have elected to target their activities not at the state level but rather at the GCC level. There may be instrumental reasons for this decision, but it provides additional evidence that citizens of the Gulf are conceptualizing mobilization at the regional level.[72]

What appears to be taking place is that two caravans – an official one and a popular one – are moving along distinct paths. The Gulf leaders created the GCC to foster some symbolic security and economic cooperation, deepened the security cooperation in ways unanticipated while failing to increase economic cooperation in ways imagined, and then departed from their previous regional efforts in favor of statism after the Gulf War. Still, the shell of the GCC continues and encourages its members to continue to bow in the direction of sustained cooperation and coordination. And another security crisis could bring home to the leaders their common interests. For example, Bahraini accusations made in June 1996 of direct Iranian involvement in the country's domestic disturbances led to a strong statement of support for Bahrain by all its GCC partners.[73] Despite its difficulties with its neighbors, Qatar has not withdrawn from the organization and shows no signs that it will. The institutional mechanisms of the GCC are well-established and available should the leaders choose to move forward with security and economic cooperation. While the post-Gulf War period can most charitably be described as a "pause" in the integrative momentum established in the 1980s, it would be wrong to discount the possibility of renewed cooperation.

While Gulf leaders might have found that their umbrella organization might have outlasted its function, an enduring legacy of the organization was to encourage the residents of the region to continue to follow the shadow of cooperation and to imagine themselves as part of the region. But the residents are doing more than imagining – they are making business deals, exchanging information, taking holidays in each others cities, and holding conferences on the "Gulf" identity. At this point we have little concrete evidence to suggest whether this transnationalism is encouraging GCC states to push harder for institutionalization than they otherwise would have, but comparative experience suggests that such sentiments, activities, and interests are likely to make their way up to formal politics and interstate negotiations. And again, any "Gulf" identity is limited, nascent, and competing with other forms of association and identification; still, that a "Gulf" identity is even part of the regional conversation is testimony to how new forms of interaction are inspiring new ways of thinking.

Conclusion

It should be clear that we think that the GCC states are a poor candidate for a security community in the near future. Its members can imagine using force against each other. Qatar and Bahrain continue to pose a menace to each other in their territorial dispute; Saudi Arabia and Qatar clashed over their border as recently as 1992. Indeed, these developments represent a retreat from the rather impressive cooperation of the 1980s. In the 1980s the GCC member states made great strides in coordinating their efforts against internal security threats and began to experiment with military cooperation and to draw plans for military integration. But the Gulf War seemed to have replaced any thoughts of regionalism with statism. Although the Gulf War was a challenge the states met, this unified response can, to a great extent, also be explained in realist terms as simple balancing behavior; and the post-Gulf War developments call into question the extent to which their ties go beyond an alliance. The failure of the group to devise a reliable method of solving problems among themselves, most notably border issues, does not bode well for anticipating new institutional mechanisms in other areas that might contribute to dependable expectations of peaceful change.

So, what can we learn from the GCC? We want to conclude by calling attention to four points related to the study of the development of security communities. The first is the importance of taking a path-dependent perspective. The very creation of the GCC established new parameters and institutional constraints and incentives for state action. The establishment of the organization forced its members to consider, if only nominally and haphazardly at first, how their policies, interests, and strategies were interdependent and might benefit from some modest cooperation. This became particularly evident when internal security threats loomed large and encouraged the GCC states to begin to coordinate their policies. Such modest coordination gently pushed and pulled the GCC to experiment further in security cooperation. By the end of the 1980s individuals and regimes were beginning to think in regional terms, due to the very establishment of the organization. The Gulf War shattered the tide of regionalism and ushered in a return to statism, but even here the presence of the GCC has provided something of a break on unbridled realism and possessive sovereignty. Although modest, there is some evidence to suggest that through their interactions they began to develop "Gulf" identities whose interests were defined in regional rather than strictly territorial terms. A path-dependent perspective reminds us that we could not conceivably trace backwards the history of the GCC to its origins through the logic of statism and realism, and part of the reason is because of how the institution helped to change the preferences, interests, and perhaps even the identities of its members.

Secondly, the case of the GCC points to obstacles rather than facilitators toward community-building. We want to mention two obstacles in particular. To begin, in chapter 2 Adler and Barnett hypothesize that security communities are organized around core states or a k-group that are able to project a sense of purpose and to pay the transaction costs that are frequently required to assemble collective action. Saudi Arabia is the logical candidate to be a core state, but to the other GCC states it looks less like a core state in a potential security community than it does a hegemon in classical realism. Although Saudi Arabia has exhibited leadership on important issues in the past, encouraging and facilitating cooperation among the GCC states, such enabling behavior is undermined by the fear that Saudi Arabia effects leadership not for purpose but rather for power. This fear of Saudi Arabia has been an obstacle toward economic and military cooperation, and we suspect that such suspicions will continue into the near future.

Another obstacle toward deepening cooperation was the recrudescence of fear among some of the ruling elites that their GCC neighbors were working against them in their own domestic politics. This obstacle is not at the social structural level   these regimes resemble each other fairly closely in terms of legitimating principles and state-society relations. Rather, it stems from pervasive fears among the ruling elites about their own stability, and about the ability of neighbors to work with their own domestic opponents (because of the great cultural and social similarities among the states) to destabilize their own individual status as ruler. Because of their mutual vulnerabilities on these sensitive domestic questions, the GCC states have been as likely to interfere in each other's domestic politics as they have been to coordinate their policies. This central role that regime security plays in intra-GCC cooperation and conflict highlights a point made by the editors in chapter 2: that having agreement on their domestic architecture and on how each player will relate to the others' domestic political scene may be as important to the development of a security community as experiments in security cooperation. We are not suggesting that a security community can only be founded among democratic states, but agreement on some fundamental organizing principles concerning the management and organization of domestic politics appears to be an important precondition for the encouragement of transnationalism and deepened interstate cooperation. Only when leaders are confident that interstate cooperation will not lead to a challenge to their own domestic position can integration move forward.

A third observation is the relationship between internal and external security in the development of a security community. In so-called weak states that lack legitimacy and whose populations' identities do not necessarily follow the flag, internal security can be as prescient and pressing for the regime as can external security. Indeed, the Gulf states were more interested in coordinating their internal security measures as they were their military policies. But such coordination on internal security measures encouraged GCC states to experiment on military cooperation and integration. In other words, spillover in this context concerned not between economic and political spheres but rather between internal and external security domains.

Fourthly, there are various elements of the intra-group process that suggest some of the traits associated with a security community. Community-building progress has been made among the six states on issues of the free movement of populations. Visas are not now required for GCC state citizens to travel to other GCC states. There has been progress toward opening up economic opportunities for citizens across state borders, but not all states have fully implemented GCC resolutions on these issues. The formation of a real common market among the six is a goal that appears almost as far off now as it did in 1981, when the GCC was formed. Perhaps the most interesting feature has been the development of a "Gulf" identity. Introduced by the Gulf leaders for symbolic and strategic purposes at the outset of the 1980s as a way to offer a rival identity to secular Arab nationalism and political Islam, this identity has become more prominent on the political landscape. The facilitation of contact at the individual level has been matched by the beginnings of development of a "Gulf" identity at the social level among populations of these states. The Gulf War was a major impetus in raising the salience of "Gulf" identity discourse throughout the region. By no means has that identity become hegemonic, but over the past fifteen years it has worked itself squarely onto the political and social agenda of the region.

While the mere existence of the GCC continues to encourage the Gulf states to think in regional terms, there is little reason to oversell the case of the GCC. But the establishment of the GCC created new incentives and opportunities for both states and their societies. Perhaps the most interesting feature, in this respect, is that while the regimes have been cautious concerning cooperation, various societal groups have begun to think in regional terms and to articulate a "Gulf" identity. At this stage we can only speculate, but it could very well be that as the idea of a "Gulf" identity grows, the incentives for the leaders to build on popular feelings of community will increase. If so, the origins of community-building were born in the insecurities of the Gulf regimes who feared domestic instability and looked to the GCC as a place to coordinate their responses and to provide an alternative identity for their citizens.

Notes

1 Joseph Kostiner, *The Making of Saudi Arabia, 1916–1936* (New York: Oxford University Press, 1993); Jill Crystal, *Oil and Politics in the Gulf: Rulers and Merchants in Kuwait and Qatar* (New York: Cambridge University Press, 1990); Rosemarie Said Zahlan, *The Making of the Modern Gulf States: Kuwait, Bahrain, Qatar, the United Arab Emirates and Oman* (London: Unwin Hyman, 1989).

2 Kostiner, *The Making of Saudi Arabia*, p. 81.

3 Nadav Safran, *Saudi Arabia: The Ceaseless Quest for Security* (Cambridge, MA: Harvard University Press, 1985), p. 79.

4 Safran, *Saudi Arabia*, ch. 10; Laurie Ann Mylroie, "Regional Security After Empire: Saudi Arabia and the Gulf," Ph.D. dissertation, Harvard University, 1985, chs. 4 and 5; J. E. Peterson, "The GCC and Regional Security," in John A. Sandwick, ed., *The Gulf Cooperation Council* (Boulder, CO: Westview Press, 1988), pp. 72–76.

5 Text in Majid Khadduri, *The Gulf War* (New York: Oxford University Press, 1988), pp. 119–20.

6 See R. K. Ramazani, *The Gulf Cooperation Council: Record and Analysis* (Charlottesville: University Press of Virginia, 1988), pp. 15–17, for the Charter of the GCC.

7 Michael Barnett, "Identity and Alliances in the Middle East," in Peter Katzenstein, ed., *Culture and National Security: Norms and Identity in World Politics* (New York: Columbia University Press, 1996), pp. 400–447.

8 See Abu Dhabi Domestic Service, May 26, 1981. Cited from *FBIS-NES*, May 27, 1981, A1–2; and Gulf News Agency, May 26, 1981. Cited in *FBIS-NES*, June 4, 1981, A10–11.

9 Joseph Wright Twinam, "Reflection on Gulf Cooperation, with a Focus on Bahrain, Qatar and Oman," in Sandwick, ed., *The Gulf Cooperation Council*, p. 23. Also see Emile Nakhleh, *The Gulf Cooperation Council: Policies, Problems and Prospects* (New York: Praeger, 1986), p. 57; Barnett interview with Bishara, New York, October 3, 1993.

10 Barnett interview with Bishara, New York City, October 3, 1993.

11 Ghassan Saleme, "Inter-Arab Politics: The Return of Geography," in William B. Quandt, ed, *The Middle East: Ten Years After Camp David* (Washington: Brookings Institution, 1988), pp. 239, 249–50. For brief overviews of the relationship between the Gulf and other Arab regions see Michael Morony, "The Arabisation of the Gulf," in B. R. Pridham, ed., *The*

Arab Gulf and the Arab World (New York: Croom Helm, 1988), pp. 3–28; and Robert Landen, "The Changing Pattern of Political Relations Between the Arab Gulf and the Arab Provinces of the Ottoman Empire," also in Pridham, ed., *The Arab Gulf and the Arab World*, pp. 41–64.

12 See, for instance, the interview with Bahraini Foreign Minister Shaykh Khalifa, *Akhbar al-Khaliji* 11 March 1981, p. 3. Cited in *FBIS-NES*, March 12, 1981, C1.

13 *Al-Ra'y al-'Amm*, November 19, 1984. Cited in *FBIS*, 234, December 4, 1984, C3.

14 Ramazani, *The Gulf Cooperation Council*, pp. 15–17, 24–25, 29–30.

15 Oman did have a low-level, but highly controversial, strategic agreement with the United States, the other Gulf states condemned its actions, and actively discouraged any greater US (or Soviet) presence in the region.

16 *FBIS-NES*, September 20, 1984, 5, 184, C1.

17 Joseph Kostiner, "Shi'i Unrest in the Gulf," in Martin Kramer, ed., *Shi'ism, Resistance and Revolution* (Boulder, CO: Westview Press, 1987), pp. 177–180; R. K. Ramazani, *Revolutionary Iran: Challenge and Response in the Middle East* (Baltimore: The Johns Hopkins University Press, 1986), chs. 3 and 8.

18 David Holden and Richard Johns, *The House of Saud* (New York: Holt, Rinehart and Winston, 1981), ch. 25.

19 "Saddam Husayn's Message to 'al-Watan' [Kuwait]: Unity and Syria," Baghdad Voice of the Masses, September 16, 1980; cited from *BBC World Broadcasts*, ME/6526/A/2, September 18, 1980.

20 Faisal S. A. al-Salem, "The Issue of Identity in Selected Arab Gulf States," in Tawfic E. Farah and Yasumasa Kuroda, eds., *Political Socialization in the Arab States*, (Boulder, CO: Lynne Rienner, 1987), pp. 47–63.

21 Nakhleh, *The Gulf Cooperation Council*, ch. 4.

22 MENA, April 4, 1985. Cited from *FBIS-NES*, 85, 66, April 5, 1985, C2–3.

23 Ramazani, *Revolutionary Iran*, pp. 131–133; Ramazani, *The Gulf Cooperation Council*, pp. 48–51.

24 Gause interview with a GCC official.

25 Ramazani, *Revolutionary Iran*, p. 132.

26 Barnett interview with Abdulla Bishara, New York City, October 3, 1993.

27 See Ursula Braun, "The Gulf Cooperation Council's Security Role," in Pridham, ed., *The Arab World and the Arab Gulf*, pp. 252–67, for an overview of GCC security cooperation.

28 J. Peterson, "The GCC and Regional Security," pp. 193–99; Erik Peterson, *The Gulf Cooperation Council* (Boulder, CO: Westview Press, 1988), pp. 201–214.

29 Anthony Cordesman, *The Gulf and the Search for Strategic Stability* (Boulder, CO: Westview Press, 1984), p. 490.

30 WAKH, January 13, 1982. Cited in *FBIS-NES*, January 15, 1982, C2. Italics added.

31 See WAKH, April 24, 1984. Cited in *FBIS-NES*, 5, 81, April 25, 1984, C1, for a list of reasons precluding greater military integration and coordination.

32 Summits meet once a year, foreign ministerial meetings every six months plus emergency meetings, and other ministerial meetings convene at longer intervals.

33 Braun, "The Gulf Cooperation Council's Security Role," p. 262.

34 Ramazani, *The Gulf Cooperation Council*, pp. 125–127.

35 Peterson, *The Gulf Cooperation Council*, pp. 113–115; Ramazani, *The Gulf Cooperation Council*, pp. 106–108.

36 Peterson, *Gulf Cooperation Council*, ch. 7; Abdullah Ibrahim el-Kuwaiz, "Economic Integration of the Cooperation Council of the Arab States of the Gulf: Challenges, Achievements and Future Outlook," in Sandwick, ed., *The Gulf Cooperation Council*, pp. 71–85.

37 Peterson, *Gulf Cooperation Council*, p. 175.

38 Nakhleh, *The Gulf Cooperation Council*, pp. 87–95.

39 This book was subsequently translated into English. Muhammad Rumaihi, *Beyond Oil: Unity and Development in the Gulf* (London: Al Saqi Books).

40 HRH Khalid Bin Sultan, *Desert Warrior: A Personal View of the Gulf War by the Joint Forces Commander* (New York: HarperCollins, 1995), pp. 248–49.

41 In fact, that the Gulf states participated in the Gulf coalition under GCC auspices while the Syrian and Arab states were integrated as individual states in the coalition provided additional evidence of the division between the Gulf Arabs and the rest of the Arab world.

42 F. Gregory Gause III, *Oil Monarchies* (New York: Council on Foreign Relations Press, 1994), ch. 4; F. Gregory Gause III, "The Gulf Conundrum," *Washington Quarterly* 20, 1 (Winter, 1997), pp. 145–165. The GCC states remain quite sensitive to a highly visible presence by American troops. Kuwait is still insistent about the limits of a US presence, stressing that there are no foreign military bases or troops. Interview with Kuwaiti Defense Minister Shaykh Sabah, KUNA, November 25, 1991. Cited in *FBIS-NES*-91–228, November 26, 1992, pp. 15–16. Saudi Arabia, for its part, keeps the United States isolated because of overt opposition to its presence; for instance, the Saudi government dismissed a religious scholar for opposing the US presence in Saudi Arabia. *FBIS-NES*-023, February 4, 1992, 24–5. See Stephen Zunes, "The U.S.–GCC Relationship: Its Rise and Potential Fall," *Middle East Policy* 2, 1 (1993), pp. 103–112, for further caveats on the US presence.

43 Interview with Barnett, Amman, August 29, 1995.

44 Interview with Barnett, April 2, 1996, Washington DC.

45 Ihsan Bakr in *al-Ahram*, June 7, 1992, p. 9. Cited in *FBIS-NES*-92–114, June 12, 1992, 9–10. The Secretary-General of the Arab League nearly pronounced the last rites of the Collective Arab Defense Pact: "At the same time it must be clear that the concept of security is the biggest responsibility of each individual state. Each state determines the needs and boundaries of its security on its own, because this concerns its people and

its future. We should basically assume that there should be no interference in any country's security. We must acknowledge and proceed from this basic principle." *FBIS-NES*-92–232, December 2, 1992, pp. 1–2. See also the "Memorandum of Understanding" signed between the Arab League and the GCC. *FBIS-NES*-92–034, February 20, 1992, p. 3.

46 *FBIS-NES*-92–241, December 15, 1992, p. 10–11.

47 Gause, *Oil Monarchies*, p. 130.

48 Ashraf Fouad, "Gulf Arab Military Integration Gains Steam," *Reuters* (on-line), January 21, 1996.

49 On Kuwait, see the April 13, 1996 communiqué of the Bahrain Freedom Movement, a London-based Bahraini opposition group, and "Kuwait arrests subversive Bahrainis," United Press International (on-line), March 31, 1997. On Saudi Arabia, see the Bahrain Freedom Movement's monthly English-language publication, "Voice of Bahrain," No. 37, January 1995, pp. 1, 3.

50 *al-Hayat*, December 21, 1994, pp. 1, 4.

51 Gause, *Oil Monarchies*, pp. 130–131.

52 "Qatar, Saudi Arabia Revive Border Body," UPI (on-line), April 7, 1996.

53 *al-Hayat*, August 24, 1994, p. 4.

54 Reuters (on-line), December 6, 1995, accessed through Gulf/2000 bulletin board.

55 Ashraf Fouad, "U.S. works to bring Gulf allies together for Qatar," Reuters (on-line), February 25, 1996.

56 "Qatar Boycotts Gulf Arab War Games," Reuters (on-line), March 5, 1996.

57 "Qatar rejects Iran's military offer, seeks French," Reuters (on-line), February 29, 1996.

58 Crystal, *Oil and Politics in the Gulf*, p. 92.

59 "Gulf Arab Ministers Recommend Eight Pct Tariff," Reuters (on-line), June 1, 1996.

60 Gause interviews in Kuwait, Spring, 1992.

61 An example is the long article on the GCC by Kuwait University political scientist Shamlan 'Issa in *Sawt al-Kuwayt*, May 28, 1992, p. 9.

62 See in particular Ghazi Algosaibi, *The Gulf Crisis: An Attempt to Understand* (London: Kegan Paul International, 1993). The author is currently the Saudi ambassador to London, and a highly respected Gulf intellectual, poet and novelist.

63 markaz dirasat al-wahda al-'arabiyya [Center for Arab Unity Studies], *'azmat al-khalij wa tada'iyyat 'ala al-watan al-'arabi* [The Gulf Crisis and Challenges for the Arab Nation] (Beirut: Center for Arab Unity Studies, 1991), p. 342.

64 See, for example, their statements reported in *al-Hayat*, August 19, 1994, p. 9, and *al-Hayat*, June 9, 1995, p. 10.

65 *al-Qabas* [Kuwaiti newspaper], May 14, 1992, pp. 1, 4.

66 *al-Hayat*, November 13, 1994, p. 5.

67 For a strong defense of the latter position, see Sa'id Abdallah Harib, "al-

shakhsiyya al-khalijiyya: al-mustalah wa al-muqawwamat" [Gulf Identity: the Term and the Fundamentals]. *Shu'un Ijtima'iyya* [Journal of Social Affairs – published by the Sociological Association of the United Arab Emirates] 35, 9 (Fall 1992).

68 Ahmad Ali al-Haddad, "tatawwur al-shakhsiyya al-khalijiyya" [The Development of Gulf Identity]. *Shu'un Ijtima'iyya* [Journal of Social Affairs – published by the Sociological Association of the United Arab Emirates] 35, 9 (Fall 1992), p. 167.

69 Shafiq Nathim al-Ghabra, "al-shakhsiyya al-khalijiyya wa tahaddiyyat al-namu" [Gulf Identity and the Challenges of Development], *Shu'un Ijtima'iyya* 35, 9 (Fall 1992), pp. 193–194; Munira Fakhru, "mahfum al-shakhsiyya al-khalijiyya" [An Understanding of Gulf Identity]. *Shu'un Ijtima'iyya* 35, 9 (Fall 1992), pp. 223–224.

70 Turki al-Hamad, "hal hunak shakhsiyya khalijiyya?" [Is There a Gulf Identity?]. *Shu'un Ijtima'iyya* 35, 9 (Fall 1992), p. 177; and Abd al-Karim Hamud al-Dukhayl, "al-shakhsiyya al-khalijiyya: al-mu'aththarat wa al-khasa'is" [Gulf Identity: Influences and Particularities]. *Shu'un Ijtima'iyya* 35, 9 (Fall 1992), pp. 208–209.

71 *al-Hayat*, July 25, 1996, p. 4.

72 *al-Hayat*, June 3, 1996, pp. 1, 6.

73 Abbas Salman, "Behrain plot suspects say they trained in Iran," Reuters (on-line), June 5, 1996.

6   Collective identity and conflict management in Southeast Asia

Amitav Acharya

Introduction: security communities and Non-Atlantic Areas

When Karl Deutsch and his associates first proposed the idea of security community, they were seeking to explain the emergence of cooperation among the developed states of the north Atlantic region. Neither they, nor most of the other scholars who have used the concept since, have taken serious note of the possibility of security communities in the developing world. This is hardly surprising as the Third World is a rather disappointing arena for investigators looking for "a group that has become integrated, where integration is defined as the attainment of a sense of community, accompanied by formal or informal institutions or practices, sufficiently strong and widespread to assure peaceful change among members of a group with 'reasonable' certainty over a 'long' period of time."[1] If anything, conditions in much of the Third World have been exactly the reverse. As several studies establish, this is where the overwhelming majority of conflict and violence in the post-Second World War period has taken place.[2]

There is another reason why the idea of security community may not seem particularly applicable to the Third World, especially from the perspective of the more recent, and largely liberal, interpretation of the Deutschian notion. According to this school, security communities require a liberal-democratic milieu featuring significant economic interdependence and political pluralism.[3] As Adler puts it:

> Members of pluralistic security communities hold dependable expectations of peaceful change not merely because they share just any kind of values, but because they share *liberal democratic* values and allow their societies to become interdependent and linked by trans-

national economic and cultural relations. Democratic values, in turn, facilitate the creation of strong civil societies . . . which also promote community bonds and common identity and trust through the process of the free interpenetration of societies . . .[4]

Adler and John Vasquez explicitly invoke the Kantian notion of democratic peace as the philosophical basis of the concept of security communities.[5] In their view, a true security community is "democratic security community."[6] Similarly, the Kantian dictum that "the spirit of commerce . . . cannot exist side by side with war,"[7] has been incorporated into the liberal interpretation of security communities.[8] To be sure, Deutsch himself was concerned with more than just economic interdependence, using a wide range of indicators to measure integration, including international trade, mail flows, student exchanges, travel and so on and so forth. But like functionalists and interdependence theorists,[9] he too assumed that the growth of transactions increased the likelihood of pacific relations among the concerned states and societies.

If the emergence of security communities is assumed to be contingent upon liberal politics and economics, then the concept would appear to have limited utility in studying Third World security dynamics. Illiberal politics tends to be the hallmark of Third World states. Regional economic interdependence and integration in the Third World, as one study concludes, had been "much more rudimentary than in Europe, more obscure in purpose and uncertain in content."[10] Moreover, the two features seem to be mutually reinforcing. In the 1970s, neo-functionalists such as Ernst Haas and Joseph Nye pointed out that the absence of domestic pluralism was a major reason why European Community-style regional integration did not flourish in the Third World.[11] This, in turn, meant that Third World regional sub-systems could not benefit from the pacific effects of interdependence. In sum, from a liberal perspective, a high dose of authoritarian politics and relatively low levels of intra-regional economic interdependence render the Third World particularly inhospitable for the emergence of regional security communities.

What then explains the fact that in Southeast Asia, the members of the Association of Southeast Asian Nations (ASEAN), defying all expectations, have not fought a war against each other since 1967?[12] Admittedly, this is a shorter time frame for judging ASEAN's claim to be a security community than that of other recognized security communities in North America and Western Europe. But the ASEAN record is a significant one, especially when compared with the pervasive conflict and violence in most other Third World regions, such as the Middle East, Southern Asia, Africa, and Central America (although, as Andrew Hurrell's contribution to this volume suggests, contemporary Latin America, especially the Southern Cone countries, may be an exception to this). What is even more remarkable is that the members of ASEAN may have evolved toward a security community without sharing liberal-democratic values[13] or a substantial degree of intra-regional economic interdependence. Thus, while ASEAN may not appear to be a full-fldged security community in the classic Deutschian sense, the absence of war among the ASEAN members since 1967 poses a challenge to the liberal conception of security communities and deserves careful scrutiny.

My proposed framework of using the idea of security community to examine the evolution and role of ASEAN is also addressed to the debate between neorealism and neoliberal institutionalism. The very idea of security community is profoundly subversive of the entire realist tradition, especially, as Andrew Linklater put it, its emphasis on "the continuing primacy of strategic interaction and the need for states to steadily advance their understanding of how to realize their national interests and outmanoeuvre and control adversaries under conditions of conflict."[14] Deutsch's work represented one of the earliest challenges to realism's belief in the necessity and inevitability of war. While contemporary neorealists tend to view the sources of change in world politics as shifts, often violent, in the distribution of power, the idea of security community denotes the possibility of change being a fundamentally peaceful and sociological process, with its sources lying in the "perceptions and identifications" of actors.[15] International relations can be conceptualized as a process of social learning and community-formation.

While neorealists find it difficult to think in terms of community in international relations, neoliberal institutionalists adopt an explicitly rationalist and materialist conception of state behavior, often ignoring the sociological and intersubjective processes underlying the emergence of cooperation. (Admittedly, this is far more true of neoliberal institutionalism than the classical integration theorists.) For neoliberal institutionalists, the emergence of cooperation is largely or primarily a function of measurable linkages and utility-maximizing transactions. In contrast, building security communities involves a highly self-conscious, socio-psychological, and "imaginative" dynamic. The idea of cooperation in a security community is deeply embedded in a collective identity which is more than just the sum total of the shared interests of the individual actors. In this respect, the concept of security community shares two of the fundamental premises of the constructivist theory of international relations, that "the key structures in the states system are intersubjective, rather than material"; and that "state identities and interests are in important part constructed by these social structures, rather than given exogenously to the system by human nature or domestic politics."[16]

Moreover, actor relationships within security communities may be qualitatively different from those associated with the idea of security institutions or regimes popular in the literature on neoliberal institutionalism. To be sure, most security communities are anchored in formal or informal institutions, including regimes,[17] which promote norms and principles of conduct, constrain unilateral preferences, facilitate information-sharing, and build mutual predictability and trust. But as I have argued elsewhere,[18] a security regime or institution may develop within an otherwise adversarial relationship in which the use of force is inhibited by the existence of a balance of power or mutual deterrence situation (for example, the common interest of the USA and the Soviet Union with regard to nuclear weapons and non-proliferation measures has been cited as an example of a security regime[19]). A security community usually implies a fundamental, unambiguous and long-term *convergence* of interests among the actors in the avoidance of war. While institutions and regimes (security or otherwise) do not always or necessarily work to "constrain" the use of force and produce cooperation, in the case of security communities, the non-use of force is already assumed. To put it bluntly, to qualify as a security community, institutions and regimes must be accompanied by the growth of "symbols, attitudes and expectations of community."[20] There is another major difference between the idea of a security regime and that of a security community. In a security regime, competitive arms acquisitions and contingency planning usually continue, although specific regimes might be created to limit the spread of weapons and military capabilities. The absence of war within the regime may be due to short-term factors and considerations, such as the economic and political weakness of actors otherwise prone to violence or to the existence of a balance of power or mutual deterrence situation. A security community not only features strict and observed norms concerning non-use of force, there must also be an absence of competitive arms acquisitions or "arms racing" within the grouping.

The differences between security communities, institutions, and security regimes could be overstated, however. A security community may develop initially as a regime. In this context, the framework proposed by Adler and Barnett is particularly useful. Modifying the Deutschian framework, they sketch a social constructivist and path-dependent approach to the development of security communities, identifying three stages in the development of such communities: "nascent," "ascendant," and "mature."[21] A nascent phase is marked by common threat perceptions, expectations of mutual trade benefits, and some degree of shared identity. The ascendant phase is marked by tighter military coordination, lessened fears on the part of one actor that others within the grouping represent a threat, and the beginnings of cognitive transition and intersubjective processes and collective identities "that begin to encourage dependable expectations of peaceful change." The main characteristics of the mature phase are greater institutionalization, supranationalism, a high degree of trust, and low or no probability of military conflicts. A mature stage may be "loosely coupled" (a minimalist version), or "tightly coupled." The latter variety is marked by an increasingly supranational identity, in which the right to use force is legitimate only against external threats or against community members that defect or return to "old ways." It is important to note that the distinction between "loose" and "tight" security communities cannot be a sharp one, and there may be considerable overlap between "nascent," "ascendant" and "mature." The attributes of an earlier stage of a security community, particularly the "nascent" stage, may indeed resemble those of a security regime. The evolutionary nature of the Adler and Barnett model to some extent narrows the gap between neo realist, neo liberal and constructivist conceptions of security cooperation, and makes it easier to conduct systematic and serious research into the development of security communities by going beyond of the classic Deutschian model.

The origins and evolution of ASEAN: threats, interests, and identities

At a first glance, the ASEAN experience does not sit easily with the suggested pathway toward security communities. There is no doubt that promoting a regional security community in the Deutschian sense was a primary objective of ASEAN's founders when they launched the grouping in 1967. The founding of ASEAN immediately followed the end of Indonesia's policy of "Confrontation" against newly independent Malaysia and Singapore, which had proved costly for Indonesia's economic development and the region's stability. Thus, preventing a repetition of such inter-state confrontation and developing a mechanism for the pacific settlement of disputes were major considerations behind ASEAN's formation.[22]

ASEAN was also a product of shared threat perceptions. Yet, the threat that its founding members were responding to was not necessarily external. That commonly perceived external threats act as a catalyst of international cooperation is usually a tenet of the realist theory of alliances. Security communities are in many ways different from alliances. A distinction can be made between a security community which is essentially inward-looking, i.e., geared toward war prevention and conflict-resolution within the grouping, and an alliance, which is an outward-looking group geared more towards common defence against external threats.[23] Nonetheless, a commonly perceived threat can moderate and inhibit conflicts among actors within a grouping and hence could be important in the early evolution of security communities.

Following its inception, external threat perceptions among the original ASEAN members (Indonesia, Malaysia, Thailand, Singapore, and the Philippines) rarely converged. For much of the 1970s and 1980s, Singapore and Thailand viewed Vietnam as a major security threat, while Indonesia and Malaysia saw China as the more dangerous, if long-term, threat to national security and regional order. The important factor behind the evolution of ASEAN regionalism, however, was a common sense of vulnerability to the enemy within, particularly the threat of communist insurgency.[24] Admittedly, the communist threat was magnified by the possibility of external backing (especially Vietnamese and Chinese), but ASEAN members recognized that the conditions that sustained insurgencies in the region had more to do with their internal social, economic and political conditions.[25]Not only were internal threats more pressing, but mutual cooperation against the transborder movement of communist guerrillas, including intelligence-sharing, mutual extradition treaties, and joint border patrols and counter-insurgency operations served as an important basis for intra-ASEAN solidarity, while bilateral border committees set up to deal with insurgents proved useful as a direct channel for handling territorial disputes.[26] The security perceptions of ASEAN members were, and continue to be, inward-looking in which overcoming insurgency and preventing a recurrence of inter-state war took precedence over organizing an alliance against a common external threat.[27]

ASEAN's origin was also influenced by the desire of the members to enhance economic cooperation for mutual gain. As with other parts of the Third World, the progress of the European Community served as an inspiration for ASEAN's own efforts. But the ASEAN members were not interested in emulating the EC model. The vision of EC's founders, for whom regional integration meant at least a partial surrender of the member states' sovereignty, was neither feasible nor desirable for the ASEAN leaders. ASEAN was conceived as a framework which will allow its members to preserve their independence and advance their national interests, rather than promote supranationalism. Instead of pursuing EC-style trade liberalisation which might would have involved major national sacrifices on the part of its economically less-advanced members (ASEAN economies not only lacked complimentarity, but were, and continue to be, at differing stages of development), ASEAN's economic objective was to improve its external economic climate through collective bargaining with its major trading partners. As one observer noted:

> ASEAN regionalism is stronger in its external relations than in intra-ASEAN cooperation. Thus, ASEAN economic regionalism takes the form of a joint effort in securing a larger external market and better terms for exports rather than in establishing a customs union or a free trade area *vis-à-vis* the non-ASEAN countries.[28]

The relatively low priority attached by ASEAN to intra-regional trade also suggests an approach to community-building that is quite different from the path outlined by Deutsch. For Deutsch, a security community is the end product, or terminal condition, of a process of integration which is driven by the need to cope with the conflict-causing effects of increased transactions. The growing volume and range of transactions – political, cultural, or economic – increases the opportunities for possible violent conflict among actors. This throws a "burden" on the actors to devise institutions and practices for peaceful adjustment and change.[29] In this sense, the attributes of a security community, such as the "institutions, processes, and habits of peaceful change and adjustment are developed in such a manner as to keep pace with the increasing volume of transaction and adjustment problems thrown upon them." But the emergence and consolidation of ASEAN took place in a climate of fairly low level of intra-regional transactions and interdependence. Even today, ASEAN's trade with non-ASEAN members is significantly higher than intra-ASEAN trade (which has rarely risen above 20 percent of the total trade of its members). Collective bargaining geared to helping the position and goals of ASEAN members in the global economy has remained the key economic role of ASEAN; it is only in the 1990s that ASEAN begun to experiment with EC-style market-integration.

Thus, the political (responding to a common internal threat) and economic (fostering greater external economic clout) imperatives outlined above, while important, were not sufficient to trigger the process of community-building in ASEAN. As Adler and Barnett remind us, progress toward a security community involves and requires the development of a collective identity. In making this assertion, they draw upon Deutsch's view of security community-building as an exercise in identity-formation. In the development of security communities, Deutsch held, "the objective compatibility or consonance of major values of the participating populations" is to be "supplemented by indications of common subjective feelings of legitimacy of the integrated community, making loyalty to it also a matter of internalized psychic compulsion."[30] Important to this process is the element of "identification," defined as "the deliberate promotion of processes and sentiments of mutual identification, loyalties, and 'we'-feelings."[31]

The work of Benedict Anderson, who shares with Deutsch an interest in the study of nationalism, also focusses on the inter-subjective and deliberate nature of the community-building process. Anderson argues that nationalism, especially in Southeast Asia, developed despite significant objective differences – ethnic, cultural, linguistic, and economic – within the territorial units brought under a centralized colonial administration. For example, thanks to the introduction of a standardized education system and centralized bureaucracy by the colonial regime seeking to meet its administrative requirements, nationalism in Indonesia emerged among disparate and distantly located ethnic groups with little previous knowledge and contact among each other. Subsequently, the indigenous elite found nationalism a powerful tool in its efforts to drive out the colonial power and consolidate its own rule, and promoted it through a "systematic, even Machiavellian, instilling of nationalist ideology through the mass media, the educational system, administrative regulations, and so forth."[32] While Anderson is concerned primarily with community-building within the nation-state, his work has obvious relevance to understanding the process of community-building between states. Like the former, the latter can be one vast exercise in collective self-imagination and identity-formation. Communities can be constructed even in the absence of cultural similarities or economic transactions between groups through the creation and manipulation of norms, institutions, symbols, and practices that significantly reduces the likelihood of conflictual behavior.

Constructivist theory owes an intellectual debt (largely unacknowledged) to both Deutsch and Anderson in presenting a sociological view of international relations in which states develop collective interests and identities within an intersubjective structure that gradually lead to a transformation of Westphalian anarchy. Constuctivists argue that collective identities among states are constructed by their social interactions, rather than given exogenously to them by human nature, domestic politics, or, one might add, the international distribution of power. Viewed in these terms, regional cooperation among states is not necessarily a function of immutable or pre-ordained variables such as physical location, common historical experience, level of economic development, shared values, cultural affinities, and ideological convergence. Rather, regionalism may emerge and consolidate itself within an intersubjective setting of dynamic interactions consisting of "shared understandings, expectations, and social knowledge embedded in international institutions and threat complexes . . ."[33]

Without a constructivist understanding, it would be difficult to explain the emergence of ASEAN. The exogenous variables in ASEAN regionalism were not conducive to the development of a collective identity. Southeast Asia, described by historian D. G. E. Hall as a "chaos of races and languages,"[34] was hardly an ideal setting for regional cooperation. The members of ASEAN were, and remain to date, remarkably divergent in terms of their colonial heritage, postcolonial political setting, level of economic development, ethnic composition, and linguistic/cultural make-up.[35] A year before ASEAN's formation, Kenneth T. Young, a former US ambassador to Thailand, observed about Southeast Asia: "This is a so-called region without any feeling for community, without much sense of shared values and with few common institutions."[36] Thus, the remarkable growth of regionalism and collective problem-solving that followed ASEAN's formation attests to the constructivist claim that irrespective of their exogenous material circumstances, "through interaction, states might form collective identities and interests,"[37] which in turn might enable them to overcome their security dilemma.

Community-building involves a certain convergence of values, although, as argued earlier, these need not be liberal-democratic values. In the case of ASEAN, anti-communism (but not adherance to liberal democracy) and a general preference for capitalist economic development (albeit state-controlled) over the socialist model,[38] served as important factors binding an otherwise diverse membership. ASEAN members were never reticent in their use of these values to articulate their distinctiveness in relation to the ideological and economic currents sweeping in the communist societies of Indo-china. Moreover, ASEAN's "free-market," "anti-communist," and "pro-Western" image gained it siginificant international recognition, and brought political and economic support from the West. Against this backdrop, ASEAN regionalism developed as a highly deliberate process of elite socialisation involving the creation of norms, principles, and symbols aimed at the management of diversity and the development of substantive regional cooperation.

This was clearly foreshadowed by a founder of ASEAN, former Foreign Minister S. Rajaratnam of Singapore. While the first ever ASEAN declaration (the Bangkok Declaration of 1967) had assured its members that the grouping would "preserve their national identities," Rajaratnam argued that this objective needed to be reconciled with the development of a "regional existence." In his view, the success of ASEAN depended on "a new way of thinking about our problems." Since ASEAN member states had been used to viewing intra-mural problems from the perspective of their national interests or existence, the shift to a "regional existence means painful adjustments to those practices and thinking in our respective countries."[39]

Collective identity and conflict management in ASEAN

Both in the Deutschian and inconstructivist formulations, collective identity is a process that leads to the "structural transformation of the

Westphalian states system from anarchy to authority."[40] In the ASEAN context, collective identity may be understood as a process and framework through which its member states slowly began to adapt to a "regional existence" with a view to reducing the likelihood of use of force in inter-state relations. Four factors have played an important role in the development of a collective identity in ASEAN. The first is the practice of multilateralism. Multilateralism was a novel concept for ASEAN members, who had no significant previous experience in regional inter-state cooperation. Bilateralism had been the preferred mode of security relations and dispute settlement. For example, border disputes between Malaysia and Indonesia, or Malaysia and Thailand, were handled by bilateral joint border committees. Defence relations among the ASEAN members, such as military exercises and intelligence-sharing, were also kept at the bilateral level. Even today, ASEAN members continue to handle intra-ASEAN disputes and defense cooperation through bilateral channels. But such bilateralism has not been exclusionary, or directed against another ASEAN member, but rather has served as a complement to multilateralism. It is widely understood and agreed within ASEAN that contentious bilateral disputes are best handled through bilateral channels; while the ASEAN multilateral framework serves as a social and psychological barrier to extreme behavior, it does not have to deal with such conflicts directly and openly. The contribution of multilateralism to community-building lies not in providing a formal institutional mechanism for conflict resolution, but rather in encouraging the socialisation of elites which facilitates problem-solving. Jorgensen-Dahl captures this aspect of ASEAN multilateralism:

> ASEAN served a useful purpose by providing a framework within which the parties could discuss their differences in a "neutral" atmosphere . . . The multilateral framework allowed the parties to remain in contact in circumstances which either had caused a collapse of bilateral channels or placed these channels under such stress that they could no longer function properly . . . Through the steadily increasing scope and range of its activities . . . it produced among government officials . . . attitudes which were much more receptive and sensitive to each other's peculiar problems, and which made compromise solutions to conflicting interests a much more likely outcome than before . . . the multilateral setting served to discourage extreme behaviour, modify extravagant demands, and inspire compromise.[41]

The second element in ASEAN's collective identity is the development of what Noordin Sopiee calls the "ground rules of inter-state relations within the ASEAN community." [42] These norms are summed up by Musa Hitam, a senior Malaysian statesman, in the following terms:

> Because of Asean, we have been able to establish the fundamental ground rules for the game of peace and amity between us all. What are these fundamental ground rules? First, the principle of strict non-interference in each other's internal affairs. Second, the principle of pacific settlement of disputes. Third, respect for each other's independence. Fourth, strict respect for the territorial integrity of each of the Asean states . . . The Asean states have declared these ground rules . . . we have enacted them, we have imbibed them, and most important, we have acted and lived by them. [43]

The Treaty of Amity and Cooperation signed at the first ever summit meeting of ASEAN leaders in Bali in 1976, outlined the norms that were to form the basis of ASEAN's long journey. These norms include: (1) "Mutual respect for the independence, sovereignty, territorial integrity of all nations"; (2) "The right of every state to lead its national existence free from external interference, subversion and coercion"; (3) "Non-interference in the internal affairs of one another"; (4) "Settlement of differences and disputes by peaceful means"; and (5) "renunciation of the threat of use of force." [44]

This normative framework of ASEAN served as the basis of its collective opposition to Vietnam's invasion and occupation of Cambodia during the 1978–89 period. ASEAN, which had earlier sought to coopt Vietnam into a system of regional order founded on these norms, now saw the Vietnamese invasion as a gross violation of the principle of non-intervention in the internal affairs of states as well as the principle of non-use of force in inter-state relations. [45] As a result, ASEAN not only organized an international campaign to isolate Vietnam, but also spearheaded the diplomatic search for a settlement of the Cambodia conflict that would undo the Vietnamese occupation. In this process, ASEAN lost no opportunity to present itself in a more favourable international light *vis-à-vis* Hanoi. Vietnamese "expansionism" was contrasted with ASEAN's "good-neighborliness" and desire for regional political stability (implying territorial and political status quo in Southeast Asia), Vietnam's alliance with the Soviet Union with ASEAN's professed goal of a Zone of Peace, Freedom and Neutrality (ZOPFAN) in Southeast Asia, Vietnam's intense nationalism and ideological fervour with ASEAN's pragmatism and developmentalism, and Vietnam's military suppression of the Cambodian rebels with ASEAN's efforts for a political settlement of the conflict. ASEAN's Cambodia posture served not only to enhance its international stature (hence giving it a distinctive identity in international diplomacy), but also to strengthen its intra-mural solidarity. It motivated ASEAN members to overcome conflicting security interests and territorial disputes within the grouping, thereby moving it further in the path toward a security community.

A third and somewhat more discreet element of identity-building in ASEAN involves the creation and manipulation of symbols. Deutsch's work suggests that institutions and organizations by themselves cannot sustain a security community in the absence of a common devotion to "some symbol or symbols representing this security community."[46] A. P. Cohen argues that when the members of a given social group develop differences in their orientations and attitudes toward community-building, then "the consciousness of community has to be kept alive through manipulation of its symbols."[47] The ASEAN experience provides interesting examples of this. The prominent ASEAN symbols in the arena of conflict-management are the so-called "ASEAN Spirit" and the "ASEAN Way." These symbols have been invoked on countless occasions to reduce bilateral tensions among the ASEAN members, especially those between Malaysia and Singapore (conflicts rooted in ethnic and nationalist tensions as well as territorial disputes), Malaysia and the Philippines (especially the dispute over Sabah), and Singapore and the Philippines (over Philippine migrant workers in Singapore). For example, when Malaysia and the Philippines broke diplomatic relations over the latter's claim to the Malaysian state of Sabah, what helped the two sides to reduce their bilateral tensions was not the formal arbitration by ASEAN (no such mechanism was available until 1976) nor mediation by fellow ASEAN members, which, with the exception of Indonesia, stayed out of the dispute, but "because of the great value Malaysia and the Philippines placed on ASEAN."[48] The moderation of the Sabah dispute, which threatened to nip the ASEAN experiment in the bud in the later part of the 1960s, was an important psychological milestone for ASEAN's conscious promotion of a security community.

Since then, ASEAN members have claimed to have developed a particular approach to conflict-reduction within the grouping that is commonly referred to as the "ASEAN Way."[49] This in itself has two main aspects.[50] The first is avoidance of formal mechanisms and procedures of conflict-resolution. This preference for informal ways in international behavior is considered by some ASEAN commentators to be a "cultural trait."[51] In the ASEAN setting, formal institutions and procedures of dispute-settlement are considered secondary to the development of social-psychological processes that facilitate conflict prevention and management.[52] This representation is at least partly a conscious effort to differentiate ASEAN from institutional mechanisms elsewhere, especially the CSCE/OSCE. For example, formal measures of confidence-building and arms control, which have proved essential in the development of a post-Cold War security architecture in Europe, are viewed in ASEAN with profound distrust. In the view of ASEAN members, adopting such measures would amount to an admission that an adversarial relationship already exists between them. Such a perception is detrimental to the development of a sense of community, or "we-feeling"within the grouping. Another example is the working of ASEAN's Treaty of Amity and Cooperation. This Treaty (under Chapter IV, Articles 13 to 17) provides for an official dispute settlement mechanism, called a High Council, consisting of ministerial level representatives from each member state. This Council, as a continuing body, is supposed "to take cognizance of the existence of disputes and situations likely to disturb regional peace and harmony" and "in the event no solution is reached through direct negotiations," to "recommend to the parties in dispute appropriate means of settlement such as good offices, mediation, inquiry or conciliation." But to this date, ASEAN members have not convened a meeting of the High Council, despite the existence of numerous intramural disputes.

ASEAN's protagonists refuse to view its failure to invoke the dispute settlement mechanism as a manifestation of weak regionalism, as some critics have suggested.[53] Noordin Sopiee argues that its chief contribution to conflict-resolution is "the intangible but real 'spirit' of ASEAN, which has been effective in "sublimating and diffusing conflicts as in actually resolving them."[54] Unlike regional multilateral organizations in Europe, Africa and Latin America, ASEAN's approach to conflict-resolution rests on an assumed capacity to manage disputes within its membership without resorting to formal, multilateral measures.

A second aspect of the ASEAN Way is the principle of consensus. The consensus approach traces its origins to traditional Indonesian

village culture, particularly its notion of *musjawarah* (consultations)
and *mufakat* (consensus). As a former Indonesian Foreign Minister
once put it, in *musjawarah,* negotiations take place "not as between
opponents but as between friends and brothers."[55] Another goal of
the process, Malaysian scholar Mak Joon Nam points out, is to create
an" amalgamation of the most acceptable views of each and every
member." In such a situation, "all parties have power over each
other."[56] In commenting on the value of consultations and consensus,
Jorgensen-Dahl observes that "a residue of goodwill based on feelings
of brotherhood and kinship may serve the same purpose as oil on
rough sea. They take the edges of the waves and make for smooth
sailing."[57]

It is easy to be skeptical of the ASEAN Way. Although ASEAN has
functioned with a bureaucratic apparatus which had been kept
deliberately small and weak, it is not as loose an institution as it
claims to be. Formal agendas, structured meetings, and legalistic
procedures are quite evident in ASEAN's approach to political and
economic cooperation (particularly in the development of the ASEAN
Free Trade Area and the recently created Southeast Asia Nuclear
Weapon-Free Zone Treaty). But the ASEAN brand of "soft regionalism," which relies primarily on consultations and consensus, serves
as a useful, if not entirely accurate, symbol of its collective uniqueness,
and has been a source of considerable satisfaction and pride for
ASEAN members in the international stage. ASEAN members have
become so confident of their approach that they have offered it as the
basis for a wider framework of confidence-building and conflict
reduction in the Asia Pacific region. For example, the ASEAN
Regional Forum, a newly created security institution for the wider
region, is self-consciously emulating ASEAN's norms (such as those
contained in the Treaty of Amity and Cooperation) and procedures
(especially the consensus method). This has meant the rejection of the
"heavily institutionalised" CSCE/OCSE, with its Conflict Prevention
Centre, Missions of Long Duration, and the Valletta Mechanism for
Peaceful Resolution of Disputes, as a possible model for conflict
resolution in the Asia Pacific region, as suggested in early Russian,
Australian and Canadian proposals.[58]

A fourth element in collective identity formation in ASEAN is the
principle of regional autonomy. This was articulated by Adam Malik,
Indonesia's former Foreign Minister and a founding father of ASEAN,
in 1975: "Regional problems, i.e. those having a direct bearing upon

the region concerned, should be accepted as being of primary concern to that region itself. Mutual consultations and cooperation among the countries of the region in facing these problems may . . . lead to the point where the views of the region are accorded the primacy they deserve in the search for solution."[59] ASEAN's quest for regional autonomy was initially shaped by a concern, prevalent in the Cold War milieu, that regional conflicts not managed at the regional level would invite intervention by outside powers, which in turn would aggravate existing intra-regional tensions and polarisation. ASEAN's declaration of a ZOPFAN in Southeast Asia in 1971 expressed its collective commitment to a non-aligned international posture. It reinforced ASEAN's normative framework for conflict regulation; apart from championing the principles of mutual non-interference, non-intervention, and non-use of force, the ZOPFAN concept also committed the ASEAN members to shy away from alliances with foreign powers, to refrain from inviting or giving consent to intervention by external powers in the domestic affairs of the regional states, to abstain from involvement in any conflict of powers outside the zone, and to ensure the removal foreign military bases in the territory of zonal states.[60] ZOPFAN became another powerful ASEAN symbol, invoked by members to underscore the danger of great power rivalry and the need for security self-reliance. Although the principles concerning foreign alliances and bases have never been seriously pursued, ASEAN has managed to keep the concept alive through verbal manipulation. Thus, Singapore, Malaysia and other ASEAN countries have stepped up cooperation with the US navy through "access arrangements," while strongly rejecting the need for foreign military "bases," while an Australian-Indonesia agreement providing for mutual consultations in the event of external threats is described as a "security agreement," not an "alliance."

Taken together, the practice of multilateralism, the ASEAN norms, the "ASEAN Way," and the principle of regional autonomy constitute the basis of ASEAN's collective identity. They have helped mobilize the attention of its members to the danger of inter-state conflict, prevented unilateral action, and served as the basis of interactions on political, economic, strategic, and cultural issues. They served as a rallying point for ASEAN members in dealing with external security challenges. Moreover, they have emboldened ASEAN members to the extent that the latter has offered the ASEAN approach to conflict management as a model for other regions to follow. ASEAN has provided both its own ideas and its institutional framework as the basis for organizing security cooperation at the wider Asia Pacific level, a process in which ASEAN claims leadership over such Great Power, as the US, Russia, Japan, and China.[61]

Avoiding war in Southeast Asia

Since 1967, Southeast Asia has come a long way in the path of regional cooperation. Kusuma Snitwongse claims that while ASEAN might not have realised its goal of security self-reliance, "its most notable achievement has been community building."[62] In the specific area of war-avoidance, Michael Leifer notes: "one can claim quite categorically that ASEAN has become an institutionalized vehicle for intramural conflict avoidance and management . . . ASEAN has been able to prevent disputes from escalating and getting out of hand through containing and managing contentious issues."[63] Although there remains a number of conflicts among the ASEAN members,[64] with the exception of the Spratlys (which is more of a China-ASEAN, rather than intra-ASEAN, problem) these are quite mild in nature.[65] Malaysia, which has a territorial dispute with every other neighbouring ASEAN member, discounts the possibility of any "serious . . . confrontation or war . . . to solve our problems with our neighbours."[66] It can be safely asserted that no ASEAN country seriously envisages war against another at present. ASEAN thus meets an important criterion for pluralistic security communities, i.e., the "increasing unattractiveness and improbability of war among the political units of the emerging pluralistic security community as perceived by their governments, elites and (eventually) populations." [67]

The mere existence of disputes and conflicts within a group does not necessarily undermine its claim to be a security community. The distinguishing feature of a security community is its "ability to manage any conflicts within the region peacefully, rather than the absence of conflict per se."[68] As Deutsch put it, "even if some of the prospective partner countries [in a security community] find themselves on the opposite sides in some larger international conflict, they conduct themselves so as to keep actual mutual hostilities and damage to a minimum-or else refuse to fight each other altogether."[69]

But has ASEAN gone beyond being a war avoidance system? While common liberal-democratic values and interdependence need not be a prerequisite for their emergence, security communities could derive greater strength and vitality from these attributes. ASEAN has moved toward greater intra-regional interdependence and integration. At the inter-state level, an ASEAN Free Trade Area has been launched, while a proliferation of "growth triangles," or sub-regional economic zones featuring freer movement of transnational capital, labor and technology, testifies to the growing appeal of "market-driven regionalism" in Southeast Asia. Apart from intra-ASEAN integration, interdependence and institution-building involving the ASEAN members and other Asia Pacific nations (including the Asia Pacific Economic Cooperation) has made rapid progress, thereby providing an additional set of disincentives to the use of force within the region.[70]

But ASEAN has no comparable aspirations to become a "democratic security community." Unlike the EU, membership in ASEAN does not require a liberal-democratic polity. Non-democratic regimes, such as those in Burma and Vietnam, have been welcomed into the ASEAN fold. Some ASEAN members have even championed the virtues of "soft-authoritarianism" as a necessary framework for political stability and economic prosperity. ASEAN also refuses to develop a collective role in the promotion of human rights in the region, on the ground that such a role would conflict with its principle of non-interference. Thus ASEAN has countered an international campaign for sanctions against the military regime in Burma with its own calls for "constructive engagement."[71] While an ASEAN security community may function on the basis of an "authoritarian consensus," it also creates the risk that regime change in a member state might alter its commitment to regional cooperation, especially if the new regime blames the ASEAN framework for having condoned or supported the repressive policies of its predecessor. Moreover, to the extent that authoritarian governments in ASEAN (as in the case of Indonesia) face increasing demands for human rights and democratic governance from their own people, the idea of regional cooperation and community-building, including mutual responsiveness and socialisation, remains narrowly confined to the inter-governmental level. This kind of regionalism does not translate into cooperation or development of "we-feeling" at the societal level, as Deutsch clearly envisaged. It is important to note that in recent years, a network of indigenous non-governmental organizations has promoted a different kind of regionalism aimed at opposing human rights abuses by the ASEAN governments. The emergence of a regional civil society in Southeast Asia opposing the official ASEAN regionalism on issues of human rights, environment and democracy attests, at the very least, to the dissatisfactions with, and incompleteness of, the community-building enterprise led by the ASEAN elites.

Another factor affecting the prospects for a security community in ASEAN relates to interactive military planning and arms acquisitions by its members. While inter-state disputes in ASEAN have been muted, the armed forces of ASEAN states continue to plan for military contingencies involving each other.[72] Moreover, significant increases in defence spending and arms imports by the ASEAN states have been blamed by some analysts on "the widely underestimated competition and latent conflict which undoubtedly exists between various of ASEAN's members."[73] To be sure, interactive arms acquisitions are not widespread within the grouping,[74] and the military build-up in the region may be explained in terms of a host of non-interactive factors (such as the increased buying power of the ASEAN members, the post-Cold War buyer's market in arms, the prestige value of armaments, and prospects for commissions from manufacturers).[75] But to the extent that an emerging security community may be characterized by a situation in which not only "war among the prospective partners comes to be considered as illegitimate," but "serious preparations for it no longer command popular support,"[76] the pesisting tendency among ASEAN members to engage in con-tingency-planning and war-oriented resource mobilization against each other suggests important limits to community-building.

ASEAN's claim to be a security community also needs to be examined in the light of its expansion to include all the ten countries of Southeast Asia. In the past, an exclusionary attitude toward membership has been important to the development of the ASEAN identity. ASEAN has refused Sri Lanka's desire to join the grouping and dismissed either India, China or Australia (although none of these had formally applied for membership) ever acquiring member-ship status. But ASEAN has always professed the vision of "One Southeast Asia," which has now emerged as an important new symbol of ASEAN's post-Cold War direction. Yet, an expanded ASEAN may be a mixed blessing. Although it will extend ASEAN's norms to the entire Southeast Asia region, one cannot say with a great deal of confidence whether the ASEAN identity and the ASEAN Way of decision-making will survive into the expanded ASEAN. The new ASEAN members have little experience in multilateralism; the problem is compounded by the fact that the new ASEAN members will bring with them their own load of bilateral and multilateral disputes, which now have to be accommodated and moderated within the ASEAN framework.[77] These impose new burdens on ASEAN regionalism which will test existing ASEAN norms and may contribute to an unravelling of the organisation. An expanded ASEAN may make it more difficult for the grouping to achieve consensus on key issues. The danger is compounded by ASEAN's decision to become deeply engaged in developing a framework for Asia Pacific security cooperation, which would involve a much larger number of actors, including most of the great powers of the contemporary international system. It is highly unlikely that the painstakingly developed ASEAN Way with its particularistic symbols and processes of socialization can be replicated at the wider regional level. The extension of ASEAN's horizons may not only dilute the ASEAN identity, but also challenge its resolve to "stay united in the face of . . . pushes and pulls exerted upon it by the dynamics of international politics and diplomacy," as Malaysia has warned with reference to the danger of ASEAN members developing divergent responses to the complex and unpredictable political, economic, and security trends in the Asia Pacific region.[78] Thus, the case of ASEAN suggests the need for considering the possibility that the evolution of security communities need not be a linear process, but one that could be subject to disruption and decline as a result of burdens imposed from inside and outside.

Finally, in contrast to security communities in Europe and North America, ASEAN's practice of multilateralism does not extend to defence matters. Despite the proliferation of overlapping bilateral security ties, such as joint exercises and training, ASEAN members are reluctant to make a serious attempt at military integration. Ostensibly, bilateral ties within ASEAN are not directed against other members and are considered adequate in promoting mutual confidence and trust. But this argument obscures fundamental differences in threat perceptions and security priorities within the grouping that detract from its claim to be a security community. As a former chief of Malaysian defense forces acknowledges:

> Multilateralism may be possible if there is a collective belief that such an arrangement would bring mutual benefit to all members concerned. In other words there must be a convergence of security interest derived from a common perception of threat facing the individual members and the region as a whole. Presently this is

217

unlikely to happen simply because of differing security interests and needs. To a large extent this has been due to the long established security alignment with extra regional powers, domestic instability or fragility of the regime in power and also the uneven political and economic developments within ASEAN states.[79]

Conclusion

The ASEAN experience certainly challenges the neorealist preoccupation with anarchy and the inevitability of war as well as the rationalist and materialist foundations of cooperation assumed by the neo-liberal institutionalists. It also permits several generalizations that may be relevant to the constructivist project. The following are especially noteworthy: (1) community-building is a self-conscious exercise in learning and collective identity formation; (2) that this learning process may begin even in an illiberal domestic and regional political-economic setting; (3) it may proceed despite cultural and other differences and may help obscure, if not fundamentally override, these differences, (4) it can be promoted through the deliberate creation of, and adherence to, norms, symbols, and habits, and (5) it may not require the presence of a commonly perceived threat from an external source.

The idea of community is both a descriptive and a normative construct, one that not only describes a social group, but shapes it in that particular way. As Ole Wæver suggests in this volume, if states act as a community, there will be one. In the case of ASEAN, the intersubjective and symbolic notion of community preceded the formal process of integration and functional linkages. It developed despite low initial levels of interdependence and transactions, and the existence of substantial cultural and political differences among its members.

For ASEAN, developing a collective identity has involved a conscious attempt at differentiating itself from a variety of competing actors and processes. Thus, for much of the 1970s and 80s, ASEAN juxtaposed itself from the ideological orientation, economic policies, and security practices of the Indo-Chinese segment of Southeast Asia. It claimed for itself an exclusive role in the promotion of regionalism in Southeast Asia. Similarly, ASEAN's economic regionalism was carefully distinguished from the European Community model. In the post-Cold War era, ASEAN has sought to define its approach to conflict management in direct opposition to the security institutions and practices in Europe. Such exceptionalism has become a key aspect of the ASEAN security discourse, and has facilitated community-building.

The exercise in collective identity formation has contributed to ASEAN's progress toward a security community by lessening the likelihood of inter-state military confrontation. Four elements have been crucial to this process: multilateralism, norms, symbols, such as the ASEAN-Way of consensus-seeking and informal and non-lega-listic decision-making procedures, and a shared quest for regional autonomy. The ASEAN experience somewhat blurs the distinction between nascent, ascendant, and mature security communities. Several characteristics of a mature security community are present in Southeast Asia. These include: multilateralism, discourse and language of community, cooperative (but not collective) security, and policy coordination against internal threats. But to describe ASEAN as a mature security community will be inaccurate in the absence of a high level of military integration, common definition of external threat, and unfortified borders. While intra-ASEAN disputes are considerably muted today, and are highly unlikely to lead to outright war, there are lingering concerns about competitive arms acquisitions and an interactive contingency planning involving ASEAN members. These factors do detract from ASEAN's claim to be a security community in the Deutschian sense.[80] But they do fit the more differentiated and graduated conceptual framework introduced by Adler and Barnett in this volume, especially the concept of a "nascent" security community. While Southeast Asia may not be Europe or North America, ASEAN's record certainly compares favourably with all other parts of the Third World. Despite its limitations, the fact that no ASEAN member has been involved in a military confrontation with another since 1967 is a significant achievement, which cannot be explained by referring either to chance or accident or to exogenous variables such as geographic proximity, cultural affinity, or a favorable international balance of power.

Notes

1 Karl W. Deutsch, "Security Communities," in James Rosenau, ed., *International Politics and Foreign Policy* (New York: Free Press, 1961), p. 98.

2 One study by Evan Luard estimates that between 1945 and 1986, there were some 127 "significant wars." Out of these, only two occurred in

Europe, while Latin America accounted for twenty-six, Africa thirty-one, the Middle East, twenty-four, and Asia forty-four. According to this estimate, the Third World was the scene of more than 98 percent of all international conflicts. Evan Luard, *War in International Society* (London: I. B. Tauris, 1986), Appendix 5.

3 See Bruce Russett's contribution to this volume.

4 Emanuel Adler, "Europe's New Security Order: A Pluralistic Security Community," in Beverly Crawford, ed., *The Future of European Security* (Berkeley, CA: Center for German and European Studies, University of California, 1992), p. 293.

5 Vasquez uses the term "The Democratic Security Community." John M. Vasquez, ed., *Classics of International Relations*, 3rd edn (Upper Saddle River, NJ: Prentice Hall, 1966), pp. 288–289.

6 On the democratic peace, see Zeev Maoz and Bruce Russett, "Normative and Structural Causes of Democratic Peace, 1946–1986," in Vasquez, ed., *Classics of International Relations*, pp. 386–400; Dean V. Babst, "Elective Governments – A Force for Peace," in Vasquez, ed., *Classics of International Relations*, pp. 381–385.

7 Immanuel Kant, "Perpetual Peace: A Philosophical Sketch," in Vasquez, ed., *The Classics of International Relations*, p. 375.

8 For a review of arguments linking interdependence and peace, see Arthur Stein, "Governments, Economic Interdependence, and International Co-operation," in Philip Tetlock, et al., eds., *Behaviour, Society, and International Conflict*, (Oxford: Oxford University Press, 1989), pp. 244–254. See also Jack S. Levy, "The Causes of War: A Review of Theories and Evidence," in Philip E. Tetlock et al., eds., *Behaviour, Society and Nuclear War*, vol. 1 (New York: Oxford University Press, 1989); Robert O. Keohane and Joseph S. Nye, *Power and Interdependence: World Politics in Transition* (Boston: Little, Brown Co., 1977).

9 On functionalism and neofunctionalism, see David Mitrany, *A Working Peace System* (Chicago: Quadrangle Press, 1966); Ernst B. Haas, *The Uniting of Europe: Political, Economic and Social Forces, 1950–1957*, 2nd edn (Stanford: Stanford University Press, 1968); Joseph S. Nye, "Comparing Common Markets: A Revised Neo-Functional Model," in Leon Lindberg and Stuart Scheingold, eds., *Regional Integration: Theory and Research* (Cambridge, MA: Harvard University Press, 1971), pp. 192–231.

10 Lincoln Gordon, "Economic Regionalism Reconsidered," *World Politics* 13 (1961), p. 245 ; See also Charles A. Duffy and Werner J. Feld, "Whither Regional Integration Theory," in Gavin Boyd and Werner Feld, eds. *Comparative Regional Systems* (New York: Pergamon Press, 1980), p. 497.

11 Joseph S. Nye, "Central American Regional Integration," in Nye, ed., *International Regionalism* (Boston: Little, Brown, 1968), pp. 381–382; Haas acknowledged that the "application [of the neo-functionalist model] to the third world . . . sufficed only to accurately predict difficulties and failures of regional integration, while in the European case some successful

positive prediction has been achieved." Ernst Haas, "The Study of Regional Integration: Reflections on the Joys and Anguish of Pretheorising," in Richard A. Falk and Saul H. Mendlovitz, eds., *Regional Politics and World Order* (San Fransisco: W. H. Freeman, 1971), p. 117. See also Ernst Haas, "International Integration: The European and the Universal Process," in Leland Goodrich and David A. Key, eds., *International Organization: Politics and Process* (Madison: University of Wisconsin Press, 1973), pp. 397–423.

12   ASEAN was formed on 8 August 1967 with five member states: Indonesia, Malaysia, Singapore, Thailand and the Philippines. Brunei became a member in 1984, while Vietnam joined in 1995. In 1997, ASEAN admitted two new members, Burma and Laos, but Cambodia's entry was postponed because of its internal political crisis. An ASEAN-10, comprising all the ten countries of Southeast Asia, remains ASEAN's official policy objective.

13   On the ASEAN members' record on democratic governance, see: Mark R. Thompson, "The Limits of Democratisation in Southeast Asia," *Third World Quarterly* 14, 3 (1993), pp. 469–484; Don Emmerson, "Region and Recalcitrance: Rethinking Democracy Through Southeast Asia," *Pacific Review* 8, 2 (1995), pp. 223–248.

14   Andrew Linklater, "The Problem of Community in International Relations," *Alternatives* 15, 2 (1990), p. 144.

15   Donald J. Puchala, "The Integration Theorists and the Study of International Relations," in Charles W. Kegley and Eugene M. Wittkopf, eds., *The Global Agenda: Issues and Perspectives* (New York: Random House, 1984), p. 189.

16   Alexander Wendt, "Collective Identity Formation and the International State," *American Political Science Review* 88, 2 (June 1994), p. 385.

17   Richard W. Van Wagenen, *Research in the International Organization Field* (1952), cited in Ronald J. Yalem, ed., "Regional Security Communities and World Order," in George W. Keeton and George Scharzenberger, eds., *The Yearbook on International Affairs* (London: Stevens and Sons, 1979), p. 217.

18   Amitav Acharya, "A Regional Security Community in Southeast Asia?" *Journal of Strategic Studies* 18, 3 (September 1995), pp. 175–200.

19   Joseph S. Nye, "Nuclear Learning and U.S.–Soviet Security Regimes," *International Organization* 41 (Summer 1987), pp. 371–402.

20   Deutsch, "Security Communities," p. 100.

21   See their contribution to this volume.

22   J. Soedjati Djiwandono, "The Political and Security Aspects of ASEAN: Its Principal Achievements," *Indonesian Quarterly* 11 (July 1983), p. 20.

23   For a discussion of the distinction between "security community" and "alliance" or "defence community," see Amitav Acharya, "Association of Southeast Asian Nations: Security Community or Defence Community?," *Pacific Affairs* 64, 2 (Summer 1991), pp. 159–178; Acharya, "A Regional Security Community in Southeast Asia?"

24 Amitav Acharya, "Regionalism and Regime Security in the Third World: Comparing the Origins of the ASEAN and the GCC," in Brian L. Job, ed., *The (In)security Dilemma: National Security of Third World States* (Boulder, CO: Lynne Rienner, 1991), pp. 143–164.

25 ASEAN's security predicament conforms to that of the Third World countries in general, where threats from within often outweigh threats from outside. On the sources of Third World conflict and insecurity, see Mohammed Ayoob, "Security in the Third World: The Worm About to Turn," *International Affairs* 60, 1 (1984), pp. 41–51; Udo Steinbach, "Sources of Third World Conflict," in *Third World Conflict and International Security*, Adelphi Papers 166 (London: International Institute for Strategic Studies, 1981), pp. 21–28; Soedjatmoko, "Patterns of Armed Conflict in the Third World," *Alternatives* 10, 4 (1985), pp. 477–493; Edward Azar and Chung-in Moon, "Third World National Security: Towards a New Conceptual Framework," *International Interactions* 11, 2 (1984), pp. 103–135; Barry Buzan, "People, States and Fear: The National Security Problem in the Third World," in Edward Azar and Chung-in Moon, eds., *National Security in the Third World* (Aldershot: Edward Elgar, 1988), pp. 14–43; Yezid Sayigh, *Confronting the 1990s: Security in the Developing Countries*, Adelphi Papers no. 251 (London: International Institute for Strategic Studies, 1990); Mohammed Ayoob, "The Security Predicament of the Third World State," in Job, ed., *The (In)Security Dilemma*; Steven R. David, "Explaining Third World Alignment," *World Politics* 43, 2 (January 1991), pp. 232–256.

26 Amitav Acharya, *A Survey of Military Cooperation Among the ASEAN States: Bilateralism or Alliance*, Occasional Paper no.14 (Centre for International and Strategic Studies, York University, April 1990).

27 Muthiah Alagappa, "Comprehensive Security: Interpretations in Asean Countries," in Robert A. Scalapino et al., eds., *Asian Security Issues: Regional and Global* (Berkeley: University of California, Institute of East Asian Studies, 1988).

28 Narongchai Akrasanee, "Issues in ASEAN Economic Regionalism," in Karl D. Jackson and M. Hadi Soesastro, eds., *ASEAN Security and Economic Development* (Berkeley: University of California, Institute of East Asian Studies, 1984), p. 72.

29 Deutsch, "Security Communities," p.99.

30 Karl W. Deutsch, *The Analysis of International Relations* (Englewood Cliffs, NJ: Prentice-Hall, 1988), p. 272.

31 Ibid., p.272.

32 Benedict Anderson, *Imagined Communities*, revised and expanded edn (London: Verso, 1991), pp. 113–114.

33 Wendt, "Collective Identity Formation and the International State," p. 389.

34 D.G. E. Hall, *History of Southeast Asia* (London: Macmillan, 1964), p. 5.

35 For an account of the state of regional cooperation in Southeast Asia prior to ASEAN's formation, see: Arnfinn Jorgensen-Dahl, *Regional Organization and Order in Southeast Asia* (London: Macmillan, 1982), ch. 2; Bernard K.

Gordon, *East Asian Regionalism and United States Security* (McLean, VA: Research Analysis Corporation, 1968), pp. 42–50; Russell H. Fifield, *National and Regional Interests in ASEAN: Competition and Cooperation in International Politics*, Occasional Paper no. 57 (Singapore: Institute of Southeast Asian Studies, 1979), pp. 3–6.

36 Kenneth T. Young, "The Southeast Asia Crisis," in Lyman M. Tondel, ed., *The Southeast Asia Crisis* (Dobbs Ferry, NY: Oceana Publications, 1966), p. 5.

37 Alexander Wendt, "Collective Identity Formation and the International State," p. 384.

38 As a founder of ASEAN and Malaysia's former foreign minister put it:

> The concept of free enterprise as they apply [sic] in the ASEAN region is the philosophical basis of ASEAN. The appreciation of this is vital in the understanding of ASEAN and its sense of direction. The countries of the ASEAN region had come together to protect the system of free enterprise as a counterpoise against communism on the one hand and monopolistic capitalism on the other. When the leaders of Malaysia, Indonesia, Philippines, Singapore and Thailand got together in Bangkok in 1967 to officiate at the establishment of the Association of Southeast Asian Nations, they were in fact making a commitment to jointly strengthen and promote the system of free enterprise in their countries in the belief that together they could harness the strength of that system to bring about the kind of national and regional resilience that would serve as a bulwark against communism.

Mohammed Ghazali bin Shafie, "Confrontation Leads to ASEAN," *Asian Defence Journal* (February 1982), p. 31.

39 Cited in C. P. Luhulima, *ASEAN's Security Framework*, CAPA Reports no.22 (San Fransisco: Center for Asia Pacific Affairs, The Asia Foundation, November 1995), p. 1.

40 Wendt, "Collective Identity Formation and the International State," p. 393.

41 Jorgensen-Dahl, *Regional Organisation and Order in Southeast Asia*, pp. 56–57.

42 Noordin Sopiee, "ASEAN and Regional Security," in Mohammed Ayoob, ed. *Regional Security in the Third World* (London: Croom Helm, 1986), p. 229.

43 Text of keynote address by Datuk Musa Hitam delivered at the East–West Conference on ASEAN and the Pacific Basin, Honolulu, October 29, 1985, pp. 5–6.

44 Tarnthong Thongswasdi, "ASEAN After the Vietnam War: Stability and Development through Regional Cooperation," PhD dissertation, Claremont Graduate School, California, 1979, p. 123.

45 On ASEAN's response to the Vietnamese invasion of Cambodia see: Chan

Heng Chee, "The Interests and Role of ASEAN in the Indochina Conflict," paper presented to the International Conference on Indochina and Problems of Security and Stability in Southeast Asia" held at Chulalongkorn University, Bangkok, June 19–21, 1980, p. 12; Tim Huxley, *ASEAN and Indochina: A Study of Political Responses*, Canberra Studies in World Affairs no. 19 (Canberra: The Australian National University, Department of International Relations, 1985); Lau Teik Soon, "ASEAN and the Cambodia Problem" *Asian Survey* 22, 6 (June 1982); Michael Leifer, *ASEAN and the Security of Southeast Asia* (London: Routledge, 1989); Muthiah Alagappa, "Regionalism and the Quest for Security: ASEAN and the Cambodia Conflict," *Journal of International Affairs* (Winter, 1993), pp. 189–200.

46 Deutsch, "Security Communities," p. 100.

47 A. P. Cohen, *The Symbolic Construction of Community* (New York: Tavistock Publications, 1985), p.15.

48 Jorgensen-Dahl, *Regional Organisation and Order in Southeast Asia*; Lau Teik Soon, *Conflict-Resolution in ASEAN: The Sabah Issue* (Singapore: University of Singapore, Department of Political Science, undated).

49 For a more detailed discussion of the "ASEAN Way" and its role in building regional cooperation, see Amitav Acharya, "Ideas, Identity, and Institution-Building: From the 'ASEAN Way' to the 'Asia-Pacific Way'," *Pacific Review* 10, 3 (1997), pp. 319–346.

50 Mak Joon Num has identified some of the key features of the ASEAN process: "(1) it is unstructured, with no clear format for decision-making or implementation; (2) it often lacks a formal agenda, issues are negotiated on an *ad hoc* basis 'as and when they arise'; (3) it is an exercise in consensus-building; (4) decisions are made on the basis of unanimity; (5) decision-making can take a long time because of the need for consensus, there is no fixed time-table, negotiations may go on as long as it takes to reach a position acceptable to all parties; (6) it is closed, behind-the-scenes, lacking transparency." J. N. Mak, "The ASEAN Process ('Way') of Multilateral Cooperation and Cooperative Security: The Road to a Regional Arms Register?," paper presented to the MIMA-SIPRI workshop on An ASEAN Arms Register: Developing Transparency, Kuala Lumpur, October 2–3, 1995, p. 6.

51 Mohamed Jawhar Hassan, "The Asean Approach to Security: Cooperative or Comprehensive?," paper prepared for the International Conference on Preventive Diplomacy for Peace and Security in the Western Pacific," jointly sponsored by the 21st Century Foundation and The Pacific Forum CSIS, August 29–31, 1996, Taipei, Taiwan, p. 12.

52 For a detailed discussion of this aspect of ASEAN, see Donald Weatherbee, "ASEAN Regionalism: The Salient Dimension," in Karl D. Jackson and M. Hadi Soesastro, eds., *ASEAN Security and Economic Development* (Berkeley, CA: University of California, Institute of East Asian Studies, 1984), pp. 259–268. Deutsch's own work suggests a close and mutually reinforcing relationship between the formal institutions and organizations

of a security community on the one hand and the social-psychological processes that create the "we-feeling" among its members on the other. One is not viable without the other. Just as a security community cannot be achieved through a "sense of community or by persuasion unaccompanied by the growth of institutions and organizations," similarly a security community will not be viable if it had "only institutions and organizations but none of the psychological processes operating in and through people." See Deutsch, "Security Communities," p. 100.

53 Michael Leifer, "Debating Asian Security: Michael Leifer Responds to Geoffrey Wiseman," *Pacific Review* 5, 2 (1992), p. 169.

54 Sopiee, "ASEAN and Regional Security," p. 228.

55 Cited in Jorgensen-Dahl, *Regional Organisation and Order in Southeast Asia*, p. 166.

56 Mak, "The ASEAN Process ('Way') of Multilateral Cooperation and Cooperative Security," p. 5.

57 Jorgensen-Dahl, *Regional Organisation and Order in Southeast Asia*.

58 Trevor Findlay, "The European Cooperative Security Regime: New Lessons for the Asia-Pacific," in Andrew Mack and John Ravenhill, eds., *Pacific Cooperation: Building Economic and Security Regimes in the Asia-Pacific* (St Leonards, Australia: Allen and Unwin, 1994), p. 238.

59 Adam Malik, "Regional Cooperation in International Politics," in *Regionalism in Southeast Asia* (Jakarta: CSIS, Centre for Strategic and International Studies, 1975), p. 160.

60 Heiner Hanggi, *ASEAN and the ZOPFAN Concept* (Singapore: Institute of Southeast Asian Studies, 1991), p. 25.

61 Amitav Acharya, "ASEAN and Asia Pacific Multilateralism: Managing Regional Security," in Amitav Acharya and Richard Stubbs, eds., *New Challenges for ASEAN: Emerging Policy Issues* (Vancouver: University of British Columbia Press, 1995), pp. 182–202.

62 She adds:

> [ASEAN] members have come to a tacit agreement not to coerce one another and to limit the scope of bargaining. Other components of community building that have emerged in the sense of shared common interests and values, even if still limited, and of belonging together; these have been placed alongside a strong sense of nationalism in the ethos of the national leadership of member countries and advanced through the processs of dialogue and consultations.

> Kusuma Snitwongse, "Meeting the Challenges of Changing Southeast Asia," in Robert Scalapino, Seijabura Sato, and Sung-Joo Han, eds., *Regional Dynamics: Security, Political and Economic Issues in the Asia Pacific Region* (Jakarta: Centre for Strategic and International Studies, 1990), p. 40.

63 "ASEAN as a Model of a Security Community?" in Hadi Soesastro, ed., *ASEAN in a Changed Regional and International Political Economy* (Jakarta: Centre for Strategic and International Studies, 1995), p. 132.

64 These include the Malaysia-Singapore dispute over the Pedra Branca island off the coast of Johor, the Malaysia–Indonesia dispute over Sipadan and Ligitan islands in the Sulawesi Sea near the Sabah-Kalimantan border, the Thai–Malaysia dispute regarding their common order, the Malaysia–Brunei dispute over Limbang and the lingering Philippines–Malaysia dispute over Sabah. Additionally, a number of disputes exists in the maritime arena over issues such as boundaries demarcation, exclusive economic zones, fishing rights and resource exploitation. The Spratly Islands disputes, widely regarded as a flashpoint of regional tension in the post-Cold War era, involves four ASEAN members, Malaysia, the Philippines, Brunei, and Vietnam, along with two non-ASEAN claimants, China and Taiwan. See Bilveer Singh, "The Challenge of the Security Environment of Southeast Asia in the Post-Cold War Era," *Australian Journal of International Affairs* 47, 2 (1993), pp. 263–277; Amitav Acharya, *A New Regional Order in Southeast Asia: ASEAN in the Post-Cold War Era*, Adelphi Paper no. 279 (London: IISS, 1993).

65 Muthiah Alagappa, "The Dynamics of International Security in Southeast Asia: Change and Continuity," *Australian Journal of International Relations* 45, 1 (May 1991), pp. 1–37.

66 *The Straits Times* (Singapore), August 17, 1990, p. 22.

67 Deutsch, *The Analysis of International Relations*, p. 281.

68 Acharya, "A Regional Security Community in Southeast Asia?"

69 Deutsch, *The Analysis of International Relations*, p. 276.

70 Hadi Soesastro, "Economic Integration and Interdependence in the Asia Pacific: Implications for Security," paper presented at the Eighth Asia Pacific Roundtable, Kuala Lumpur, June 5–8, 1994, p. 1; Robert A. Scalapino, "Challenges to the Sovereignty of the Modern State," in Bunn Nagara and K.S. Balakrishnan, Proceedings of the Seventh Asia–Pacific Roundtable, *The Making of a Security Community in the Asia-Pacific* (Kuala Lumpur: ISIS Malaysia, 1994), p. 50.

71 Amitav Acharya, "Human Rights and Regional Order: ASEAN and Human Rights Management in Southeast Asia," in James Tang, ed., *Human Rights and International Relations in Asia-Pacific* (London: Frances Pinter, 1995), pp. 167–182.

72 See for example, Tim Huxley, "Singapore and Malaysia: A Precarious Balance," *Pacific Review* 4, 3 (1991), pp. 204–213

73 Tim Huxley, "South-East Asia's Arms Race: Some Notes on Recent Developments," *Arms Control* 11, 1 (May 1990), pp. 69–76.

74 Amitav Acharya, *An Arms Race in Post-Cold War Southeast Asia? Prospects for Control*, Pacific Strategic Papers no. 8 (Singapore: Institute of Southeast Asian Studies, 1994).

75 Panitan Wattanayagorn and Desmond Ball, "A Regional Arms Race," *Journal of Strategic Studies* 18, 3 (September 1995), pp. 147–174.

76 Ibid., p. 276.

77 Hari Singh, *Vietnam, ASEAN and Regional Cooperation in Southeast Asia*,

Eastern Asia Policy Papers no.17 (Toronto: University of Toronto – York University Joint Centre for Asia Pacific Studies, 1996).

78 Amitav Acharya, "The ARF Could Unravel," in Derek da Cunha, ed., *The Evolving Pacific Power Structure* (Singapore: Institute of Southeast Asian Studies, 1996).

79 Gen. Hashim Mohammed Ali, "Prospects for Defence and Security Cooperation in ASEAN," paper presented to the conference on: "ASEAN and the Asia-Pacific Region: Prospects for Security Cooperation in the 1990s," Manila June, 5–7, 1991, p. 5.

80 In a previous paper, "A Regional Security Community in Southeast Asia," *Journal of Strategic Studies*) I had chosen to characterize ASEAN as a "security regime" rather than a "security community." But this assessment was based on the classic Deutschian notion, rather than the more differentiated interpretation provided by Adler and Barnett. The concept of security regime as developed in my earlier paper shares many features of the "nascent" phase of pluralistic security communities as understood by Adler and Barnett

7 An emerging security community in South America?

Andrew Hurrell

I

The paucity of major wars in Latin America constitutes a major challenge to international relations theory and provides especially fertile ground for thinking about the nature of security communities. For the first half-century following independence, the region was beset by persistent and widespread wars of state formation and nation building, both internal and external. In this, as in so many other ways, Latin America foreshadowed the pattern of subsequent postcolonial conflicts and, by no stretch of the imagination, could be viewed as constituting a security community. However, since the late nineteenth century both the number and the intensity of interstate wars between Latin American states have been remarkably low – despite the existence of large numbers of protracted and militarized border disputes, many cases of the threatened use of force and of military intervention by outside powers, high levels of domestic violence and political instability, and long periods of authoritarian rule.[1]

Explanations follow predictable lines. Realists and neorealists look to geopolitical location, to the varying degree of insulation from extra-regional influences, and to the hegemonic or policing role of, first, Britain and then the United States. Within the region, they highlight the emergence of relatively autonomous regional balances of power (for example between Brazil, Argentina and Chile), as well as other material factors which worked to restrain conflict – the absence of transport links, borders that were geographically removed from centres of political and economic activity, and military technologies that made it extremely difficult to bring power to bear in offensive wars of conquest. Liberals look to shifting patterns of domestic politics, to the fortunes of democratization within states, to the quality and level of interdependence among states, to the pacifying impact of the region's insertion into the global economy, and to the role of institutions in helping states to maximize common interests. Marxists see the international relations of the region as reflective of developments in global capitalism with first Britain and then the United States intervening and manipulating local relationships in pursuit of their economic interests. Finally, international society theorists and constructivists stress the extent to which a shared cultural and historical experience, particular patterns of state formation and ongoing international interaction all combined to produce a strong regional diplomatic culture – a regional society of states which, although still often in conflict, conceived themselves to be bound by a common set of rules and shared in the workings of common institutions.

Rather than analyze historic patterns of conflict and cooperation across the region as a whole, this chapter concentrates on the southern cone and examines the relationship between Brazil and Argentina the extent of their historic rivalry, the shift from rivalry to cooperation that developed through the 1980s and 1990s, and the emergence of institutionalized economic and political cooperation in the form of Mercosur (The Southern Common Market). There are two reasons for adopting this approach. The first follows from the idea of a security community – a group of states in which "there is real assurance that the members of that community will not fight each other physically, but will settle their disputes in some other way."[2] Within such a community there must be dependable expectations of peaceful change, with military force gradually disappearing as a conceivable instrument of statecraft. A security community, then, necessarily involves the non-expectation of war of a very particular kind. Even if we can identify a zone of relative peace and even if we can see and hear much that suggests the existence of a security community, we need to look beyond positivist correlations across a large number of cases and examine instead the quality and internal constitution of a particular relationship and the causal mechanisms that may explain the emergence of a stable peace.

A meaningful security community cannot rest on the simple inability to fight (because of technology or geography), nor on a stable balance of deterrent threats, nor on coming together in the face of an external threat – all factors typically stressed by neorealists. But nor can it be based solely on instrumental interest-driven cooperative strategies of the kind analyzed by neoliberal or rationalist institutionalists. Although institutionalists stress the ways in which institutions promote cooperation, institutions remain rooted in the realities of power and interests and the core assumption of states as rational egoists allows only a very limited place for the redefinition of interests and identities. It is precisely the possible emergence of a situation in which cooperation goes beyond instrumental calculation and in which the use of force declines as a tool of statecraft that opens the door to constructivist theories. Building on constructivist insights, this chapter highlights the importance of historically constructed interests and identities, of learning and ideational forces, and of normative and institutional structures within which state interests are constructed and redefined.

Secondly, Brazil/Argentina represents both a very *significant* case because of the size and intrinsic importance of the two states, and a *hard* case because of their long tradition of rivalry and competition. As Robert Burr notes, "The theme of Argentine-Brazilian rivalry and struggle for influence in South America is the oldest of all the Latin American conflicts."[3] Rivalry (here in its etymologically purest sense) goes back to the recurrent conflict between the Spanish and Portuguese empires over the east bank of the Rio de la Plata and over control of the river system. Following the Portuguese invasion of the Banda Oriental (later Uruguay) in 1817, the newly independent Brazil and Argentina fought over the territory between 1825 and 1828. There was further protracted competition for influence in Uruguay between 1839 and 1852, culminating in the successful Brazilian military and diplomatic support for the overthrow of the Argentinian dictator Rosas in 1852. Further disputes, war scares and periodic arms races occurred in the period from the Paraguayan War (1864–1870) to the First World War, especially during the tenures as foreign minister of Rio Branco in Brazil and Zeballos in Argentina with tension particularly high in the years 1908–10. Moreover, by the mid-nineteenth century the language of power balancing had become well established as the dominant frame of reference for understanding the relationship.

Although military conflict was avoided, high levels of mutual threat perception continued through the twentieth century and, in stark contrast to the logic of a security community, the possibility of war and the importance of military preparedness were constant themes in strategic and diplomatic discussion.[4] Brazilian diplomacy and military circles saw a constant Argentinian threat to dominate the Spanish-speaking buffer states and to encircle and isolate Brazil, perceptions that were exacerbated during the Chaco War (1932–35) and World War II.[5] Thus, to give one example, Goes Monteiro, minister of war 1945–46 described Perón's Argentina as "the true Nazi menace in the Americas" which was "gearing itself for a military clash with Brazil." And, in the early 1960s, Itamaraty described rivalry with Argentina is the "most powerful and persistent determinant" of foreign policy.[6]

Finally, it is too easy to see Latin America as an area with shared values, language, culture, an explanatory move which underplays the distinctiveness of Brazil: linguistically distinct as a Portuguese-speaking country; culturally distinct as a result of the differing patterns of Portuguese colonialism (and, very importantly, decolonization); racially distinct because of the small size of the Indian population and the large section of the population of African origin; and, until 1889, politically distinct as a monarchy in a continent of republics. For cultural models and for political ideas Brazilian elites looked (and still look) not to their neighbors or indigenous traditions but first to Europe and subsequently to the United States. The separation of Brazil from the rest of the region also resulted from the pattern of economic development established during the colonial period and the extent to which economic ties in both the colonial and postcolonial periods were tied firmly to the core capitalist countries. And finally, from the time of Rio Branco in the early twentieth century down to the 1970s, Brazil looked to the United States as a prime means of balancing the power of Argentina, a tactic which only served to reinforce the distance and difference between Brazil and its neighbours.[7]

And yet by the end of the 1980s a dramatic shift had taken place in the enduring rivalry between Brazil and Argentina. In the economic sphere, moves towards institutionalized economic cooperation gathered pace in the mid-1980s and proved far more resilient and successful than many predicted. These began with a series of bilateral economic agreements between Brazil and Argentina and were taken further by the creation of Mercosur in 1991 and by the successful creation of a common external tariff on January 1, 1995. In the security field, rapprochement involved confidence building measures, arms control agreements with cooperative verification schemes, shifts in military posture towards defensive orientation and declining levels of military spending, as well as a security discourse that avoids the rhetoric of the balance of power and that contrasts sharply with the extreme geopolitical doctrines of the 1960s and 1970s.

There is, then, a good deal of unexpected cooperation that stands in need of explanation and that provides strong *prima facie* grounds for taking the idea of a regional security community seriously. To explore these issues, this chapter addresses three questions. First, how might we explain the end of the enduring rivalry between Brazil and Argentina and the *process* of greater cooperation? Secondly, is it in fact correct to analyze the *character* of relations that had emerged by the mid-1990s in terms of a security community, and, if so, what kind? And finally, what are the *boundaries* to this community and to what extent are the developments between Brazil and Argentina indicative of more general trends within South America?

II

The simplifying rationalist assumptions of both neorealism and institutionalism provide a powerful tool for unravelling the ways in which external constraints and the structure of the international system shape the foreign policy options of all states, but especially of relatively weak states. They are good at explaining the logic of strategic interaction when the identity of the actors and the nature of their interests is known and well understood. Yet such accounts fail to provide sufficient analytical purchase on the sources of state interest, on the critical junctures and break points when actors come to redefine and reinterpret the nature of their relations, and on the role of interaction and institutions in reinforcing these redefinitions. This section presents an alternative, broadly constructivist, account of the three principal stages in the move away from rivalry and competition towards the emergence of loosely knit security community.

Phase I: The easing of rivalry, 1975–1985

Relations in the early 1970s between Brazil and the other major states of the region varied from cool to openly hostile and the idea of a regional security community would have appeared quite absurd. There were three principal areas of discord. Firstly, there was a steady increase in rivalry for influence in the buffer states of Bolivia, Paraguay and, to a lesser extent, Uruguay. The second focus of friction developed over the use of hydroelectric resources of the Paraná river. Argentinian opposition had been growing in the late 1960s but reemerged as a bitter source of discord in mid-1972 and continued to dominate relations until 1979. Thirdly, the nuclear rivalry between Brazil and Argentina, visible since the Brazilian decision in the late 1960s to move ahead with the acquisition of nuclear technology, grew more intense and was sharpened immensely by the 1975 Brazil–West German nuclear agreement, the largest ever transfer of nuclear technology to a developing country.

These tensions resonated so powerfully because of the long tradition of rivalry, but were fueled by the extremely rapid economic development of the Brazilian "economic miracle" which rekindled historic fears of Brazil's expansionist and hegemonic ambitions, as well as by the rhetoric of *Brasil potência* that dominated the foreign policy discourse of the Médici government (1969–1974). The image stressed by the Médici government was of a rapidly developing middle power moving towards First World status and having little in common with the other countries of the region. The reassertion of the special relationship between Brazil and the United States that followed the 1964 military coup sharpened the traditional Spanish-American view of Brazil as a trojan horse for US imperialism and it was in this period that the view of Brazil as a "sub-imperialist" power was most prevalent, a perception strengthened by the lack of Brazilian interest in regional economic integration. Indeed, although Brazil continued with rhetoric of the need for Latin American unity, its attitude towards regional organizations was at best ambiguous. On the one hand, multilateral regional organizations could usefully complement Brazil's economic diplomacy and help prevent the emergence of a united anti-Brazilian grouping. On the other, as an economically more advanced country, it was increasingly wary of any moves towards integration that would involve making concessions to weaker members. Above all, during this period Brazil was reluctant to allow Latin American economic or political solidarity to interfere with its own bilateral relations with the United States.

Finally, rivalry was viewed on both sides through the prism of the geopolitical doctrines that were so influential both within the military establishments and beyond. Thus Spanish-American fears were heightened by the very visible influence within the Brazilian government of geopolitical theories with their starkly Hobbesian view of international life, their talk of "moving frontiers" and "platforms for expansion," and their assertion of Brazil's historic mission to regional predominance (its *vocação de grandeza*).[8] On the other side, Argentinian attitudes to the region were shaped both by equally extreme geopolitical doctrines, as well as by virulent territorial nationalism and a powerful mythology of territorial dispossession.[9]

It is worth stressing the degree to which tensions between Brazil and Argentina fitted a more general pattern. Indeed, during the 1970s and into the early 1980s the prospects for sustained cooperation and the emergence of a security community in South America appeared extremely poor. Even if the region had been relatively pacific, most commentators were predicting that South America was becoming more conflictual and more like the rest of the developing world. "There are significant reasons to expect more conflict of various kinds between Latin American states."[10] "All this points to a new era of international politics in Latin America: an era characterized by power politics and realism during which the myth of regional unity will be replaced by rivalries among regional powers . . ."[11] Or again:

> For many years it was possible to consider South America as a region of peace in comparison to so many other areas of the world. For a number of reasons, this state of affairs began to change markedly in the middle and late 1970s and reached a dramatic and bloody climax in the Anglo-Argentine Falklands/Malvinas conflict of 1982. There are few informed optimists today who would predict that the South Atlantic war was an isolated event that could not be repeated in some other battlefield of the Western Hemisphere.[12]

There was consensus too on the reasons for this pessimism. First, the struggle for natural resources had, it was argued, drastically increased the stakes of many historic border disputes: hydroelectric resources on the River Paraná between Brazil and Argentina, access to off-shore oil, fishing and seabed minerals in the case of Chile and Argentina (and, in many Latin American minds, Britain and Argentina); access to oil once more in the border disputes between Peru and Ecuador, Venezuela and Guyana, and Venezuela and Colombia. Secondly, the reemergence of superpower rivalry in the Third World had increased the stakes and ideological intensity of regional insecurity, above all in Central America. Thirdly, many saw the overall decline of United States hegemony and the virtual death by 1982 of the Inter-American Military System as reducing the ability of Washington to maintain "discipline" within its own sphere of influence. And finally, many noted the continued prevalence of extreme geopolitical thinking amongst the militaries of the Southern Cone and the fact that arms spending and the capabilities of national arms industries appeared to be increasing. Not only was the Falklands/Malvinas War of 1982 a worrying sign that extreme forms of territorial nationalism had not disappeared, but the debt crisis that broke in 1982 led to the collapse of intraregional trade flows and the further erosion of the already stagnant economic integration schemes inherited from the integrationist wave of the 1960s, such as the Andean Pact, the Central American Common Market (CACM) and LAFTA (replaced by ALADI in 1980).

This pattern of relations between Brazil and its Spanish-speaking neighbours which varied from coolness to outright hostility began to change in the late 1970s. An early sign of change was Brazil's proposal in November 1976 for the creation of an Amazon Pact to assist the joint development of the Amazon Basin. After considerable initial difficulties, Brazil was successful in overcoming the suspicions of the seven other countries involved and the treaty was signed in 1978. Economic relations with Latin America expanded and by 1981 Latin America's share of total Brazilian exports (18.4 percent) surpassed that of the United States for the first time. There was also an important shift in political attitudes and evidence of the growing "latin-americanization" of Brazilian foreign policy could be seen in the unprecedented range and frequency of political contacts between Brazil and other governments in the region.

It was within this context that we can locate the first signs of rapprochement with Argentina. Following a low point when Argentina blocked the transshipment of Brazilian goods to Chile, negotiations over the Itaipu and Corpus dams began again in July 1977 and in October 1979, Brazil signed an agreement with Paraguay and Argentina which effectively ended the thirteen year dispute. A further indication of change was the start in 1978 of the FRATERNO exercises between the two navies. In May 1980 Figueiredo visited Buenos Aires (the first visit by a Brazilian president since 1935) during which a package of ten agreements was signed. These included an agreement on joint arms production and nuclear cooperation, covering joint research and the transfer of some nuclear materials. In August 1980 Videla paid a return visit to Brasilia, during which a further seven protocols and conventions were signed extending the nuclear agreements. In 1981 three additional agreements were signed in the nuclear field between Argentina's NARC and Brazil's Nuclearbras.

After this initial improvement, relations cooled in the early 1980s when Galtieri returned to playing bandwagoning strategy offering close support to Washington in Central America. Yet during the Falklands/Malvinas war Brazil supported Argentinian claims; supplied some aircraft and permitted some transshipment of Argentinian agricultural produce via Brazilian ports. Indeed, it is significant that even the announcement of Argentina's achievement of a uranium enrichment capacity in 1983 did not affect the process of rapprochement.

How might we explain this period? The most dominant liberal theory, rationalist institutionalism, has very little to say. Institutionalists are concerned with understanding cooperation *after* the parties have come to perceive the possibilities of joint gains. Yet this misses out what is often most puzzling: how historic enemies and rivals come to view each other as legitimate players in a potentially cooperative enterprise or game? Before we get to active *cooperation* we have to explain the joint acceptance of *coexistence* and the willingness of the parties to live together within a framework of agreed legal and political rules. By contrast, neorealism appears to take us a considerable way in understanding how the process of desecuritization gets underway and the initial triggers for change by focusing on the dynamics of a double set of strategic triangles: Argentina, Chile and Brazil on the one hand, and Argentina, Brazil and the USA on the other. For Argentina, the desire for better relations came from recognition by the Videla government of its internal weakness and the country's declining power position *vis-à-vis* Brazil, combined with the marked deterioration in Argentinian–Chilean relations over the Beagle Channel dispute following the 1977 arbitral award in favour of Chile. Tensions over the Beagle Channel brought the two countries to the brink of war in October/December 1978. As Tulchin puts it: "The armed forces were mobilized, coffins were shipped to the south, and the national radio played martial music for long periods."[13] The seriousness of the threat underlined the logic of rapprochement with the old adversary, Brazil.[14]

Equally explicable within a neorealist framework, it had become clear by this time that the special relationship between Washington and Brasilia had unravelled – the most visible signs being the bitter disputes of the Carter years over human rights and nuclear proliferation. When the USA cut off military assistance to Argentina in response human rights abuses during the dirty war, there was a clear convergence of positions within the second strategic triangle with both countries angrily denouncing US policy and adopting a parallel positions in face of breakdown of superpower détente. The old

Argentinian fear of Brazil as a "sub-imperialist" power had therefore become increasingly outdated and irrelevant.

On the Brazilian side, the most important factor was the growing perception that its earlier regional policy had been thoroughly counter-productive. Talk of Brazil's emergence as a great power and Golbery's geopolitics had merely served to exacerbate Spanish-American fears and threatened to create the very situation that Brazil feared, namely the formation of a united anti-Brazilian grouping. Moreover, such a policy had become an obstacle to other more important Brazilian goals, especially the expansion of economic ties and the promotion of Brazilian exports (especially non-traditional and manufacturing exports). Finally, as the relationship with Washington unravelled, so the need for alternative relationships became more pressing. If the central theme of Brazilian policy in the 1970s was to diversify its external relations and to increase the range of its foreign policy options, then it became increasingly illogical to all but exclude Argentina from that process. These changing calculations of interest were reflected in a significant shift in the language used to describe foreign policy. By the mid-1970s the notion of Brazil as an aspiring member of the First World and of a special relationship with Washington (Golbery's "loyal bargain" in which support for Washington would be traded for an acknowledgement of Brazil's special role in ther region) had given way to an emphasis on Brazil as a developing country, a member of the Third World and, increasingly, of Latin America.

Finally, rapprochement was assisted by the nature of the issues and the ways in which they played into these broader themes. In the first place the structure of bargaining over Itaipu was altering. Since the late 1960s Brazil's policy had been one of hegemonic unilateralism. "The Itaipu dam was designed to make maximum use of the hydro-electric potential of the Paraná River with no consideration given to the negative externalities on Argentine uses of the river."[15] Moreover, once construction had begun, time worked to Brazil's advantage, especially as Argentina's attempt to internationalize the issue brought so little advantage. However, when in 1976 Argentina decided to go ahead and build its own dam further downstream at Corpus, the situation changed: by altering the height of its dam it could impose some costs and affect the viability of Itaipu; moreover by continuing the dispute it could block Brazil's desire to improve its relations with Latin America.

The late 1970s also saw important shifts in the nuclear field. In Brazil the increasingly evident failures of the official program and of the West German technology on which it was based opened the way to the development of the so-called parallel programs. In developing this parallel program Brazil had much to gain from cooperating with Argentina's more advanced nuclear technology, whilst, on the other side, Argentinian officials had increasingly concluded that a nuclear arms race would be costly and counterproductive. Moreover, whilst both countries continued to see the acquisition of nuclear technology as important to their long-term development (and perhaps, at some later point, military) objectives, both faced increasingly stringent financial constraints, increasingly serious technological problems, and a common interest in resisting attempts by outside powers to limit the proliferation of nuclear technology. There was, then, both an internal technological logic to cooperation and strong external pressures making for this initial move towards cautious cooperation.[16]

Although a straightforward interest-based explanation takes us a good way, it is worth pausing here and reflecting on how little this account has said about the kinds of states with which we are dealing and at how historic interaction came to shape both the limits of conflict and possibilities of cooperation. There may be some examples of true Hobbesian conflict (perhaps holy wars, inter-civilizational conflicts, heavily ideologized wars). Yet most protracted conflicts take place against a background of shared understandings and established legal and diplomatic institutions. In the case of Brazil–Argentina, the social character of relations is especially important. What we find is a long history, not of Hobbesian conflict, but rather of recurrent rivalry and conflict, often with military overtones, combined with periods of cooperation within a very "thick" social environment.[17] The language of community and of a common Latin American identity did not therefore suddenly appear in the 1980s, but had deep historical roots. Alongside the recurrent fears and suspicions, the post-war period saw a number of previous moves to cooperation, especially between Vargas and Perón in the early 1950s and between Quadros and Frondizi in 1961.[18]

This is in itself something of a puzzle, especially for the neorealist. Why, after all, if states are naturally power seeking has the security dilemma in the region not been more acute? What accounts for the striking gap between the savage rhetoric of the Brazilian geopoliticians and their failure to seek regional hegemony based on active military power – a move that would surely deepened the security dilemma and precluded the emergence of a security community?

The neorealist stress on geopolitical location is undoubtedly important. At least in this century there has never been a convincing need for a serious defensive capability against extra-regional powers which would have upset the regional balance of power and led to the destructive interaction between regional and extra-regional power balances that has so bedeviled the Middle East or the Indian subcontinent. But beyond this neorealism does not take us very far. Whilst distance, lack of communication may explain the limited contact and conflict with Brazil's other neighbors, the relationship with Argentina had always been close and intense. Moreover, on neorealist logic, as the two states consolidated, modernized and industrialized the chances of confrontation should have increased. Equally, whatever the earlier impact of hegemonic policing by Britain and then the USA, this was less than in the rest of Latin America and declined steadily after 1960. Finally, it is often argued that Brazil was a geopolitically satisfied power, a state that had gained enormous areas of territory from its neighbours through both diplomacy and coercion in the late nineteenth and early twentieth centuries. It therefore had little interest or incentive in hostile relations with Argentina. Yet, in the first place, security dilemmas do not depend on whether states seek only security or wish to maximize power, on whether they are defensive or offensive positionalists. And, secondly, the idea of a "satisfied Brazil" or a "revisionist Argentina" begs many questions about the character and historical construction of states that simply cannot be answered within the intellectually impoverished world of neorealism.[19]

It is impossible to give a full alternative account here, but a number of points can be made. First, a constructivist would want to look in far more detail at the patterns of state formation in the region and the emergence of governments and militaries that did not place great emphasis on external power projection. Indeed, a case might be made for a Latin American *via media*: namely that, particularly after the wars of independence and state formation, Latin American states were successful enough to avoid the civil strife, disintegration and secession that characteristic of so many other parts of the postcolonial world; but weak enough to escape the destructive dynamic between state-making and war-making that was such a feature of the European Westphalian order (and which is perhaps visible in the case of Chile).

Secondly, it is important to ask why, after the difficult years of state-building and, in particular, after the Paraguayan War, the two countries in general avoided (or managed to contain) the kinds of intense militarized conflict that, counterfactually, might have seemed probable. An answer might begin by recognizing the degree to which this is a period in Brazil in which domestic political power swings away from the center and towards the regional oligarchies, in which the army is severely weakened (to the point of having great difficulty in suppressing domestic revolts such as Canudos and Contestado), in which the foreign ministry (*Itamaraty*) dominates the management of the countries many border disputes, and in which a pacific diplomatic culture comes to be established and considered "normal." In Argentina, relations were overwhelmingly focused on Europe and the "central objective of its foreign policy was the resolution or diminution of political friction between states in order to permit greater freedom for international commerce."[20] On this view, whilst war had been central to the process of state/nation building in Argentina, it ceased to be so. Argentinian leaders may not have liked their neighbors but realised that economic development, immigration and foreign capital all required peace. Moreover, as Tulchin also argues, it was in this period that balance of power and geopolitical thinking was eclipsed by both eurocentric and idealist frames of reference (many of whose themes reappear in the Argentina of the 1990s).

Thirdly, as developmentalism and industrialization develop after 1930 often under authoritarian governments and as the two countries come into ever closer relations and acquire ever greater means of damaging each other, why has the security relationship not been worse? Again, any convincing answer would need to look at the particular role of the military as agents of domestic modernization, at the extent to which military professionalization and modernization was largely inner-directed, responding to domestic failures and aimed at integrating national territory, at upholding domestic order and at promoting economic development. This is especially relevant for understanding why Brazil – unlike, say, India or China – is a country whose governments have not placed a particularly high priority on expanding regional influence, especially in the power political and military arena, even when it has had the capabilities to do so. What becomes such a "natural" and taken-for-granted feature of the regional landscape is in fact the result of a specific set of historical processes.

Phase II: The strengthening of cooperation, 1985–1990

From mid-1980s, the momentum of cooperation picks up. In November 1985 Presidents Sarney and Alfonsín signed an agreement which covered nuclear issues and energy cooperation and which set up a commission to examine economic cooperation.[21] In July 1986 the signature of the Ata para a Integração (Integration Act) established the Economic and Cooperation and Integration Programme (PICE). Under PICE 24 bilateral protocols were signed, followed by the Treaty of Integration and Cooperation in November 1988 and the Treaty of Integration, Cooperation and Development in August 1989. This envisaged the creation of a free-trade area between the two countries within a ten year period.

In addition to the launching of agreements on economic cooperation the second half of the 1980s saw increased stability in the security relationship. The logic of nuclear cooperation visible in the late 1970s reasserted itself and was strengthened by the serious failings of both nuclear programs despite large financial and political investments.[22] Cooperation was visible in the various nuclear cooperation agreements signed between 1985 and 1987. Increased mutual confidence on the nuclear question followed from a far greater degree of transparency and the gradual emergence of more explicit confidence building measures: for example Alfonsín's decision to place CNEA under civilian control within the foreign ministry; the creation in 1985 of joint working groups involving members of the nuclear bureaucracies and nuclear industries; the signature under PICE of Protocol 11 on information in the case of nuclear accidents and Protocol 19 on areas for joint research and development; increased technical visits; the prior notice (to Argentina) of Sarney's speech in September 1987 announcing that Brazil had "dominated" the nuclear fuel cycle with the navy's domestically built gas centrifuge enrichment facility; and the transformation of the working groups in 1988 into a formal binational Permanent Committee on Nuclear Affairs. Most visibly, confidence was enhanced by Sarney's visits to Argentina's nuclear facilities in 1987 and 1988, and Alfonsín's visit in 1988 to the hitherto officially unacknowledged Brazilian facility at Aramar.[23]

How to explain this period? Again, liberal institutionalism faces serious problems. Institutionalists stress the extent which cooperation is viewed as a functional and self-interested response by states to the problems created by regional interdependence and institutionalists are keen to stress the extent to which increasing interdependence creates the "demand" for regimes. Yet in this case rapprochement developed against a background of, and as a response to, *declining* regional interdependence. Moreover, this approach stresses the critical role of institutions in fostering and developing regional cohesion. Yet in this case the role of institutions has been limited and has tended to follow from the success of earlier moves to rapprochement.

Some accounts of this period suggest that neorealist theory has nothing useful to say. Philippe Schmitter, for example, argues that: "[F]rom a neorealist perspective ... nothing bodes favorably for an increase in cooperative behaviour within the subregion."[24] Such a conclusion however, ignores the extent to which increased cooperation reflected a convergence of foreign policy interests and perspectives, born of common external pressures and of the erosion of alternative policy options. For much of the post-war period, major Latin American states tended towards a policy of constrained balancing: active efforts to diversify away from the USA but falling short of close and direct alignment with major US antagonists (both because of the high direct and indirect costs of such a move and because of the absence of a domestic constituency – except under conditions of social and nationalist radicalization). However the grand (and always excessive) hopes of diversification were already wearing thin by the beginnings of the 1980s and looked still less secure as the decade progressed. Moreover, as the prospects for diversification waned, so the centrality of the United States was reasserted but in ways that provoked or intensified tensions between Washington and the region. Thus, cooperation was based both on the absence of the kinds of alternative options that Brazil and Argentina had sought to develop in the 1970s and on a common rejection of US policy across a number of issues.

In Argentina, foreign policy under Alfonsín was built around the image of Argentina as a Western, non-aligned and developing country. Relations with Washington were strained as a result of the lingering resentment over Washington's support of Britain in 1982 and persistent differences over the Central American crisis, Argentina's strongly non-aligned stance, the management of the debt crisis, and a range of trade and investment issues. In Brazil there was a high level of continuity between the military period and the New Republic, nowhere more so than in the continuation of the frictions that had increasingly come to characterize US–Brazilian relations since the mid-1970s. Under Sarney such friction centred around debt management and Brazil's 1987 debt moratorium, trade issues (especially investment access and intellectual property rights in the informatics and pharmaceutical sectors), nuclear policy and arms exports, and environmental questions. Continuity was also visible in the continued importance of national autonomy and the protection of national sovereignty as policy goals. This could be seen in the continuation or expansion of such stereotypical projects as the country's informatics regime, the nuclear program, or the national arms industry. Increased cooperation was therefore born, at least in part, of the need to present a united front against a hostile world. The severity and uniformity of the economic crisis served to underline common interests and common perspectives between the two countries. The negative external environment reemphasised the need to broaden and strengthen the regional market and to institutionalize the economic interdependence that had been growing through the 1970s, but which had fallen back so dramatically in the early 1980s.

Interest-based accounts also draw attention to power political factors within the region. On the one hand, the continued preoccupation of the Argentinian military with Chile and with the Malvinas and South Atlantic. On the other the shift in the concerns and threat perceptions of the Brazilian military, away from Argentina and towards the Amazon region. This reflected fears of subversion seeping down from the Caribbean (Cuba, Grenada, Suriname), a spillover of guerrilla violence from the Andean region and the need to reassert control over the extremely rapid and increasingly disorderly development of the Brazilian Amazon. From the mid-1980s, the Brazilian military laid great emphasis on the Amazon and occupied the major role in the formulation of policy towards the region. This trend continued into the 1990s and discussions of national defense planning and procurement policy have focused less and less on the possibility of inter-state conflict with Argentina and ever more on the need to police borders in the North, to control flows of gold miners, to counter *narcotraficantes*, and to prevent the "internationalization" of the Amazon region.

However, whilst shared foreign policy interests were important, it is impossible to ignore the importance of the transitions to democracy that are occurring in both countries (and throughout the region). In the first place, democratization involved the (albeit incomplete) shift in political and bureaucratic power away from the military, both generally and, very importantly, in the management of regional foreign policy. Itamaraty and San Martin (the foreign ministeries of Brazil and Argentina respectively) became the dominant agencies in the whole process of political cooperation and economic integration and controlled the working groups on technical and nuclear cooperation. Secondly, democratization also laid the political foundation for increased transparency on which more specific confidence building measures were later to be built. This was particularly important in the nuclear field with a series of Brazilian congressional hearings and increased discussion of Brazil's parallel nuclear program in the press and public (for example through the work of the Brazilian Physics Society).

Thirdly, it is very important to note that we are not dealing here with a "democratic peace" between two well-consolidated democracies but rather with contested processes of *democratization*. Particularly in this phase the shared interests and perhaps shared identities came rather from a common sense of vulnerability: the shared conviction that democracy in both countries was extremely fragile and that non-democratic forces were by no means out of the game (witness the military rebellions in Argentina in April 1987, January 1998 and December 1990). This provided a shared sense of common purpose between a limited group of politicians and government officials (rather than between political, let alone public, opinion more generally).

Fourthly, and especially in Argentina, this led to the overt use of foreign policy as a means of protecting fragile and newly established democracies. In part this reflects the close and very concrete link between conflict resolution abroad and democratic consolidation at home – the need to promote regional pacification in order to deprive the nationalists of causes around which to mobilize opinion, to demand a greater political role, or to press for militarization and rearmament. Regional peace therefore becomes central to the maintenance of successful civil–military relations at home. But it also reflected the perceived importance of building up the idea and the rhetoric of external support: the idea of a club of states to which only certain governments are allowed to belong and in which cooperation becomes the international expression and symbol both of new democracies and of the end of old rivalries. Democratization, rather than democracy *per se*, therefore mattered a great deal and this case provides an important counter-example to the argument that democratizing regimes are more aggressive and war-prone than other kinds of states.[25] The leading actors on both sides *believed* democratization to have been very important in redefining the interests of the two states and in reshaping their identities and their sense of common purpose. In so doing, one of Deutsch's essential conditions for a security community, namely the compatibility of major values, becomes reasonably well established.

But democratization, it bears repeating, was not the only factor and does not provide a single magic key to understanding cooperation. A simple Kantian account is difficult to reconcile with the relative pacificism of both civilian and military governments in the region historically and with earlier patterns of conflict and cooperation between Brazil and Argentina. It tells us little about the successful resolution of conflict in the period immediately before the transition to civilian rule in Brazil and Argentina and downplays or ignores the other factors pressing for cooperation, especially from outside the region. Moreover, as the nuclear issue demonstrates, there are many cross cutting pressures and relationships. The military remain politically significant, especially in Brazil with the persistence of "authoritarian enclaves," a domestic role recognized in the 1988 constitution, the absence of a civilian minister of defense and continued military control over "strategic activities." Although democratic politicians and foreign ministries undoubtedly make the running, the extent of continued military power suggests that rapprochement cannot be seen in terms of a simple struggle between civil and military authorities. Equally, the limits to nuclear cooperation under Sarney and the domestic debates over ratification of the Quadripartite Agreement in the 1993 underscore the extent to which nuclear nationalism was by no means limited to the military.

Phase III: Secure cooperation vs divergent identities, 1990–1996

The inauguration of Carlos Menem in Argentina in July 1989 and Fernando Collor in Brazil in March 1990 witnessed a significant effort to relaunch the somewhat flagging process of economic cooperation. In July 1990 they agreed to establish a full common market by the end of 1994. In March 1991 the Treaty of Asunción creating Mercosur was signed between Brazil, Argentina, Paraguay and Uruguay, entering into force in November 1991. Bureaucratic and political ties and visits become ever denser and the symbolism of integration continues (for example, Cardoso's first act as president in January 1995 was a meeting with the presidents of Mercosul and of Bolivia and Chile). There was also important progress in the security and arms control field. In September 1990 Collor formally rejected any Brazilian desire to acquire nuclear weapons and, in a symbolic gesture largely intended for US consumption, closed the weapons testing facility at Serra do Cachimbo and included some greater civilian oversight of the continuing nuclear research. The 1990 Joint Declaration on a Common Nuclear Policy created a system of jointly monitored safeguards in the form of the December 1991 agreement between Brazil, Argentina, the IAEA and a newly formed bilateral agency for controlling nuclear materials (ABACC). This opened the way for full implementation of the Tlatelolco Regime. Finally, the Mendonca Agreement (which included Chile) of September 1991 extended arms control to cover chemical and biological weapons.

Two factors stand out in explaining this phase. In the first place, increasingly institutionalized interaction sets up a process of internalization and enmeshment which does not merely alter material incentives but reinforces changes in attitudes. As we have seen, military contacts began in the 1980s as exploratory meetings designed to find out what the other side was doing. By the early 1990s greater confidence and an increased awareness of common interests led to increased institutionalization which in turn provided a framework for new patterns of strategic interaction. In a similar way, this period sees a gradual but steady creation of interest-groups and networks within the state favouring integration. The network of binational working groups established under the 1986 agreements and, still more, the intergovernmental structures of Mercosur acquired a degree of bureaucratic autonomy (and insulation from the on-going political and institutional crisis in Brazil). Not only was the habit of consultation growing but a small group of officials was increasingly able to push the integration agenda forward and to work together to try and find solutions to problems. Moreover, the institutionalization of visits, exchanges by presidents and officials was leading to a broader "habit of communication" of the kind that has been so important within Europe. Although the shared sense of vulnerable new democracies is less visible in this phase, the domestic process of democratization remains important. In Argentina, for example, the foreign ministry was able to secure a progressively greater role in "security" affairs and, with the backing of Menem, to force the military to accept a series of unpalatable decisions on weapons and nuclear policy.

Secondly, as with democratization in the mid-1980s, the definition of interests and understandings of identity shift very significantly in this period, above all because of changes in economic policy and economic thinking. The relaunching of economic integration needs to be understood against a set of shared and widely held perceptions of the external environment: that economic multilateralism was under threat and that a three-bloc world was emerging; that the end of the Cold War was leading to the "marginalization" of the region; that the success of US military power in the Gulf signalled a "unipolar moment" in which there was little choice but to come to terms with the realities of US power; and that economic globalization had undercut the viability of existing economic policies. Partly as a result policy in both countries moves increasingly in parallel directions: questioning of existing economic models based on ISI, high tariffs, and a large role for the state, and moving towards market liberalism, placing greater reliance on market mechanisms, seeking to restructure and reduce the role of the state, and laying greater emphasis on integration in world markets.

This shift towards market liberalism had a profound impact on the way Latin American states define the core goals of foreign policy – military security, economic prosperity and political autonomy – and the range of acceptable trade-offs between them (recall the degree to which state-centred ISI strategies fitted with the military's strategic interests and purposes). It also fed into regional policy in a number of ways. Firstly, its most important impact was to make the region more outward looking and more dependent on the international economy at precisely the time when the overall pattern of international relations was in a state of great flux and uncertainty. It increased Latin American interests in the continued existence of a more or less open, multilateral world economy. But it also altered the options when global multilateralism appeared to be under threat, increasing the importance of regional and sub-regional economic liberalization. Secondly, the fact that the two countries were moving together (if still unequally) towards economic liberalization provided a potentially more promising basis for sub-regional economic cooperation than old-style ECLA prescriptions. As a result, the specific character of integration changes significantly in this phase: away from balanced, sector-specific agreements based on specific reciprocity of the kind that had dominated the 1986–1989 period (with a heavy focus on the capital goods sector); and towards generalized, linear and automatic reductions in levels of protection. What we see, then, is the idea of Mercosur as a reflection of the need for competitive modernization, as "a platform" or a "regional laboratory" for modernization and competitive insertion in the world economy" – as the new discourse expresses it – and as a way of bringing together the internal and external agendas of economic liberalization.

The reasons for these changes are partly to be found in purely domestic developments: the discredit and failure of previous development policies built around import substitution in which wide-ranging subsidy programs and extensive direct state involvement in industry had played a major role; the increased recognition of the need for effective stabilization; and, most importantly, the analytically distinct but temporally interconnected, fiscal, political and institutional crises of the state. But these changes in economic policy are impossible to understand without reference to the critical impact of structural changes in the global economy: the increased pace of the globalization of markets and production, and the dramatically increased rate of technological change. This led to a powerful Latin American *perception* that dynamic economies are internationalized economies; that growth depends on successful participation in the world economy; that increased foreign investment is central to the effective transfer of modern technology; and that the increased rate of technological change has undermined projects that aim at nationally based and autonomous technological development.

Neorealists (and radical IPE theorists) can certainly point to important political factors that help explain the parallel shift towards market liberalism. They highlight the role of direct external pressure from both states and multilateral agencies and the increasing tendency to make economic assistance conditional upon moves towards economic and political liberalization. Moreover, neorealists can also highlight the continued hegemonic "policing role" of the USA in forcing change in precisely those areas that had been previously been central to Brazilian–Argentinian rivalry. It is difficult, for example, to explain the shifts in nuclear policy, missile technology or arms exports without some reference to the consistent pressure applied by Washington. But neorealism can tell us nothing at all about the ways in which systemic or structural economic factors have interacted with domestic factors to produce new definitions of state interest, supported by new sets of domestic political coalitions. Its picture of the international system misses out entirely the ways in which both competitive dynamics and the consequent definition of state interests are affected by changes in the global economic system and by the changing character of the "transnational whole" within which states and the state system are embedded. Interests and identities are being reshaped through this period as interaction with the global political and economic system creates a complex process of socialization. It is tempting here to argue that peace follows from the inherently pacific character of democratic liberalizing "trading states." Yet such an explanatory move is difficult to square with similarly democratizing and liberalizing states (such as Colombia, Peru, Venezuela) in parts of the region that very clearly do not comprise a security community (see below). Rather than classic liberalism, one might point to the emergence of broadly liberal developmental states that face a common predicament in adjusting to changes in the global economy and that see regional cooperation as providing both a shelter and a platform, and whose understandings of power, autonomy and independence have been modified (but not transformed) in ways that facilitate cooperation.

III

By the mid-1990s it was clear that a major break had taken place in the historic rivalry between Brazil and Argentina in the sense that previous disputes had been settled; that diplomatic, military and economic resources were no longer committed to opposing the other side; and that the two countries were enmeshed in an increasingly dense process of institutionalized cooperation across a range of issues. As we have seen, neorealist factors and forces certainly played an important role, especially as triggers for change in the first stage of rapprochement. Equally, shifting material incentives have been consistently important and, as the process of cooperation has become denser, institutions have indeed come to provide important functional benefits and helped states capture common gains. But whilst power and interest have been important, it is impossible to produce a credible account without understanding, first, the particular historical construction of the states involved; secondly, the processes by which both interests and identities are created and evolve; and thirdly, the ways in which interaction and enmeshment reinforce these changes.

The change in the overall quality of relations is undoubtedly bigger than the sum of its (often instrumentally driven) parts.

In order to justify the claim that the quality of the relationship has indeed undergone significant change and that a loosely knit security community has emerged, let us look at the evolution of transactions, organizations and institutions, beginning in the all-important military sector. Here there is strong evidence that the two countries no longer fear war or prepare for war against each other. In the first place, borders are no longer actively fortified. On one side, Brazil has increasingly (and unilaterally) redeployed troops away from the South. On the other, Argentina has given up its policy of "empty provinces" under which, until the 1980s, no valued economic activities, and few bridges or transport systems were developed in the northern provinces as part of a geopolitical doctrine of strategic denial in the face of a Brazilian threat. Not only has such thinking disappeared, but increased infrastructural integration has become a central part of the Mercosur project.

Secondly, a successful and well established series of confidence building measures has resolved previous points of dispute, fostering increased trust and establishing more general principles of transparency and cooperation. In addition to the formal arms control regimes discussed above, by the mid-1990s chiefs of staff were meeting twice a year as part of a broadening pattern of interservice contacts. There has also been some examples of more active cooperation – for example the AREX joint exercises between the navies and the training of Argentinian pilots on the Brazilian aircraft carrier; or the September 1996 joint army exercises which were the first time that Brazilian troops have been on Argentinina soil since the Paraguayan War. Although these are mostly symbolic, these may gradually lead to more concrete discussion of shared threats and security challenges (as is already happening between the two navies). Other illustrations of these trends include closer consultation between the militaries on peacekeeping and preparation for peacekeeping operation; the April 1996 agreement between Brazil, Argentina and Paraguay which established a new tripartite body to coordinate security in the frontier area, aimed especially at drugs, contraband and terrorism; and a further agreement, also signed in April 1996, for closer cooperation in the nuclear and space sectors.

Thirdly, there has been gradual civilianization of security issues and more secure civilian control over the military. In Argentina there has been a steady increase in the effectiveness of civilian control, with a civilian minister of defense, the creation of a unified command structure, civilian control of military enterprises and their subsequent privatization, the absence in the constitution of any domestic political role, and the ending in 1994 of conscription. The military were forced to accept the ending of the Condor II program and Argentina's entry into the MTCR Missile Technology Control Regime. Military spending fell from 4 percent in 1990 to 2 percent of GNP in 1993 and the Argentinian military have moved furthest in developing new roles and attitudes, especially with the increased participation in multilateral peacekeeping operations (to the extent that half of all officers have participated in such operations). In Brazil the military has been more able to maintain its autonomy and its control over strategic programs (and to resist the creation of civilian led ministry of defense). But military spending is low (around 0.8 percent of GNP) and the arms industry that attracted so much attention in the 1970s has unravelled, with the effective bankruptcy of the three largest firms and the cancellation or postponement of ambitious programs to produce a main battle tank, a ground attack aircraft, a satellite launcher and a nuclear submarine. Above all, in both countries the military have accepted the importance of regional cooperation and of maintaining confidence building measures.

This security relationship has been embedded in an increasingly dense process of economic integration and transactions, organizations and institutions in this sector have increased dramatically. Exports within Mercosur have more than doubled as a share of total exports since 1990, with Mercosur absorbing around 30 percent of Argentina's exports and 22 percent of Brazilian exports. Although there were certainly many difficulties in the 1990–1994 period caused most obviously by the divergence of economic policies between the two countries and the differential speed of economic liberalization and tariff reductions, the two countries were able to agree on the implementation of a common external tariff that came into effect on January 1, 1995. Although certainly different from the EU or NAFTA, Mercosur is much more than a trade agreement and the deep integration agenda encompasses investment, dispute settlement, physical integration, labour issues, energy and macro-economic coordination. Although difficulties continue, the security relationship is more firmly rooted in a continuing process of economic integration than had appeared conceivable ten years ago.

Two points can be made about the relationship between economic and political processes. First, politics, economics and security are continually intertwined (in very different ways to the "twin-track" EC/NATO model) and the positive reinforcement between them was particularly important in sustaining the momentum of cooperation. For example, in the late 1980s, security cooperation made much of the running when, despite the flurry of agreements, economic cooperation was slow and erratic. Secondly, economic regionalism has become important to security and political stability, not because the costs of fighting became too high according to some abstract measure; but rather because it has helped to stabilize the redefinitions of interest that occurred in the 1980s and because it promotes an ongoing process of socialization and enmeshment. It has done this through a double process of internalization, the first element of which involves material changes in bureaucratic procedures, domestic legal arrangements, domestic coalitions; and the second subjective element of which involves changes in the way in which politically salient individuals think and act.

As we have seen, the process of increased cooperation has been strongly statist project. The development of transnational social networks has not been significant factors in either the ending of rivalry or the moves towards cooperation and Deutsch's emphasis on social transactions in such fields as trade, migration, tourism, or cultural exchanges does not appear relevant in this case. If we look for evidence of interaction and internalization, then this is mostly to do with changes within the bureaucracies and the growth of institutionalized interaction among an ever broader range of bureaucratic actors. There is, however, evidence that the success of integration is leading to an expansion in the range of actors involved – for example the greater organization of business interests and the creation of more formalized involvement of those regions and provinces most closely affected by integration.[26]

The increased density of interaction processes and the growth of organizations and institutions in the security, economic and political sectors has had an important impact on both the power structures and cognitive structures. Understandings of the role of power have shifted both within Mercosur and between Mercosur and the rest of the sub-region. Power and relative power still matters, especially to many in Argentina who fear that deep integration with Brazil is bringing excessive dependence, who believe that too much autonomy has been given up, and who are keen to maintain direct reciprocity, both in terms of economic exchanges and in other areas of cooperation. Yet, as with Germany within the EU, the problem of Brazilian power is no longer understood in military terms and the idea of actively opposing Brazilian power has largely disappeared. The neorealist may be tempted to argue that the objective balance of power has shifted so far against Argentina that conflict has become impossible (as in the case of Mexico and the USA) and that elites in Buenos Aires are merely bowing to the inevitable.[27] Yet, first, without examining shifts in identity and conceptions of interest it would be hard to understand how and why Argentinian political and military leaders came to accept this "objective" truth in this period rather than any other – how great does the imbalance of power have to be to produce cooperation? And, secondly, whilst such an approach may help explain why rivalry ended, it is unclear that it could explain Argentinian willingness to embark on both increased security cooperation and deep economic integration with the erstwhile threatening hegemon.

A further important aspect concerns the idea of a powerful core to which outside states no longer respond by balancing behaviour, but rather view as a zone of peace and security in which membership is valued. There are some signs of such a development as Mercosur becomes more firmly established and the process of expansion has moved forward, first with the 1996 agreement on Chilean association and then with the advanced negotiations for Bolivian and Venezuelan association. Here again power considerations do not disappear, in this case the notion that a strong regional grouping will be better able to negotiate with the USA – a belief which explains the Brazilian emphasis on turning Mercosur into a South American grouping. Yet power alone cannot explain the shift in attitudes towards Brazilian power and the growth in the value placed on inclusion within the organization.

Power, then, is a social phenomenon that is inseparable from the cognitive structures and webs of meanings in which it is embedded. Here it is critical to distinguish between the emergence of a genuinely shared collective identity on the one hand (Deutsch's "we-feeling" and mutual loyalty); and shifts in individual identities and interests in ways that facilitate cooperation on the other. As the previous section sought to demonstrate, the move from rivalry to cooperation has had a great deal to do with the separate but parallel shifts in the foreign policies of Brazil and Argentina. As a result of democratization and economic liberalization, it becomes much easier to speak of a compatibility of major values, shared ways of organizing society domestically, and a shared system of intersubjective meanings.

There is some evidence that shared values have come to play a significant role in the process of cooperation itself. Thus the rhetorical emphasis on democracy was certainly a central feature of the 1985–1990 period: the sharp discursive break in the way in which cooperation is conceived: the constant iteration of a shared Latin American identity; the repeated emphasis that the emerging community was to be a democratic; the way in which the agreements and presidential meetings explicitly sought to provide mutual support for the process of democratic consolidation. This was carried on by both language and symbols (for example, the building of "friendship bridges" or the inclusion of a commitment to Latin American integration in the 1988 Brazilian constitution). It is also worth noting the differential treatment of undemocratic regimes in Paraguay and Chile (their exclusion from economic agreements and, in Brazil's case, the suspension of arms sales to Chile). More recently, there has been a steady move, first towards joint action to maintain the democratic basis of Mercosur (as in the joint Brazilian–Argentinian involvement in the attempted coup in Paraguay in 1996); and the formal enunciation of democratic criteria for the admission of future members (the June 1996 *Declaração Presidencial sobre o Compromisso Democrático no Mercosur*).

Overall, then, there has been a sustained move away from the logic of anarchy and towards the logic of community, to that extent that a loosely-knit security community can be said to exist around Mercosur. Yet, against this, the Deutschian language of "we-feeling" and mutual loyalty risks overstating the strength and density of cooperation, and the limits to the idea of security community have to be acknowledged. In the first place, the successes in the field of cooperative security have mostly been of a negative (but still important) kind: relaxing tension, reducing threat perceptions via confidence building measures and arms control regimes, preventing backsliding and the reappearance of balance of power discourses.[28] There has been only rather modest steps towards the more activist components of cooperative security such as agreeing on developing plans for joint action or constructing a collective security system. Whilst Argentina has argued for more elaborate ideas of cooperative security both sub-regionally and within the OAS, Brazil has proved resistant: because of its unwillingness to be constrained by regional multilateral institutions (equally visible in its dislike of proposals to strengthen the military capabilities of the OAS); because the debate on force restructuring and new professional roles for the armed forces has moved less far than in Argentina. Thus, when Argentina proposed 180 days' notice on military exercises and also advanced notification of arms purchases, Brazil (and Chile) rejected the idea.

A second limitation is the weak level of institutions in the regional governance structure. As outlined above, this is true in the security realm. But it is also true in the economic field with no desire on the part of Brazil to move towards a more institutionalized intergovern-mental system, let alone a supranational one. This is the result of both foreign policy divergences (discussed below) but also reflects the interests of the larger partner unwilling to see its scope for unilateral action curtailed (cf the parallel with the USA in NAFTA). The habit of dialogue is certainly well established but forms of management that are not subject to immediate, day-to-day political interference (whether from São Paulo industrialists or regional politicians) are only weakly established. As the arguments over car exports and industrial policy demonstrated, conflict management relies on overtly political bargaining at the highest political, rather through institutionalized dispute settlement procedures. In addition, despite the general moves to liberalization, it is striking just how far the two sides continue to insist on reasonably specific reciprocity, with aspects of the earlier sector-specific concerns still visible. Institutions and procedural rules matter because successful integration inevitably creates instability and a new range of problems that have to be managed – for example the expansion of Mercosur beyond the southern cone opens a range of security issues that are far more serious and threatening than those within the southern cone.

Finally, and most importantly, the successes of cooperation have to be set against both important foreign policy divergences and the conflicting identities that underpin them. During the period from 1993 to 1995 the foreign policy interests of the two countries moved apart and Mercosur's place in the respective foreign policies and "world views" of the two countries became more ambiguous and contested. Argentina came to lay very great stress on improving and intensifying relations with the United States and Western Europe. This involved a policy of grand gestures, sometimes quite extreme and quite remote from immediate interests (such as support for the USA over the Gulf or Haiti, or the country's voting record in the UN), as well as a strong emphasis on the country's commitment to liberal values. These steps were designed to underline in strong and symbolic terms the extent of the historic shift in the country's international stance and to overcome Argentina's negative and unreliable image. Argentina also played a leading role in giving greater teeth to the OAS's charter commitment to democracy and, in a further striking rejection of earlier thinking, supported the use of coercion to restore democratic regimes. Particular during 1993/94 there was vigorous debate about the relative position of relations with Brazil and Mercosur on the one hand and early membership of NAFTA on the other.

Brazilian policy, by contrast, remained more ambiguous and the elements of continuity remain far more pronounced. Foreign policy speeches lay great emphasis on the idea of "universalism" and of the country as a "global trader" whose fundamental interests lie in global multilateralism and political diversification. Although great efforts have been made to improve relations with Washington, although the costs of previous confrontation have been appreciated, and although fear of exclusion from regional developments forced Brazil to participate even when opposed (eg on the role of the OAS in promoting democracy), Brazilian policy on hemispheric cooperation and integration remained ambivalent and hesitant. This reflected a deep rooted belief that Brazil is different and is powerful enough to stand apart. Thus whilst it is certainly true that Brazil has been unable to resist the need to redefine and improve its relations with Washington, it has also sought to maintain its freedom of action by strengthening the viability of sub-regional options. This logic would explain the Brazilian decision in October 1992 to launch its so-called "Amazonian initiative" and the announcement by President Franco in October 1993 of the proposal to expand Mercosur into a South American Free Trade Area.

It is possible to analyze these differences in narrow instrumental terms, for example to view Argentinian policy in terms of the desire to "trade" political support for concrete economic benefits, especially in the light of the underlying fragility of the Cavallo economic policy and its high dependence on the maintenance of investor confidence. But as Roberto Russell has argued, external incentives did not *necessarily* led to the dramatic pro-western policies of the Menem government.[29] Rather differences in foreign policy reflect a deeper divergence in the ways in which elites in the two countries conceive of their place in the world and current debates about identity only make sense when viewed within a longer-term historical context. Thus Argentinian foreign policy under Menem has been built around a conscious rejection of the idea of Argentina as a "third world" country and natural member of the NAM; of a conception of nationalism defined in terms of opposition to the US; and of an "exceptionalist" account of Argentina's place in the world. This has also involved growing doubts about the idea of Latin America as representing any kind of collective identity. Thus di Tella has spoken of the Latin America as a "cartographical illusion." Instead of a common regional identity, we have seen a reversion to an older image of Argentina as an essentially Western and European country that has little in common with the other countries of the region. On this view, cooperation is secure and important, but, as one senior Argentinian diplomat has put it "integration is not identification." In Brazil on the other hand there continues to be a good deal of emphasis on the differences between the country and other parts of the region, and on the need for independence. There has also been a revival of the image of Brazil as a "consensus builder" or "interlocuteur" between North and South (apparent in the 1970s). In response to Mexico's defection, it is also interesting to note the conscious effort to redefine regional cooperation in terms of a "South" rather than "Latin" American identity. Constructivism, then, helps us understand both the ways in which more expansive notions of community may emerge, but also the ways in which historically embedded identities constitute important obstacles to cooperation.

IV

If we can indeed speak of an emerging security community around the Mercosur countries, what are its boundaries? The most immediate issue concerns Chile. The long history of territorial conflict with Argentina and of the shared perception of territorial losses at the other's expense go back to the early days of state formation in the 1820s. In addition Chile has long been part of the balance of power system in the southern cone and balance of power thinking and, later, geopolitical analysis is deeply engrained in the military establishments of the two countries. A protracted arms race and the renewal of conflict over the islands in the Beagle Channel brought the two countries close to war in the 1970s.

Since then, there have been many positive developments. Starting with the 1984 Treaty of Friendship and Cooperation which settled the Beagle Dispute, twenty-three out of the twenty-four outstanding border disputes have been settled (the twenty-fourth has been agreed by governments but is stuck in congress). Chile has taken part of a number of arms control and confidence building measures (in particular the Mendonca Declaration of 1991 on chemical and biological weapons signed by Brazil, Argentina and Chile). Contacts between the military establishments have grown in frequency and density since 1986 and in November 1995 a memorandum of understanding on security affairs was agreed with Argentina.[30] Diplomatic and political exchanges have flourished based on a convergence of market liberal economic policies and undoubtedly assisted by the 1989 presidential elections in Chile. In addition by 1995 Chile had decided to shift to seek closer relations (although not membership) with Mercosur, signing an association agreement in June 1996. Hitherto Chile had been forthright in its prioritization of NAFTA membership. All this can be taken as evidence of Chile's inclusion an expanding security community in the Southern Cone.

On the other hand there remain grounds for hesitancy. Securing domestic political support for the delineation of historically contested boundaries has not been easy.[31] In 1992, for example, 17 percent of Argentinians and 37 percent of Chileans thought that military threats were likely or very likely. But the more important issue concerns the position of the Chilean military. In part this has to do with the continued political role of the military which is much stronger than in Brazil and which, for example, enjoys continued control over the level and content of defense spending (significantly higher than in Brazil or Argentina). But, more importantly, it has to do with the military's underlying assumptions about their role and the nature of regional international politics. The Chilean military (and especially the army) has shown very little interest in peacekeeping operations and discussion of new security issues and its doctrine, procurement and planning remains focused on the traditional roles of power projection and the protection of borders.

Finally, if there is an emerging loosely coupled security community in the southern cone and a consolidated security community involving Canada, the USA and Mexico, what is the status of the region in between? The first point to make is that the popular idea that this sub-region has become increasingly pacific since the late nineteenth century needs to be treated with considerable caution, especially when one considers the whole spectrum of armed conflict. Balancing behaviour and balance of power discourse has been extremely common and the possibility of using force as part of foreign policy has been taken for granted by the militaries of many South and Central American states. In this sub-region there have been seven international conflicts in the twentieth century. Military interventions involving the USA have been still more common, as have civil wars and very high levels of social violence. As discussed at the start of this chapter, trends in the 1980s pointed towards increasing conflict with violence between Peru and Ecuador, serious tensions between Argentina and Chile and Venezuela and Colombia, and an internationalized set of civil wars in Central America.

Since then it is possible to highlight positive developments: the success of regional pacification in Central America, involving confidence building measures, regional mediation efforts and an active role for the OAS and UN; the growth in the 1980s of new forms of political concertacion in the 1980s; the spread of economic integration and cooperation agreements; and the reinvigoration of the OAS, not least with its new found determination to uphold its Charter commitment to democracy and its actions in Peru, Guatamala and Haiti.[32] In addition, Latin American arms imports declined from around 8 percent of the world total in 1981 to 6.5 percent in 1987, to 3.8 percent in 1991. Latin American arms exports declined from 0.46 percent of world total in 1981, to 1.5 percent in 1987, to 0.37 percent in 1991.

Yet there are very serious difficulties with the notion of even a loosely coupled security community in this area, reflecting the increased social and economic heterogeneity of the region as a whole. In the first place, specific border conflicts remain far from settled, most obviously given the war between Peru and Ecuador which flared up in early 1995, but also between Venezuela and Colombia where tensions have been fed by guerrillas, drugs, and illegal immigration and where the two sides mobilized in 1987 and 1993. These conflicts certainly pose problems for liberal approaches that stress the importance of democracy and growing economic interdependence.[33] Secondly, although activity and discussion has certainly increased dramatically, the OAS is very far from providing an effective security system, of either collective or cooperative security.[34] Third, and closely related, there is the position of the United States. Historically, the USA has never been consistently opposed to the use of force in the region. On the one hand, it has sometimes chosen to remain disengaged from international tensions (as with Peru/Ecuador in 1939/1941 or with Chile/Argentina in the 1970s). On the other hand, Washington has been willing to use military force itself, to support or actively promote the use of force by others (as in Central America in the 1980s), and to resist multilateral security arrangements both regionally and within the UN that would seriously curb its traditional unilateralism. The end of the Cold War has done little to alter this historical pattern. Finally, there is the difficult question of civil wars and social violence. Partly because of the relative success of state- and nation-building and the absence of secessionist movements; and partly because of the lack of the kinds of international involvement that characterized Central America in the 1980s, most of this violence is contained within the borders of states. Yet the levels of violence have been very high (165,000 killed in Colombia in the 1980s alone). If, as Deutsch originally argued, security communities have to do with groups of *people*, as well as collectivities, integrated to the point that they will not fight each other, then it becomes impossible to hide behind the distinction between international wars and other forms of social conflict. Precisely how one deals with the relationship between social and international violence is not clear. Yet continued high levels of social conflict and the privatizaion of violence provides a further reason for doubting the existence of even a loosely coupled security community.

Conclusion

Although no doubt possessing common attributes and sharing an "elective affinity," the Latin American case provides important grounds for doubting that regional "anarchies" are everywhere alike or that we can meaningfully talk of a Westphalian system whose essence remains unchanged and whose logic applies universally. Security communities are not illusions, deceptive islands of peace in a self-help system whose logic carries with it the ever present danger of a return to war and conflict. This chapter has argued that a loosely coupled, if still imperfect, security community can be identified within Mercosur, built around the changes that have taken place in the core relationship between Brazil and Argentina. It is a bounded community, with Chile's position still ambiguous and with the rest of South America still beset by a range of traditional and non-traditional security challenges.

This chapter has also argued that the move away from rivalry and conflict between Brazil and Argentina cannot be reduced either to power considerations or to a narrow set of issue-specific, instrumentally driven cooperative moves. Rather the process of cooperation challenges both neorealist and neoliberal theories, highlighting by contrast: first, the critical importance of the historical construction of states and of historically specific patterns of interaction; secondly, the ways in which a series of separate but parallel shifts in interests and identities facilitated cooperation; thirdly, the extent to which these shifts were the product of both domestic and international factors and were reflected in, and powerfully reinforced by, the on-going process of interaction and the creation of institutionalized cooperation; but, finally, the way in which barriers to cooperation need to be understood as much as the product of continued divergent identities as of material obstacles and disincentives.

Notes

I would like to thank the editors, David Mares, Andres Fontana and Charles Kupchan for their helpful comments on earlier versions of this chapter.

1 Twentieth century interstate wars in South America consist of: Bolivia–Paraguay, 1931/35 (Chaco War); Peru–Colombia, 1932 (Leticia War); Peru–Ecuador, 1939–41, 1981, 1995; Britain–Argentina, 1982 (Falklands–Malvinas War).

2 Karl W. Deutsch et al., *Political Community in the North Atlantic Area* (Princeton: Princeton University Press, 1957), p. 5.

3 Robert N. Burr, "The Balance of Power in Nineteenth-Century South America: An Exploratory Essay," *Hispanic American Historical Review* 35, 1 (February 1955), p. 98.

4 Some recent accounts seriously underplay the extent of previous conflict and hence the difficulties of rapprochement. Reiss, for example, mistakenly believes that the two countries had never seen each other as enemies or even adversaries. Mitchell Reiss, *Bridled Ambition: Why Countries Constrain Their Nuclear Capabilities* (Washington: Woodrow Wilson Centre Press, 1995), p. 52.

5 Because of military fears and suspicions, the first direct bridge between the two countries was not built until 1938.

6 Both quoted in Stanley E. Hilton, "The Argentine Factor in Twentieth-Century Brazilian Foreign Policy Strategy," *Political Science Quarterly* 100, 1 (Spring 1985), pp. 32 and 34.

7 For the classic study of this subject see E. Bradford Burns, *The Unwritten Alliance: Rio-Branco and Brazilian–American Relations* (New York: Columbia University Press, 1966).

8   Geopolitical rhetoric could not be further from the language of security communities. To give a flavour taken from Brazil's most influential geopolitician, Golbery do Couto e Silva: "The insecurity of the citizen within the nation and the insecurity of one state in relation to the others, the omnipresent vision of war – civil war, subversive war or international war – dominate the world of our time ..." *A Geopolítica do Brasil* (Rio de Janeiro: José Olympio, 1967), p. 13.

9   On the way in which this image of Argentina's regional role was constructed historically and embedded in the education system and the mental maps of elites see Carlos Escudé, "Argentine Territorial Nationalism," *Journal of Latin American Studies* 20 (1988), pp. 139–165.

10 Gregory F. Treverton, "Interstate Conflict in Latin America," in Kevin J. Middlebrook and Carlos Rico, eds., *The United States and Latin America in the 1980s* (Pittsburgh: University of Pittsburgh Press, 1986), p. 582.

11 Gordon Mace, "Regional Integration in Latin America: A Long and Winding Road," *International Journal* 43 (Summer 1988), p. 426.

12 Jack Child, *Geopolitics and Conflict in South America: Quarrels Among Neighbours* (New York: Praeger, 1985), p. 3. Along similar lines see Michael Morris and Victor Millán eds., *Controlling Latin American Conflicts* (Boulder, CO: Westview, 1983); For a more nuanced and sckeptical view, see Walter Little, "International Conflicts in Latin America," *International Affairs* 63, 4 (Autumn 1987), pp. 589–601.

13 Joseph S. Tulchin, *Argentina and the United States: A Conflicted Relationship* (Boston: Twayne Publishers,1990), p. 146.

14 On the close coincidence the worsening of relations with Chile and the course of negotiations over Itaipu, see Moniz Bandeira, *Estado Nacional e Política Internacional na América Latina* (Brasilia: Editora Universidade de Brasilia, 1993), p. 240.

15 See Maria Regina Soares de Lima, "The Political Economy of Brazilian Foreign Policy: Nuclear Energy, Trade, and *Itaipu*," PhD. dissertation, University of Vanderbilt, 1986, especially pp. 395–408.

16 See Mónica Serrano, "Brazil and Argentina" in Mitchell Reiss and Robert S. Litvak eds., *Nuclear Proliferation after the Cold War* (Washington: The Woodrow Wilson Center Press, 1995), pp. 238–239.

17 See Helio Jaguaribe, "Brasil-Argentina: Breve Análise das Relações de Conflito e Cooperação," in *O Novo Cenário Internacional* (Rio de Janeiro: Editora Guanabara, 1986).

18 The relationship between balance of power discourse and the language of fraternal cooperation is often very close and Hilton provides many examples of what one might call the strategic use of cooperative security discourse on the part of the Brazilians. Thus Rio Branco in 1909: "We should treat Argentina with real fraternity, but without neglecting our defenses for a single moment." Or Vargas in 1934: "Our policy has been one of cordial friendship with Argentina. We should continue it, but we need to take military precautions." Hilton, "The Argentine Factor," pp. 36

and 37. For details on post-war moves to cooperation see Juan Archibaldo Lanús, *De Chapultepec al Beagle, Política Exterior Argentina, 1945–1980* (Buenos Aires, Emecé, 1984), chap. 4, and Bandeira, *Estado Nacional*, chaps. 5 and 6.

19 On the use of additional assumptions to salvage realist arguments, see Alexander Wendt, "Constructing International Politics," *International Security* 20, 1 (Summer 1995), p. 78.

20 Joseph S. Tulchin, "Una perspectiva histórica de la política argentina frente al Brasil," *Estudios Internacionales* 13, 52 (Oct./Dec. 1980), p. 464.

21 On the details of this process see Sonia de Camargo, "Caminhos que se juntam e se separam: Brasil e Argentina, uma visão comparativa," *Política e Estrategia* 10, 3 (1986), pp. 372–403; and Sonia de Camargo, "Brasil e Argentina: A integração em questão," *Contexto Internacional* 9 (1989), pp. 45–62

22 See Reiss, *Bridled Ambition*, especially pp. 54–58; and Thierry Riga, "Une approche coopérative de la non-prolifération nucléaire: l'exemple de l'Argentine et du Brésil," Working Paper no. 29 (New York and Geneva: UNIDIR, 1994).

23 For details of the evolution of the nuclear relationship, see Monica Hirst and Héctor Eduardo Bocco, "Cooperação nuclear e integração Brasil-Argentina," *Contexto Internacional* 9 (1989), pp. 63–78. See also Thomas Guedes da Costa, "A Idéia de Medidas de Confiança Mútua em uma Visão Brasileira," *Contexto Internacional* 14, 2 (1990), pp. 297–308.

24 Philippe C. Schmitter, "Change in Regime Type and Progress in International Relations," in Emanuel Adler and Beverly Crawford, eds., *Progress in Post War International Relations* (New York: Columbia University Press, 1991), p. 96.

25 See Edward D. Mansfield and Jack Synder, "Democratization and the Danger of War," *International Security* 20, 1 (Summer 1995), pp. 5–38.

26 See Monica Hirst, "La Dimension Politica del Mercosur: Atores, Politizacion e Ideologia," FLACSO, Buenos Aires, Serie de Documentos (November 1995).

27 This argument is made by David R. Mares, "Equilibrios Estrategicos y Medidas de Confianza Mutua en America Latina: La historia de una relacion ambigua y compleja," in Francisco Rojas Aravena, ed., *Balanco Estrategico y Medidas de Confianza Mutua* (Santiago: FLACSO/Woodrow Wilson Center, 1996).

28 On the limits and weaknesses of the non-proliferation regime as it affects Brazil and Argentina, see Serrano, "Brazil and Argentina," pp. 242–247.

29 Roberto Russell, "Los ejes estructurantes de la política exterior Argentina," *America Latina/Internacional* 1, 2 (1994), pp. 5–26.

30 See Augusto Varas and Claudio Fuentes, *Defensa Nacional, Chile 1990–1994* (Santiago: Libros Flacso, 1994), esp. ch. 5.

31 See Augusto Varas and Isaac Caro eds., *Medidas de Confianza Mutua en América Latina* (Santiago: FLACSO, 1994), especially chaps. 6 and 9.

32 For an assessment of regional initiatives see Carl Kaysen et al., *Collective Responses to Regional Problems: The Case of Latin America and the Caribbean* (Cambridge, MA: American Academy of Arts and Sciences, 1994).
33 One might want to salvage some notion of security cooperation by highlighting the degree to which the Peru/Ecuador conflict illustrates a particular pattern of limited border conflict: the use of force not designed to seize large areas of territory or to "win," but rather as a diplomatic instrument to force the issue back onto the agenda and to try and win concessions at the diplomatic negotiations that, as both sides know, will inevitably follow. There is, then, a clear willingness to use force, but this is a limited conception of force within a strong diplomatic culture. Indeed the importance of the Latin American predilection for international law is not that it obviates conflict but that it may provide a framework for its management and limitation.
34 For an analysis of the increased activity, see Andres Fontana, "Seguridad Cooperativa: Tendencias Globales y Oportunidades Para El Continente Americano," Working Paper, ISEN, Buenos Aires, May 1996.

8 Australia and the search for a security community in the 1990s

Richard A. Higgott and Kim Richard Nossal

Introduction

When Karl Deutsch and his colleagues proposed the concept of "security community,"[1] their focus was on groups rather than single states. Given the necessarily plural nature of "community," it might be wondered how a single-country case study might assist in the retrieval of Deutsch's concept of security community. We argue that the case of Australia is indeed useful, because of the country's shifting location in global politics. While such changes are by no means unique, few political communities have as self-consciously sought to "relocate" themselves, in economic, diplomatic, and security terms as Australia did in the 1980s and 1990s. Between 1983 and 1996, the Australian Labor Party (ALP) governments of Bob Hawke and Paul Keating pursued an undisguised "push into Asia." While this hardly represented an Australian "defection" from the West, as Samuel Huntington put it,[2] there can be little doubt that the ALP was seeking to "move" Australia from being a European/American-oriented community to being a nation in, and of, the Asia Pacific.

In addition, however, we argue that the Australian case offers analytical insights into foreign policy transformation. We will argue that a combination of post-imperial history, geo-strategic location, and national politico-economic development provided the impetus for the pursuit of a liberal internationalist foreign policy that can foster the growth of security communities in the post-Cold War era.

Australia, we suggest, has increasingly become a state in international politics that sits uneasily between two worlds in security terms. The first is the Anglo-American world of Australia's nineteenth-century origins and twentieth-century development. Like other settler societies – such as Canada, New Zealand, and South Africa – Australia evolved from colonies that Britain either established or seized from others. Created by an act of the British Parliament in 1901, Australia was not independent, but a self-governing and non-sovereign dominion of the British Empire. While it acquired formal sovereignty from Britain with the Statute of Westminster in 1931 along with the other dominions, a sense of independence from Britain took longer to develop, with Australia only fully coming of age during the years of American hegemony in the middle and later years of the twentieth century.

While early on those living in Australia developed a distinctive identity and culture – perhaps best exemplified by the thousands of words that are distinctly Australian and not inherited from England – the links to Europe and the United States were powerful and pervasive. Until recently, all but a minority of Australians had familial roots in the United Kingdom and Ireland. While the institutions of the community – political, economic, social, educational, religious, cultural, sporting – evolved their own distinctive Australian characteristics, most of those institutions could be traced in some fashion to one or both of the two imperial centres, British or American. National identity tended to be an admixture of British and indigenous symbols.[3]

Likewise, for much of the twentieth century, Australian wealth was linked to a global imperial economy centered in England. The cultural referents of Australians tended to be European and American. Security was intricately bound to the security of empire – first the British Empire, and then, after Britain had demonstrated its inability (if not unwillingness) to defend Australia from the predations of imperial Japan in the early 1940s, the global defense networks of the United States in the Cold War era.

Australia's other world is that of the Asia Pacific.[4] A consequence of globalization in the 1960s and 1970s, Australia's location in the international division of labor changed, shifting the basis of wealth away from Britain and Europe. And when the government in Canberra discarded its discriminatory "White Australia" policy in the early 1970s,[5] the ethnic mix of Australians, particularly in the cities, was radically altered. And, as the country's location changed, Australia's political, bureaucratic, educational, and corporate elites pushed the idea that Australia was also a member of the Asia Pacific region, a country in Asia, and a part of an Asian "neighborhood." This resulted in what one journalist breathlessly termed the progressive "Asianization" of Australia.[6]

But, we will argue, Australia's two worlds do not sit easily with one another. The shift from one security community – the alliance between Australia, New Zealand, and the United States – to another, more nascent, and more ambiguous, community in Asia, perhaps best exemplified by the Australia-Indonesia Agreement on Maintaining Security of 18 December 1995, has not been easy. In particular, there has been a domestic reaction to the attempt to change Australia's security location. Following the defeat of the ALP in the March 1996 elections, the Liberal/National Coalition government of John Howard backed away from the ALP's aggressive Asian policy, instead adopting a pro-American "tilt" in its foreign policy. Likewise, the "push into Asia" also spawned views like those of Pauline Hanson, an independent member of Parliament, who in her maiden speech warned that Australia was being "swamped by Asians."[7]

Our argument proceeds in five parts. We begin with a brief overview of the "old" world of Australia's security in the post-1945 period. Next we examine the changes of the 1980s and 1990s and survey the efforts to move to develop a new security location. The third section looks at the "new" world of Australian security, including the 1995 security agreement with Indonesia, and the aftermath of the defeat of Labor in the March 1996 elections. The fourth and fifth parts contrast Australian and Asian perspectives on community. We examine Canberra's propensity to build "community" in international politics, and how that affected efforts to shift Australia's security location. We then turn to Asian views of Australia's membership in regional community, and survey the obstacles to the achievement of a security community in the Asia Pacific given the lack of shared sense of "we-ness" so necessary for the flourishing of a security community.

The "old" world of Australian security

Rich, developed, liberal-democratic, and sparsely populated, Australia is located on the southern margins of the Asia Pacific.[8] Historically, Australians tended to perceive themselves as being far removed from what was seen as the cultural and economic "homeland" of Britain. The only other neighbor in the immediate vicinity "like" Australia was New Zealand; by contrast, the other neighbors immediately to the north – populous, poor, non-industrialized, undeveloped, and non-democratic – were regarded by most Australians primarily as a threat, either to the racial purity of the Australian nation, or to the security and well-being of the Australian state.[9] Thus, in the first four decades of nationhood after Australia was created in 1901, the government sought to provide security for the nation by insulating Australia from its neighbors, isolating itself from the natural dictates of geographic proximity, and seeking "a great and powerful friend"[10] to provide the physical security that a small nation with a vast coastline could not provide for itself against such putatively predatory neighbors. In such a lonely, fragile, and essentially insecure location, "community" was hardly possible.

If community with their northern neighbors was seen as impossible, Australians did nonetheless develop a Deutschian "security community" after the Second World War. The inability of Britain to defend Australia against Japan, and the widespread view in Australia that the United States had "saved" the country from the Japanese, prompted both the government and ordinary Australians to swap patrons. In security terms, they turned from one "friend" who was no longer either so great or so powerful to one who clearly was both. The arrangements that grew out of American involvement in the Pacific war and solidified during the emergent Cold War constituted a security community. The community was institutionalized via a formal alliance between Australia, New Zealand and the United States (ANZUS),[11] and given concrete manifestation through Australian participation in both the Korean and Vietnam wars. Security links with Britain (and, in the South Pacific, France) remained strong. While Britain was no longer the major alliance partner, military and intelligence arrangements flourished in the wider context of the Western alliance during the Cold War. Thus, this community was marked by huge geographic distances between its members, confirming Michael Barnett's observation, made in the context of the Israeli–American security relationship, that shared identities need not be tied to spatial proximity.[12]

Despite the distances that separated its members, it nonetheless was a "security community" in the Deutschian sense. First, the members of that community regarded it as inconceivable that force would be used against one another in the settlement of disputes. Secondly, the organization of the security arrangements was an on-going confirmation of what Adler and Barnett call the "we-ness" of the group members: Australians, New Zealanders, Americans, and Europeans. And it confirmed the concomitant necessary "they-ness" of Asians (an "otherness" that persisted even when Australian troops were used to provide security to Asian states, such as in Korea in the early 1950s, or South Vietnam during the 1960s, or Malaysia and Singapore via the Five Power Defence Arrangement).

Thirdly, security and the economy went hand in hand. On the one hand, Australia's security arrangements reflected the country's economic ties. In the two decades after 1945, Australia's economic links were with Britain, the United States, and Japan. In 1945, close to half of all Australian imports came from Britain; by 1970, the United States was supplying a quarter of Australia's imports and Britain another quarter. In the 1950s and into the 1960s, the bulk of Australian exports went to Britain, eventually to be replaced by Japan in the mid-1960s. Likewise, economic links reflected, and reinforced, security: Australia was a keen participant in the Colombo Plan, seeing economic development as a means of avoiding internal and external subversion from Communism.

Relocating Australia's security community

By the late 1960s, Australia's location in the international system shifted. It began with changes in patterns of trade, accelerated by the growth of the Japanese economy in the 1960s, British membership in the European Economic Community in the early 1970s, the solidification of the Japanese–Australian trading relationship in the 1970s, and the growth of the newly industrializing countries in the 1970s and 1980s. By the 1980s, the shift had become pronounced: the Asia Pacific region, including the South Pacific, Southeast Asia, Northeast Asia, and North America, accounted for two-thirds of Australia's exports and imports. By contrast, Britain's role as a trading partner – but not its role as a source of foreign investment[13] – had diminished dramatically: just over 3 percent of Australian exports went to Britain; and only 2 percent of Australian imports came from Britain. In short, by the 1980s, Australia was more significantly integrated in economic terms into the Asia Pacific than any other Western industrialized state.

This change in economic location was accompanied by a shift in the emphasis of foreign policy. Australian policy-makers began to attach an increasing importance to both multilateralism and regionalism, particularly in economic policy. Disputes over agricultural trade with the United States prompted Canberra to try and find solutions to the threats to its economic security in multilateral fora. At the outset of the Uruguay Round, Australia took the lead in organizing the Cairns group, countries committed to the liberalization of agricultural trade. Likewise, Australia began looking to regional organizations as a forum for the discussion of economic conflicts in which it and its major trading partners were increasingly involved. For example, it was instrumental in the formation of the Asia Pacific Economic Cooperation (APEC) forum in 1989.[14]

The changing location of Australia in the global economy also altered the country's bilateral relationship with the United States. In the view of some, economic issues in the bilateral relationship began to assume greater importance.[15] The result was that the historical priority that had been placed on military security and the ANZUS alliance declined somewhat – even before the end of the Cold War. Although the alliance was still deemed important, it no longer dominated the relationship, bringing into sharp relief the different theoretical directions that the foreign economic policies of the two allies took in the late 1980s and early 1990s. As the United States became more of a realist in foreign economic policy, Australia pursued a more liberal institutionalist approach. These differences frequently spilled into the security domain. For example, James Baker, the United States secretary of state, strongly condemned the proposal by Gareth Evans, Australia's minister for foreign affairs and trade from 1988 to 1996, to establish a Conference on Security and Cooperation in Asia (CSCA) modelled on the Conference on Security and Cooperation in Europe.[16]

At the same time, there was a marked change in the international politics of Australia's region during the 1980s. Most importantly, the security community that had been the hallmark of international relations in the South Pacific began to fray somewhat with the decision of the French government to blow up the *Rainbow Warrior*, the Greenpeace vessel spearheading opposition to French nuclear tests in the South Pacific.[17] Although Australia, New Zealand, and other South Pacific states had been increasingly at odds with France over the French nuclear testing program that had begun with atmospheric tests in 1966, the *Rainbow Warrior* bombing was the first occasion when one of the members of the Western alliance in the South Pacific had used force against another.

The fracture deepened when the New Zealand Labour government

270

of David Lange, largely in response to the bombing, adopted a policy that barred nuclear-powered and nuclear-armed ships from New Zealand harbors. The United States, worried about the precedent that would be set for other American allies, responded harshly. It imposed sanctions against New Zealand, including a ban on high-level contacts; it downgraded the country from an "ally" to a "friend," and effectively suspended its membership in ANZUS.[18]

These disputes also affected Australia. The Australian government of Bob Hawke might have been displeased at Lange's policy, and, as Coral Bell notes, New Zealand's suspension from the alliance actually brought the United States and Australia closer together.[19] But Washington's harsh reaction served to remind Australians of the limits of American tolerance of divergence within its security arrangements in the Pacific. Likewise, the unsympathetic response of both London and Washington to the bombing led some Australians to wonder whether Britain or the United States would defend Australian security when antipodean interests conflicted with those of the metropolitan powers – as they so clearly did in the *Rainbow Warrior* case.[20]

At the same time, changes were occurring in the composition of Australian society. For the seven decades after the federation was founded in 1901, Australian immigration policy was marked by an undisguised effort to keep the country racially pure. It was a remarkably successful policy: in 1947, for example, 97.9 percent of all Australians had been born in Australia, Britain, Ireland, or New Zealand.[21] However, the "White Australia" policy was by slow degrees liberalized in the 1960s,[22] and finally discarded after the Australian Labor Party (ALP) under Gough Whitlam came to power in 1972.[23] It was replaced with a universal, ethnically blind policy. The pattern of immigration – and the ethnic face of Australia – changed. By 1991–2, Britain was still the largest single source of settlers arriving in Australia – 13.5 percent. But that year over half of Australia's new immigrants were from Hong Kong (12 percent), Vietnam (9 percent), the Philippines, India, China, Taiwan, Malaysia, Sri Lanka, and New Zealand. The Asian-born population grew considerably, from 1.3 percent of the population in 1971 to 2.5 percent in 1981 to 4.3 in 1989.[24]

These changes all prompted a widespread rethinking of Australian identity among the contemporary Australian intellectual, corporate, and policy-making elite in the 1980s and early 1990s. The transition being experienced by Australia was widely seen as an opportunity to mold and consolidate a new national identity and a new international role for Australia distinct from that which for so long had been conditioned by the Anglo-American connection. The story of the intellectual struggle to reshape Australia's identity has been told in detail elsewhere.[25] However, this reconsideration of identity was also reflected in the changing nature of Australian foreign and security policy.

The major element in the redefinition of national identity was a subtle downplaying of links with a British and American past, and instead the embrace of a new Asian future. Sir Robert Menzies, prime minister from 1949 to 1966, had declared himself to be "British to the boot heels," an Anglophilic view that gave way in the 1960s to Harold Holt's pro-Americanism, best captured in his catch-cry "All the way with LBJ." In the 1980s, Bob Hawke would discover Australia's "Asian future"; by the early 1990s, as one critic noted, Paul Keating's prime ministership could be characterized by the slogan "It's all the go with Tokyo."[26]

According to this redefinitional exercise, it was time for Australia to abandon the 200 years of struggle against "the reality of its own geography," to use the words of Australia's foreign minister between 1988 and 1996, Gareth Evans.[27] Australia should no longer view itself as an Anglo-American outpost, a transplanted European nation in Asia. Rather, Australians should come to terms with their geography, and admit that their country was part of the Asian region. Not that Australians were "Asians," but rather that, in the words of Gareth Evans, "The old perceptions . . . based on "Asian" and "European" identities, are losing their utility."[28]

Part of this coming to terms often meant forging an identity that was more robustly different from the past. That is why, for example, in the 1990s Keating tried so hard to replace the symbolic links to a British past with new symbols. He argued that to close what he called the Australian "branch office of empire,"[29] it was necessary to replace the ensign and its Union Flag with an indigenous flag; and to cut the umbilical cord to the British Crown and instead create a republic. In the end he and the ALP were defeated in the March 1996 elections before such symbolic changes could be made, but the debate over redefining identity was nonetheless sharpened by such efforts.

As Stephen FitzGerald reminds us, it is important to recognize that the main proponents of such a redefinition were mostly institutional: "The Australian discovery of Asia has been dominated by institutional engagement: governments – Commonwealth [i.e., federal] and state – political parties, government departments, business corporations, university administrations, media organisations . . ."[30] And while there were numerous proponents of the Asian idea at the governmental level in the 1980s and 1990s, there can be no doubt that the most vigorous was Gareth Evans, the minister for foreign affairs and trade in the Australian Labor Party governments of Bob Hawke and Paul Keating. In numerous speeches after he was appointed to the portfolio in 1988, Evans pushed the idea that Australia should be seen as a country that is part of Asia; that Asia is Australia's future; that Asia is "where we live." As he wrote in 1991: "Our future lies, inevitably, in the Asia Pacific region. This is where we must live, must survive strategically and economically, and find a place and a role if we are to develop our full potential as a nation."[31] While Meg Gurry has shown that such attempts to conceptualize the importance of Asia to Australia can be traced back to the 1940s,[32] Evans's efforts to turn Australia, in his words, from an "odd man out" in Asia to an "odd man in," were more persistent and more coherent than in the past. To be sure, this quest occasionally took an odd turn. For example, in Brunei in July 1995 for the annual Association of Southeast Asian (ASEAN) foreign ministers' meeting, Evans argued that Australia and New Zealand should be issued invitations to the Asia–Europe Economic meeting then being planned for Bangkok in 1996. He buttressed his argument with a new map, whose projection portrayed Australia as being in the center of an East Asian hemisphere. Rather than the flat distortions of a Mercator projection, Evans's map looked as though "it was drawn by someone staring out of a space capsule as it orbited over Australia."[33]

The "new" world of Australian security

Not surprisingly, such a dramatic relocation had an impact on the attitudes of Australians about external threats to their well-being, and on their definition of the protection needed to mitigate those threats; this is especially the case in attitudes toward alliance structures and regional neighbors.

First, there has been a dramatic change in the nature of threat perception in Australia. For much of the twentieth century, concern focussed on threats to sovereign integrity posed by those who could invade Australian territory, most palpably seen in the invasion scares of the early 1940s. By the 1980s and 1990s, by contrast, many Australians had begun to define security more broadly, with greater threats seen in the economic realm than from invasion.[34] For example, assertive American economic policies were seen as causing damage to Australian well-being: indeed, facing huge losses in export earnings because of American export enhancement programs, an Australian foreign minister, Bill Hayden, would go so far as to wonder aloud whether the United States was still Australia's friend.[35] Likewise, a threat was seen in the declining autonomy of the state over the control of national economic well-being in an era of globalization; the suggested solution was greater liberalization and openness.[36]

Secondly, the changing nature of threat perception and the "push" into Asia produced a contradiction in Australian policy toward the region. The contradiction can be simply stated: the government does not believe that its neighbors pose any threat to the security of Australia; however, the government spends approximately AUD$10 billion a year to defend Australia against threats to its security that could only come from its neighbors.[37]

The paradox had its beginnings in the policy of "defence self-reliance" – a doctrine that proposed remaining under the US-backed ANZUS umbrella, but acquiring the capability to defend Australia against all but a major aggressor without having to depend on a "great and powerful friend." While this policy dates back to Richard Nixon's Guam doctrine of 1969, the Australian government enshrined the idea in its 1987 defense white paper.[38] Becoming self-reliant within ANZUS necessitated a AUD$25 billion program of capital acquisition to ensure that the Australian Defence Forces had the appropriate capabilities to defend against military attack.[39] In the meantime, however, the government would seek "to strengthen the commonality of strategic interests" between Australia and the countries of the region, mainly by encouraging "security cooperation."[40]

Canberra's policy on regional security was sharpened two years later. In a Ministerial Statement issued in December 1989,[41] Evans outlined plans for relations with Australia's neighbors for the 1990s. The statement advocated the adoption of a policy of "comprehensive engagement" in Southeast Asia. Much of the discussion of how Australia would provide for its security focused on the military aspects of Australian security, and indeed was generally consistent with the precepts of the 1987 defense white paper. In addition, the statement did feature an extended discussion of "non-military

274

threats" – the environment, health problems such as AIDS, drugs, and illegal migration.[42]

The 1989 Statement can be seen as an attempt by a foreign minister to allay concerns in Southeast Asia that Australia's defense policy was directed at them.[43] Indeed, Evans continued to try to soothe Australia's neighbors, claiming for example in February 1990 that Canberra would seek "active participation in any gradually emerging sense of shared strategic and security interests" in the region. Although he was manifestly sceptical of "a sort of 'common Southeast Asian home' security concept on Gorbachevian lines," Evans did indicate that "Australia wants to be constructively involved in any dialogues" on regional security.[44]

Between 1989 and 1994 Evans tried out a number of different conceptions of security for application in the region.[45] He finally settled on "cooperative security" as the most appropriate approach in a regional context.[46] However, the idea of cooperative security did not originate in Australia: due acknowledgement needs to be located elsewhere, especially in Canadian policy and intellectual circles.[47] However, Evans did embrace the idea of cooperative security as part of his pursuit of good international citizenship, seeking to occupy the high moral ground that was so often in the past the preserve of Scandinavians and Canadians.

But the embrace of cooperative security by Evans exposed a tension within the foreign policy-making community in Canberra between the Department of Foreign Affairs and Trade (DFAT) on the one hand, and the defense establishment on the other. While DFAT eagerly embraced the newer conceptions of security implicit in the "habits of dialogue" associated with cooperative security, the defense establishment – including its intellectual arm, the Strategic and Defence Studies Centre at the Australian National University – remained more diffident and "old-style realist" on such questions. This led to a discrepancy between the rhetoric of Australian security policy in the Asia Pacific region, and the substance of Australian defence policy on such matters as weapons procurement and defense preparation.[48]

For Evans, the problem was particularly acute, for he was unable to solve the basic contradiction in Australia's security policy. Australia might be "pushing" into Asia, but Australia's defense policies were still designed to protect the country from threats that could come from nowhere else but regional neighbors. Moreover, when the Keating government adopted a new white paper on defense in 1994, it was unwilling to resolve this basic contradiction. The foreign minister sought to soothe; the defense white paper was blunt:

> [O]ur region is one of great dynamism, strategically as well as economically. The next fifteen years will see great change in our strategic environment. With the end of the Cold War, important new uncertainties have emerged about the future strategic situation in Asia. Economic growth will increase the power of nations in our region, and political change may make their policies less predictable. Because of these uncertainties, we acknowledge the possibility that our security environment could deteriorate, perhaps quite seriously in the future. We recognise that at some time in the future armed force could be used against us and that we need to be prepared to meet it.[49]

To be sure, the authors of the white paper wriggled mightily to escape the obvious implications of this prudential analysis, dwelling at length on the range of Australia's engagement with the Asian region, and stressing defense cooperation with both close ASEAN neighbors and the states of Northeast Asia.

But the essence of the paradox remained: for all the desire on the part of the country's elites to "relocate" Australia as part of Asia, there was little willingness to alter the definition of identity sufficiently to admit that Australia's Asian neighbors did not pose a risk to the country's well-being.[50]

However, the tensions in this approach did not deter Evans from pursuing the cooperative security idea, focussing in large part on the great powers. For example, in March 1995, he bruited the idea of a "security grouping" in Asia to balance, as he put it, "the minuet of the giants" in the Asia Pacific.[51] Likewise, Prime Minister Keating stressed that Australia, while not wanting to set up a "non-China block," had no wish to "be in the Chinese orbit."[52]

Nor, importantly, did these tensions in approach deter the ALP government from engaging in highly secret negotiations with Indonesia, the results of which were revealed in December 1995. The Australia–Indonesia Agreement on Maintaining Security was a concrete manifestation of the simultaneous pursuit of security cooperation and cooperative security, and an attempt to resolve the contradictions implicit in the defense white paper. The agreement was not an alliance or a pact. It was simply an "agreement on maintaining security." The operative articles of the agreement outline limited commitments "to consult at ministerial level about matters affecting their common security and to develop such cooperation as would benefit their own security and that of the region" (article 1); "to consult each other in the case of adverse challenges to either party or to their common security interests . . ." (article 2); and "to promote . . . mutually beneficial cooperative activities in the security field" (article 3).[53] In short, it was, as Keating put it, a declaration of trust between the two countries.

The agreement was, however, an important symbol of the "new" world of Australian security. First, the language of the agreement embraces the concepts of both cooperative security (championed by Foreign Affairs) and security cooperation (the approach of choice in the Department of Defence). Second, the signing ceremony on 18 December 1995 was equally symbolic of "Australia in Asia": held in Jakarta, it was attended by the entire upper foreign affairs/defence echelon of the Australian government – the prime minister, Paul Keating; the deputy prime minister, Kim Beazley; the minister for foreign affairs, Gareth Evans; the minister for defence, Robert Ray; the chief of the defense forces, General John Baker; and the former chief, General Peter Gration, who had negotiated the treaty. (Indeed, according to DFAT, it was the most senior delegation to have ever left Australia.) The security agreement thus shifted Australia's security stance considerably, and went some distance to resolving the contradictions inherent in the 1994 defense white paper.

But the domestic uneasiness that had been growing towards Australia's new security position reasserted itself after the general elections of 2 March 1996. The new conservative coalition of the Liberal Party and National Party under John Howard pledged to continue Labor's policy of engagement with the region, but it was clearly not as committed as Labor to the "new" security arrangements. For example, while in opposition, Alexander Downer, Howard's minister for foreign affairs, had criticized Keating for having damaged Australia's international reputation with his "obsession" with Asia;[54] and once in office, Downer quickly became embroiled in a tiff with Australia's Asian neighbors over development assistance. More importantly, the Howard government left in no doubt its preference for facets of the "old" world of Australian security: the July 1996 AUSMIN talks between Australian and United States officials at the ministerial level were given considerably more prominence by the Coalition than by Labor. And the prime minister himself distanced himself from Evans's rhetoric, asserting that Australia was in fact not faced with "a choice between its history and its geography."[55]

Australian perspectives on community in the Asia Pacific

The Australian attempt to "relocate" itself more firmly as part of Asia has thus been somewhat ambiguous. On the one hand, Australian elites generally support a redefinition of identity, a "push" into Asia, and a relocation of Australia in the region. On the other hand, those same elites have found it difficult to include a security dimension to the relocation as the Australian government seeks to come to terms with the altered structures of the international system in the post-Cold War era, and the changed neighborhood in which it finds itself.

The Australian government embraced some of the key assumptions of "security community" in its foreign policy. Much of the Australian engagement in the Asia Pacific – whether through APEC, the ASEAN Regional Forum, in its efforts at "middle power" diplomacy to bring peace to Cambodia,[56] or its bilateral agreement with Indonesia – featured a persistent emphasis on establishing processes by which the states of the region can engage in peaceful change.

More importantly, there was a firmly held belief among Australian policy-makers that "community" exists in the Asia Pacific – this notwithstanding multiple definitions of what constitutes the region.[57] This should not be surprising: Australian foreign policy-makers, like those of many other countries, tend to see the world in essentially Grotian terms, accepting an understanding of international politics as the politics of an anarchical *society* – as its favourite international relations son, Hedley Bull, put it[58] – rather than the anarchical *system* insisted on by the devotees of Kenneth Waltz.[59]

With but few exceptions,[60] most Americans, practitioners and scholars alike, tend to find notions of "society" in international politics quaintly eccentric at best, downright dangerous at worst. But those in many other countries have little problem with the more robustly Grotian perspectives of the so-called "English school" of international politics. Certainly such perspectives inform the praxis of Australian foreign policy, with the result that, for those who make Australian foreign policy, the idea of community flows naturally from an understanding of world politics as a paradox – a society of sovereign states that exists in an anarchical condition where no one has the right to command and no one is obligated to obey.

The ready acceptance of community at the international level also explains why the notion of Australia as a "good international citizen" featured so prominently in Australian foreign policy discourse under Labor. But what exactly did this mean? After all, evoking the notion of citizenship takes one into the deep water of political theory and state-society relations. It can be argued that the government's invocation of citizenship in international politics was informed by the same normative approach that informs its approach to community.

When he was still at Monash University in Melbourne, Peter Lawler evoked the possibility of a "good state" in international politics.[61] Borrowing from Václav Havel and rejecting the predominant negative view of the state, Lawler reminds us that Havel's exercise in state theory also has an international dimension, the central element of which is the notion of "moral" foreign policy. At its simplest, such an approach rejects traditional realist understandings of international relations in favor of some variant of communitarian/liberal internationalism. This is not to suggest that the resulting foreign policy is not "realist." Rather it is an approach to foreign policy that rejects Waltzian neo-realism's instrumental blindness to the potential for the development of norms and social learning as a vehicle for positive transformation in international relations. Such a position rests on a belief that contemporary change in the global Westphalian order is limiting the ability of states to behave in unrestrained "sovereign" manner; instead, there is a belief in the enhanced need for greater cooperation, and a concomitant belief that cooperative endeavors can be advanced by social learning and concerted policy action among like-minded states.

These assumptions were clearly evident during Gareth Evans's tenure as foreign minister, manifesting themselves at a policy level in the Australian commitment to institution-building in the Asia Pacific region. In this way, an understanding of international relations usually described as "idealist" found its way into the "real world" of world politics. This normative position privileged a post-hegemonic, multilateralist approach to international relations,[62] but without Kantian overtones.[63] The state-centric imperatives of the security communities approach – underwritten by traditional notions of national interest, where cooperative endeavours are negotiated between states – fitted well with the optimism in Australia and more broadly within the Asia Pacific that community could indeed be built in the region.

Australia's devotion to APEC provides an illustration of these assumptions at work, and in keeping with the kind of state behavior

Richard A. Higgott and Kim Richard Nossal

one would expect of a state committed to the idea of community at the regional level. To be sure, one can identify "real" Australian interests in APEC. But Canberra's willingness to invest the intellectual capital and diplomatic effort to APEC is not simply a tactical exercise. Rather, the genuine cognitive readjustment discussed in the previous section pushed Australian elites into initiatives of neighborliness and "good citizenship," often taking the form of institution-building.[64]

Likewise, assumptions of "community" are clearly reflected in the Australian embrace of cooperative security. Such a community-oriented approach flowed from two factors, one general, the other specific. First, as we have noted elsewhere,[65] the evolution of a conscious "middle power" foreign policy orientation represented the logical response to a recognition of Australia's changing structural location in the global order. Community-focused notions such as "cooperative security" fitted well with the normative focus of middle-power diplomacy.

Secondly, more specifically, thinking about "cooperative security" in Australia came out of the development of a post-Cold War epistemic community of scholars and practitioners (with the international relations, peace research and strategic studies community in the Research School of Pacific and Asian Studies at the Australian National University at its epicentre) working on questions of "alternative security" – alternative in the sense of being underwritten less by realist notions of balance and deterrence and more by the search for the development of new institutional arrangements appropriate to the enhancement of confidence-building.

These ideas found easy access to policy-makers because of the generally cosy relationship-some would say too cosy[66] – between academics and policymakers in Canberra. When this facility for easy input of new thinking was combined with the growing recognition among policymakers of Australia's structural redefinition of itself as "part of Asia" and a changing understanding of the nature of the Western alliance system at the end of the Cold War, cooperative security found its way easily into the language – and the praxis – of Australian foreign policy. As a policy option, it suited a changed understanding of Australia's location in the Asia Pacific. With its emphasis on confidence-building, conflict prevention, and "habits of dialogue," cooperative security offers an alternative, indeed *cooperative*, language of security to be pitted against more orthodox *state-centric* understandings of security as peace though strength. In this

280

regard, cooperative security is predicated on what Adler and Barnett see as central to a research program on security communities: "the development of shared understandings, transnational values and transaction flows to encourage community building."[67]

While Australian foreign policy has always been underwritten by conceptions of self-interest, the embrace of cooperative security nevertheless represented a wider normative exercise: an attempt to recraft interstate politics in the region in a manner that minimized traditional realist understandings of states as pre-social actors. Nonetheless, for all the Australian willingness to search for and build community in the Asia Pacific, policymakers in Canberra are only slowly sorting out their differences, as the shifts in policy evident with the Howard government demonstrate. The result is a significant ambiguity. In official discourse, one sees clear efforts to build a new "security community" in Asia, using notions like cooperative security and bilateral consultative measures such as the security agreement with Indonesia. In practice, however, Australia's security community still remains very much tied to the "old" world of the ANZUS-based alliance, and many parts of the "new" world of Asia continue to be seen as threatening to Australian interests.

Building a "security community" in the Asia Pacific?

As Australians surveyed the post-Cold War era, they saw possibilities for achieving some sense of community in their new neighborhood, perhaps even a "security community." But even if Australians were to embrace wholeheartedly the idea of such a community with their neighbors, what is the prospect for the achievement of a comparable security community to the one that they enjoyed while enveloped in the skirts of the American hegemon during the Cold War? We argue that there are a number of difficulties with the creation of a security community in the Asia Pacific.

The first is the problem of boundary – in other words, how is a community based on region going to be defined given that there is little consensus on what constitutes the region? While there are connections between economic understandings of region and security understandings of region, the two do not automatically overlap. Australia is in that group battling to see an Asia Pacific-wide understanding of an *economic* region (in contrast to a more narrowly defined East Asian understanding). But in the *security* context, Australians remain skeptical: at this stage, a nascent security community appears to be forming around ASEAN and its dialogue partners in the ASEAN Regional Forum (ARF), but not much more broadly.

A second problem is that, unlike the ANZUS-based security community, there is in the Asia Pacific no region-wide shared ideology of community. Indeed, some Asian members believe that there is a distinctly "Asian way" to cooperation. In the view of the key proponents of this idea, such as Noordin Sopiee, and Kishore Mahbubani, head of Singapore's foreign ministry,[68] there is in Asia a legitimate and culturally derived alternative to Western Cartesian approaches to statecraft, an approach which emphasizes the importance of informal, non-binding, non-legalistic interaction, and which stresses consensus and giving "face." In such a view, economic and security arrangements need not be sanctified by some form of institutional or legal framework; instead, indissoluble networks, heavily glued by trust and long-standing personal contacts developed over time, are assumed to be more important in holding agreements together.

Moreover, Mahbubani argues that there is a uniquely Asian "corporate culture" on security that combines aspects of the Western understanding of national sovereignty (especially respect for the non-interference in the affairs of other states) with resistance for other aspects of Western understandings of sovereignty (such as the acceptance of a right to intervention in the event of the abuse of universalistic assumptions on issues such as human rights) and with an Asian approach to managing difference – especially ensuring that "face" is not lost in interstate conflicts.[69]

While a specifically "Asian way" should not be thought of as impossible or dismissed out of hand,[70] it does pose an obstacle to the achievement of a security community. Australians may have an approach to international politics that is distinct from the "American way," but Australian diplomacy remains essentially Westphalian, its foreign policy essentially Cartesian, and its defense policy essentially Hobbesian. Certainly Australians tend not to engage in statecraft in the "Asian way," as Keating's wrangle with Mohammed Mahathir in 1993 and Downer's quarrels over the Development Import Finance Facility (DIFF) in 1996 demonstrate. More importantly, in the eyes of Asians themselves, Australians will always lack that most important quality for seeing security in an "Asian" manner: Asianness.

And this leads inexorably to a third problem: Australians such as Evans may deny the utility of identity based on geographic/ethnic constructs such as "Europe," or "Asia," or "North America," but this is clearly not the view of many Asians. Australia, simply put, is not *seen* to be "Asian" by Asians. As Mahathir has said, calling Australia an Asian country has no meaning whatsoever. This has considerable implications for the development of security community, which depends so heavily on the evolution of a common identity, or a "we-ness," as Adler and Barnett put it. Moreover, there are clear differences between Australia and its Asian neighbors over such issues as human rights. For their part, political leaders in the region tend to be ambivalent about Australia. While some find the Australian presence useful diplomatically, others regard Australia with some distrust for several reasons, including an annoyance with Australian preaching on human rights, or Australian hostility to the Malaysian concept of an East Asian Economic Caucus, or, the security agreement notwithstanding, Australian views on the Indonesian occupation of East Timor.

These three problems pose considerable obstacles for the achievement of a security community in the region. If the bedrock of a definition of security community is the belief that states of a region will not settle their differences by military means, then the nature of the security discourse in the Asia Pacific – in the broadest sense of including Southeast and Northeast Asia, the South Pacific, and the western seaboard of the Americas – is not that of a security community in the sense that we might think of Scandinavia or Western Europe.

But at the same time it is clear that what underlies the security dialogue in the region is an attempt to erect an architecture that will allow for the future development of such a community, even though this is not always explicitly stated. That exercise has been helped by the willingness of governments throughout the region to make use of a "two track" security dialogue – one "track" is a purely government-to-government set of relationships; the other "track" involves discussions between and among non-governmental and quasi-governmental actors. "Track two" diplomacy designed to enhance regional transparency and confidence-building in the region has occurred in numerous settings: the ASEAN Institute for Strategic and International Studies (ISIS) Roundtable Meetings, the Canadian North Pacific Cooperative Security Dialogue, and the evolving agenda of the Council for Security Cooperation in Asia Pacific (CSCAP). While there is no agreement on the value of these exercises,[71] on occasion, the tracks have converged. For example, the ARF, a government-to-government undertaking, has been deeply affected by "track two" diplomacy.[72]

Moreover, if we expand the notion of a security community to include contributing towards global or even regional governance – aspiring to provide the necessary institutions to enhance economic and social interdependence – then the intellectual history of the Asia Pacific in the last decade has been quite encouraging. While APEC might not be the last word in regional governance, if we look at the processes of information exchange and enhanced communication over economic matters that have accompanied the increased economic interdependence in the Asia Pacific since its creation in 1989, APEC has certainly been more significant in creating a sense of community than was envisaged by critics like Miles Kahler.[73] While the constraints on the continued development of APEC should not be underestimated,[74] it has potential as a catalyst in the future: APEC's facility for enhancing an understanding of notions of "community at a regional level" while at the same time doing nothing to threaten the sovereign integrity of the ruling regimes in many of its member states is important. Most of the Asian states support APEC as an informal regional structure, but are wary about possible encroachments on their sovereignty. In contrast to the development of the European Union, APEC is not an exercise in the pooling or sharing of sovereignty rather than consolidating the power of states within the context of an evolving tradition of Asia Pacific economic diplomacy.[75]

It is thus too early to say that the economic and security dialogues of the Asia Pacific represent the consolidation of a regional pluralistic security community – if we take such a community to mean a situation, "in which states identify sufficiently with each other that force is no longer seen as a means of resolving disputes."[76] But there are epistemic institutional tendencies in train which are assisting the development of specific norms, values, and regional identities. These developments are not, of course, either teleological or uniform in the impact on the various member states of the differing groupings, as the contest of differing groupings to be "the voice" of region attests. Moreover, the evolution of regional economic and security discourses in the Asia Pacific over the last decade attests to the role of region-builders "inventing" (by writing, talking, workshopping, and proselytizing) new spatial political and economic identities.[77]

Australia has contributed to this epistemic process. Reflecting its desire for acceptance, and demonstrating what we have argued was entrepreneurial leadership,[78] Australia was at the forefront of efforts to advance the debate over the virtues of regionalism – seeking to convince its regional neighbors of the virtue of open regionalism and market-led integration in the economic domain, and the virtues of multilateralism in the security domain. It was able to do this because Australia has a sophisticated foreign policy bureaucracy and an intellectual community with linkages to intellectual elites elsewhere in the region.[79]

These ideational influences did not, of course, take place in a materialist vacuum. They tended to be a reflection of the growing complexity of a globalized economy on the one hand, and the need for a more regionally-focused security discourse after the Cold War on the other. Economic regionalization has been a response to changing structures in the regional economy. However, the institutional arrangements that are accompanying this economic regionalization need to be seen in this broader structural context. Similarly, the evolution of a regional security discourse since 1991 must be seen as a response to the changing nature of regional security questions after the collapse of the Soviet Union.[80] Regional agents are *consciously responding* to the wider structural constraints and opportunities in their desire to develop appropriate institutions.

Our analysis does not suggest the decline of egoistic behaviour by states in the region. Interest can exist within a concept of community. But state-based interest and an evolving regional identity, based on an enhanced understanding of diffuse reciprocity within regional relations, are not mutually exclusive. Moreover, as the evolution of regional exercises in economic and security cooperation such as APEC and ARF have demonstrated, these new forms of interaction themselves create forms of interest and action new to the region.

The standard responses of realists might be that these developments are in their infancy; they are not sufficiently embedded; and that therefore they should be treated with skepticism. There can be no denying that these developments are neither well developed nor embedded, but we question the appropriateness of skepticism. Skeptics make few allowances for learning; instead, they work on the assumption that Asian diplomacy is destined to repeat the mistakes of European diplomacy in the past (inevitably the referent point for realist scholarship).

Likewise, skeptics are prone to see communities as immutable. But communities do fold, as the events of post-Cold War Eastern and Central/Southern Europe tell us. And that suggests that understandings of community can develop elsewhere – especially if we adopt a somewhat "minimalist" understanding of the concept of the kind outlined by Adler and Barnett – the development of shared values and beliefs; the existence of numerous and varied points and venues of contact and interaction; and the development of a longer-term relationship built not only on interest but also including the development of some sense of obligation and trust.

Our aim here is not to over-estimate the degree to which a sense of community is developing in the Asia Pacific, nor the role played by Australia in that process. Rather, it is to suggest that the processes are much more complex than most analyses imply. Simple economistic theories of regional cooperation predicated on enhanced welfare, or gravity models of enhanced cooperation emanating from increased intra-regional trade, do not tell us everything. The story of intellectual contact between the states of the region in the 1980s and 1990s – those of bodies such as the Pacific Basin Economic Council (PBEC) and Pacific Economic Cooperation Council (PECC) in the economic domain and Institute for Strategic and International Studies (ISIS) Roundtables in the security domain – demonstrate the evolution of transregional elite networks and movements providing not insignificant transregional bonds and permanent, issue-focused, interactions.[81]

Conclusion

In this chapter, we describe Australia as moving between two security communities, an "old" and a "new." In his study of Australian politics in the 1980s, Paul Kelly described the passing of the "certainties" of Australia's "old" world: White Australia, tariff protection, centralized wage-fixing, state paternalism, and imperial benevolence. Prominently featured in Australia's "new" world, and its "new" certainties, is Asia, and Australia's attempted relocation in the region.

And yet accessing the "new" world of the Asian neighborhood has clearly been difficult. Australian policy-makers have tried hard to foster a sense of community in the Asia Pacific, and, we have argued, they have had considerable success, particularly with economic institutions like APEC. Their efforts have laid the foundations for continued development in this area.

But on the issue of a security community in the region to replace the ANZUS-based security community that was for so long Australia's anchor, we are less sanguine. While the security agreement with Indonesia of December 1995 is suggestive of a new security architecture for the Asia Pacific, it is unlikely that the architecture that eventually emerges will resemble the security communities sketched out by Deutsch and his colleagues forty years ago. Rather, it is likelier that the security architecture in the Asian part of the Asia Pacific will be built around China, confirming the suggestions of those who have argued for a distinctive "Asian way" of diplomacy. There is little agreement on whether the smaller states of the region will be able to balance possible rogue behavior by a major regional power such as China, which has in the past demonstrated its willingness to put domestic politics ahead of regional economic cooperation. For while China has engaged in positive initiatives in the region, such as mediation in Cambodia, tensions with Beijing at their center continue to affect regional security politics. Whether the issue is the Spratly Islands, or the autonomy of Hong Kong, or the future of Taiwan, regional security will depend on the way in which smaller states in the region relate to China; and this, in turn, will surely influence the evolving security architecture in the Asia Pacific.

And even if a security community with a distinctive Asian quality does emerge in the twenty-first century, we are not convinced that Australia will find a home in that community. For all of the profound changes experienced by Australia in the 1980s and 1990s, for all of its apparent readiness of its elites to embrace an "Asian future," we argue that in security matters at least it is likely to remain in a liminal location for the foreseeable future.

On the one hand, Australia will continue to experience the "old" world of security based on the engagement of the United States in the Pacific. In other words, while some Australians may argue that the United States can no longer be counted on to guarantee Australian security, many Australians will continue to believe that in the event of an overt physical threat to Australia, the United States will, as it did in the early 1940s, "save" the country. Such a belief may have no foundation in reality as the United States redefines its interests in the Pacific; but only in the event of a crisis will Australians know for sure whether their security would be backstopped by the United States.

On the other hand, the processes of economic and socio-cultural globalization will continue to push Australia into the Asia Pacific. But, paradoxically, we suggest, that new world will remain, tantalizingly, just beyond reach, put there by the politics of identity: for both Australia's neighbors in Asia and most ordinary Australians themselves will continue to be unwilling to embrace that sense of "weness" that Adler and Barnett rightly argue is so important for the development of community.

The Australian experience, we suggest, has implications for the retrieval of security community as both analytical concept and as normative prescription for peace-building in the post-Cold War period. This single case study confirms the observation by Adler and Barnett that identity is the single most important *necessary* condition for the achievement of security community. Moreover, that sense of "we-ness," as Adler and Barnett put it, must be fully reciprocal among the members of a security community. It is not enough to have one country try to define itself as part of a community; that sense of community must be widely shared.

Notes

We would like to thank Ann Capling, Stuart Harris, James Morley, and J. L. Richardson for comments on initial drafts of this paper, and the Social Sciences and Humanities Research Council of Canada for support through research grant 410–95–1085.

1 Karl Deutsch et al., *Political Community and the North Atlantic Area* (Princeton: Princeton University Press, 1957).

2 Samuel P. Huntington, *The Clash of Civilizations and the Remaking of World Order* (New York: Simon & Schuster, 1996), pp. 151–154.

3 The Australian flag is the British blue ensign with a Southern Cross in the fly; the coat of arms features an emu and a kangaroo propping up a shield that clearly has its origins in the heraldry of feudal England; coinage has a distinctly antipodean obverse but the British monarch on the reverse; the national anthem, prior to the adoption of "Advance Australia Fair" in 1984, was officially God Save the Queen.

4 There is a large literature on what exactly constitutes the "Asia Pacific." The definition of the region remains contested, but in Australian discourse, the "Asia Pacific" tends to mean those countries that are routinely invited to the Asia Pacific Economic Cooperation (APEC) summits.

5 Neville Meaney, "The End of 'White Australia' and Australia's Changing Perceptions of Asia, 1945–1990," *Australian Journal of International Affairs* 49 (November 1995), pp. 171–189.

6 Greg Sheridan, "Australia's Asian Odyssey," in Sheridan, ed., *Living With Dragons: Australia Confronts its Asian Destiny* (St Leonards, NSW: Allen and Unwin, 1995), pp. 3–18.

7   Australia, *Commonwealth Parliamentary Debates*, House of Representatives, September 10, 1996, 3860–63.

8   Bruce Grant, *The Australian Dilemma: A New Kind of Western Society* (Sydney: McDonald Futura, 1983).

9   T. B. Millar, *Australia in Peace and War*, 2nd edn (Canberra: Australian National University Press, 1991), chs. 1–3; Alan Dupont, *Australia's Threat Perceptions: A Search for Security*, Canberra Papers on Strategy and Defence 82 (Canberra: Strategic and Defence Studies Centre, Australian National University, 1991), chs. 1–2; and Richard A. Higgott and Jim George, "Tradition and Change in International Relations in Australia," *International Political Science Review* 11, 4 (1990), pp. 423–38; Desmond Ball and Pauline Kerr, *Presumptive Engagement: Australia's Asia-Pacific Security Policy in the 1990s* (Canberra: Allen and Unwin, 1996).

10 As Australia's great-power protectors are known in Australian political discourse: for example, Norman Harper, *A Great and Powerful Friend: A Study of Australian American Relations between 1900 and 1975* (St Lucia, Qld: University of Queensland Press, 1987).

11 Desmond Ball, *A Suitable Piece of Real Estate* (Sydney: Hale & Iremonger, 1980); Henry S. Albinski, *ANZUS, the United States and Pacific Security* (Lanham, MD: University Press of America, 1987); Coral Bell, *Dependent Ally* (Melbourne: Oxford University Press, 1988).

12 Michael Barnett, "Identity and Alliances in the Middle East," in P. Katzenstein, ed., *The Culture of National Security* (NY: Columbia University Press, 1996), pp. 400–44.

13 By the early 1990s, Britain was still a significant source of foreign direct investment in Australia (AUD$49.1 billion), just behind the United States (AUD$54.2) and Japan (AUD$50.8); likewise, a third of Australian foreign investment overseas went to Britain. Australia, Australian Bureau of Statistics, *International Investment Position, 1990–91*.

14 Andrew F. Cooper, Richard A. Higgott, and Kim Richard Nossal, *Relocating Middle Powers: Australia and Canada in a Changing World Order* (Vancouver: University of British Columbia Press, 1993), chs. 3–4.

15 Richard Higgott, "From High Politics to Low Politics: The Ascendancy of the Economic Dimension in Australian–American Relations," in John Ravenhill, ed., *No Longer an American Lake: Alliance Problems in the South Pacific* (Berkeley: Institute of International Studies, University of California, 1989).

16 Richard A. Higgott, "From American Hegemony to Global Competition: US Foreign Policy and Australian Interests after the Cold War," in Robert Cushing, John Higley, Michael Sutton and Sidney Weintraub, eds., *The Challenge of NAFTA, the Pacific, Australia and New Zealand* (Austin: University of Texas Press, 1993).

17 On July 10, 1985, agents of the French foreign intelligence service, the *Direction générale de la Sécurité extérieure*, planted a bomb on the Greenpeace boat while it was docked in Auckland harbor, killing a Greenpeace

member on board. Ramesh Thakur, "A Dispute of Many Colours: France, New Zealand and the 'Rainbow Warrior' Affair," *The World Today* 42 (December 1986), pp. 209–214.

18 Stuart McMillan, *Neither Confirm Nor Deny* (Wellington: Allen and Unwin, 1987).

19 Coral Bell, *Australia's Alliance Options: Prospect and Retrospect in a World of Change*, Australian Foreign Policy Papers no. 1 (Canberra: Australian National University, 1991), pp. 36–37.

20 When the British prime minister, Margaret Thatcher, was asked if the condemnation of state-sponsored terrorism by the 1986 G-7 summit, which included France, was not a little hypocritical, she responded: "The two are totally different . . . there is no point in wasting time on that question." Quoted in Thakur, "A Dispute of Many Colours," p. 213.

21 Australia, Australian Bureau of Statistics, *Year Book Australia 1988* (Canberra, 1988), p. 264.

22 Charles Price, "Immigration: 1949–1970," in Gordon Greenwood and Norman Harper, eds., *Australia in World Affairs, 1966–1970* (St Kilda, Victoria: Cheshire/Vancouver: University of British Columbia Press, 1974), pp. 171–205.

23 Meaney, "End of 'White Australia'"; also Henry S. Albinski, *Australian External Policy under Labor* (Vancouver: University of British Columbia Press, 1977), pp. 111–112.

24 Gareth Evans and Bruce Grant, *Australia's Foreign Relations in the World of the 1990s* (Melbourne: Melbourne University Press, 1991), p. 327.

25 For example, Grant, *Australian Dilemma*; Bruce Grant, *What Kind of Country: Australia and the Twenty-First Century* (Ringwood, Victoria: Penguin, 1988); Paul Kelly, *The End of Certainty* (St Leonards, NSW: Allen and Unwin, 1992).

26 *Australian Financial Review*, October 1, 1992, 16.

27 Evans and Grant, *Australia's Foreign Relations*, p. 326.

28 Quoted in *Far Eastern Economic Review*, August 17, 1995, p. 26.

29 Richard Higgott, "Closing a Branch Office of Empire: Australian Foreign Policy and the UK at Century's End," *International Affairs* 70, 1 (1994), p. 41.

30 Stephen FitzGerald, "Ethics and business," p. 162.

31 Evans and Grant, *Australia's Foreign Relations*, p. 326.

32 Meg Gurry, "Identifying Australia's 'region': from Evatt to Evans," *Australian Journal of International Affairs* 49 (May 1995), pp. 17–31.

33 *Far Eastern Economic Review*, August 17, 1995, p. 26; the map is reproduced in Ball and Kerr, *Presumptive Engagement*, p. 5.

34 Richard Higgott, *The Evolving World Economy: Some Alternative Security Questions for Australia*, Canberra Papers in Strategy and Defence no. 51 (Canberra: Strategic and Defence Studies Centre, Australian National University, 1989).

35 Higgott, "From High Politics to Low Politics," pp. 153–58.

36 Ross Garnaut, in his report to the Australian government, *Australia and the Northeast Asian Ascendancy* (Canberra: Australian Government Publishing Service, 1990), stressed the importance of liberal, internationally oriented economic growth to Australian interests.

37 Pauline Kerr and Andrew Mack, with some understatement, characterize this as "a certain tension" in Australian defense policy: "The Future of Asia Pacific Security Studies in Australia," in Paul M. Evans, ed., *Studying Asia Pacific Security* (North York: Joint Centre for Asia Pacific Studies, 1994), p. 37.

38 Australia, Department of Defence, *The Defence of Australia 1987* (Canberra: Australian Government Publishing Service, 1987).

39 Graeme Cheeseman, *The Search for Self-Reliance: Australian Defence Since Vietnam* (Melbourne: Longman Cheshire, 1993).

40 *Defence of Australia 1987*, p. 6.

41 *Australia's Regional Security* is reproduced in Greg Fry, ed., *Australia's Regional Security* (Sydney: Allen and Unwin, 1991), pp. 163–216.

42 *Australia's Regional Security*, paras. 124–134.

43 Graeme Cheeseman, "The Military Dimensions of Australia's Regional Security Posture," in Fry, ed., *Australia's Regional Security*, p. 85.

44 Gareth Evans, "Ministerial Response," in Fry, ed., *Australia's Regional Security*, p. 150.

45 Kim Richard Nossal, "Seeing Things? The Adornment of 'Security' in Australia and Canada," *Australian Journal of International Affairs* 49 (May 1995), pp. 33–47.

46 Gareth Evans, *Cooperating for Peace: The Global Agenda for the 1990s and Beyond* (Sydney: Allen and Unwin, 1993) and Evans, "Cooperative Security and Intra-state Conflict," *Foreign Policy* 96 (Fall 1994), pp. 3–20.

47 The intellectual lineage of cooperative security, particularly in an Asia Pacific context, can be traced to David Dewitt's "Common, Comprehensive, and Cooperative Security," *The Pacific Review* 7 (Spring 1994), pp. 1–16. Indeed, both *Cooperating for Peace* and Evans's 1994 article in *Foreign Policy*, which won the Grewemeyer Prize, drew on, but did not acknowledge, Dewitt's work. Peter Lawler, "Cooperative Security: Core Assumptions and Presumptions," *Working Paper* no. 10 (Melbourne: Centre for International Relations, Monash University, 1994); Nossal, "Seeing things?"; and *Campus Review* (Australia), August 3–9, 1995.

48 This difference can be seen by comparing Evans's article in *Foreign Policy* and the Adelphi Paper, *Towards a New Balance of Power in Asia* (1994), by Paul Dibb, former Defence Department bureaucrat and now Head of the Strategic and Defence Studies Centre at the Australian National University (ANU).

49 Australia, Department of Defence, *Defending Australia: Defence White Paper, 1994* (Canberra: Australian Government Publishing Service, 1994), p. 4.

50 For critical essays on the 1994 White Paper, see Graeme Cheeseman and

Robert Bruce, eds., *Discourses of Danger and Dread Frontiers: Australian Defence and Security Thinking after the Cold War* (Canberra: Allen and Unwin, 1996).

51 Quoted in Stuart Harris, "Australia–China Political Relations: From Fear to Friendly Relations?" *Australian Journal of International Affairs* 49 (November 1995), p. 247.

52 *The Economist*, December 23, 1995/5 January 1996, p. 87.

53 Quoted in Australia, Department of Foreign Affairs and Trade, *Insight*, February 12, 1996, p. 9.

54 *Nikkei Weekly*, March 11, 1996, p. 19.

55 Richard Woolcott, "A Mature Alliance." *Weekend Australian*, August 3–4.

56 On Australia's Red Book proposals for the establishment of peace in Cambodia, see Cooper, Higgott, and Nossal, *Relocating Middle Powers*, pp. 149–152.

57 Richard A. Higgott and Richard Stubbs, "Competing Conceptions of Economic Regionalism: APEC versus EAEC in the Asia Pacific," *Review of International Political Economy* 2, 3 (1995), pp. 549–68; also the contributions in Ariff Dirlik, ed., *What Is In a Rim? Critical Perspectives on the Pacific Region Idea* (Boulder, CO: Westview Press, 1993).

58 Hedley Bull, *The Anarchical Society* (London: Macmillan, 1977).

59 Kenneth Waltz, *Theory of International Politics* (Waltham, MA: Addison Wesley, 1979).

60 For example, the emerging American constructivist school as exemplified by such work as Alexander Wendt, "Collective Identity Formation and the International State," *American Political Science Review* 84 (June 1994), pp. 384–396.

61 Peter Lawler, "Constituting the Good State," in Paul James, ed., *Critical Politics: From the Personal to the Global* (Melbourne: Arena Publications, 1994), pp. 153–154; also Lawler, 'The Good Citizen Australia," *Asian Studies Review* 16, 2 (1992), pp. 241–250.

62 Richard Higgott, "Towards a Non-Hegemonic International Political Economy," in Craig Murphy and Roger Tooze, eds., *The New International Political Economy: International Political Economy Yearbook*, vol. 4 (Boulder, CO: Lynne Rienner, 1991).

63 The notion of Australia as a good international citizen in the 1980s and 1990s was *not* informed by any notion of radical cosmopolitanism in international relations. Even if he insisted on a universal conception of human rights, appeals to universal morality or imaginings of an international community imbued with cosmopolitan values were not part of the day-to-day discourse of Gareth Evans.

64 Senior Australian scholars-cum-diplomats, such as Stuart Harris, Ross Garnaut, and Peter Drysdale are among the principal exponents of regional community; Peter Drysdale, *International Economic Pluralism: Economic Policy in East Asia and the Pacific* (New York: Columbia University Press, 1988) and "Open Regionalism: A Key to East Asia's Economic

Future," *Pacific Economic Papers* 197 (1991); Garnaut, *Australia and the Northeast Asian Ascendancy*; and Stuart Harris, "Varieties of Pacific Economic Cooperation," *The Pacific Review* 4, 4 (1991), pp. 301–311; Richard Higgott, "Pacific Economic Cooperation and Australia: The Role of Knowledge and Learning," *Australian Journal of International Affairs* 46, 2 (1992), 182–97.

65　Cooper, Higgott, and Nossal, *Relocating Middle Powers.*

66　See the critical essays in Cheeseman and Bruce, eds., *Discourses of Danger.*

67　Adler and Barnett, chapter 2, this volume

68　Kishore Mahbubani, "The Pacific Way"" *Foreign Affairs* 74 (January–February 1995), pp. 101–111; Noordin Sopiee, "An Asian Way to APEC," *Japan Times*, September 19, 1994, 2.

69　Mahbubani, "Pacific Way," pp. 115–118.

70　Some may assert that Asia will follow the same path as Europe in the last two centuries, where industrialization and development were accompanied by war. However, this denies an ability to learn from the past. As Mahbubani notes, "it is not an accident that a region that has experienced some of the greatest wars of the twentieth century is now the most peaceful." "Pacific Way," p. 114.

71　For some, like Buzan and Segal, these meetings are mere ephemera that have little chance of bearing fruit. For others, such fatalistic assessments do not give foreign policy-makers enough credit for being able to learn. Barry Buzan and Gerald Segal, "Rethinking East Asian security," *Survival* 36, 2 (1994), pp. 3–22, and J. L. Richardson, "The Asia Pacific: Geo-Political Cauldron or Regional Community?" Working Paper, 1994/6 (Canberra: Department of International Relations, Australian National University, 1994).

72　Pauline Kerr, "The Security Dialogue in the Asia Pacific," *The Pacific Review* 7, 4 (1994), pp. 397–409.

73　Miles Kahler, "Institution-building in the Pacific," in Andrew Mack and John Ravenhill, eds., *Pacific Cooperation: Building Economic and Security Regimes in the Asia Pacific* (Boulder, CO: Westview Press, 1994).

74　For example, Higgott and Stubbs, "Competing Conceptions of Economic Regionalism," pp. 549–568.

75　Richard A. Higgott, "Economic Cooperation in Europe and Asia: A Preliminary Comparison," *Journal of European Public Policy* 2, 3 (1995), pp. 361–383.

76　Adler and Barnett, Chapter Two, this volume, citing Alexander Wendt, "Anarchy is What States Make of It: The Social Construction of Power Politics," *International Organization* 46 (Spring 1992), p. 386.

77　On the general theme, Iver Neuman, "A Region-Building Approach to Northern Europe," *Review of International Studies* 20, 1 (1994), pp. 53–74; for a specific discussion on the Asia Pacific, Richard Higgott, "Ideas, Interests and Identity in the Asia Pacific," *The Pacific Review* 7, 4 (1994), pp. 367–381.

78 Cooper, Higgott, and Nossal, *Relocating Middle Powers*, ch. 1.
79 Australia's Department of Foreign Affairs and Trade established well-developed networks in the region, partly because of the large number of ASEAN diplomats who had their original training in Canberra. Moreover, many members of the Asia Pacific's policy communities attended Australian universities. Drysdale, *International Economic Pluralism*; Harris, "Varieties of Pacific Economic Cooperation"; and Larry Woods, *Asia Pacific Diplomacy: Non-Governmental Organizations and International Relations* (Vancouver: University of British Columbia Press, 1993).
80 Muthiah Alagappa, "Regionalism and Security: A Conceptual Investigation"; Barry Buzan, "The Post Cold War Asia Pacific Security Order: Cooperation or Conflict?"; Joseph Camilleri, "The Asia Pacific in a Post-Hegemonic World," all in Andrew Mack and John Ravenhill, eds., *Pacific Cooperation*.
81 Stuart Harris, "Policy Networks and Economic Cooperation: Policy Coordination in the Asia Pacific," *The Pacific Review* 7, 4 (1994), pp. 381–97.

9 The United States and Mexico: a pluralistic security community?

Guadalupe Gonzalez and Stephan Haggard

Although Karl W. Deutsch and his colleagues invoked the USA – Mexican relationship in their study of pluralistic security communities, bilateral relations between the United States and its southern neighbor have fallen far short of a relationship that rests on trust and common identity. From Mexico's independence through its revolution in the early twentieth century, the USA intervened repeatedly in Mexico. American acquiescence in Lázaro Cardenas' expropriation of Dutch, British and American oil companies in 1938 was a turning point and crucial test for Franklin D. Roosevelt's noninterventionist Good Neighbor Policy. During World War II, the two countries crossed the threshold of a loosely coupled security community, initiating a fifty-year period during which both sides have enjoyed "dependable expectations of peaceful change."[1] With the end of the war, however, the incentives for close cooperation dissipated and bilateral relations became less institutionalized and more *ad hoc*.

The signing of the North American Free Trade Agreement (NAFTA) opened a new era of cooperation and institution building. Nonetheless, collaboration between the two countries remains segmented and the extent of mutual confidence limited. In the USA, both the substantive content and dispute-settlement procedures of the NAFTA reflected quite substantial *distrust* of Mexico. Despite greater economic cooperation – some of it *ad hoc*, and crisis-driven – the 1980s produced heightened American concerns over drug trafficking and the stability of Mexico's dominant-party system. Bilateral conflict over immigration deepened, contributing to the revival of American nativism. The militarization of the American side of the border stands as a telling indicator of unresolved policy conflicts and a low level of trust.

For Mexico, the NAFTA required not only an opening of the

economy but a controversial redefinition of Mexican nationalism. Yet despite the new cosmopolitanism in Mexican foreign policy, the asymmetry in the bilateral relationship, the vulnerability associated with proximity and high interdependence, and domestic political constraints have placed strong limits on the extent to which the ruling party can compromise national sovereignty. As in the United States, the level of trust is low.

This chapter examines the history of US–Mexican relations through a Deutschian lens. What we hope to add to an extensive literature on this complex bilateral relationship is a long-historical perspective and an effort to be more systematic about the causal factors that have affected the prospects for cooperation over time.[2] We begin with some theoretical observations on the difficulty of achieving cooperation under conditions of large power asymmetries, where the central challenge is not the traditional security dilemma but how to tie the hands of the more powerful partner. We argue that the main determinants of cooperation lie not in the extent of transactions or interdependence, which have been a source of conflict, but in the extent to which policy in the weaker partner converges with the interests of the stronger; domestic politics thus plays a central role in the theoretical argument we advance.

Theory and context: cooperation under asymmetry

The theoretical problem of how to achieve cooperation under conditions of asymmetry can be introduced by placing US–Mexican relations in a hemispheric context. To date, the Western Hemisphere has been a "community manqué" that has perennially fallen short of the Deutschian ideal. Latin American states have long created substantial security problems for themselves.[3] But the main barrier to hemispheric security cooperation has been the tremendous differential in power between the USA and its Latin American neighbors. Asymmetry has bred an American penchant for unilteralism and a reluctance to renounce its "right" to intervene. The use of a wide variety of policy instruments to influence its Latin American and Caribbean neighbors, and an unwillingness to be bound by international institutions – even those of its own making – have undermined hemispheric security cooperation.

The story of continental expansionism under the banner of Manifest Destiny, the reach for a hemispheric sphere of influence with the

Monroe Doctrine, and America's flirtation with overt imperialism in the late-nineteenth and early-twentieth centuries are well known. The years of the Pan-American Union (PAU) (1889–1945) coincided with the period of the most extensive US intervention in the region.

With Roosevelt's Good Neighbor policy, the USA renounced interference in Latin America and sponsored a sequence of inter-American conferences that established consultative mechanisms on security and defense questions; the onset of global war spawned further American efforts to orchestrate hemispheric cooperation.[4] In the immediate post-World War II era, collective security initiatives flowered. The Inter-American Treaty of Reciprocal Assistance, or Rio Treaty was signed in 1947, and in 1948 the PAU was reorganized into the Organization of American States. Latin American nations naturally hoped that these institutions might check American unilateralism.

But US planners were hesitant to tie American hands. At the San Francisco conference, the American delegation was explicit that no regional security commitment would override its "rights" under the Monroe Doctrine.[5] By the time of the US intervention in Guatemala in 1954, the Cold War had brought a new set of motives for intervention to the fore. The subsequent clash between rhetorical commitment to the principle of non-intervention and American unilteralism constitutes a recurrent theme in the history of inter-American relations.[6] The Panamanian operation of 1989, US orchestration of the invasion of Haiti in 1994, and the continuing Cuban embargo show that the end of the Cold War did not put an end to US interventionism.

The US penchant for intervention in the hemisphere and the failure to construct successful regional institutions have had an enduring effect on Latin American foreign policies. Latin American countries have typically built their foreign policy on a firm commitment to international law and the principles of sovereignty and non-intervention; this was particularly true in Mexico. Since the mid-nineteenth century, Mexico has developed and sustained a defensive and non-militaristic concept of national security that rejected the use of force as a legitimate instrument for solving external disputes and strongly defended the sovereignty norm.[7] This doctrine evolved in a series of unilateral diplomatic statements, typically in response to conflicts with, and threats from, foreign powers.[8]

Latin American concern about the political dominance of the United States has had an important economic corollary: fear of economic imperialism and dependence. Until the economic reforms of the 1980s, Latin America's economic policy exhibited a high degree of skepticism about integration into world markets; again, Mexico was no exception. Periodic efforts by the United States to orchestrate hemispheric or regional economic cooperation, such as the Alliance for Progress and the Caribbean Basin Initiative, reflected security rather than economic objectives and were viewed with suspicion in many Latin American capitols.

Deutsch and his colleagues saw economic transactions and interdependence as a force for political cooperation and the building of community. It is not altogether clear why this would be the case, however. Conflicts over trade, the protection of foreign investors' property rights, and debt have been recurrent features of hemispheric economic relations; yet again, Mexico is no exception in this regard. Nor is the logic of "spillover" from economic to other issues self-evident under conditions of asymmetry; to the contrary, we would expect smaller countries to be wary of efforts to link issues.

In sum, the main barrier to the creation of a security community in the hemisphere is not the traditional realist one of overcoming a security dilemma among equals; no Latin American state on its own has ever posed a direct military threat to the United States. Rather, the problem is the high asymmetry of power between the USA and the countries of the Western Hemisphere, the American tendency for intervention and unilateralism, and the defensive foreign policy and general distrust that these American practices have elicited.

Under what conditions is this asymmetrical security dilemma likely to be mitigated? One answer is a realist one. Though unable to constitute a military threat on their own, small countries can pose threats through their alliances. Latin American countries, and particularly Mexico, could pose a traditional security challenge to the USA if they engaged in extra-hemispheric balancing; the Monroe Doctrine sought to foreclose precisely such an eventuality.[9] In contrast to Cuba under Fidel Castro, Chile under Salvador Allende, or Nicaragua under the Sandinistas, Mexico has never attempted such an overt anti-American alignment itself. But the *threat* of such alignments during World Wars I and II resulted in substantial US accommodation.[10]

Periods of American involvement in great-power war or examples of extra-hemispheric military alignments on the part of Latin American countries are hardly the norm, however; indeed, the lack of any meaningful security challenge has probably been a deterrent to the construction of a durable bilateral security system.[11] Rather, the threats that have produced intervention and unilateralism and weakened the extent of institutionalized cooperation lie in other areas; we focus on three.

The first is the willingness and capacity of the smaller power to protect the property rights and economic interests of the larger. Conflicts over the expropriation of investments, debt repayment, and the climate for American firms have constituted a leitmotif of the US–Mexican relationship since the nineteenth century. Prospects for wider cooperation are clearly enhanced, though by no means guaranteed, when challenges to American economic interests are muted.

A second cluster of issues we will call "cross-border externalities"; negative but unintended consequences that arise from geographic proximity. In the nineteenth and early twentieth centuries, cross-border banditry was a nagging issue. In the second half of the twentieth century, immigration, drug flows, and transborder environmental problems have been considered security questions. These externalities have increased in political importance in recent years, but Mexico's interest and capacity in controlling them has not necessarily kept pace.

These two factors are in turn affected by a third, more profound consideration: perceptions by the more powerful actor of the underlying political stability, and thus reliability, of the smaller one. As Peter Cowhey has argued, states do not simply look at the policy pronouncements of their diplomatic interlocutors; they look through those pronouncements to the underlying institutional arrangements which determine the capacity to make credible commitments.[12] When Mexico has been stable, the United States has generally been tolerant of – or disinterested in – the nature of its domestic politics. During periods of political uncertainty or instability, US diplomatic attention has focused on internal politics more intently, the likelihood of intervention increases, and the possibility for cooperative relations built on mutual trust declines. With unambiguous transitions to democracy elsewhere in the hemisphere, and Mexico appearing less stable than at any time since the Revolution, the dominant party system has come under increasing US scrutiny.

In sum, the United States' relations with the countries of the Western Hemisphere, including Mexico, must be understood as a problem of cooperation under asymmetry. Traditional military threats can arise in such a setting through the alliance behavior of the smaller party, but the more typical security challenges are economic and political. A necessary (though not sufficient) condition for cooperation and community is the extent of *convergence* around the interests of the larger power, including a willingness and capacity to protect economic interests and to control cross-border externalities. More profoundly, prospects for cooperation rise when politics in the smaller country appears adequately stable to sustain such commitments.

To explore these ideas, we divide the history of US–Mexican relations into three unequal parts: the oscillations in the relationship from Mexican independence through the revolutionary period (in which we include the Cardenas presidency, 1934–40); the shift to a loosely coupled security community in the 1940s; and the evolution of more institutionalized cooperation since 1970.

From the dismantling of Mexico through the Revolution (1823–1940)

The history of US–Mexican relations prior to 1940 shows no linear trend toward greater cooperation, nor any pattern that can be associated with the extent of "transactions" between the two countries. During America's first half-century of relations with independent Mexico (1821–1876), the weakness of central political control allowed the United States to expand at Mexico's expense. During much of the long reign of Porfirio Díaz (1876–1911), political stability and economic liberalism combined to produce increasingly close political and economic ties. However, economic integration *followed* rather than preceded important policy and political changes in Mexico. Cordiality snapped with the descent into revolution. The collapse of political order, extensive cross-border externalities emanating from the revolution and basic challenges to American property rights combined to make Mexico one of the first targets of a new liberal interventionism. The new interventionism was reversed with Roosevelt's Good Neighbor policy, but that policy was not really tested until the nationalization of the oil industry in 1938, to which the United States ultimately acquiesced.

Both American and Mexican historians have noted that the balance of power between the two countries at the time of Mexico's independence in 1821 was surprisingly symmetrical.[13] In 1821, Mexico's territory was 1,710 million square miles compared to 1,788 million in the United States, and Mexico had only one million fewer inhabitants (6.1 vs. 7.2 million). Yet the secession of Central America (1823) and Texas (1836), the war with the United States (1846), and the fixing of the boundaries between the two countries in the Treaty of Guadalupe Hidalgo (1848) and the Gadsden Treaty or Treaty of Mesilla (1853) yielded a much-reduced Mexico.

Differences in political development were clearly a factor in this remarkable divergence. In the United States, a robust and stable republican form of constitutional government provided the foundation for economic growth, immigration, and territorial expansion. By contrast, the collapse of Agustin Iturbide's Imperial regime in 1823 was followed by nearly six decades of revolts against the center, *coups d'etat*, and civil war. During the period, Mexico was governed under two monarchical attempts (Iturbide's and Maximiliano de Habsburgo's Imperial regimes), one conservative, centralist and clericalist constitution (1836), one moderate liberal (1824) and one radical liberal constitution (1857). Between 1821 and 1857 there were fifty changes of the presidency, thirty-six different governments, and over one hundred different foreign ministers.

The inability to establish a functioning central state, in turn, made it difficult not only to make credible commitments but to deter foreign intervention. In the early years of its independence, Mexico faced Spain's effort to recuperate its colonial territories in 1829, French intervention to collect debts in 1838 (the so-called Pastry War), the joint British, Spanish and French intervention of 1862, and Napoleon III's imposition of Maximiliano de Habsburgo as the head of a conservative-monarchist regime (1863–1867). By far the most momentous intervention for the course of Mexican history, however, was the war with the United States.

The early diplomacy between the two countries centered on US efforts to secure a favorable definition of the border, to counter British influence in Mexico, and to reach a commercial agreement. The USA succeeded in the last goal with a Trade Treaty in 1832, but in general the US–Mexican relationship in the middle decades of the nineteenth century was characterized by successive diplomatic ruptures and US violations of Mexican territory. *Contra* Deutsch, it was precisely interdependence of a particular sort that ultimately sparked war: the movement of American settlers into the sparsely populated and weakly-controlled northern border region of Mexico, Texas' declaration of independence in 1836, persistent claims by residents against a weakened and unstable Mexican government, and the American annexation of Texas in 1845 in the wake of strong "transnational" lobbying. The war settlement contained in the Treaty of Guadalupe Hidalgo (1848) contained several concessions to Mexico, but Josefina Zoraida Vázquez and Lorenzo Meyer are not altogether exaggerating when they assert that the terms of the settlement are "among the harshest imposed by a winner upon a loser in the history of the world."[14] In combination with the Gadsen Purchase of 1853, the war cost Mexico nearly half of its territory.

After 1877, US–Mexican relations entered a new phase.[15] The territorial settlements of mid-century proved enduring, political relationships were cooperative, and economic integration between the two countries expanded rapidly. Some of this change must be attributed to the United States. Following the Civil War, commercial or dollar diplomacy generally took precedence over territorial aggrandizement; where the USA did expand its territory, it was no longer at Mexico's expense.

Yet it was ultimately domestic developments in Mexico that made accommodation possible. First and most important was the consolidation of political authority under Porfirio Díaz. Díaz resolved the nagging problems of cross-border banditry, cattle thieves and Indian raids, partly by the gradual assertion of Mexico City's authority over the northern part of the country, partly by an agreement with the USA in 1882 that permitted troops of both countries to cross the border in hot pursuit.

Diaz also settled outstanding economic disputes and adopted a liberal economic posture. Through a set of important policy changes in the 1880s and 1890s, the Mexican regime opened the door to American immigration and foreign investment in land, mining, and above all railroads. By 1911, Luis Nicolau d'Olwer estimates that foreign investors controlled 98 percent of the mining sector, 100 percent of oil, 87 percent of power, and 94 percent of banking. Only 3.5 percent of all foreign investment was in manufacturing, but it accounted for 90 percent of total manufacturing investment.[16]

The collapse of political stability in Mexico that followed the breakdown of the Diaz regime generated intense bilateral conflict. The reasons can be found both in new challenges to the American economic interests that had flourished during the Porfiriato and the growth of cross-border externalities during the armed phase of the revolution. The suspension of payments on Mexico's external debt in

1912, increased taxation of the oil industry, and the accumulation of tremendous claims against Mexico for damages to US lives and property were all direct results of the revolution. So was the reversal of the more liberal stance toward the property rights of foreigners contained in the Mexican Constitution of 1917.

Throughout the civil war, US policy ranged from diplomatic pressure and withholding diplomatic recognition to economic sanctions, military threats and outright intervention.[17] During the summer of 1912, the Taft administration saw a threat to US oil and financial interests in the weak democratic regime of Francisco Madero; US actions contributed to undermining that government. Woodrow Wilson's policy toward Mexico, by contrast, sought to achieve political stability through democracy and opposition to the dictatorial Victoriano Huerta regime. Seizing on a pretext in April 1914, Wilson ordered the Atlantic fleet to Mexico and occupied the port of Veracruz.

The rejection of American interventionism in Mexico was universal, however, extending even to those who were its beneficiaries. Even prior to seizing power in August 1914, the anti-Huerta Constitutionalists opposed Wilson's interventionism. When Wilson accepted the joint offer from Argentina, Brazil and Chile to mediate bilateral disputes, Venustiano Carranza refused to participate. The so-called Carranza Doctrine rejected any foreign involvement in Mexico's internal affairs regardless of its origin, scope and nature and condemned any domestic faction that would look abroad for support. Carranza ordered the US forces to evacuate Veracruz "without linking their departure to the pretexts for their arrival,"[18] a request Wilson promptly ignored in ordering two further interventions against Mexico.

The initiation of the German U-boat strategy and the Zimmermann telegram proposing a German-Mexican alliance in early 1917 changed the security context and jolted US policy. Wilson did not abandon his effort to influence the course of the Mexican Revolution, but great power threats produced important concessions to the new government and contributed to its very survival.

The end of the war in November 1918 once again increased US freedom of maneuver in the hemisphere, in part by definitively weakening European rivals.[19] American diplomacy quickly focused on the outcome of the Mexican revolution. There is an ongoing historiographical debate over the extent to which the revolution was explicitly anti-foreign and anti-American in its origins and conduct.[20] There can be little doubt, however, that the Constitution of 1917 marked a strong assertion of Mexican nationalism, particularly in its new stipulations with respect to labor, agriculture, and the government's assertion of its final control over all natural resources (Arts. 3, 27, 33, and 130).

Asserting these rights in a constitution was one thing; enforcing them was another. The governments of Alvaro Obregon (1920–24), Plutarco Elias Calles (1924–8) and the weak presidents over whom Calles exercised control (1928–34) made significant concessions to the USA while attempting to maintain their nationalist credentials, uphold the Constitution, and consolidate domestic political authority. Three issues were at stake: the interpretation of the Constitution with respect to the protection of foreign property rights, particularly in the oil sector; the payment of claims arising out of the revolution; and the repayment of foreign debt.

Through Supreme Court rulings in 1921 and 1927, the Mexican government signalled that it would not retroactively enforce the provisions of Article 27 that granted subsoil rights to the state as long as companies had developed their holdings (undertaken a "positive act"). A succession of finance ministers reached agreements on Mexico's debt: in 1922 (de la Huerta-Lamont), 1924 (Pani-Lamont) and 1930 (de la Oca-Lamont). Each had to be renegotiated when the Mexican government proved unable to meet them and in 1932, Mexico suspended all debt payments indefinitely. By that time, however, Mexico was not alone; European and American creditors could do little to enforce their claims. In the so-called Bucareli Agreements of 1923, private meetings between representatives of the American and Mexican presidents, the claims question was also put to rest. Ultimately, claims settlement went the way of Mexico's debt repayment plans; however at the time they were enough for Obregon to secure diplomatic recognition from the USA.

The compromises of the 1920s were not the final word on the revolution, however. In seeking to build an independent political base against his conservative Sonoran predecessors, Lazaro Cardenas turned to organized labor and the peasantry for support and developed a populist and nationalist program that included increased land redistribution, increased worker rights and the selective expropriation of foreign investment. Though the agrarian reform was a point of bilateral contention – nearly 40 million acres of land belonging to Americans were affected – the most important conflict was unquestionably the nationalization of the oil industry in 1938.

Revolution, wartime cooperation and the "special relationship" (1940–1970)

American restraint in the wake of the nationalization showed that the Good Neighbor policy did in fact extend to Mexico. Within two years of the oil nationalization, bilateral relations had improved and become more institutionalized than at any time in previous history. The reasons have to do with strategic calculations in the USA arising from the onset of global war and a fundamental shift in the nature of the Mexican regime. However, we argue that the bilateral relationship did not develop the penumbra of trust that signals deeper community and much of the institutionalized cooperation that emerged during the war was reversed following it.

Despite obvious distress and disappointment, the Roosevelt administration's response to the nationalization was that Mexico was entitled to expropriate if the companies received prompt and fair compensation; it was the Mexican proposal to delay compensation that constituted the official source of conflict. Lorenzo Meyer makes much of the fact that the Roosevelt administration backed up its early diplomatic notes with a variety of economic sticks as well as carrots, signalling its interest in reversing the decision by unilateral pressure if at all possible.[21] The United States also sought to invoke international law by suggesting that the case be referred to binding international arbitration.

However the acceptance of the nationalization and the unwillingness to even contemplate the use of force are even more striking. The government's economic actions had less force than Meyer suggests; despite the suspension of regular silver purchases the USA continued to buy from Mexico and the oil quota proved temporary. Even the idea of seeking binding arbitration fell by the wayside in 1940 in favor of a bilateral commission.[22]

Why such restraint on the part of the USA? Certainly partisanship mattered; the utter intransigence of the oil companies suggests that the US response would have been quite different during the Republican twenties. However the USA was also increasingly constrained by developments in Europe. Vazquez and Meyer are worth quoting on this point:

> They could not resort to force, for that would destroy a policy more vital than oil to the US government: the creation of an inter-American

alliance within the setting of the Good Neighbor policy. Nor were they willing to encourage Cardenas's internal enemies for fear that the resulting instability might lead to the replace of his administration by a more conservative one. In the Mexican context, that could open the door to fascist and Falangist groups.[23]

The American interest in securing Latin American political and economic cooperation and deterring any possible German advances in the hemisphere increased steadily after 1939, and with it the willingness to make strategic compromises.

Such compromises were made much easier by a crucial turning point in Mexican politics and economic policy: the reversal of Cardenas's nationalist-populist experiment.[24] A coalition of conservative politicians supported Manuel Avila Camacho's compromise candidacy against Cardenas's chosen successor in the presidential election of 1940. The end of Cardenismo opened the way for a new business-state alliance in support of industrialization, cemented by a new set of opportunities for import-substitution during the war. The ruling party increasingly used its organization of labor and the peasantry not for mobilizational purposes but as a powerful instrument of social control.

The political grounds had been laid for a new policy course and with it, a tacit economic understanding with the United States.[25] The first sign of rapprochement was the settlement of outstanding economic disputes. In 1941 and 1943 agreements were signed on the terms of compensation to the oil companies; Mexico was to pay $30 million dollars in annual installments rather than the $450 million immediate payment sought by the companies. By the end of 1946, the debt problem had been resolved by a series of accords, again on terms highly favorable to Mexico.

The second step in the process of bilateral accommodation was building the joint military and economic efforts required by the war against Germany, Italy and Japan.[26] In 1942 Mexico declared war on the Axis powers and entered for the first (and last) time into a formal military alliance with the United States. The action came in response to the sinking of the Mexican oil tankers *Potrero del Llano* and *Faja de Oro* by German submarines; the Mexican government based its decision in terms of "legitimate defense" involving limited military action in the conflict.[27] Military cooperation reached unprecedented levels during World War II. In 1941, Mexico and the United States signed an agreement with respect to the transit of military aircraft and the installation of radar stations in Baja California, although Mexico refused American proposals of building naval bases on the Mexican Pacific coast. In January 1942 the Joint Mexican–United States Defense Commission was established to coordinate military action and facilitate Mexican purchases of military equipment.[28] Mexico also agreed that its citizens living in the United States could be recruited into the US army (around 250,000 Mexicans participated into the USA armed forces) and contributed in a symbolic way by sending an airforce squadron to the Philippines.

The most significant aspects of closer bilateral cooperation during the war were not military, but economic. In 1941, the USA signed an agreement to purchase Mexican output of a number of raw materials and in December 1942, after years of wrangling and delays, the countries reached a reciprocal trade treaty. A Mexican–American Economic Cooperation Commission established in 1943 provided a forum for settling trade disputes, and the United States began to extend economic assistance. Economic cooperation extended to the labor market. In 1942 Mexico and the United States signed the first of a series of agreements that would permit the contracting of about 200,000 workers (*braceros*) to work in the USA, mainly in the railroad and agricultural sectors.[29]

With the end of the war, the factors that had contributed to the forging of a loosely coupled security community were reversed. The United States no longer feared Mexican expropriations, political instability, or Mexican collaboration with extra-hemispheric enemies. American foreign policy took on the global scope of the superpower that it had become and the salience of Latin America in general, and Mexico in particular, fell sharply. The bilateral relationship underwent a process of fairly rapid deinstitutionalization; not until the 1970s were official bilateral mechanisms of consultation to reach the level achieved during the war.[30]

The formal alliance was quietly terminated in 1945. Bilateral military relations became increasingly distant and nascent military cooperation through the consultative mechanisms never solidified. Broader foreign policy interests also diverged. The United States sought to orchestrate multilateral security cooperation in the hemisphere and began to intervene unilaterally in cases deemed a Communist threat. Mexican foreign policy and strategic thinking, by contrast, reverted to principle, opposing military participation in international collective security operations and raising its voice in support of international legal norms. Mexico did not directly challenge the United States over the Cold War, but through a number of actions, it signalled an independent foreign policy course.[31] Mexico did not break diplomatic relations with the Soviet Union and did not send a military contingent to participate with the UN forces in the Korean War. It was the only major Latin American country not to sign a bilateral military aid treaty with the United States. Mexico also opposed the US intervention against the reformist government of Jacobo Arbenz in Guatemala (1954), the exclusion of Cuba from the OAS in 1961, the 1964 trade embargo against the government of Fidel Castro and the military invasion of the Dominican Republic in 1965. Mexico was behind the idea for a nuclear-free zone in the Americas, resulting in the Treaty of Tlaltelolco (1967).

Economic cooperation also underwent a process of deinstitutionalization. During the war, Mexico could square a protectionist industrial policy with a reciprocal trade agreement because American exports were in short supply and the US demand for Mexican exports was high. With the end of the war, the country faced new balance of payments constraints and protectionist pressures from the industries born during the war. In 1947, the two countries agreed to a provisional change in the reciprocal treaty to allow outright prohibitions on imports of manufactures covered by the accord; Mexico also unilaterally imposed high tariffs on a number of items not covered by the agreement. Because of proximity and growing American investment, bilateral trade continued to grow, but not as a result of formal cooperation. Unable to reach terms on a revision of the bilateral accord, it was terminated in 1950. The USA continued to grant Mexico MFN status, but informally. Mexico refused to enter the GATT.

The seeds of later conflict over immigration were also sown in the early postwar years. After hard negotiations a second *bracero* agreement was signed after the war, but it was increasingly undermined by the ability of US growers to hire illegal workers; Mexico even asked the US government to fine employers that violated the agreement. In the early 1960s, pressure in the US to slow the influx of Mexican workers increased and in 1964, Mexico decided not to request that the program be renewed. Immigration policy entered a long period of unilateralism.

The only area in which institutionalized cooperation endured was in the management of border issues. The International Boundary and

Water Commission, founded in 1944, has continued to meet continuously throughout the postwar period and the successful negotiation of the Chamizal territorial dispute in 1963, the foundation of the US-Commission for Border Development and Friendship (CODAF) in 1966, and the definitive settlement of several water disputes in the early 1970s showed that cooperation was possible. However, this largely technical cooperation was the exception that proves the rule; the experience did not extend to other issue-areas where more ad hoc and informal means of bilateral problem-solving prevailed.

Both American and Mexican analysts have been at somewhat of a loss over how to characterize the first half of the postwar period. Olga Pellicer captures both the strengths and weaknesses of the early postwar relationship when she notes that it was the longest crisis-free era in the history of US–Mexican relations.[32] On the one hand, the United States accepted the nationalist and corporatist elements of the Mexican post-revolutionary political regime and Mexico's relatively independent foreign policy because more vital US interests in political stability and economic growth were served. Some analysts have even characterized the period as the "special relationship" or "era of good feelings."[33] On the other hand, the ease of the relationship resulted as much from American indifference as from convergence on common norms. The relationship was weakly institutionalized. Mexico and the United States constituted a security community during this period in that there were expectations of peaceful change, but it was a community of only the most loosely coupled sort.

The current era: economic integration and political conflict (1970–1995)

Any analysis of the current phase of US–Mexican relations must begin with the NAFTA, which represents an altogether new level of cooperation and institution-building.[34] The NAFTA was made possible by profound changes in Mexican economic policy and by a new willingness to address at least some of the cross-border externalities that plagued the bilateral relationship.

Yet the implications of the NAFTA for the formation of a security community remain unclear. The NAFTA has proven durable in the face of crisis because of the economic interests that benefit from it, but wider political support on both sides of the border remains shallow and falls far short of community or common identity. Although the NAFTA appears to be extremely wide-ranging in its scope, it does not address quite critical economic issues such as macroeconomic policy and exchange rate coordination, explicitly excludes labor market integration, and has no social dimension.[35] When the United States has cooperated with Mexico on macroeconomic issues, it has been in the wake of severe economic crises and American policy has reflected a complex mix of economic self-interest, accommodation, and profound suspicion of Mexico's reliability.

Even if we grant that the bilateral economic relationship *is* becoming more institutionalized, a crucial issue for evaluating the Deutschian approach is whether closer economic integration has spilled over into broader political and security cooperation.[36] We tackle this issue by looking at three additional policy areas. In the realm of high foreign policy, the end of the Cold War and its Central American manifestation has facilitated broader foreign policy and defense cooperation. Nonetheless, deeply rooted disagreements on principle remain. The evidence for the collective management of cross-border externalities is also mixed. Environmental cooperation has expanded, but cooperation over drugs has proven difficult. The politics of immigration has become deeply divisive, and goes directly to constructivist concerns with identity; far from creating community, deepening labor market integration has spawned nativism and an anti-immigrant reaction. Finally, Mexico's domestic political arrangements have come under increasing scrutiny in the USA, a development that reveals the profound differences that continue to separate the two countries.

The NAFTA: the ambivalent nature of economic cooperation

It is difficult to explain the NAFTA on the basis of the *level* of interdependence between the two countries. Mexico's overwhelming dependence on the United States market has been a fixed feature of the relationship throughout the entire postwar period. Mexico's significance as a trade and investment partner for the United States has remained relatively constant as well. A constant level of economic exchange should not generate a change in the level of political cooperation; something else must have changed.

Changes in US foreign economic policy were one component of the equation. Through both its trade policy and influence on the international financial institutions, the United States became increasingly insistent over the 1980s that developing countries undertake liberalizing reforms. The willingness of the United States to resort to administrative trade policy measures also was an important stimulus to both Canada and Mexico to enter into a regional agreement; both countries sought to limit US abuse of dumping and subsidies law through the elaboration of a regional dispute settlement process.[37]

The NAFTA cannot be understood without reference to policy convergence: the profound liberalization measures undertaken by Mexico after 1982. These dramatic changes can be traced to the increasing structural and political problems in the Mexican growth model that began to appear in the late-1960s, the policy failures of the Luis Echeverría (1970–76) and Jose Lopez Portillo (1976–82) administrations, and the prolonged economic crisis that ensued in the 1980s. The crisis resulted in the ascent of the technocratic wing of the PRI and their private sector allies and the defeat of the nationalist countercurrents that had resurfaced in the 1970s.

The political economy of Echeverria's turn toward a mild form of populism in the early 1970s has been well documented;[38] of relevance here were its foreign economic policy correlates. The administration completed the nationalization of the mining and infrastructure sectors, and passed two general laws – the Law to Promote Mexican Investment and Regulate Foreign Investment and the Law on the Transfer of Technology and the Use and Exploitation of Patents and Trademarks – that made Mexico's stance toward multinational corporations substantially more restrictive. Industrial policy efforts in particular sectors, particularly automobiles, added further restraints. Echeverria also took a leadership role in the Group of 77's ill-fated effort to advance a New International Economic Order and in dramatically expanding Mexico's diplomatic relations with other Third World countries.[39]

Most analysts have emphasized the discontinuities between Echeverria and his successor, Lopez Portillo.[40] The economic crisis at the end of the Echeverria administration guaranteed that Lopez Portillo would initially be preoccupied with stabilizing rather than expanding the economy, and in general he moved the presidency back toward the right. However, the oil boom also provided opportunities to extend and even deepen Echeverría's nationalism. At the economic level, oil – and the borrowing that it permitted – allowed Mexico to continue its protectionist, "public-expenditure-led-growth" strategy in an even more aggressive and ultimately disastrous fashion.[41] Lopez Portillo did not reverse Echeverría's nationalist posture toward foreign investors, ultimately took an extremely tough stance with the Carter administration in negotiations over the sale of natural gas and rejected accession to the GATT. In his last act as president, Lopez Portillo nationalized the banking system; although this action did not directly affect American banks, it was cloaked in strongly worded nationalist rhetoric.[42]

A more assertive Mexican foreign economic policy did not mean the absence of efforts to institutionalize greater bilateral cooperation. To the contrary, Mexico's oil reserves sparked renewed American interest in Mexico to relieve American dependence on less reliable Middle Eastern sources. In 1977, the Carter administration proposed the creation of a bilateral consultative structure that constituted one of the most important institutional innovations in the postwar period. The collapse of the bilateral gas talks in late 1977 and the subsequent deterioration of bilateral relations spurred a wide-ranging review of US–Mexican relations by the National Security Council in 1978 (summarized in Presidential Review Memorandum No. 41 or PRM-41) and the creation of a new Coordinator of Mexican Affairs.

These structures increased the range of bureaucratic interactions between the two countries, but the binational consultative mechanisms and their national counterparts lacked decision-making authority.[43] They proved of little relevance in mediating the major economic and political conflicts between the two countries during the period, including the aftermath of the national gas controversy. As a presidential creation, the Coordinator of Mexican Affairs did not outlast the Carter presidency; on assuming office, Ronald Reagan promptly dismantled all that his predecessor had built.

The debt crisis forced the wide-ranging economic policy reforms of the Miguel de la Madrid (1982–88) and Carlos Salinas (1988–1994) administrations and set the stage for the NAFTA.[44] Mexico's commitment to free trade with the USA and Canada is a stunning turnaround in policy. With some important exceptions, NAFTA provisions also grant national treatment to foreign investors and eliminate a host of export and local content requirements. In 1989 and 1990, the government independently launched a series of deregulation initiatives, accompanied by privatizations that provided further opportunities for foreign investment in important sectors including finance, road transport, petrochemicals, and telecommunications, each the subject of its own market access chapter under the NAFTA. The NAFTA also codified intellectual property standards which go beyond those negotiated in the Uruguay Round.

The second accomplishment of the NAFTA is the creation of consultative and dispute settlement institutions designed to oversee and extend the agreement's substantive commitments.[45] Chapter 20 of the NAFTA established a trilateral Trade Commission of cabinet-level representatives to oversee implementation of the agreement, adjudicate disputes, and supervise the work of the NAFTA's eight committees, five subcommittees and seven working groups. Chapter 19 established a dispute settlement procedure for antidumping and countervailing duty actions that constitute the NAFTA's most novel institutional innovation.[46] Each country retained its own antidumping and countervailing duty laws, but *ad hoc* binational panels superseded national judicial review of final determinations by domestic courts. The panels would not act on, nor create, common rules, but they could rule on whether administrative actions were in line with domestic law.

On closer inspection, however, the NAFTA's institutional structure only partly reflects trust and convergence on common norms. The evolution and design of the labor and environmental side agreements (discussed in more detail below) reflected skepticism both about the content of Mexican law and its enforcement. Only with explicit commitments to change administrative law procedures were the United States and Canada willing to permit the extension of Chapter 19 to Mexico; further legal convergence would require constitutional changes that are highly unlikely to occur.

Moreover, economic diplomacy between the two countries in the period culminating in the NAFTA was not limited to the trade policy agenda. Bilateral relations since 1976 have been littered with a series of economic crises of varying intensities, most notably in 1976, 1982, 1986–8, and 1994–5. These crises did elicit responses from the United States that revealed Mexico's special relationship with its Northern neighbor. The willingness of the United States to coordinate two major financial bailouts (1982 and 1995), to push for favorable Brady Plan terms in 1990, to use its influence with the IMF, and to extend direct financial assistance of its own were partly self-interested actions. Not only did the US economy and American investors stand to lose directly from Mexico's financial misfortunes, but detailed studies of particular crises show a concern with the broader political risks from a Mexican "meltdown."[47] Nonetheless, Mexico was a beneficiary of this American concern, and received treatment and terms unavailable to other larger debtors. These crises also meant that the new bilateral relationship was forged at a time of profound Mexican vulnerability. Severe external constraints weakened Mexico's hand in bargaining not only with the United States, but the IMF, World Bank, and commercial banks as well. Efforts to appease foreign creditors were implicated in each crisis episode, just as the need to secure NAFTA passage led the Salinas administration to make substantial concessions to both the Bush and Clinton administrations. The submission of Mexican law to supranational scrutiny and the crisis atmosphere and external pressures that surrounded the NAFTA combined to make policy change even more controversial in Mexico than it was in Canada and the United States.

Salinas' commitment to the NAFTA was but one component of a profound "technocratic revolution" in Mexican politics which required not only changes in economic policy but a fundamental redefinition of Mexican nationalism. In his third *informe* in 1991, Salinas argued: "Historically, nationalism has responded to an external threat. Today that threat has become the prospect of remaining outside, at the margins of the worldwide integrationist trend ... To fail in that challenge would be to weaken oneself and succumb."[48] However this stance generated strong opposition forces that could become more salient as Mexico democratizes. Moreover, an examination of attempted cooperation in other areas demonstrates that the integrationist logic did not extend in a straightforward way from economics to other issues.

High politics: the USA, Mexico and regional conflicts

Although the bilateral relationship has increasingly been defined in economic terms, the United States and Mexico have also had to deal with more traditional diplomatic disputes. In general, these disagreements have centered on Mexican opposition to US intervention in the hemisphere; Mexico protested US intervention in Guatemala in 1954, the Dominican Republic in 1965, and Chile at the end of the Unidad Popular government in 1973. Mexico provided support to the United

States during the Cuban missile crisis, but the two countries have consistently disagreed with respect to Cuba's position in the hemisphere. Mexico's overt political support for Castro has waxed and waned, but its opposition to the US effort to isolate Havana has been consistent and often pointed.

The United States tolerated these disagreements with Mexico, in part out of a recognition that they were rooted in a complex domestic political strategy on the part of the PRI to appease and contain the left.[49] Moreover, until the 1980s Mexico was largely content to state its views or resort to symbolic gestures without undertaking foreign policy actions that might have more substantive consequences.

With the coming of the Central American conflicts and the Reagan administration's aggressive response to them, however, Mexico's foreign policy profile changed, reflecting a depth of disagreement that one would not typically associate with the idea of a pluralistic security community.[50] First, Mexico consistently argued that the conflicts in Central America had to be interpreted as the result of anachronistic political systems, economic underdevelopment, and high levels of poverty and inequality. The Mexican government recognized that internal developments could have international ramifications for other parties, but consistently rejected the idea that the internal wars were a manifestation of the US–Soviet conflict. The Carter administration had initially been sympathetic to these views, but the invasion of Afghanistan and the end of US–Soviet détente pushed the USA away from this position even before Ronald Reagan came to office.

The second component of Mexican policy was its support for negotiated settlements. Mexico's effort to coordinate an alternative to the Reagan strategy began with its surprising joint statement with France on El Salvador (August 28, 1981), and took regional shape with the formation of the Contadora Group (Colombia, Panama, Venezuela and Mexico) in January 1983. Over the remainder of the 1980s, myriad conflicts ensued between the regional-multilateral approach to a negotiated settlement and the unilateral and aggressively interventionist strategy pursued by the Reagan administration. The USA and the Contadora countries differed on key issues, including the role of Cuba in any settlement, the way to restrain and monitor the regional arms buildup, and the nature of the political conditions that would be attached to any final agreement, if any. The Reagan administration did everything in its power either to undermine the Contadora initiative, circumvent it, or turn it in the direction of US policy interests. When the Reagan administration did finally acquiesce to a negotiated approach, it was not through the Contadora process but under a new regional initiative launched by President Oscar Arias of Costa Rica. US–Mexican conflicts were not limited to the modality of reaching a peace settlement; they spilled over into more direct challenges to US policy. These challenges included strongly worded statements at the UN against the commercial embargo of Nicaragua and in support of the International Court of Justice ruling that US military and para-military activities, including aid to the Contras, constituted violations of international law.

The end of the Cold War revealed that American intervention in the hemisphere had deeper roots, and had long joined geostrategic motivations with both economic interests and a Wilsonian gloss. This Wilsonian side of American diplomacy surfaced after 1989 in US efforts to revitalize the OAS following a decade of disuse dating to the Malvinas/Falklands dispute. The Clinton administration showed an interest in reviving the OAS as an instrument for protecting democracy and human rights in the hemisphere and combatting a host of non-traditional security threats.

However, Mexico has been no less opposed to intervention on these grounds than it has been on the basis of realpolitik. Since the 21st General Assembly meeting of the OAS in June 1991, when these initiatives were first discussed, Mexico has shown skepticism about the use of multilateral institutions for political purposes. In 1991 Mexico killed a draft resolution that proposed the automatic expulsion from the OAS of any member in which the democratic system was overthrown as a result of a *coup d'etat*. Mexico's opposition was in part self-interested, but also rested on principle and pragmatism, questioning, for example, whether it was either appropriate or productive to intervene to promote democracy. In 1992, Mexico moved actively against the expulsion of the Fujimori government from the OAS, arguing that it would do little to restore democracy. The Mexican government voted against a proposal making democratic government a requirement of OAS membership and adamantly opposed the idea of expanding the definition of human rights to include political topics such as elections or extending the legal jurisdiction of the Interamerican Commission of Human Rights to play a monitoring role in these areas. Immediately after the Summit of the Americas adopted a

Declaration of Principles in December 1994 reaffirming the commitment of the OAS to actively preserve and defend democratic institutions in the hemisphere, President Ernesto Zedillo stated bluntly that Mexico did "not accept the imposition of democracy from outside" and that each nation's domestic political system was an issue that "concerns only its people, and it is not an issue that can be resolved through foreign interference."[51]

Mexico's activism toward the Central American conflicts already marked a subtle departure from its traditionally non-interventionist position, even if policy was articulated in an effort to balance US intervention. To avoid diplomatic isolation, Mexico has continued to make subtle adjustments in its non-interventionist stance since 1989. Mexican opposition to hemispheric intervention in Haiti was half-hearted, and the country supported the active diplomatic role played by the OAS during the constitutional crisis in Guatemala in 1993.[52] Nonetheless, the general insistence on the inviolability of the sovereignty and non-intervention norms with respect to political issues shows that there are limits on the redefinition of nationalism attempted by Salinas in the economic sphere. These limits are also visible in the management of cross-border externalities.

Managing externalities: the environment, drugs, and migration

In asymmetric relationships, security challenges are not likely to be the traditional military ones. Cooperation will also hinge on the willingness and capacity of the weaker party to manage cross-border externalities that are seen as posing a threats. Three such issues gained salience in the 1980s and 1990s: the environment, drugs, and immigration. Each is characterized by a very different levels of cooperation, institutionalization and trust.

The strongest case for policy convergence leading to the creation of new, community-like institutions is in the environmental area.[53] The longest-standing bilateral institution between the two countries is the International Boundary and Water Commission (established in 1944), which has provided a forum for the ongoing management of a number of water and sewage problems. In 1983 the two countries reached an important agreement on protecting and improving the border environment (known as the La Paz Agreement), which created six functional working groups and was subsequently extended through the negotiation of additional annexes.

The NAFTA substantially increased the scope of bilateral environmental cooperation. In the United States, environmental and labor groups allied to exploit the NAFTA opening and push their issues onto the trade agenda (though for some groups with the ultimate objective of killing the agreement altogether). There is also evidence of growing demand for improved environmental legislation in Mexico, although the course of Mexican policy was influenced above all by efforts to keep the broader economic negotiations on track. The Bush proposal for a North American Commission for the Environment and the Bush-Salinas agreement on an Integrated Environmental Plan for the Mexican-US Border Area (IBEP) were the first responses to the domestic political pressures emanating from the USA, followed in rapid succession under the Clinton administration by revised environmental provisions in the NAFTA itself, the negotiation of the environmental side agreement, the creation of a bilateral Border Environmental Cooperation Commission (BECC) and North American Development Bank (Nadbank), and the re-crafting of the IBEP into a new bilateral Border XXI Plan. Nor do these national initiatives exhaust the range of cooperation, which increasingly extends to subnational governments on both sides of the border as well.[54]

The significance of the increasingly complex web of environmental agreements and institutions for the forging of a North American community is far from clear, however. The NAFTA and the environmental side agreement were designed to allay fears that cooperation with Mexico would necessarily dilute national standards and reflected substantial distrust of Mexico, particularly with respect to enforcement. The North American Commission for Environmental Cooperation (NACEC) has the authority to oversee the implementation of national environmental laws. Environmental groups have subsequently used the Commission process against both the United States and Canada, but its initial design clearly targeted Mexico. Despite these new institutions, the USA has not refrained from highly controversial efforts to extend its environmental laws extra-territorially to maquilas located on the other side of the border. On balance, though, one must see the web of environmental institutions as signalling the emergence of community-like norms and processes.[55] The NACEC, BECC and Nadbank not only have supranational components, but they all allow for direct participation and legal standing on the part of businesses, NGOs and citizens.

The segmented nature of institutionalized cooperation becomes clear when we turn to the management of illicit drug flows and immigration. The control of drugs constitutes a mixed case: the USA and Mexico have a long history of formal cooperation, including both Mexican participation in multilateral protocols and since 1975 a rapidly growing array of bilateral agreements.[56] By the late 1980s, this cooperation was increasingly grounded on a convergence of interests, particularly the growing Mexican recognition that drug-trafficking posed profound challenges to the integrity of the country's political institutions. However, the two countries views of the underlying source of the problem continue to diverge quite substantially.[57]

Since the 1970s, the United States has focused overwhelmingly on the control of supply rather than domestic demand.[58] This is to be achieved by two means: destroying crops and laboratories and interdiction of shipments. The first of these two strategies results in a recurrent game in which the United States provides a combination of incentives (in the form of financial and technical assistance) and pressure to get Latin American countries to undertake costly eradication programs, despite the fact that the industry is geared overwhelmingly toward supplying USA rather than local demand.

Following tensions with the United States over half-hearted eradication efforts, culminating in the costly and controversial Operation Intercept at the border in 1969, the Echeverria administration initiated closer cooperation with the USA and a "campana permanente" against drugs in 1975. A number of bilateral accords followed between 1975–80, ranging from financial assistance for aerial crop destruction to allowing the presence of American agents for the purpose of information-gathering. Yet over time, the capacity of the drug industry to adapt, the closing of other international sources of supply, the growth of Mexico as a transshipment route for cocaine and continuing American demand all meant that there was little correlation between Mexican eradication efforts and the actual flow of drugs.

Partly out of frustration, the Reagan and Bush administrations shifted the emphasis to the second prong of the prohibition approach: interdiction. Although the de la Madrid and Salinas administration continued Mexican commitment to combat drug-trafficking (as reflected in budget allocations), the shift in American emphasis naturally created a new set of bilateral tensions. The kidnap and murder of a DEA agent in Mexico in 1985 focused Congressional and media scrutiny in the USA on corruption in the Mexican police forces. Though these concerns were warranted, the incident raised concerns about sovereignty in Mexican politics. This was particularly true given that the United States moved to pursue traffickers unilaterally through the extra-territorial extension of US law, the kidnapping and expatriation of suspects, and the "certification" process initiated in 1986 that implied sanctions against non-cooperation.[59] US drug policy was becoming increasingly unilateral.

The control of immigration poses the most profound challenge for the bilateral relationship, and is the area in which institutionalized cooperation is least developed.[60] The NAFTA explicitly excluded any consideration of immigration, and through the mid-1990s, cooperation on the topic has been relatively limited: a binational study commission; a series of Memoranda of Understanding in 1996 that did little more than reiterate current law and practice on the rights of legal and illegal Mexican nationals in the USA; and Mexican cooperation on a "deep repatriation" program and some strengthening of the persecution of "polleros."

At one level, the key challenge appears to be the one of integrating developed and developing countries. The United States is increasingly seeking to limit the flow of immigrants, both legal and illegal, because of the downward pressure these workers place on wages and the strain they place on a variety of social services. The evidence for this view appears abundant, from increasingly restrictionist immigration legislation (particularly 1990 and 1996), to initiatives that limit the access of undocumented immigrants to various government services (California's Proposition 187 of 1994 and the federal welfare reform bill of 1996). For its part, the Mexican government faces high levels of under- and unemployment and as a result has little interest in closing an important employment escape valve and source of remittances. Officially, the Mexican government acknowledges the right of the United States to control its borders, though it has also insisted that the USA respect the human rights of all persons within its borders regardless of their legal status. However, it has held the position that the Mexican Constitution prohibits the government from restricting its citizens from leaving the country.[61]

In fact, the problem is substantially more complex than this simple portrait would suggest. The United States has actively or tacitly cooperated with Mexico in *encouraging* cross-border labor flows in the past, first through the Bracero Program (1949–1964) and thereafter through lax or selective enforcement.[62] Although the maquiladora program and the NAFTA were sold in part as means for controlling illegal immigration, both have contributed to the problem by accelerating migration to northern Mexico, some of which inevitably spills across the border. As a result, the labor markets in the two countries have become increasingly integrated in a number of important agricultural, manufacturing and services segments.[63] Both the 1986 Immigration Reform and Control Act [IRCA] and the 1996 immigration legislation continued this ambivalence toward Mexican immigrants. On the one hand, the 1986 bill finally threatened (albeit weakly) to rely on employer sanctions as a means of enforcement; the 1996 bill sought to strengthen these provisions. On the other hand the IRCA granted an amnesty that allowed naturalization of certain classes of undocumented immigrants. Both the 1996 bill, Proposition 187, and welfare reform have encouraged a rush to naturalize on the part of permanent residents, further encouraged by a fundamental change in Mexican law that would permit dual citizenship. At the insistence of Texas growers, the IRCA created a Special Agricultural Workers program that became a major source of illegal labor flows; this program was even expanded under the 1996 legislation.

The issue of immigration is of particular interest because it raises most clearly the issues of identity that are at the heart of a constructivist approach to international community-building. In a nation of immigrants, the question of national identity is always problematic. The large Mexican-American population in the United States, which encompasses second-generation (and older) citizens, naturalized citizens, permanent residents, and undocumented aliens, compounds the politics of the issue; though by no means uniformly supportive of more open immigration policies, the electoral salience of Mexican-Americans in Texas has acted as a counterweight against restrictionism and may in the future in California as well.[64] Moreover, it is difficult to disentangle pragmatic concerns about the adverse effects of immigration on particular classes of people from various forms of racism and nativism which are impervious to empirical argument about the net economic and social benefits of immigration. Nonetheless, careful studies of initiatives such as California's Proposition 187 have demonstrated fairly convincingly that such nativist sentiment played some role in the vote even when controlling for economic factors.[65]

A second and final indicator of distrust between the United States and Mexico with respect to both drug trafficking and immigration is the increasing militarization of the border.[66] Although this has been a gradual process, it might be dated to Operation Alliance in 1986, an effort to coordinate field operations both among a host of US agencies as well as bilaterally with Mexico. As Lemus notes, however, "Alliance became a more unilateral project once it became obvious that the Mexican government was having problems coordinating its own drug control policy and was not willing to participate in joint projects," due primarily to longstanding concerns about sovereignty; this changed only marginally in the early 1990s with the formation of several binational Border Task Forces targeted at four principal drug-trafficking organizations.[67] The defining characteristics of Alliance, which have been continued and even deepened under the Clinton administration, are a blurring of the customs, immigration, and drug control functions, the devotion of increasing number of police and para-military personnel to the border, and the increasing use of direct military assistance, including primarily the national guard but also Special Operations, intelligence and other support from regular military units. Though this military support has largely been limited to backup and logistic functions, including road- and fence-building, the placement of military forces on the border stands in stark contrast to the rhetoric of openness that characterizes the dialogue on trade and investment issues.

The willingness and ability of Mexico to manage various political and societal externalities has been an important determinant of the overall relationship. With respect to the environment and the management of illicit drug trafficking, interests have converged to some extent and we are witnessing new levels and forms of cooperation. However, Mexico's capacity to control these externalities has not always kept pace with American demands; as a result, the United States has come to see broad areas of the bilateral relationship as threatening and resorted to unilateral, and even quasi-military, means of handling them. Moreover, the politics of immigration and the revival of anti-Mexican sentiment shows that the two countries are a long distance from achieving a common sense of community and identity.

Mexico's politics

The issue of identity and differences in political culture are raised most fundamentally by the recurrent and increasing conflicts between the two countries over Mexico's dominant party system. Prior to the crises of the 1980s, the benefits the United States enjoyed from Mexico's political stability were enough to bury any doubts it might have about the authoritarian face of PRI dominance. American academics vigorously debated the nature of Mexico's political system but these controversies did not spill over into the policy arena; even during the Carter era, when America's Wilsonian traditions resurfaced, political repression, electoral fraud, and human rights abuses did not figure at all in bilateral diplomacy.

That began to change following the debt crisis, and interestingly the pressure came as much from the right in both the USA and Mexico as it did from the left. Beginning with the local elections in Chihuahua in 1983, where the opposition PAN scored some of its first electoral victories, through the closely-contested elections of 1988 and 1994, the American media began to cover Mexican politics more aggressively. Human rights advocates had long noted the existence of abuses in Mexico and a dense transnational "democracy network" emerged in the late-1980s and early 1990s made up of NGOs, domestic and international election observer organizations, private foundations, international secretariats of political parties, particularly European social democratic ones, and groups of scholars.[68] However more traditional policy analysts in the US also began to express concerns that the combination of severe economic distress and closed politics constituted a recipe for "instability" and increased cross-border spillovers, particularly in the form of more immigration. With the transition to democracy elsewhere in the hemisphere, Mexico even came under scrutiny from other Latin American countries. In 1990, the president of Panama openly criticized Mexican electoral fraud and Mario Vargas Llosa labeled the country a "perfect dictatorship" in a televised roundtable.

Beginning in 1994, a series of events combined to once again put the issue of Mexico's political stability on the table: the murder of PRI presidential candidate Luis Donaldo Colosio and the controversial selection of a politically weak successor in Ernesto Zedillo, the Zapatista rebellion in Chiapas, an upsurge of opposition electoral challenges at the state and local levels, and the emergence of a new, leftist guerilla challenge in 1996. The profound economic crisis at the outset of the new *sexenio* in December 1994–January 1995 raised new doubts, which were deeply politicized in the United States by President Clinton's effort to secure Congressional support for assistance to Mexico and Congress' efforts to attach conditions to that support. In general, the Clinton administration was restrained in its response to these events; it would hardly have been helpful to underline the country's political fragility when attempting to secure passage of the NAFTA and multilateral and bilateral financial support during the crisis of 1994–5. However, subtle changes were afoot, including public statements about the importance of impartial electoral processes and a more critical stance in the State Department's annual report on human rights than had been seen under the Bush administration.

The Mexican government has made some tactical compromises on the question of external surveillance. For example, the government's opposition to international observation of elections began to erode in 1993 in response to internal and external pressures to guarantee the credibility of the 1994 elections. Reforms of the Federal Code of Electoral Organizations and Procedures in May 1994 introduced a compromise by accepting the presence of "foreign visitors" to observe Mexican elections while continuing to oppose their accreditation to provide information, oversight or more formal supervision.[69] Arguably, the government's response to the Chiapas uprising was conditioned by foreign scrutiny as well, as Salinas showed some restraint in the use of military force and made promises to investigate any human rights abuses that might have occurred. Denise Dresser has gone farther, arguing that a number of the political initiatives of the early 1990s could be traced in part to foreign pressures.[70]

In general, however, the response of Mexico to these external pressures has been to draw sharp lines of demarcation between its new internationalism in the economic sphere and its openness to external political scrutiny. In his third *Informe de Gobierno*, for example, Salinas acknowledged that internationalization implied greater foreign comment on domestic politics, but declared that "the day that Mexico refers domestic political questions to outside decision it will have forfeited its sovereignty." The concern was not merely an academic one. Between 1985 and 1994 the PAN lodged seven protests with the Inter-American Human Rights Commission of the OAS accusing the Mexican government of electoral violations; other opposition parties followed the PAN's example. The Mexican government roundly rejected both the accusations and the resulting IAHRC resolutions, arguing that they violated the principle of non-intervention and that the IAHRC lacks competence to judge electoral processes. The fact that Mexican political forces would themselves appeal to outsider agencies to adjudicate disputes suggests clearly that the definition of Mexican nationalism, long monopolized by the PRI, is now being contested more vigorously than at any time in the past.

For numerous reasons, the United States has been reluctant to press Mexico on political reform. But a restraint born of prudence and instrumental calculations is a long distance from the existence of common political norms. Perhaps in no other area is the difference between the United States and Mexico as profound as in this one; until Mexico has achieved something resembling a modern democratic political form, it is impossible to imagine its relations with the United States enjoying the intangible sense of community that suffuses the US–Canadian relationship.

Conclusion: US–Mexican relations in historical perspective

Our overview of US–Mexican relations seeks to make three points, one about the past, one about the present and one about the future prospects for cooperation. In contrast to Deutsch, our history does not find the main motor of cooperation between the two countries to lie in increased transactions or ties of interdependence. Traditional security concerns have periodically played a role in forcing US accommodation to Mexico, particularly in the 1940s and to a lesser extent with concerns about energy and national security in the 1980s. But a necessary (if not sufficient) precondition for cooperation is convergence: the extent to which Mexico adopts policies that are conducive to US interests.

Our second point is that the extent of convergence shows no linear trend over time or across issues. Viewed from a distance, the US–Mexican relationship bears a number of the hallmarks of a Deutschian PSC. Force appears to have been ruled out as a means of settling disputes in the 1940s, and the bilateral association is becoming increasingly institutionalized. A second layer of increasingly dense cooperative ties is developing between subnational governments along the border, between NGOs and civic groups, and of course between the private sectors of the two countries; therein a Deutschian might well find tales to tell about the significance of growing transactions.[71]

However, our historical review suggests that cooperative relations need not be institutionalized and that institutionalized relations need not be cooperative; in important ways, the US–Mexican relationship was less conflictual under the Porfiriato and the golden age of "desarrollo establizador" than it is in the present. Following the research direction laid down by Deutsch's neofunctionalist contemporaries, particularly Ernst Haas, we find that "cooperation" and "community" are difficult to gauge in the aggregate and that economic cooperation and the development of regional institutions in some areas can coexist with substantial policy conflict in others. When cooperation has extended into new areas, it appears to result less from a substantive logic of spillover than from functionally-specific policy convergence or direct political pressures from the USA.

If this leaves an ambiguous portrait of a complex relationship, we are clear on one point: the USA and Mexico are still a long way from a deep or tightly coupled Deutschian security community. The reasons are in part economic; integration between proximate developed and developing countries is bound to engender important conflicts with respect to labor and immigration questions. However, the sources of distrust run deeper: to the resurgence of a divisive identity politics on both sides of the border and to Mexico's still-unfinished transition to fully democratic rule.

Notes

1 Karl Deutsch et al., *Political Community in the North Atlantic Area* (Princeton: Princeton University Press, 1957), p. 6.

2 Among the many studies are Josefina Zoraida Vázquez and Lorenzo Meyer, *The United States and Mexico* (Chicago: University of Chicago Press, 1985). Susan Kaufman Purcell, ed., *Mexico–United States Relations* (New York: The Academy of Political Science, 1981); George W. Grayson, *The United States and Mexico: Patterns of Influence* (New York: Praeger, 1984); Howard F. Cline, *The United States and Mexico* (Cambridge: Harvard University Press, 1961); Karl M. Schmitt, *Mexico and the United States, 1821–1973* (New York: John Wiley and Sons, 1974); Luis G. Zorrilla, *Historia de las Relaciones entre Mexico y los Estados Unidos de America: 1800–1958* (México DF: Editorial Porrúa, 1965), vol. 1.

3 See David Mares, *Violent Peace* (New York: Columbia University Press, forthcoming).

4 For a succinct summary of this history, see David Rock, "War and Postwar Intersections: Latin America and the United States," in Rock, ed., *Latin America in the 1940s: War and Postwar Transitions* (Berkeley: University of California Press, 1994), pp. 22–35.

5 Gaddis Smith, *The Last Years of the Monroe Doctrine 1945–93* (New York:

Hill and Wang, 1994), ch. 2; Peter H. Smith, *Talons of the Eagle: Dynamics of US–Latin American Relations* (New York: Oxford University Press, 1996), p. 124; Roger Trask, "The Impact of the Cold War on United States-Latin American Relations, 1945–49," *Diplomatic History* 1, 3 (Summer 1977): pp. 271–284.

6 See Cole Blaiser, *The Hovering Giant: USA Responses to Revolutionary Change in Latin America* (Pittsburgh: University of Pittsburgh Press, 1976); Arthur P. Whitaker's early post-war analysis in *The Western Hemisphere Idea: Its Rise and Demise* (Ithaca: Cornell University Press, 1954); Gordon Connell-Smith, *The United States and Latin America: An Historical Analysis of Inter-American Relations* (New York: Wiley, 1974); Bryce Wood, *The Dismantling of the Good Neighbor Policy* (Austin: University of Texas Press, 1985); and Smith, *Talons of the Eagle.*

7 Raúl Benítez Manaut, "Sovereignty, Foreign Policy and National Security in Mexico, 1821–1989", in H. P. Klepak, ed., *Natural Allies?: Canadian and Mexican Perspectives on International Security* (Ontario: Carleton University Press, 1996) pp. 57–87; Guadalupe González, "The Foundations of Mexico's Foreign Policy: Old Attitudes and New Realities," in Rosario Green and Peter Smith, eds., *Foreign Policy in US–Mexican Relations* (La Jolla: University of California, San Diego, Center for US–Mexican Studies, 1989), pp. 21–42.

8 The Juárez Doctrine on mutual respect (following the French intervention of 1861); the Carranza Doctrine on foreign intervention (following the US occupation of Veracruz in 1914); the Estrada Doctrine on diplomatic recognition (1930); and the Drago Doctrine on the use of force for the collection of foreign debts.

9 Gaddis Smith entitles his recent history *The Last Years of the Monroe Doctrine 1945–93* (New York: Hill and Wang, 1994). Intervention in Chile, the Central American wars, and persistent American efforts to isolate Cuba are the most obvious examples of extra-hemispheric alliances sparking tough US responses.

10 Michael Desch, *When the Third World Matters: Latin America and United States Grand Strategy* (Baltimore: Johns Hopkins University Press, 1993).

11 Michael J. Dziedzic, "Mexico and the United States Grand Strategy: the Geo-Strategic Linchpin to Security and Prosperity," in John Bailey and Sergio Aguayo Quezada, eds., *Strategy and Security in US–Mexican Relations Beyond the Cold War* (La Jolla: Center for US–Mexican Studies, University of California, San Diego, 1996), pp. 63–83.

12 Peter Cowhey, "Domestic Politics and International Commitments: The Cases of Japan and the United States," *International Organization* 47 (1993): pp. 299–326.

13 Karl Schmitt, *Mexico and the United States*, pp. 44–48; Vázquez and Meyer, *The United States and Mexico*, chs.1 and 2; George W. Grayson, *The United States and Mexico: Patterns of Influence* (New York: Praeger Publishers, 1984), ch. 2; Lorenzo Meyer, "The United States and Mexico: The Histor-

ical Structure of Their Conflict", *Journal of International Affairs* 43, 2 (Winter 1990): pp. 251–271.

14 *The United States and Mexico*, p. 49.

15 On the transformation of the US–Mexican relationship, see Thomas David Schoonover, *Dollars Over Dominion: The Triumph of Liberalism in Mexican–United States Relations, 1861–1867* (Baton Rouge: Louisiana State University Press, 1978).

16 Luis Nicolau d'Olwer, "Las inversiones extranjeras," in Daniel Cosío Villegas, ed., *Historia Moderna de México. El Porfiriato: La vida Económîca* (Mexico, DF: Editorial Hermes, 1974).

17 For overviews, see P. E. Haley, *Revolution and Intervention: The Diplomacy of Taft and Wilson with Mexico, 1910–1917* (New York: Cambridge University Press, 1970) and Friedrich Katz, *The Secret War in Mexico: Europe, the United States and the Mexican Revolution* (Chicago: University of Chicago Press, 1981).

18 Vazquez and Meyer, *The United States and Mexico*, p. 112.

19 See Joseph Tulchin, *The Aftermath of War: World War I and US Policy Toward Latin America* (New York: New York University Press, 1971).

20 Katz and Knight question the anti-American character of the Mexican revolution while Castañeda and Meyer emphasize its nationalist face. Peter Knight, *US–Mexican Relations 1910–1940: An Interpretation* (La Jolla: Center for US–Mexican Studies, University of California, San Diego monograph no. 28, 1991) and Katz, *The Secret War in Mexico*; Jorge Castaneda, "Revolution and Foreign Policy: Mexico's Experience," *Political Science Quarterly* 78 (1963), pp. 391–417; Lorenzo Meyer, *Mexico and the United States in the Oil Controversy, 1917–1942* (Austin: University of Texas Press, 1972).

21 These actions included the suspension of regular silver purchases, the imposition of oil quotas, vetoes of Export-Import Bank loans, and delay in completing a bilateral trade treaty. Meyer, *Mexico and the United States Oil Controversy*, pp. 200–213.

22 See Bryce Wood, *The Making of The Good Neighbor Policy* chs. 8 and 9 and Irwin F. Gellman, *Good Neighbor Diplomacy* (Baltimore: Johns Hopkins University Press, 1979), pp. 49–55.

23 *The United States and Mexico*, p. 151; Desch, *When the Third World Matters*, ch. 3.

24 Ariel José Contreras, *México 1940: Industrialización y crisis politica* (México DF.: Siglo XXI, 1977); Nora Hamilton, *The Limits of State Autonomy* (Princeton: Princeton University Press, 1982).

25 Olga Pellicer de Brody and Esteban L. Mancilla, *El entendimiento con los Estado Unidos y la gestación del desarrollo establizador* (México DF.: El Colegio de México, 1978).

26 See Blanca Torres, *México en la Segunda Guerra Mundial, Historia de la Revolución Mexicana, Periodo 1940–52* (México DF: El Colegio de México, 1979) and Stephen R. Niblo, *War, Diplomacy and Development: The United*

States and Mexico, 1938–54 (Wilmington Delaware: Scholarly Resources Inc., 1995).

27 Raúl Benítez Manaut, "Sovereignty, Foreign Policy and National Security in Mexico," p. 67.

28 John A. Cope, "In Search of Convergence: US–Mexican Military Relations into the Twenty-first Century", in Bailey and Quezada, eds., *Strategy and Security in US–Mexican Relations*, p. 191.

29 Richard B. Craig, *The Bracero Program: Interest Groups and Foreign Policy* (Austin: University of Texas Press, 1971); Manuel Garcia y Griego, "The Importation of Mexican Contract Laborers to the United States, 1942–1964: Antecedents, Operation and Legacy," in Peter G. Brown and Henry She, eds., *The Border that Joins: Mexican Migrants and US Responsibility* (Totowa, NJ: Rowman and Littlefield, 1983).

30 David Ronfeldt and Caesar Sereseres, *The Management of US–Mexican Interdependence: Research Results from 1977–78* (Santa Monica: The Rand Corporation, 1990).

31 Héctor Aguilar Camín and Lorenzo Meyer, *In the Shadow of the Mexican Revolution. Contemporary Mexican History, 1910–1989* (Austin: University of Texas Press, 1993), p. 196.

32 Olga Pellicer de Brody, "A Mexican Perspective," in Susan Kauffman Purcell, ed., *Mexico–United States Relations* (New York: Academy of Political Science, 1981), p. 7.

33 Mario Ojeda characterized the long period of non-conflictive interaction but limited concord from 1950 to 1970 as the "special relationship. " Mario Ojeda Gomez, *Alcances y Límites de la Política Exterior de México* (México DF: El Colegio de México, 1976). See also Olga Pellicer de Brody and Esteban L. Mancilla, *El Entendimiento con los Estados Unidos*. The "era of good feelings" is from Howard F. Cline, *The United States and Mexico* (Cambridge, MA: Harvard University Press, c. 1963), pp. 307–332.

34 The literature on the NAFTA is vast, but influential American treatments include Nora Lustig, Barry P. Bosworth, and Robert Lawrence, eds., *North American Free Trade: Assessing the Impact* (Washington DC: The Brookings Institution, 1992); Gary Clyde Hufbauer and Jeffrey J. Schott, *NAFTA: An Assessment*, rev. edn (Washington DC: Institute for International Economics, 1993); Robert Pastor, *Integration with Mexico: Options for USA Policy* (New York: Twentieth Century Fund, 1993); Manuel Pastor and Carol Wise, "The Origins and Sustainability of Mexico's Free Trade Policy," *International Organization* 48, 3 (1994), pp. 459–490.

35 On this failing, see Jaime Ros, "Mexico in the 1990s: A New Economic Miracle?" in Maria Lorena Cook, Kevin J. Middlebrook, and Juan Molinar Horcasitas, eds., *The Politics of Economic Restructuring: State-Society Relations and Regime Change in Mexico* (La Jolla: Center for US-Mexican Studies, 1994); Manuel Pastor and Carol Wise, "Challenges to Western Hemispheric Integration: Free Trade is Not Enough," *SAIS Review* 2 (1995), pp. 1–16.

36 The concept of spillover was articulated by Ernst B. Haas, *The Uniting of Europe* (Stanford: Stanford University Press, 1958), which was contemporaneous with Deutsch's transactional approach.

37 See Stephan Haggard, *The Developing Countries and the Politics of Global Integration* (Washington DC: The Brookings Institution, 1995), ch. 2; Miles Kahler, "Orthodoxy and Its Alternatives: Explaining Approaches to Stabilization and Adjustment," in Joan Nelson, ed., *Economic Crisis and Policy Choice* (Princeton: Princeton University Press, 1990), pp. 33–61.

38 See Leopoldo Solis, *Economic Policy Reform in Mexico: A Case Study for Developing Countries* (New York: Pergamon, 1981); Carlos Arriola, *Los empresarios y el estado, 1970–1982* (México DF: Universidad Nacional Autónoma de México/Miguel Angel Porrua, 1988).

39 See George W. Grayson, *The United States and Mexico: Patterns of Influence* (New York: Praeger, 1984), pp. 42–48.

40 See Judith Teichman, *Policymaking in Mexico: From Boom to Crisis* (Boston: Allen and Unwin, 1988).

41 See George Grayson, *The Politics of Mexican Oil* (Pittsburgh: University of Pittsburgh Press, 1980); Edward F. Buffie, "Economic Policy and Foreign Debt in Mexico," in Jeffrey D. Sachs., ed., *Developing Country Debt and Economic Performance*, vol. 2 *Country Studies: Argentina, Bolivia, Brazil and Mexico* (Chicago: University of Chicago Press, 1990), pp. 431–443.

42 See Sylvia Maxfield, *Governing Capital: International Finance and Mexican Politics* (Ithaca: Cornell University Press, 1990), ch. 6.

43 Cathryn L. Thorup, "US Policy-making toward Mexico: Prospects for Administrative Reform," in Green and Smith, eds., *Foreign Policy in US–Mexican Relations.*

44 Structural reforms began in earnest with the stabilization efforts of 1985–86, when the government initiated a trade liberalization, intensified bilateral trade consultations with the United States on a number of technical issues, and launched the negotiations that led to Mexican accession to the GATT. For an analysis of the political economy of the de la Madrid period, see Robert R. Kaufman, Carlos Bazdresch, and Blanca Herredia, "Mexico: Radical Reform in a Dominant Party System," in Stephan Haggard and Steven B. Webb, eds., *Voting for Reform* (New York: Oxford University Press, 1994). For a concise overview, see Nora Lustig, *Mexico: the Remaking of an Economy* (Washington DC: The Brookings Institution, 1992). For an "official" Mexican view, see Pedro Aspe, *El Camino Mexicano de la Transformación Económica* (Mexico DF: Fondo de Cultura Económica, 1993).

45 See Rafael Ferndández de Castro, "Explaining Cooperation in US–Mexican Relations: the Emergence of a Process of Institutionalization," unpublished PhD dissertation, Georgetown University, 1996, ch. 3.

46 Gilbert R. Winham, "Moving WTO Dispute Settlement toward the Model of Administrative Review," unpublished ms, Dalhousie University, October 1995 and Beatriz Leycegui, "A Legal Analysis of Mexico's

Antidumping and Countervailing Regulatory Framework," in Beatriz Leycegui, William B.P. Robson, and S. Dahlia Stein, *Trading Punches: Trade Remedy Law and Disputes Under NAFTA* (Washington DC: National Planning Association, 1995).

47 See, for example, Joseph Kraft, *The Mexican Rescue* (New York: Group of Thirty, 1984).

48 Carlos Salinas de Gortari, *Tercer Informe de Gobierno*, Nov. 1, 1991.

49 Gaddis, *Last Years*, p. 226; Olga Pellicer de Brody, *Mexico Frente a la Revolucion Cubana* (México DF: El Colegio de México, 1972).

50 See Robert Pastor, *Whirlpool: USA Foreign Policy Toward Latin America and the Caribbean* (Princeton: Princeton University Press, 1992), ch. 4; René Herrera and Mario Ojeda, "La política de México en la región de Centroamérica," *Foro Internacional* 23, 4 (April–June, 1983), pp. 423–440; René Herrera Zuniga and Manuel Cavarría, "México en Contadora: una búsqueda de límites a su compromiso en Centroamerica," *Foro Internacional* 24, 4 (April–June, 1984), pp. 458–483; and Claude Heller, "US and Mexican Policies toward Central America," in Green and Smith, eds., *Foreign Policy in US–Mexico Relations*.

51 Quoted in Guy Gosselin and Jean-Philippe Thèrien, "The OAS and Inter-American Regionalism," paper prepared for the 37th Annual Convention of the International Studies Association, San Diego, CA April 16–20, 1996, p. 5.

52 Luis Herrera-Lasso, "Mexico in the Sphere of Hemispheric Security", in Bailey and Aguayo, eds., *Strategy and Security in US–Mexican Relations*, pp. 41–49.

53 Marc A. Stern, "Mexican Environmental Policy Revisited," *Journal of Environment and Development* 2 (Summer 1993). On the institutional configuration that has evolved in the 1990s, see Fernandez de Castro, "Explaining Cooperation," ch. 4.

54 See Paul Ganster, "Environmental Issues of the California-Baja California Border Region," Southwest Center for Environmental Research and Policy, Border Environmental Research Report No.1, June 1996.

55 For a succinct summary of the institutions, see Richard Opper and Mark J. Spalding, "Mexico Border Environment Regulation," in Carole Stern and Christian Volz, eds., *1996 Wiley Environmental Law Update* (New York: John Wiley and Sons, 1996).

56 See Maria Celio Toro, *Mexico's "War" on Drugs: Causes and Consequences* (Boulder, CO: Lynne Rienner, 1995), pp. 5–36.

57 For a more extended theoretical analysis of the issue, see Guadalupe González, "Condicionantes de la cooperación hemisférica para el combate al nacrotráfico: interdependencia y asimetría," México DF: Centro de Investigación y Docencia Económicas, Documento de Trabajo No. 13, 1993.

58 Peter H. Smith, "The Political Economy of Drugs: Conceptual Issues and Policy Options," in Smith, ed., *Drug Policies in the Americas* (Boulder, CO: Westview Press, 1992).

59 See Toro, *Mexico's "War,"* pp. 64–66.
60 The literature on the topic is voluminous, but the standard introduction is Wayne Cornelius and Jorge A. Bustamante, eds., *Mexican Migration to the United States: Origins, Consequences, and Policy Options* (La Jolla: Center for US–Mexican Studies, University of California, San Diego, 1989). See also Wayne Cornelius, Philip L. Martin and James Hollifield, eds., *Controlling Immigration: A Global Perspective* (Stanford: Stanford University Press, 1994).
61 *Migration News* 3, 8 (August 1996).
62 Kitty Calavita, *Inside the State: the Bracero Program, Immigration, and the I.N.S.* (New York: Routledge, 1992).
63 See Wayne A. Cornelius, "Mexican Migration to the United States: Introduction," in Cornelius and Bustamante, ed., *Mexican Migration to the United States*.
64 Gregory Rodriguez, "The Browning of California," *The New Republic,* September 2, 1996, pp. 18–19.
65 See Bruce E. Cain, Karin MacDonald, and Kenneth F. McCue, "Nativism, Partisanship and Immigration: An Analysis of Prop [sic] 187," paper presented to the Annual Meeting of the American Political Science Association, San Francisco, August 29–September 1, 1996.
66 See the statements of witnesses before the House National Security Committee Subcommittee on Military Personnel, Hearing on Use of Military Forces in Border Security, March 15, 1996, Santa Ana California.
67 Gabriela Lemus, "US–Mexican Border Drug Control: Operation Alliance as a Case Study," in Bruce M. Bagley and William O. Walker III, eds., *Drug Trafficking in the Americas* (New Brunswick: Transaction Publishers, 1994), p. 431.
68 Denise Dresser, "Treading Lightly and without a Stick: International Actors and the Promotion of Democracy in Mexico," in Tom Farer, ed., *Beyond Sovereignty: Collectively Defending Democracy in the Americas* (Baltimore: Johns Hopkins University Press, 1996), pp. 316–342.
69 Rolando Cordera and Jose Woldenberg, "Las nuevas reformas al COFIPE," *Cauderno de Nexos* 71 (May 1994), pp. 2–3.
70 Dresser, "Treading Lightly." Stephen J. Wager and Donald E. Schulz, *The Awakening: the Zapatista Revolt and Its Implications for Civil-Military Relations and the Future of Mexico* (US Army War College, Strategic Studies Institute, 1994).
71 On these relations, see for example Cathryn Thorup, "The Politics of Free Trade and the Dynamics of Cross-Border Coalitions in US–Mexican Relations," *Columbia Journal of World Business* 26, 11 (Summer 1991), pp. 12–26.

10 No fences make good neighbors: the development of the Canadian–US Security Community, 1871–1940

Sean M. Shore

The durable peace between the United States and Canada has nowadays become an afterthought. It is simply unimaginable to most observers, except perhaps in satire,[1] that the two North American countries[2] could fight a war over any issue that is likely to arise. As 5,000 miles (and 125 years) of undefended border attest, neither side regards the other as even a potential military threat, despite the fact that interstate anarchy supposedly makes war an ever-present possibility.[3] Conflicts materialize and are resolved without the expectation that they might lead to violence. The United States and Canada thus constitute a striking example of a pluralistic security community (PSC).

How and why did this PSC arise? I will argue that it was produced by two enduring and causally related processes which together promoted a sense of community and the assurance that the US and Canada would settle their disputes through pacific means. First and foremost, after the Civil War, the United States and Canada *demilitarized* their border. Initially, this process was based on domestic political incentives, not warm sentiment. Prior to the Cold War, Americans were generally unenthusiastic about military spending and large peacetime armies because they feared domestic repression and adventurism. American policymakers also believed that force was unnecessary and unsuitable for effecting their desired annexation of Canada. For its part, Canada disarmed after 1867, when it achieved quasi-autonomy and could pass the defense buck to Britain and spend its money more effectively elsewhere.

However unintended, the undefended border resulting from these policies was a powerful trust-generating mechanism: the longer the two sides refrained from arming, the more trustworthy they appeared to one another. This argument borrows from recent constructivist critiques of neorealism. The latter approach, especially in the strict form propounded by Kenneth Waltz, argues that international anarchy generally precludes trust because there is no international government, equivalent to a domestic Leviathan, which can ensure the physical safety of states.[4] States that entrust their security to others will be systematically punished, if not exterminated. Those that remain will be prone to engaging in arms competition with their neighbors because of the security dilemma. Put simply, the enduring facts of unequal power and the lack of enforcement capabilities compel states to consider all others to be potential threats.

However, as Alexander Wendt argues, anarchy by itself tells us very little about what sorts of threats states are likely to perceive and act upon. According to Wendt, it is what actors *do* that determines how they relate to one another:

> The first social act creates expectations on both sides about each other's future behavior: potentially mistaken and certainly tentative, but expectations nonetheless. Based on this tentative knowledge, ego makes a new gesture, again signifying the basis on which it will respond to alter, and alter again responds, adding to the pool of knowledge each has about the other, and so on over time. The mechanism here is reinforcement; interaction rewards actors for holding certain ideas about each other and discourages them from holding others. If repeated long enough, these 'reciprocal typifications' will create relatively stable concepts of self and other regarding the issue at stake in the interaction.[5]

Thus, the level of threat in a given interstate relationship is a function of the quality of prior interaction; where those interactions are peaceful, states can internalize positive images of one another, and come to expect friendly behavior in the future. They can *learn* to trust one another, in the sense that their theories about the "Other" can be revised in light of new evidence.[6]

The mutual demilitarization of the border prompted just this sort of learning in the US–Canadian case. Although major disputes arose from time to time, prolonged demilitarization made policymakers and mass publics increasingly confident that force would not be used to resolve them. With no immediate military threat from across the border, war seemed more distant and unlikely; this in turn diminished the need for military preparations. The undefended border thus generated self-fulfilling prophecies of peace.

World War I triggered the second key political process, in which Canadian and American elites began to *imagine a shared North American identity*. Policymakers and scholars on both sides of the border compared the histories of Europe and North America, and found in them two different political styles: the former based on perpetual bloodshed, militarism, intrigue, and autocracy, the latter on the century of peace, the undefended border, democratic institutions and Anglo-Saxon heritage. The widespread acceptance of "North American" values by elites and mass publics transformed the US–Canadian peace from a taken-for-granted, implicitly accepted state of affairs to a consciously celebrated institution. This "immunized" the community against the possibility of a renewed security dilemma.

Together, these processes produced (and later reflected) new understandings of "Self" and "Other" in the United States and Canada; the two countries "learned" to see their relationship in a different way. Previously held attitudes of hostility and fear were reformulated in light of the new evidence of the undefended border and the discourse of "North Americanism." "We-feeling" and dependable expectations of peaceful change slowly replaced antagonism.[7] In short, behavioral changes precipitated the cognitive and affective changes necessary to realize a transnational community.[8]

This chapter will proceed in three steps. First, because of Canada's peculiar semi-colonial situation prior to the 1930s, I will address the question of Canada's autonomy *vis-à-vis* Britain and whether it interacted with the USA as an independent entity. I will then trace the historical development of demilitarization and "North Americanism," and examine how they promoted expectations of peaceful change. I conclude with a discussion of some implications for future research on PSCs.

The question of Canadian autonomy

Any discussion of the US–Canadian pluralistic security community is necessarily complicated by the fact that before the 1931 Statute of Westminster, Canada was not a formally independent state. Instead, it was a self-governing colony of the British Empire, and hence not sovereign. Prior to 1867, Canada was not even unified; Nova Scotia, New Brunswick, Prince Edward Island, and Canada (Ontario and Quebec) were administered individually, and had little autonomy from London. Confederation in 1867 created a united Canada with full domestic autonomy, but US–Canadian diplomacy was still officially channeled through Whitehall until 1927. Not until 1909 did Canada even have its own Department of External Affairs. Because of this, Americans frequently treated Canada as if it were merely an adjunct of British power. Even when they acknowledged Canada as a separate entity, they did not always know what to make of it. As W. L. Morton notes: "What Canada was, was unclear; it was covered by none of the definitions in the text books in the State Department."[9]

Although pre-1931 Canada might not have been a sovereign state, can it be considered an independent actor? For the years 1783 to 1867, the answer is an unambiguous "no". The various colonies of British North America were simply too divided and had too little autonomy. During this period, Britain dominated US–"Canadian" relations. However, after confederation in 1867, Canada was partly independent of Britain and thus could be legitimately treated as a quasi-autonomous actor. First, not all of Canada's foreign relations were actually channeled through or directed by Britain. In addition to numerous unofficial contacts it had with Washington, the Dominion was free to determine its own tariffs, and, crucially, had the right and responsibility of developing its own defenses against invasion. The Royal Navy would of course be available in case of emergency, but Canada was expected to do much of the work in maintaining its military preparedness. Ottawa was therefore given license to assess the level of threat from the USA and respond accordingly. If it felt militarily threatened, it could expand its fortifications, maintain a standing army, and train and equip an effective citizens' militia. Conversely, if it held "dependable expectations of peaceful change," it could allow its defenses to lapse.

Canada's internal cohesion and state strength also improved markedly after 1867. Previously, the St. Lawrence/Great Lakes communities had limited interactions with the Maritime colonies, and very little contact with the Pacific colony at Vancouver. The social distance between francophones and anglophones was as great. As a result, there was no consequential Canadian identity which distinguished North American Britons from the homeland. This lack of differentiation began to change with confederation. The Conservative government of Sir John A. Macdonald helped merge the disparate colonies into a united Canada with its "National Policy," centered around mercantilist economic practices and the building of transcontinental railroads to link various sections of the country. As historian Donald

Warner notes, these railroads "brought closer contact between the provinces and better understanding. The Nova Scotia 'Bluenose' learned that the Manitoban and Ontarian [were] very like himself and, amazing discovery, all were citizens of a common country."[10] Physical integration and national economic policies had an important effect on how Canadians identified themselves.

Later, Liberals like Sir Wilfrid Laurier and O. D. Skelton supported a Canadian identity as a counterweight to the British connection. This connection, while usually popular, became unwelcome when London was perceived to have sold Canada's interests short, as in the Alaskan boundary dispute.[11] Canadian participation in the Boer War also helped forge a Canadian identity. Newspaper accounts of the war stressed Canadian participation, and as historian Desmond Morton argues, "[t]roops who departed as 'soldiers of the Queen' returned as self-conscious Canadians."[12] Most importantly, successive administrations were able to build francophone–anglophone coalitions, mitigating ethnic divisions.[13] Although it is clear from the closeness of the recent vote on Quebec's independence that Canada's national identity has never been fully institutionalized, Canadians have considered themselves distinct from Britons *per se* since the nineteenth century because of instrumental, strategic, and economic processes.

Finally, from time to time Americans acknowledged Canada's autonomy, and thus extended Ottawa a measure of recognition that was tantamount to sovereignty. By 1885, US Secretary of State Thomas Bayard was already referring to Canada as an independent nation,[14] and in 1890, Congress held a series of hearings specifically on US–Canadian relations. During these hearings, a commerce official testified that Canada was really an independent actor which "use[d] the British flag as a screen behind which she violate[d] treaty stipulations."[15] The USA also recognized Canada's "international personhood" in forming the International Joint Commission on boundary waters in 1909. Although the IJC treaty was signed by British representatives, it was negotiated by Canadians, and only Canadians and Americans participated on the commission itself. To be sure, American officials still debated Canada's *de jure* status into the 1920s, but increasingly treated it as a *de facto* independent actor.

To summarize, prior to 1867 "Canada" was simply a convenient label for Britain's North American colonies. These colonies had no internal or external sovereignty, and were unable to act independently of London. After confederation, however, the Dominion of Canada became increasingly state-like. It gained complete domestic autonomy, control of national defense and trade policy, increasing internal cohesion, limited de facto control over its foreign policy, and a measure of recognition by the United States. Therefore, although the imperial connection will make it necessary to occasionally consider Anglo-American relations as a whole, this chapter will largely consider post-confederation Canada to be an independent actor.

Demilitarization and trust

In the 1870s, the United States and Canada began to tackle what is probably the most difficult task in the development of a security community: they learned to trust one another not to use force, even in the absence of deterrence. As I show below, this trust was produced by the "world's longest undefended border," itself a product of domestic political incentives in both countries. The longer the border remained undefended, the less tangible that military threats seemed to policymakers. Slowly but surely, the United States and Canada internalized benign images of one another and came to expect peaceful relations, eventually reaching the point where war was unthinkable to all but a very few Americans and Canadians.

The Defended Border, 1814–1871

Historically, two domestic political pressures had driven the United States to curtail spending on military forces directed at Canada. First, a large military was actually inconsistent with the US's primary goal *vis-à-vis* Canada, annexation. Nearly all Americans desired annexation, at least in principle; as Albert Weinberg put it, continental union was "perhaps the most serious as well as the most persistent sentiment in the history of American expansionism."[16] After the War of 1812, though, American annexationists believed that force was unsuitable for achieving this union. Canadians, after all, were North American cousins, "bone, as it were, of our bone, flesh of our flesh, deriving their origin from the same Anglo-Saxon source."[17] Forcible annexation of these cousins, while probably not difficult from a military standpoint, would be "rape-like imperialism," and unbecoming of American democracy.[18] Even peaceful pressure was deemed unnecessary by many. Canada would be drawn by the dynamism of the USA and would voluntarily join the Union, in what could be called the "gravitational" theory of annexation. An 1869 newspaper editorial spelled out the policy implications of this theory: "Should [Canadians], in obedience to a natural law of centripetal force, gravitate to us, we will welcome them cordially . . . but until they are ready to come to us, we have not the slightest disposition to interfere in or influence their affairs."[19]

Naturally, the more Americans proclaimed their annexationist desires, the less they endeared themselves to Canadians, and the less likely peaceful annexation actually became. This was most strikingly demonstrated in the debates surrounding the ratification of a trade agreement in 1911. Canada had sought such an arrangement with the United States on and off for decades, but when the USA finally agreed, Canadian Conservatives raised the specter of annexation to defeat the treaty, and the Liberals, in the next election. Greatly contributing to the Conservative cause were the many insensitive and counterproductive remarks made by President William Howard Taft, House Speaker Champ Clark, and others who predicted Canadian annexation as a result of trade reciprocity.[20] As Weinberg noted, the USA had used "the technique of a blustering Petruchio" in its wooing, with predictable results.[21] Importantly, though, American annexationism eschewed the use of force, and therefore opened up the possibility of disarmament.

The USA was also able to resist or eliminate bureaucratic and legislative pressures in favor of a militarized border. The framers of the US Constitution worried that a large standing army subject to central control would be an instrument of oppression.[22] They therefore established citizens' militias to provide most day-to-day defense, and disbanded regular armies whenever their immediate tasks were completed. They also vested the powers to raise and support the military, and to declare war, in Congress, an institution meant to be directly accountable to citizens who were reluctant to pay high taxes and send their children off to war. Finally, they helped create a political culture in which military officers were politically marginalized and peacetime war planning shunned.[23] Because of these ideas and institutions, the USA had a strong preference for small peacetime armies.

Nevertheless, an Anglo-American security dilemma compelled the USA to defend the border anyway. During the War of 1812, the USA had attacked Canada, and failed to conquer it mainly because of incompetence.[24] Britain, still committed to a North American empire, was not going to rely on this incompetence indefinitely. It therefore prepared to defend Canada, except on the Great Lakes, where an early arms control agreement had been reached.[25] The United States responded in kind.

In the 1820s, the British built expensive fortifications at Quebec and Halifax, and dug canals to allow warships to bypass Niagara Falls on their way to the upper Great Lakes. They continued to appropriate funds (more than £500,000) to upgrade existing forts and build new works at Kingston, Ontario and elsewhere through the 1840s. The United States spent somewhat less on border defense: of $8,250,000 spent on fortifications between 1816–1829, only $208,000 was targeted for works along the "Lake Frontier." Later on, however, the USA did appropriate more money for works at Detroit, Buffalo, Niagara, Oswego, and Rouse's Point, NY, and constructed its own canal system which linked the Watervliet, NY, armory to the Great Lakes/St. Lawrence system. [26]

There were also several military crises in US–Canadian relations which spurred active preparation for war. In 1837, Canadians led by William Lyon Mackenzie and Louis-Joseph Papineau rebelled against British authority and demanded more extensive democracy. Although the USA remained officially neutral, Americans provided both moral and material support for the rebels, leading to several clashes along the border with loyal Canadians and British regulars. Things came to a head in the *Caroline* affair, when Loyalist troops discovered an American supply ship for the rebels on the Niagara River. They attacked its crew, set it aflame, and sent it over the falls, actions which obviously upset the Americans. The problem was exacerbated when one of the troops involved, Alexander McLeod, later boasted in a New York tavern that he had personally killed an American in the incident. McLeod was arrested, prompting Britain to threaten war if he were convicted. An acquittal ended the crisis.[27]

From 1839 to 1842, the two sides almost fought over the proper boundary between Maine and New Brunswick, a problem eventually solved through the Webster–Ashburton Treaty which granted most of the disputed territory to the United States. Boundary problems continued from 1844 to 1846, as the United States and Britain argued over the Oregon territory. Sticking to a campaign promise, President James Polk insisted on a line at 54° 40′ north latitude, which would have cut off Canada's access to the Pacific and given the valuable port at Vancouver to the USA. When London stood firm and threatened war, though, the two countries were able to reach a compromise at the 49th parallel.

Another war scare arose during the American Civil War. Even before Confederate troops fired on Fort Sumter, Secretary of State William Seward advocated a war against Britain as a means of diverting attention from the USA's internal problems; President Abraham Lincoln quashed the idea, arguing that the USA could afford only one conflict at a time. Once hostilities began, Britain implicitly supported the Confederacy, and this generated much hostility toward Britain in the North. Several incidents compounded the problems: the *Trent* affair, when Union sailors illegally seized a British vessel carrying Confederate agents; the *Alabama* raids, conducted by a Confederate vessel built in British shipyards; and the St. Albans raid, when Confederates based in Canada staged an attack (consisting mostly of a bank robbery) on a Vermont town. Britain and Canada worried that if the South were defeated, Washington would turn its huge and battle-trained armies northwards to punish the British for their transgressions and to add large swaths of free territory which could politically swamp the South in a rebuilt Union. London hastily dispatched 14,000 troops to Quebec, and made provisions for calling out 38,000 members of the Canadian militia. The United States countered by appropriating $900,000 in 1862 for defenses along the Canadian border.[28]

Post-Civil War demilitarization

Ironically, though, the Civil War opened the door to the demilitarization of the border by triggering the political reorganization of British North America. The victory of the Union, coupled with the rise of Germany under Bismarck, had put Britain in a difficult position: if it wanted to meet the German threat, it had to somehow extricate itself from North America, which now appeared indefensible and which had become a drag on British resources. Benjamin Disraeli expressed the sentiment of many others in Whitehall and Parliament when he complained:

> We must seriously consider our Canadian position, which is most illegitimate. An Army maintained in a country which does not even permit us to govern it! What an anomaly! . . . Power and influence we should exercise in Asia; consequently in Eastern Europe; conse-

> quently in Western Europe; but what is the use of these colonial
> deadweights which we do not govern?[29]

To resolve these problems, Britain made two key decisions. First, in an effort to forestall absorption by the United States, it encouraged the divided and weak colonies of British North America to form their own union, which was achieved in 1867. Secondly, Britain quit the day-to-day defense of the continent in 1871, and left that task to the new Dominion government.[30] These decisions saved Britain money, and allowed it to devote more attention and resources to the European balance of power.

Like Britain, the Dominion was unwilling to defend its border against the United States. As Erik Yesson has noted, Canada's sovereignty was still divided after confederation, and therefore it had incentives to "pass the buck" on defense to Britain. Ottawa was free to appropriate funds for defense, but it could also expect to utilize the sizable resources of the British Empire, and this was a powerful disincentive to military spending. London, in turn, declined to pay for a Canadian military, thus passing the buck back to Ottawa. The end result was that Canada had virtually no border defenses.[31]

For its part, the USA was even less willing to arm the Canadian border after the Civil War than it had been before. Weary soldiers wanted to return home (and they did – the Army was reduced from 1,034,064 in May 1865 to 11,000 in 1866), and the few troops that remained were sent south to enforce Reconstruction and to compel the removal of the French-installed Emperor of Mexico.[32] Furthermore, Americans still clung steadfastly to the "gravitation" theory of annexation, and had received a very generous settlement of Civil War-era differences with Britain in the 1871 Treaty of Washington.[33] They therefore had no foreign policy goals *vis-à-vis* Canada requiring a large military.

With neither the USA nor Canada wanting to devote resources to defense, arms racing ceased and the security dilemma dissolved. The hitherto mythical undefended border became reality.[34] Data compiled and presented to Congress in 1903 shows that spending on American fortifications along the Canadian border stopped by the mid-1870s. Money for improving Forts Wayne (Detroit), Ontario (Oswego, NY), Niagara, and Montgomery (Rouse's Point, NY) dried up in 1867. Other border forts in Maine and New York were "zeroed out" in 1875, and had been appropriated very little for several years prior.[35] Many others lost their defensive function entirely: some were simply dilapidated, others had been turned into training barracks, and some even became dance halls. A tour of duty in upstate New York became something less than a tense affair: "In 1884 life at Fort Ontario included lawn tennis, fashionable attire, swimming lessons for children, and boating."[36] Until the Spanish-American War, the United States also maintained a very small standing army (approximately 27,000), nearly all of which was utilized in Indian operations.[37]

A similar situation obtained on the other side of the border. Between 1871 and 1876, as Canada built transcontinental railroads and other infrastructure, it cut defense spending by two-thirds, and allowed its fortifications to lapse.[38] The Canadian militia was very ineffective, listed on paper at around 40,000 part-time soldiers, but averaging fewer than 19,000 from 1876 to 1896.[39] It demonstrated some usefulness as a fighting force in suppressing a rebellion in Manitoba in 1885, and coping with periodic raids from the Fenian Brotherhood (an organization dedicated to liberating Ireland from Britain by attacking overseas imperial possessions like Canada). For the most part, though, the militia served political, not military purposes. It was a cheap and innocuous form of pork barrel, a fact widely acknowledged at the time:

> For eminently political and practical reasons, the government preferred an oversized, badly equipped, and ill-trained military organization. A large force with a purported forty thousand members looked good on paper. More regiments meant more officers and more small communities where favours could be granted. Of course, a militia with too many officers, too little training, and worn-out equipment had little fighting value. No professional soldier believed that the sham battle or ceremonial review that climaxed a twelve-day summer camp was a preparation for war. Instead, such spectacles pandered to the conceit of politicians and militiamen and the pleasure of tax-paying spectators.[40]

According to Kenneth Bourne, Canada's homegrown naval defenses, and its "regular army," were just as feeble:

> The Canadians had . . . established a Department of Marine and Fisheries and gradually assembled a fleet for the protection of the fisheries. But by 1896 there were still only five vessels, none of them large or built for war, though each had a nine-pounder gun. Their combined crews, amounting to only a little more than three hundred men, formed the entire Canadian naval militia . . . The position with

regard to troops was no less disappointing. In 1883 the Canadian parliament had at last voted a small permanent force, but by 1887 it still amounted to a mere 773 men.[41]

After the US Civil War, then, both countries stopped defending their border. Their reasons for doing so, at least initially, had little to do with friendship: Canada counted on the Royal Navy to deter the United States, while Washington disarmed because of domestic pressures and preferences. The much-heralded "world's longest undefended border" was thus a product of economic incentives, narrowly-defined self-interest, and, in the American case, confidence in Manifest Destiny.

The undefended border as source of trust

Over time, however, demilitarization in North America "outgrew" these supports, and became self-sustaining. By permanently halting material preparations for war along the border, both states visibly signaled their non-aggressive intentions toward one another.[42] As a result of this new evidence, Americans and Canadians reevaluated their previously hostile attitudes, and came to expect peace in their relations.

Admittedly, the USA's trust in Canada was overdetermined, in that even a well-armed Canada posed little military threat to the United States. So long as Canadians knew their limitations, the USA had nothing to fear from them. American preponderance thus facilitated a certain kind of trust, one that would have been more difficult to come by had Canada been more powerful. Even so, American commentators occasionally voiced concern that Canada might someday pose a threat to the USA. In the 1870s, for example, some feared that Canada's new Royal Military College would produce generations of soldiers trained on the Prussian model, putting less well-trained American troops at a disadvantage. Others thought that Canada might someday try to seize Portland, Maine, in an attempt to lessen their dependence on the often ice-bound base of Quebec. These commentators were reassured, though, by the fact that Canada showed little inclination to develop its military potential.[43] Canada's behavior, not just its relative weakness, fostered peaceful expectations.

Canada's trust in the USA was *not* overdetermined. It knew full well that an armed and motivated United States could defeat it.[44] But this knowledge did not translate into fear because after the Civil War, the USA demobilized its massive army and allowed its border forts to decay. Canadians could see this demilitarization quite clearly, and they inferred American benevolence from it. As historian Richard Preston notes, "Canadians could read American official publications, or go to see the forts. They concluded that the United States had no thought of the invasion of Canada."[45] With the USA clearly disinclined to militarize the border or forcefully press annexation, attack grew to seem very improbable to Canadians of virtually all political stripes.[46] By 1878, Prime Minister Alexander Mackenzie noted that a majority of Canadians thought that the only military Canada needed "was a volunteer force to keep domestic order and protect the frontier against the Fenians." Mackenzie himself supported more extensive military preparations, not against the United States, but against Russia, which was posing a more direct and tangible threat to the British Empire. Even General Edward Selby Smyth, assigned to the task of refurbishing the Canadian military in the 1870s, was forced by the available evidence to accept that the USA posed no military threat.[47]

Some might argue that this Canadian "trust" was really a function of American hegemony. Canada, being much smaller and weaker, feared antagonizing the USA with arms buildups or other potentially inflammatory actions. As a result, what appears to be trust was really a case of "hiding" or "bandwagoning."[48] There are two reasons, though, to reject this argument. First, the hiding hypothesis is belied by Canada's willingness to challenge the United States on important issues when its interests were threatened. This willingness was most prominently shown in the 1903 Alaskan boundary dispute, in which Canadians disputed the long-standing Russian/American claim to a wide panhandle which included all the inlets and islands south to the 54° 40' line (and which thereby left the Canadian Yukon landlocked). When a British negotiator sided with American arbitrators, Canadians were furious, although most historians agree that the decision was correct from a legal standpoint.[49]

More importantly, the evidence suggests that Canadian leaders were reassured by the USA, not fearful of it, as the bandwagoning and hiding hypotheses would imply. This trust was demonstrated in secret testimony given by Prime Minister Sir John A. Macdonald at an Imperial Defence Conference in 1880. At the conference, Macdonald explicitly rejected the idea that the United States and Canada would ever go to war, basing his assessment not on the effectiveness of deterrence, but on expectations about American attitudes and behavior:

> [M]y opinion is, that from the present aspect of affairs, and from a gradual improvement in the feeling between the people of the United States and the people of Canada, that the danger of war is annually decreasing, so much so that it is in the highest degree improbable that there will ever be a war between England and the United States, except for causes altogether unconnected with Canada of which I cannot judge.[50]

To a surprising extent, Canadians even trusted the USA during the 1895 Anglo-American confrontation over Venezuela. In this confrontation, Britain disputed Venezuela's boundary with Guyana, which had become a critical matter when gold was discovered in the region. President Grover Cleveland invoked the Monroe Doctrine in response, and threatened war (which would have inevitably involved Canada). The British eventually backed down, anxious to avoid adding the US to their growing list of enemies. This war scare spurred British and Canadian officers to reconsider the American threat for about a decade, but, as Richard Preston notes, "the people of Canada were not greatly disturbed" by the crisis. "Many of them believed that they understood American political behavior better than did the British. They dismissed Cleveland's message as meant for domestic consumption; there was an election in the offing."[51] Clearly, two decades' experience with a demilitarized USA had led Canadians to expect peaceful change, even in the midst of a serious crisis.

Additional evidence of Canada's trust can be found in its behavior during the First World War. Under the terms of confederation, Britain granted Canada the right of determining the extent of its participation in any overseas armed conflict. Although any act of war passed in London was binding on the whole empire, this meant only that the Dominion would be a belligerent under international law. Canada did not have to physically participate in any imperial conflict. Nevertheless, Canadians did choose to participate in 1914, and in great numbers. In the first three years of the war, Canada sent nearly half a million troops to Europe, as well as nearly all its heavy artillery and modern equipment. This left it utterly defenseless against a still-neutral United States. Canada also must have known that while fighting Germany and Austria, Britain would certainly be unable to deter the USA, let alone defend against an American invasion. To be sure, many Canadian leaders were quite worried in 1914 and 1915 about the possibility of sabotage conducted by German-American groups, but they assumed that the US government itself had benevolent intentions.[52]

War planning staffs on both sides were still active, even into the interwar period. As late as 1926, Col. James "Buster" Brown was working on Canadian Defence Scheme No. 1 against American invasion, and in the United States, the Army War College developed Plan "Red" for war with Britain and Canada. But because of the persistent lack of any tangible threat, and the strong civilian control of both militaries, these plans were mainly paper exercises, with almost no political impact.[53]

Military historian Henry Gole argues that training and education were the main goals of Plan Red:

> War with England [and by extension, Canada–SMS] became increasingly improbable with every passing year, but Red was exercised regularly from 1905 to 1940. Only by assuming England was the foe could planners conjure up a study in the American north or in the North Atlantic requiring a maximum effort by the US Army and the US Navy.

He adds: "If students were to plan for the defense of the east coast, they had to willingly suspend reality in the 1930s and permit our probable friends – Britain and Canada – to wear the villain's cape."[54] Although both sides planned for war, this planning was not politically relevant, in the sense that it was detached from the realities existing on the ground. These plans were destined to remain just that – plans so long as the primary civilian authorities considered Anglo-American war a far-fetched prospect.

To summarize, after the Civil War, the enduring fact of the undefended border led the United States and Canada to trust one another not to use force, even in the absence of credible deterrence. Because for decades they posed no tangible and immediate threat to one another, peace became a taken-for-granted aspect of their relationship.

Constructing a shared identity

Arguably, though, these beliefs might have been tenuous so long as they relied on domestic preferences for an undefended border. If for whatever reason (e.g., domestic upheaval, new political coalitions, influential new ideas) these preferences changed, the undefended border, and trust along with it, might have evaporated.

This did not happen, because in the 1910s and 1920s, Canadians and Americans began to form a transnational community, characterized by common values and a shared political identity. As I show below, policymakers and scholars on both sides began to conceive of North America as a political unit distinct from Europe, with its own pacific style of politics. They found that North America had enjoyed uninterrupted peace since 1815 because of cultural similarity, democracy, openness, the undefended border, and the enlightened use of arbitration and other depoliticized methods of conflict resolution. This self-congratulatory discourse effectively whitewashed the serious conflicts that had afflicted US–Canadian relations over the years, including the *Caroline* Affair, the Venezuela Crisis, the *Alabama* and Fenian raids, and boundary disputes over Maine, Oregon, Alaska, and the straits of San Juan de Fuca. It was the perception of history, though, not the actual facts, which was decisive. The widespread celebration of North American values took the tacit cooperation which had characterized the US-Canadian relationship and transformed it into an explicit norm. In so doing, it made trust part of Canadian and American self-identification. From this point forward, Canadians trusted Americans, and vice versa, because that was how North Americans were "supposed" to behave. Individuals and groups who behaved otherwise (e.g. by advocating the need for defenses, or even the possibility of war) were outside the accepted bounds of politics, and were duly chastised or ignored.

Making the community plausible: transnational interactions

Scholars of nationalism have argued in recent years that ethnic and political identities are socially constructed; i.e., they are not predetermined, objective, or "natural," but are instead intersubjectively held myths about the origins and histories of communities.[55] To say that communities are "imagined," though, is not to say that they are imaginary. For an identity to be accepted, it must resonate at some level with the beliefs and experiences of individuals.

Prior to the Civil War, the beliefs and experiences that would make a North American community seem plausible were mostly lacking.[56] Indeed, Canadians and Americans were often quite hostile to the notion that they formed a community. English Canada had, after all, been created by Loyalists fleeing the thirteen colonies; they deliberately detached themselves from the North American community. According to W. L. Morton, Americans reciprocated this antipathy, albeit in a paternalistic way. Americans tended to see Canada's attachment to Britain as deluded and artificial, and they were continually frustrated by Loyalist sentiment:

> Americans tended to see . . . the structure of Canadian politics as that of the domination of the country's government and economy, by a small, influential, pro-British group which by indoctrination and pressure kept Canada from finding its true destiny in union with the United States.[57]

For many years as well, some Americans stubbornly and foolishly maintained that parliamentary systems were anti-democratic and tyrannical.[58] They therefore could not accept that British Canada could ever be part of the North American experiment in democracy.

After the Civil War, however, the undefended border helped to support identification between Americans and Canadians. It did so in two ways: (1) by reducing tensions which might have kept the peoples apart; and (2) by promoting extensive transnational interactions between the two societies.

Social psychologists have demonstrated that the mere division of people into groups, even trivial or *ad hoc* groups, is enough to produce in-group favoritism and out-group hostility.[59] This dynamic is, in turn, greatly reinforced when groups compete over scarce resources or have conflicting goals.[60] Therefore, if the US–Canadian border had remained armed and hostile after the Civil War, ongoing security competition might have sustained sharp distinctions between Canadian and American identities. Because the border was undefended, though, in-group/out-group differentiation could be mitigated; less conflict meant less need to define the "Self" in contrast to the "Other."

Furthermore, as William R. Thompson has recently shown, the establishment of peace in North America permitted increasing liberalism and openness in the two countries.[61] During the Civil War, President Lincoln temporarily instituted the use of passports for crossing the border. Had US–Canadian relations remained hostile and militarized, strong border controls and limited transnational interactions might have become the norm, especially as enforcement capabilities improved on both sides. After 1871, détente and the undefended border allowed the two societies to freely interact in a wide variety of areas, thus generating the experiences necessary for a shared identity to emerge.

Probably the most obvious form of interaction generating shared experiences was interpersonal contact. Historically, populations drifted across the border in both directions (but mainly south), as individuals moved in search of jobs and available land. For these purposes, the international boundary often seemed irrelevant, as noted by historian James Shotwell: "Even in my own boyhood [the 1870s and 80s], people moved freely back and forth across the international line. We had relatives who went over to Michigan and farther west, and we thought no more of it than if they had moved out of Middlesex into the adjacent County of Lambton."[62] Between 1860 and 1900, the United States absorbed approximately 930,000 Canadian immigrants.[63] Many others went south on a temporary basis, to pursue educational opportunities (among them future Prime Minister William Lyon Mackenzie King, who attended Harvard, where he met Franklin Roosevelt). Movement in the opposite direction was more limited: the largest such migration sent 160,000 Minnesotans and Dakotans to the Canadian prairie in search of farmland between 1896 and 1914.[64] Even so, by 1931, there were 344,000 American-born permanent residents in Canada.[65]

Transnational flows of ideas and popular culture were also extensive. Around the turn of the century, improvements in technology and increased literacy spurred the growth of a commercialized mass publishing industry in North America, which meant that anglophone Canadians and Americans were increasingly exposed to the same (usually American) ideas. Hundreds of thousands of Canadians read *Ladies' Home Journal, McCall's,* and the *Saturday Evening Post,* and increasingly, they ignored British publications; for every dollar spent on British magazines, Canadians spent $100 on American magazines. In total, 300 separate American titles, amounting to 50 million copies, were purchased annually in Canada in the 1920s.[66] Similar processes were at work in the realm of social clubs, as Canadians flocked to join Rotary Clubs, Lions, and Kiwanis; in entertainment, with the dominance of American radio and Hollywood (98 percent of films shown in Canada were Hollywood-made); and in sports, as Canadians and Americans followed professional baseball and the National Hockey League.[67] As a result of these processes, Canadians came to share more in common with Americans than they did with the British.

Perhaps the most widespread interactions were economic relations, particularly international trade, investment, and labor union membership. Here again, the relations were usually quite lopsided. In general during this period, and especially after the turn of the century, the United States exported more goods and capital to Canada than vice versa. Even though the USA had terminated trade reciprocity with Canada during the Civil War, by 1876, Americans exported $44 million worth of goods to Canada, outpacing even the British. Canadians, in turn, sent roughly $30 million in goods back across the border.[68] By 1900, the USA was exporting more than $100 million of goods annually to Canada, and importing $58 million. The corresponding figures for 1913 were $436 million to $140 million; and for 1920, $800 million to $464 million. US imports accounted for roughly 70 percent of Canada's trade during most of the interwar period.[69] In addition, by the 1920s, Americans had invested $3.8 billion in Canada, nearly twice the figure invested by Britons.[70] By the 1930s, even though trade had dropped off dramatically as a result of tariff wars and the Great Depression, it was evident to most observers that an integrated continental economy had emerged.

Much the same was occurring to the labor movements in the two countries. In 1902, American Federation of Labor President Samuel Gompers successfully drove the Knights of Labour from the leadership of the Trades and Labour Congress, Canada's largest labor organization, and replaced them with AFL-sponsored candidates. From then on, the Canadian labor movement was fused with its American counterpart; until World War II, at least 60 percent, and as much as 90 percent, of Canadian union members joined "international" unions.[71]

These transnational relations helped to homogenize (mostly Americanize) the two societies, and made the idea of a specifically "North American" way of life seem intuitively plausible. This homogenization was noticed as early as 1890, in a letter submitted to a US Senate hearing on Canadian relations:

> Within the memory of many now in active life Canada was not only decidedly anti-republican, but was intensely British or monarchial [sic]. An American who crossed the boundary realized that he was in a foreign country; he was received there with suspicion. The dress, the speech, the manners, and the customs of the people were intensely English. The railways, the hotels, and the stage lines were English. Today . . . , all is radically changed.

The author went on to note how similar Canadians were to Americans in local and federal systems of government, education, manners, taste in magazines and newspapers, real estate markets, and economic activities, and then added: "They are our cousins, and we may well be proud of our relationship with them."[72] By the interwar period, the mixing of the two societies had been so extensive that they seemed to some observers to have become a single people. As historian J .B. Brebner noted in 1931, "It is unnecessary to make much comment on how similar ways of living are, wherever one turns in North America. The facts are obvious."[73] This sentiment was expressed even more directly by Prime Minister Mackenzie King in the House of Commons: "relations [with the USA] are so intimate and continuous that some people in Canada seem to imagine that they are not foreign relations at all."[74]

Canadians, generally being on the "receiving end" of American goods, culture, and tourists, often resented this homogenization. For example, Canadian scholar Harold Innis forcefully argued in 1952 that the USA exercised a sort of hegemony over Canada, and used the press, film, and the radio to reshape Canadian preferences along American lines:

> We are fighting for our lives. The pernicious influence of American advertising reflected especially in the periodical press and the powerful persistent impact of commercialism have been evident in all the ramifications of Canadian life. The jackals of communications systems are constantly on the alert to destroy every vestige of sentiment toward Great Britain holding it of no advantage if it threatens the omnipotence of American commercialism.[75]

Similarly, Tory MP Charles H. Dickie suggested in 1927 that Canada had become an appendage of the American empire: "[Americans] are effecting an economic conquest of Canada without going to war with us, as I am sure they never expect to do."[76] Canadian nationalists tried to resist American dominance in a variety of ways, with the rejection of free trade in 1911, restrictions on American cultural exports, and the establishment of the Canadian Broadcasting Corporation in 1932. Despite their efforts, an integrated North American way of life was slowly but surely built after the American Civil War.

Writing the North American story

The foundations for a distinctive North American identity had thus been built by the first decades of the twentieth century. This did not mean, however, that this identity had actually been articulated. North

Americans may have shared a way of life, and a uniquely demilitarized political relationship, but they were not necessarily conscious of this fact, nor did they assign it any particular significance. Their trust and shared identity was still implicit and taken for granted, rather than explicit and a source of pride.

Two political processes brought US–Canadian similarities to the forefront of political discourse. First was the creation of the International Joint Commission on boundary waters in 1909. Still functioning today, the IJC consists of six commissioners (three Americans, three Canadians), who coordinate the work of twenty-four technical boards governing issues such as the diversion of water from the Great Lakes, hydroelectric power facilities, and water quality. This organization has been remarkably successful as a tool of conflict resolution: of the more than 110 cases decided by the IJC, all but four have been settled unanimously; and in these four divided decisions, only two were split along national lines.[77]

However, the real importance of the IJC, as well as various other methods of nonviolent conflict resolution,[78] was not to ensure that US–Canadian disputes would be resolved peacefully. The undefended border had already done that. Rather, the IJC's role was more symbolic; it became a concrete example of the supposed North American preference for the depoliticized, rational, and nonviolent settlement of disputes. The IJC was a source of pride for scholars and policymakers on both sides of the border, and was frequently presented as a model for peace elsewhere. In his 1922 biography of Sir Wilfrid Laurier, Canadian Undersecretary of State O. D. Skelton noted of the IJC:

> In its explicit recognition of Canada's international status, in the optional provision for reference to the commission of any subject whatever in dispute between the two countries, in the permanent character of the joint body, and, not least, in the adoption for the first time in international practice of the far-reaching provision that individual citizens of either country might present their cases direct [sic], without the State acting as intermediary, the experiment was a distinctive North American contribution to a sane international polity.[79]

US Secretary of State Charles Evans Hughes offered a similar perspective in 1923 when he suggested that other countries might learn to overcome their propensities for war if they followed the North American lead and devised IJC-like commissions.[80] Thus, the IJC made Americans and Canadians more aware of their distinctiveness as North Americans.

Even more important for the explicit recognition of a North American identity was the onset and aftermath of World War I. Psychologists and sociologists have long argued that identity is based on difference: the recognition of a "we" depends on a simultaneous recognition of a "they."[81] The war had turned Europe into North America's "they." Canadians and Americans saw how in Europe, authoritarianism and militarism had triggered the most extensive bloodshed the world had ever seen. North Americans, on the other hand, had been farsighted enough to leave their border undefended and to resolve conflicts peacefully. Put in terms used by Emanuel Adler, North America became a "cognitive region," recognized by policymakers and scholars as constituting a distinct cultural area with its own brand of politics.[82]

One of the earliest Canadian proponents of this dichotomy was Prime Minister Sir Wilfrid Laurier. Laurier did not love the United States, and he certainly resented Canada's dependence on it. Nevertheless, he recognized that the USA and Canada had learned to overcome the "vortex of militarism" that was the "curse and blight" of Europe.[83] Similarly, Americans, who had always viewed themselves apart from Europe, began to include Canada in their "exceptionalist" discourse during World War I. Thus, in a private letter in 1914, Theodore Roosevelt wrote: "I cannot help hoping and believing that in the end nations will gradually get to the point that, for instance, Canada and the United States have now attained, where each nation, as a matter of course, treats the other with reasonable justice and friendliness and where war is unthinkable between them."[84] This last quote displays a recurring theme in this discourse: the idea that the North American democracies were destined to save Europe by providing a shining example of how to structure international politics. This argument was most forcefully made by the Rev. James Macdonald in a 1917 lecture:

> These two North American democracies are, indeed, Europe's second chance . . . North America inherited a world idea, not for her own sake, but for the world's. The United States and Canada are trustees for all humanity. Before the world's judgment seat we must give account of our stewardship.[85]

Concurrent with the drift towards global war was the 100th anniversary of the Treaty of Ghent (ending the War of 1812), which heightened the contrast between North American and European practices.[86]

In the interwar period, the celebration of "North Americanism" continued, and even intensified, as it became evident that another European war was in the offing. Franklin Roosevelt was surely wrong in 1936 when he said, "On both sides of the line we are so accustomed to an undefended boundary three thousand miles long that we are inclined perhaps to minimize its vast importance."[87] In fact, US and Canadian policymakers sang the praises of the undefended border, the hundred-years' peace, and "matchless harmony" on almost every imaginable occasion. Secretary of State Henry Stimson's 1932 Dominion Day greetings give the flavor of countless other speeches:

> My message is more than one of formal greeting. It is not merely a courteous word of remembrance such as might be exchanged between distant and dissociated nations. It is a message framed upon a common outlook, common tradition, common language and literature, and upon a relationship which is unique among the great peoples of the world. It is a message not only of good wishes but of understanding and affection.[88]

Historians, especially those Canadian-born, also had a hand in promoting this discourse. Particularly important were James Shotwell and the other contributors to the twenty-five–volume history of US–Canadian relations sponsored by the Carnegie Endowment for International Peace. These historians were less inclined than were statesmen to romanticize the undefended border and the years of peace, but they explicitly sought to use North American relations as a model for the rest of the world. As Carl Berger notes, for Shotwell, "the examination of Canadian-American relations was intended to serve a further purpose which overshadowed the simple historical satisfaction of describing the past. Shotwell's main concerns were world peace and internationalism and it was these twin goals which that in his mind justified the financial support that the [Carnegie] series received and constituted its chief relevance for world history."[89]

The political impact of shared identity

The pervasive discourse of North Americanism took the trust already implicit in the US–Canadian relationship, and turned it into a source of identification. Even when domestic political actors behaved in ways contrary to those identities, they were unable to undermine the basic trust that existed between Americans and Canadians.

This was clearly demonstrated in the reaction to a violation of the norm of the undefended border in 1935. In secret testimony at a Congressional hearing on the need for improved frontier air defenses, General Charles Kilbourne requested funds for the building of an air base near the Canadian border, "camouflaged" under the heading "intermediate stations for transcontinental flights." The subterfuge, he explained, was necessitated by the "Canadian situation": he "did not want to accentuate anything that would look as though we contemplated passing away from the century-old principle that our Canadian border needs no defense," but he thought that an air base could be built in the Great Lakes region "without attracting any attention." Later in the same hearing, General F. M. Andrews expressed fear that Canada might join a hypothetical enemy coalition, or be defeated by one, which would require the US to contemplate preemptive strikes.[90]

When the testimony was subsequently published, there was a strong negative reaction from the American side, while Canadians hardly noticed the incident at all. Franklin Roosevelt upbraided Andrews, Kilbourne, and Military Affairs Committee Chairman John J. McSwain in a clumsily phrased letter, noting that "this Government not only accepts as an accomplished fact the permanent peace cemented by many generations of friendship between the Canadian and American people, but expects to live up to not only the letter, but also the spirit of our treaties relating to the permanent disarmament of our three thousand miles of common boundary."[91] In a press conference, he added that "so far as every Government official in this country is concerned . . . we are certainly going to do nothing to arm ourselves in any form, either offensively or defensively, against Canada."[92]

Roosevelt was not the only one to weigh in on the issue. Senator Arthur Capper of Kansas complained that "the people of this continent did not even suspect that our own Army officers were guilty of [this] species of insanity"; and Representative Louis Ludlow found that "[i]n view of the matchless harmony that has enabled two Nations with 3,000 miles of common border to dwell side by side in perfect peace for 118 years, there is something tragically pathetic in the testimony" given by Andrews and Kilbourne. Many major newspapers, including the *Washington Post* and *New York Herald Tribune*, also joined in the condemnation.[93] Americans clearly found talk of preemptive strikes against Canada inconsistent with their identity as North Americans. Although an air defense bill did eventually pass, Roosevelt and others had made plain that war with Canada was not to be considered, except in cases where the latter had already been defeated by a hostile power (primarily, the Germans or Japanese). War plans came to reflect this.[94]

Canadians, for their part, dismissed the entire episode. Ottawa's first response was to note that "The government . . . had been disposed from the first to not take the matter seriously except for its possible effects on Canadian public opinion." The *Globe and Mail* regretted all the "foolish publicity given to an irritating subject," while the *Montreal Gazette* noted that "Canadians by and large did not take the episode seriously and were inclined to laugh heartily at the absurdity of the whole affair."[95] The *Ottawa Citizen* even defended the American air base plan: "the failure of this country [Canada] to take adequate steps for defense against invasion on either coast is tending to make it imperative on the United States to do something about defense of the northern frontier."[96] Clearly, Canadians "knew" that the USA, as a North American nation, had no aggressive intentions, and they interpreted the air base plan accordingly.

The vehemence with which the air base plan was denounced in the US, and the ease with which it was ignored in Canada, suggests that the two sides had internalized a North American identity that assumed and celebrated peaceful relations between the USA and Canada. This identity "immunized" North America against the reemergence of a security dilemma, and in so doing, institutionalized the North American pluralistic security community.

Conclusions

The history of the US–Canadian relationship suggests three implications for our understanding of PSCs generally. First, it demonstrates a path to PSC development not addressed in Adler and Barnett's introduction. Their three-stage model (nascent, ascendant, mature) begins with a conscious search for increased security and cooperation. With increased cooperation and diffuse reciprocity, states can develop shared meanings and identities, and slowly begin to demilitarize their relationship. Ultimately, states might cease preparing for war with one another entirely, at which point they have become a mature PSC.[97]

As shown above, the United States and Canada essentially reversed this causal logic. After barely avoiding a war during the American Civil War, they demilitarized their border almost immediately. This demilitarization preceded and produced trust: the undefended border led the two sides to revise their previously hostile images of one another, and to substitute dependable expectations of peaceful change. Once the tensions in this relationship had been reduced, the USA and Canada could begin to build a shared identity which institutionalized the PSC. Hence, contrary to the Adler and Barnett model, the undefended border was an initial cause, as well as an indicator, of the North American PSC.

Two factors are responsible for the differences in these historical paths. First, Canada's divided sovereignty, and general lack of foreign policy autonomy, made a conscious search for community impossible. Canada could cooperate tacitly with the United States, but it could not authorize "search missions" to promote cooperation or create international institutions without Britain's approval. Until Canada gained more autonomy in the interwar period, the North American PSC was by necessity spontaneous and "loosely coupled." Secondly, different international environments may also have played a role. The path outlined by Adler and Barnett seems more appropriate in situations where would-be PSC members face a common threat which compels them to cooperate, and which creates incentives for states to highlight their similarities and downplay their differences. An example might be the West European states, which after World War II had to simultaneously address the "German question" and the Soviet threat. Until World War I, though, the USA and Canada faced no common threat, and had a relatively insignificant legacy of war and aggression to overcome. Consequently, they had very little incentive for formal security cooperation. Only after Canadians and Americans realized what they had achieved did they begin to search for ways to strengthen their relationship, starting with the creation of the Permanent Joint Board on Defense in August, 1940.

There are good reasons to believe that this precise path toward stable peace in North America could not be replicated elsewhere. There are simply too many peculiarities: Canada's semi-sovereign status from 1867 to 1931; British extended deterrence; shared Anglo-Saxon culture and political institutions; American republican institutions; a thinly populated, geographically isolated, and (by Europeans, at least) largely unexplored continent. This case can, however, be used to make *contingent generalizations* about the development of other security communities.[98] The specific causal relationships identified in this study (e.g. between demilitarization and trust, or between transnational interactions and shared identity) might operate in cases which share the same or similar sets of variables. Thus, although the Canadian–American relationship is highly unrepresentative of international politics as a whole, it can still suggest possible pathways along which other PSCs might be developed.

Secondly, the US–Canadian case suggests the importance of political learning in the development of security communities. As the literature on learning demonstrates, actors' beliefs and preferences are not static, but are instead acquired through experience and reflection. New behavior or new ideas can lead actors to revise their preexisting images of one another and generate new understandings of their relationship. This kind of reevaluation was a vital component of the development of the US–Canadian security community. Prior to the 1870s, the USA and Britain/Canada had been "locked" into a security dilemma in large part because of hostile images and expectations about future aggression. After the Civil War, though, these expectations were falsified by the undefended border. As a result, the two sides began to "understand" one another in more pacific terms, even if there was still antagonism and miscommunication. Demilitarization had provided a "cognitive punch" which directed the two sides to reevaluate their prior beliefs.[99]

Thirdly, this case illustrates the path-dependent nature of PSC development.[100] When the USA and Canada decided to stop defending their border, they set in motion a self-reinforcing pattern of behavior. Mutual demilitarization generated positive feedback in the form of trust and dependable expectations of peaceful change, which in turn supported continued demilitarization. With neither side posing a military threat to the other, it became increasingly unlikely that they would revert to their pre-Civil War pattern of behavior. The institutionalization of the undefended border made it unlikely that they even *could*; domestic actors supporting renewed militarization (e.g. Selby Smyth) gradually lost the ability to impose their preferences on the political system.

Positive feedback from demilitarization had a similar effect on the construction of a shared US–Canadian identity. The undefended border facilitated transnational relations, by supporting open, liberal political systems in both countries.[101] These transnational relations in turn begat more transnational relations, as economies and cultures became more tightly integrated, and individuals formed more cross-border relationships. Eventually, Canadian and American ways of life were inextricably linked.

This is not to suggest that a US–Canadian security community was an inevitable outcome; there were many historical junctures at which it could have come unraveled. Had the Venezuelan crisis escalated, for example, the PSC might have collapsed rather spectacularly, as American troops invaded Canada. However, once the process began, it gained momentum and was increasingly difficult to halt. Peaceful expectations reinforced peaceful practices, and vice versa, making the undefended border and 150 years of peace seem the normal state of affairs, and war the subject of farce.

Notes

I would like to thank Emanuel Adler, Mike Barnett, Bruce Cronin, Jeff Gayton, Mike Lipson, Rob McCalla, Stéphane Roussel, John Sigler, David Tarr, John Herd Thompson, Joe Underhill-Cady and two reviewers at Cambridge University Press for their helpful comments and criticism.

1 See, for example, Michael Moore's recent film *Canadian Bacon* (1995).

2 Strictly speaking, of course, North American also includes Mexico and Central America, but in this essay, I will use "North America" to refer only to the United States and Canada. For an argument supporting a "North America of the Two," see William T. R. Fox, *A Continent Apart* (Toronto: University of Toronto Press, 1985), pp. 3–12.

3 The classic text on the relationship between anarchy and war is of course Kenneth N. Waltz, *Man, the State, and War* (New York: Columbia University Press, 1959).

4 See Kenneth N. Waltz, *Theory of International Politics* (Reading, MA: Addison-Wesley, 1979).

5 Alexander Wendt, "Anarchy Is What States Make of It: The Social Construction of Power Politics," *International Organization* 46 (Spring 1992), pp. 391–425. The quote is taken from page 405.

6 Emanuel Adler's definition of learning is the one used here: "the adoption by policymakers of new interpretations of reality, as they are created and introduced to the political system by individuals and institutions." Adler, "Cognitive Evolution: A Dynamic Approach for the Study of International Relations and Their Progress," in Emanuel Adler and Beverly Crawford, eds., *Progress in Postwar International Relations* (New York: Columbia University Press, 1991), p. 52. For a thorough review of the literature on learning, see Jack S. Levy, "Learning and Foreign Policy: Sweeping a Conceptual Minefield," *International Organization* 48 (Spring 1994), pp. 279–312.

7   On "we-feeling" and "dependable expectations of peaceful change," see Karl W. Deutsch et al., *Political Community and the North Atlantic Area* (Princeton: Princeton University Press, 1957), pp. 5, 36.

8   For a social psychological explanation of this phenomenon, see Daryl J. Bem, "Self-Perception Theory," in Leonard Berkowitz, ed., *Advances in Experimental Social Psychology*, vol. 6 (1972) (New York: Academic Press, 1972), pp. 1–62.

9   W. L. Morton, *The Canadian Identity* (Madison: University of Wisconsin Press, 1961), p. 61.

10 Donald F. Warner, *The Idea of Continental Union* (Lexington: University of Kentucky Press, 1960), p. 150.

11 In this dispute, the lone British representative on an international arbitration board voted to certify US ownership of the entire Alaskan panhandle. This action convinced Prime Minister Laurier that Canada needed to take more control of its affairs.

12 Desmond Morton, *A Military History of Canada* (Edmonton: Hurtig Publishers, 1990), pp. 116–117.

13 The first Canadian government after confederation was built on a political alliance between Ontarian Sir John A. Macdonald and Québécois George-Etienne Cartier. In 1896, Sir Wilfrid Laurier became the first French-Canadian prime minister of Canada.

14 J. Bartlet Brebner, *The North Atlantic Triangle* (New York: Columbia University Press, 1945), p. 247.

15 Testimony of Joseph Nimmo, Jr. in *Relations With Canada*, United States Senate Report 1530, part 2, 51st Congress, 1st session (Washington: GPO, 1890), p. 887.

16 Albert K. Weinberg, *Manifest Destiny* (Chicago: Quadrangle Books, 1963), p. 379.

17 ibid., p. 363.

18 Force was of course acceptable in incorporating those "outside the family," such as Cubans, Mexicans and Filipinos.

19 Quoted in Warner, *Continental Union*, pp. 95–96.

20 Taft claimed that Canada was at a "parting of the ways," and that "the bond uniting the dominion [Canada] to the mother country [was] light and almost imperceptible"; trade reciprocity would help break this bond. More graphically, Clark thought reciprocity would hasten the day when "the American flag [would] float over every square foot of the British-North American possessions clear to the North Pole." See W. M. Baker, "A Case Study of Anti-Americanism in English-Speaking Canada: The Election Campaign of 1911," *Canadian Historical Review* 51 (December 1970), p. 439.

21 Weinberg, *Manifest Destiny*, p. 380.

22 Daniel Deudney, "The Philadelphian System: Sovereignty, Arms Control, and the Balance of Power in the American States-Union, circa 1787–1861," *International Organization* 49 (Spring 1995), pp. 203–204.

23 Samuel Huntington notes that historically, war planners in the United States had always been politically marginalized. He recounts a story in which President Woodrow Wilson, upon learning that the Army was beginning to prepare for a possible war with Germany, orders an investigation and demands that the officers involved be relieved of duty. *The Soldier and the State* (Cambridge, MA: Harvard University Press, 1957), p. 144.

24 See Edgar W. McInnis, *The Unguarded Frontier* (Garden City, NY: Doubleday, Doran & Co., 1942), chapter 6.

25 In 1817, US and British negotiators concluded the Rush–Bagot agreement, which sharply limited naval deployments on the Great Lakes and nearby waters. On Lakes Superior, Erie, Huron, and Michigan, each side was limited to two ships of 100 tons each, with a single eighteen-pound cannon; on Lake Ontario, and Lake Champlain, the limit was one such ship apiece. Although it was occasionally violated over the years, particularly at the end of the nineteenth century, this agreement effectively halted a naval arms race between the two countries.

26 The data on expenditures comes from C. P. Stacey, "The Myth of the Unguarded Frontier, 1815–1871," *American Historical Review* 56 (October 1950), pp. 6, 15.

27 See Albert B. Corey, *The Crisis of 1830–1842 in Canadian–American Relations.* (New Haven: Yale University Press, 1941), especially chapters 3, 4, and 9.

28 For a thorough account of US–Canadian relations during the Civil War, see Robin Winks, *Canada and the United States: The Civil War Years* (Montreal: Harvest House, 1971). Britain's decision to deploy troops is discussed on p. 82.

29 Quoted in Gwynne Dyer and Tina Viljoen, *The Defence of Canada*, vol. 1 (Toronto: McClelland & Stewart, 1990), p. 117.

30 See C. P. Stacey, "Britain's Withdrawal from North America, 1864–1871," *Canadian Historical Review* 36 (September 1955), pp. 185–198; and D. G. Creighton, "The United States and Canadian Confederation," *Canadian Historical Review* 39 (September 1958), pp. 209–222.

31 Erik G. Yesson, "State Sovereignty, Democratic Institutions, and Stable Peace: Comparative Evidence from 19th-Century North America and 20th-Century Europe," presented at the 1995 Annual Meeting of the American Political Science Association, Chicago.

32 Paul J. Scheips, "Darkness and Light: The Interwar Years, 1865–1898," in Maurice Matloff, ed. *American Military History* (Washington: Office of the Chief of Military History, US Army, 1969), p. 282.

33 By the terms of this treaty, the *Alabama* claims and the San Juan de Fuca boundary dispute were submitted to international arbitration, and in both cases, the result was favorable to the United States. The treaty also opened the St. Lawrence in perpetuity to American shipping, and granted reciprocal rights to fisheries, again benefiting the United States (Nova Scotia's fisheries were far more productive than the US's). Canadians, in

turn, received the right to navigate the Lake St. Clair canal (between Lakes Huron and Erie), and three Alaskan rivers. They did *not*, however, receive any compensation for the Fenian raids, although these were comparable in scope to the *Alabama* raids. To add insult to injury, by the terms of the 1825 Anglo-Russian Treaty on Alaska (inherited by the US in 1867), Canadians had already possessed the right to navigate those three rivers.

34 Indeed, according to historian C. P. Stacey, 1872 marked the date when the undefended border ceased to be a myth. See Stacey, "The Myth of the Unguarded Frontier."

35 *Analytical and Topical Index to the Reports of the Chief of Engineers and Officers of the Corps of Engineers, United States Army*, vol. 3, US House of Representatives Document no. 439, 57th Congress, 2nd session (Washington: GPO, 1903), pp. 1493–1504.

36 Richard Preston, *The Defence of the Undefended Border* (Montreal and Kingston: McGill-Queen's University Press, 1977), p. 86

37 Scheips, "Darkness and Light."

38 D. Morton, *A Military History of Canada*, p. 94.

39 Dyer and Viljoen, *The Defence of Canada*, vol. 1, p. 147. Desmond Morton notes that the manpower problem became so acute that the senior Québécois militia unit, the 4th *Chasseurs Canadiens*, simply evaporated. Morton, *A Military History of Canada*, p. 94

40 Ibid.

41 Kenneth Bourne, *Britain and the Balance of Power in North America* (London: Longmans, 1967), pp. 318–9.

42 *Material* preparation for war is emphasized for two reasons. First, "paper preparations," i.e. war plans, are generally not visible to other states, and hence cannot communicate intent or promote trust. Second, most states will assume that others have *some* plans directed against them. Their reaction to this knowledge, however, depends upon how they appraise the political significance of that planning. If policymakers in state A devote few material resources to defense directed at state B, then B might believe that A's military planners are politically marginalized, or that the plans themselves may be mere paper exercises designed to keep the planning staff busy. I discuss the significance and political impact of Canadian and American war planning more concretely below.

43 Preston, *The Defence of the Undefended Border*, p. 65.

44 Sir John A. Macdonald noted in 1880 that "Not being a military man, I cannot speak of the possibility of defending Canada; but I have generally understood it to be the opinion of the leading military men that, beyond holding certain points, the Americans, from their immense power and superiority, could go where they liked and do what they pleased in the country." Quoted in Alice R. Stewart, "Sir John A. Macdonald and the Imperial Defence Commission of 1879," *Canadian Historical Review* 35 (June 1954), p. 123.

45 Preston, *The Defence of the Undefended Border*, pp. 58–9.

46 The Liberal Party was particularly sanguine about the prospects for peace. Liberals thought annexation unlikely, and forcible annexation nearly impossible, because they assumed that the US, as a constitutional democracy, "abjured the use of force." Preston, *The Defence of the Undefended Border*, p. 80. Canadian Tories, while generally less friendly to the United States, also expected peaceful relations.

47 Ibid., pp. 65–7.

48 On bandwagoning, see Stephen Walt, *The Origins of Alliances* (Ithaca: Cornell University Press, 1987). On hiding, see Paul Schroeder, "Historical Reality vs. Neorealist Theory," *International Security* 19 (Summer 1994), pp. 108–148.

49 See John Herd Thompson and Stephen J. Randall, *Canada and the United States: Ambivalent Allies* (Athens, GA: University of Georgia Press, 1994), pp. 67–69; C.P. Stacey, *Canada and the Age of Conflict*, vol. 1 (Toronto: Macmillan of Canada, 1977), p. 87; J.L. Granatstein and Norman Hillmer, *For Better or For Worse: Canada and the United States to the 1990s* (Toronto: Copp Clark Pittman, 1992), p. 32.

50 Quoted in Stewart, "Sir John A. Macdonald," p. 122.

51 Preston, *The Defence of the Undefended Border*, p. 126.

52 See Granatstein and Hillmer, *For Better or For Worse*, pp. 59–63.

53 Preston, *The Defence of the Undefended Border*, pp. 193–5, 227; C. P. Stacey, *Canada and the Age of Conflict*, vol. 2 (Toronto: University of Toronto Press, 1981), pp. 155–158. For a discussion of why paper planning is not evidence that states expect to fight, see Stephen R. Rock, *Why Peace Breaks Out: Great Power Rapprochement in Historical Perspective* (Chapel Hill: University of North Carolina Press, 1989), pp. 22–23. For a contrary view, see Floyd W. Rudmin, *Bordering on Aggression* (Hull, PQ: Voyageur Press, 1993).

54 Henry G. Gole, War Planning at the US Army War College, 1934–1940: The Road to Rainbow, PhD dissertation, Temple University, 1991, pp. 10, 31.

55 See Benedict Anderson, *Imagined Communities*, 2nd edn. (London: Verso Press, 1991).

56 Allan Smith demonstrates that some Canadians viewed North America as a political, cultural, and geographic unit as early as the 1820s. They were, however, limited in number until after the Civil War. See "The Continental Dimension in the Evolution of the English-Canadian Mind," in Smith, ed., *Canada: An American Nation?* (Montreal & Kingston: McGill-Queen's University Press, 1994).

57 Morton, *The Canadian Identity*, p. 59.

58 Even as late as 1890, an American commentator referred to Canada's government as follows: "The Dominion government is essentially a political party government, the leader of the party in power being at once chief of the executive branch and boss of the legislative branch of the Government; in a word, a partisan autocrat." *Relations with Canada*, p. 1234.

59 See Henri Tajfel, "Experiments in Intergroup Discrimination," *Scientific*

American 223 (November 1970), 96–102. For a recent application in international relations, see Jonathan Mercer, "Anarchy and Identity," *International Organization* 49 (Spring 1995), 229–252.

60 See Muzafer Sherif, *Group Conflict and Cooperation: Their Social Psychology* (London: Routledge & Kegan Paul, 1966), and Donald M. Taylor and Fathali M. Moghaddam, *Theories of Intergroup Relations* (New York: Praeger, 1987), chapter 3.

61 William R. Thompson, "Democracy and Peace: Putting the Cart Before the Horse?" *International Organization* 50 (Winter 1996), 141–174.

62 James T. Shotwell, "A Personal Note on the Theme of Canadian-American Relations," *Canadian Historical Review* 28 (March 1947), pp. 31–43. The quote is taken from pp. 35–36.

63 Samuel E. Moffett, *The Americanization of Canada* (Toronto: University of Toronto Press, 1972), p. 10.

64 Thompson and Randall, *Ambivalent Allies*, figure on p. 18.

65 Granatstein and Hillmer, *For Better or For Worse*, p. 88.

66 Mary Vipond, "Cultural Nationalism," in Norman Hillmer, ed., *Partners Nevertheless: Canadian-American Relations in the Twentieth Century* (Toronto: Copp Clark Pittman, 1989), p. 236.

67 Thompson and Randall, *Ambivalent Allies*, chapters 4 and 5.

68 Moffett, *The Americanization of Canada*, p. 80.

69 C. P. Stacey, *Canada and the Age of Conflict*, I, pp. 358–9; II, pp. 434–435.

70 Granatstein and Hillmer, *For Better or For Worse*, pp. 86–87.

71 Thompson and Randall, *Ambivalent Allies*, pp. 82–85, 141.

72 Testimony of Francis Wayland Glen, *Relations with Canada*, pp. 877–882.

73 J. Bartlet Brebner, "Canadian and North American History," *Canadian Historical Association Annual Report* (Ottawa, 1931), p. 41.

74 *Debates of the House of Commons*, May 24, 1938, p. 3177

75 Harold A. Innis, *Changing Concepts of Time* (Toronto: University of Toronto Press, 1952), p. 19.

76 *Debates of the House of Commons*, April 11, 1927, p. 2275.

77 This data is given in Richard Bilder, *When Neighbors Quarrel: Canada–US Dispute Settlement Experience*, University of Wisconsin Institute for Legal Studies Working Papers Series vol. 8, no. 4 (Madison, 1987), p. 55.

78 Among these methods and institutions are international arbitration, informal transgovernmental networks, and, of course, *ad hoc* diplomacy. See Bilder, *When Neighbors Quarrel*; P. E. Corbett, *The Settlement of Canadian-American Disputes* (New Haven: Yale University Press, 1937); Annette Baker Fox, Alfred O. Hero, Jr., and Joseph S. Nye, Jr., *Canada and the United States: Transnational and Transgovernmental Relations* (New York: Columbia University Press, 1976); K. J. Holsti, "Canada and the United States," in Steven L. Spiegel and Kenneth N. Waltz, eds., *Conflict in World Politics.* (Cambridge, MA: Winthrop Publishers, 1971); and Erik B. Wang, "Adjudication of Canada–United States Disputes," *Canadian Yearbook of International Law* (1981), pp. 158–228.

79 O. D. Skelton, *The Life and Letters of Sir Wilfrid Laurier*, vol. 2 (New York: The Century Co., 1922), p. 363.

80 Charles Evans Hughes, *The Pathway of Peace* (New York: Harper and Brothers, 1925), p. 16.

81 See Mercer, "Anarchy and Identity," pp. 241–243.

82 Emanuel Adler, "Imagined (Security) Communities: Cognitive Regions in International Relations," *Millennium*, 26, 2 (1997), pp. 249–77.

83 Skelton, *Life and Letters of Sir Wilfrid Laurier*, II, p. 293.

84 Elting E. Morison, ed., *The Letters of Theodore Roosevelt*, vol. 7 (Cambridge, MA: Harvard University Press, 1954), p. 795.

85 James A. Macdonald, *The North American Idea* (New York: Fleming H. Revell Co., 1917), p. 73.

86 The anniversary was greeted with the formation of "peace committees" in the US, Canada, and Britain. Future Prime Minister Mackenzie King was the first to propose the idea in Canada.

87 *The Public Papers and Addresses of Franklin D. Roosevelt*, vol. 5 (New York: Random House, 1938), p. 277.

88 United States Department of State, *Press Releases*, vol. 7 (Washington, GPO: 1932), p. 6.

89 Carl C. Berger, "Internationalism, Continentalism, and the Writing of History: Comments on the Carnegie Series on the Relations of Canada and the United States," in *The Influence of the United States on Canadian Development: Eleven Case Studies*, ed. Richard A. Preston. (Durham, NC: Duke University Press, 1972), p. 41.

90 United States House of Representatives, Committee on Military Affairs, Hearings. *Air Defense Bases*. 74th Congress, 1st session (Washington: GPO, 1935). Kilbourne's testimony is found on pp. 11–23, and the quote above is taken from p. 17. Andrews's testimony is on pp. 60–64.

91 *The Public Papers and Addresses of Franklin D. Roosevelt*, IV, p. 142. It is interesting and instructive that FDR referred to the "treaties relating to the permanent disarmament" of the border. With the exception of the Rush-Bagot agreement, which was not a treaty, and which could be terminated by either party on six months' notice, there were no treaties on Canadian-American disarmament. Roosevelt, like many Canadians and Americans, just took the existence of such treaties for granted.

92 *Complete Presidential Press Conferences of Franklin D. Roosevelt*, vol. 5 (New York: Da Capo Press, 1972), selection 268.

93 Capper's speech, and the newspaper editorials, appear in the *Congressional Record*, 74th Congress, 1st session, May 9, 1935, p. 7206; Ludlow's speech appears on p. 8265.

94 Preston, *The Defense of the Undefended Border*, p. 226.

95 Quoted in Rudmin, *Bordering on Aggression*, p. 119.

96 Quoted in "Canadians Amused by Air Base Talk," *New York Times*, May 5, 1935, Sec. IV, p. 7.

97 Adler and Barnett, this volume.

98 See Alexander L. George, "Case Studies and Theory Development: The Method of Structured, Focused Comparison," in Paul Gordon Lauren, ed., *Diplomacy: New Approaches in History, Theory, and Policy* (New York: Free Press, 1979).

99 On the concept of a "cognitive punch," see Adler, "Cognitive Evolution," p. 55.

100 On path dependence, see Stephen D. Krasner, "Sovereignty: An Institutional Perspective," *Comparative Political Studies* 21 (April 1988), pp. 66–94.

A neo-Kantian perspective: democracy, interdependence, and international organizations in building security communities

Bruce Russett

In this chapter I explore elements of a partial but arguably nascent global security community. To think about such a global scope requires treating the concept of security community somewhat loosely, and surely it applies unevenly, to some regions more strongly than to others. At one end of the spectrum, some "hot spots" manifest no security community whatsoever; other parts of the global system have plausibly reached the stage of ascendant (South America) and even mature (Europe) security communities. Overall, true interstate conflicts have become rare with the end of the Cold War, just as intrastate conflicts have multiplied.[1] So what we must do here is to consider elements – partial and potential as well as actual – of a global security community. In doing so we take the hard case, focusing on global processes and institutions and thereby push the envelope of this discussion on security communities. What seems to be transpiring, at the very least, is a blurring and extension of the boundaries of regional security communities, as they exist or as they are emerging.

By focusing on the global parts, particularly the United Nations, I do not imply that everything about these organizations works as intended. Rather, I am trying to capture the essential vision of many of the founders of the UN, previous commentators, and recent contributions to the discourse on reforming the UN.[2]

A Kantian framework

As a way of introducing some of these elements in a Kantian framework, begin with a puzzle about the end of the Cold War. For this purpose the question is not simply why did the Cold War end, but rather: why did it end before the drastic change in the bipolar distribution of power, and why did it end peacefully? Neither of these questions is well answered within the framework of a neorealist analysis. In November 1988 Margaret Thatcher proclaimed, as did other Europeans, that "the Cold War is over." By spring 1989 the US State Department stopped making official reference to the Soviet Union as the enemy.[3] The fundamental patterns of East–West behavior had shifted toward those of a nascent security community, beginning even before the circumvention of the Berlin Wall and then by its destruction in November 1989. All of this precedes the unification of Germany (October 1990) and the dissolution of the Warsaw Pact (July 1991). Even after those events, the military power of the Soviet Union itself remained intact until the dissolution of the USSR at the end of December 1991.[4] None of these events was resisted militarily. Indeed, by fall 1990 the United States and the Soviet Union were cooperating closely against Iraq, formerly a Soviet ally.

Any understanding of the change in the Soviet Union's international behavior, before its political fragmentation, and in time reciprocated by the West, demands attention to the three legs on which the liberal vision of Immanuel Kant's *Perpetual Peace* stands:

1. Substantial political liberalization and movement toward democracy in the Soviet Union, with consequent changes in free expression and the treatment of dissidents at home, in the East European satellites, and in behavior toward Western Europe and the United States.[5]
2. The desire for economic interdependence with the West, impelled by the impending collapse of the Soviet economy and the consequent perceived need for access to Western markets, goods, technology, and capital. Obtaining that access would require a change in Soviet military and diplomatic policy, and would constrain that policy subsequently.
3. The influence of international law and organizations, as manifested in the Conference on Security and Cooperation in Europe (CSCE) and the human rights basket of the Helsinki accords and their legitimation and support of political dissent in the communist states. Whereas the UN itself was not important in this process of penetrating domestic politics, the CSCE as an intergovernmental organization, and the various human rights INGOs, most certainly were.[6]

These same three pieces – consolidation of democracy, economic interdependence, and transnational institutions – constituted the basis whereby Jean Monnet, Konrad Adenauer, and other founders of the European Community sought to foreclose the possibility of yet another great war in Europe. Peace among representative democracies, economic interdependence, and international law clearly emerge in a free translation and late-twentieth century reading of Kant's 1795 work.[7] It is also a view consistent with a definition of human security recently espoused as the protection of states, and their populations, from mortal danger.[8] It is a view subversive of authoritarian and autarchic concepts of state sovereignty, in the interest of popular sovereignty in control of states (liberal internal systems) operating with substantial autonomy but embedded in, and therefore supporting and actively promoting, the production of liberal states in an interdependent international system. It is a view ultimately of a global authority structure, weak but with enough teeth to defend itself against illiberal challengers. In this it is a dynamic view of sovereignty.[9]

Ever since the Treaty of Westphalia, state juridical sovereignty has been the fundamental legal and ideological principle (and also myth) undergirding the world system. The United Nations, as an organization comprising sovereign states, is neither a world government nor an assembly of peoples. Yet states' practical sovereignty has in many areas been eroded. Some of these erosions have happened consciously and voluntarily – most strikingly in the case of the European Union, in other instances by a variety of treaty commitments binding states to common legal norms and procedures. Others have been involuntary, as when extreme violation of human rights or humanitarian distress becomes the basis for international intervention in what would normally be the domestic affairs of a state (e.g., Iraq, Haiti). Sometimes the collapse of civil authority (e.g., Somalia) may mean that there is no government capable of exercising the practical rights of sovereignty to which the country is nominally entitled. A normative fracture exists between Article 2(7) of the Charter, forbidding the UN "to intervene in matters which are essentially within the domestic jurisdiction of any state," and the broadened scope of authority under Article 39 "to maintain or restore international peace and security."

Conceptually, a Kantian view fits nicely with the thesis of the former UN Secretary-General Boutros-Ghali that democracy, economic development and interdependence, and peace are inextric-

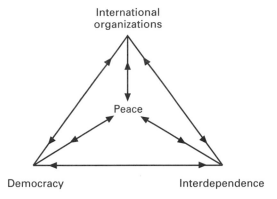

Figure 11.1   The development of security communities

ably linked, in something of a triangle of positive feedbacks, with the United Nations and other international organizations able to make direct contributions to each. Boutros-Ghali makes this thesis explicit in his *Agenda* reports, first on peace, then on development, and finally on democratization.[10] Figure 11.1 illustrates this system.

It does not matter what item one places at any particular corner of the triangle, but for the sake of this discussion peace belongs at the center. The triangular image serves as a description and prescription for an ordered, just, and peaceful society at the domestic or international levels, with wide and equal political participation yet protection of minority rights, equality of opportunity with sharp limits on rents that are derived from control of a market by powerful political or economic actors, and institutions to facilitate and promote cooperation with some – but minimal – elements of coercion.

The basic perspective holds that each of these is interacting and mutually supportive, internationally and domestically as well, in a dynamic mutually reinforcing system. For example, each of the other elements is, or can be, supported and encouraged by international organizations; in turn, a world where international organizations can flourish must be one where peace, development, and democracy also flourish in most of the constituent states. Hence all the arrows go in both directions, to emphasize the mutual feedbacks. Again, this is a conceptual and theoretical schema. The empirical evidence for each of the links is in some instances weak and contradictory, and in any case I could not possibly review it in detail here. Nor would I deny that there can also be some contradictions and negative feedbacks. But there is enough evidence for most of the links to allow us to take "the whole ball of wax" seriously, if still somewhat speculatively. We begin with the linkages in the lower half of the figure, among democracy, economic development and interdependence, and peace, proceeding only later to the linkages to and from international organizations.

Democracy and peace

At the international level, the causal arrow from democracy (and perhaps human rights more generally) to peace is arguably the most solidly established generalization of the lot. It is not uncontested, but in my view the critics have yet to seriously dent the "democratic peace" proposition. To this point in time, no one to my knowledge has seriously argued the opposite (that democracies are *more* likely to fight each other than are other states); at most a few articles have held that, especially for particular times and places, the positive association does not appear, or if so is not statistically significant. I have responded to some of these critiques elsewhere, and refer the reader to that response. The response depends less on refuting a few particular critiques than on the now voluminous theoretical elaboration and empirical evidence (statistical and historical) which support not just the basic "democracies rarely fight each other" proposition, but, in the style of a progressive research program, move to elaborations of the program to such topics as alliance behavior, winning wars, military expenditures, and signaling. I characterize the state of the evidence as akin to that about the causal effect of smoking on lung cancer: autarchies are not the sole cause of war (nor is smoking the sole cause of lung cancer); not every autocracy or smoker experiences war or cancer; the micro-causal mechanism is still in some dispute; and some folks still haven't got the message. But the evidence is stronger than most of what we use as the basis for public policy.[11]

For the security community perspective, it is important to note that the "democracies rarely fight each other" effect is specific to democracies. It depends on particular normative perspectives on the rightness of fighting others who share a commitment to peaceful conflict resolution, and on the absence of need to fight those who have political institutions that support peaceful conflict resolution internationally. It may apply to a degree to states which, though not especially democratic, nevertheless share some of the normative perspectives and institutional restraints typical of democracies. But little evidence suggests it is generalizable to other broad categories of political and cultural similarity (e.g., Islamic states, military governments, communist states). Whereas there surely are specific examples of similar "we feelings" that inhibit war-making, applying that expectation broadly risks frequent refutations unless one makes it virtually tautological. (If we don't fight them, despite some opportunity and perhaps cause to do so, it must be because we share mutual identity and we-feeling.) Deutsch's emphasis on compatibility of values rather than similarity seems sounder. I doubt, therefore, that it is necessary to make expectations of a global security community – however distant that may seem – dependent upon widespread acceptance of ideas of global citizenship or adoption of a common global culture. Globally, as well as within states, the need is to create institutions reflecting democratic principles which can protect cultural diversity while preserving a wider sense of common identity.

Within countries the evidence about peace and democracy may be less well developed, but it is still strong. Whereas civil wars do occur within democracies, they are relatively rare. The extreme cases of governments slaughtering their own citizens and otherwise engaging in massive violations of human rights are overwhelmingly concentrated in authoritarian and totalitarian states. Stable democracies, with guarantees of minority rights against majority tyranny, offer means of peaceful conflict resolution and are less likely to experience severe ethnic conflict.[12]

The return arrow plausibly also operates at both the international and national levels. Since democracies usually – 80 percent of the time – win their wars against authoritarian states, and leaders of states who lose wars are more likely to be overthrown, an evolutionary mechanism may operate from democracy to peace.[13] Wars are nonetheless dangerous to democracy. In Charles Tilly's famous aphorism, "the state makes war, and war makes the state." A common criticism of the Cold War, sometimes in terms of Harold Lasswell's prescient "garrison state" concept, was that it strengthened authoritarian political forces on both sides. International threats, real or perceived, enhance the forces of secrecy and repression in domestic politics. Relaxation of international threats to security reduces the need, and the excuse, for repression of democratic dissent.[14] Similarly, domestic insurgencies frequently lead to the suspension of democratic liberties by the threatened central authorities.

Peace and economic interdependence

As for the effect of economic interdependence on peace, a long tradition – partly Deutschian and constructivist, partly straight-out rational and nineteenth-century liberal – argues in favor of the proposition. The nineteenth-century liberal version derives primarily from a viewpoint of rational economic interest: it is hardly in my interest to fight you if in fact my markets, my sources of supplies, raw materials, and other imports are in your country. If my investments are located in your country, bombing your industry means, in effect, bombing my own factories. The Deutschian argument is that economic exchange becomes a medium for communicating perspectives, interests, and desires on a broad range of matters not the subject of the economic exchange, and that these communications form an important channel for conflict management. Both these versions probably operate empirically. In these ways dense linkages of economic interdependence are part of a wider variety of international transactions that help build a sense of shared identity among peoples.[15]

It is true that there is a competing proposition, that in many circumstances economic ties, especially in the form of asymmetrical dependence rather than true interdependence, do not promote peaceful relations. The final judgment is not yet in. The preponderance of systematic evidence for at least the post-World War II era, however, suggests that mutual economic interdependence, measured as the share of dyadic trade to GNP in the country where that trade is proportionately smaller, is strongly associated with peaceful relations in subsequent years. This is so even after the now-customary controls – distance, alliance, relative power, democracy, and wealth or economic growth rates – are included in the equation and prove also to have positive independent effects.[16] To this should be added the possibility of an interaction between democracy and interdependence with a stronger effect than just the additive one. For example, Lisa Martin argues within the context of the principal-agent framework that in order to reach credible agreements with other states, democratic executives have to persuade, and accommodate themselves to the perspectives of, their legislatures. In doing so, they make it more likely that they will be able to keep their commitments, that the commitments won't become unglued in quick or arbitrary fashion. She applies this, appropriately, both to security issues and issues of trade and economic interdependence. From it one can plausibly impute not just the direct arrow from democracy to peace, but one running from democracy to interdependence and then to peace. Another kind of interaction may be seen in some "two-level games," whereby interdependence brings extra-state actors into the domestic political process to a degree facilitated by a pluralistic political system.[17]

The possibility of reciprocal effects – states do not allow themselves to become too economically dependent on states with whom they are in military conflict or anticipate such a possibility – is of course also plausible and likely; a full sorting-out of these relationships is in progress.

Democracy and interdependence

The final set of relationships concerns the base of the triangle, between democracy and economic interdependence. At the international level, it may be that economic interdependence supports democracy; at least the European Union seems to operate on this principle, requiring all applicants for admission to the common market to demonstrate their commitment to stable democratic rule and human rights. In the other direction, democratic states presumably feel their security less threatened by other democratic states, and hence can enter into relationships of economic interdependence for absolute gain without worrying as much about the relative gains that so centrally impact the realist model of relationships. One would therefore expect more trade between democracies than between democracies and non-democracies, or between two non-democracies, holding constant other relevant cultural and economic influences.[18] Economic interdependence typically is greater between states with competitive markets (somewhat more common in democracies) than operating under state or private monopolies.

Purely at the domestic level, the relation between economics and democracy requires a conceptual shift away from simply economic interdependence to a broader focus on income levels and distribution, and to a focus on peaceful means of conflict resolution and the maintenance of stable democracy. These relationships are somewhat problematic and in dispute. Most scholars readily agree that there is an association between democracy and per capita income, and that economic development facilitates democratization. But they do not agree on whether any significant causality operates from democracy to development, nor fully on the causal relationship between economics and domestic political stability and peaceful conflict resolution. The role of free markets is also part of the discussion. Arguably, a key component of economic development is the determination of peaceful processes of economic interdependence more by market considerations than by state fiat or ethnic preference. As this debate is both voluminous and also not central to the focus of this chapter I will simply summarize my understanding of the results.[19] Nevertheless, these relationships are important to the triangular perspective of the Secretary General.

- Economic development and democracy are strongly correlated; the causal arrow seems to be from development to democracy, rather than the other way. There are nonetheless a fair number of exceptions, with successful democracy in poor countries like India, and strong resistance to democratization in Singapore (as rich as France). But once a democracy reaches an income level of $6,000 per capita ($1985 dollars), it is "impregnable and can be expected to live forever."[20]
- Democracy does not in any systematic way inhibit economic growth, nor does autocracy promote it. For every authoritarian government that represses political opposition while promoting growth, several dictatorial kleptocracies steal billions of dollars from their people (e.g., Zaire). The generalization that political opposition must be repressed in the interest of development is a lie.
- Great inequality of incomes severely reduces the likelihood of establishing or preserving stable democracy. Inequality damages the sense of common identity in a community.
- Gross economic inequality is more likely to damage economic growth than to promote it.

International organizations and peace

Let us now turn to the role of international organizations – potential as well as actual. The same kind of statistical analysis that has established a relation between democracy and peace, and at least since 1950 between economic interdependence and peace, has recently found an additional, independent relationship between peace and dense networks of intergovernmental organization membership.[21] Here I focus primarily on the UN and its associated bodies – in promoting peace, democracy, and development and interdependence. We can treat the different parts of the United Nations, and other intergovernmental organizations and international nongovernmental organizations (INGOs), as instances of institutions capable of carrying on some of various processes of international transformation:

1. Coercing norm-breakers
2. Mediating among conflicting parties
3. Reducing uncertainty by conveying information
4. Expanding material self-interest to be more inclusive and longer term
5. Shaping norms
6. Generating the narratives of mutual identification

These possibilities range from standard liberal understandings of institutions as facilitating the rational pursuit of self-interest in ways that also serve existing mutual interests, to "teaching" a set of norms and appropriate political organization that may sharply revise actors' preferences and sense of their self-interest.[22] To illustrate them I draw on a perspective on the United Nations which I characterize as "the three UNs." Although the UN is not neatly and formally divisible into three separate sets of functional agencies, it can be helpful to group its activities under these three headings and purposes.

The direct relationship of international organizations to peace is straightforward, and largely derivable from realist theories of international relations rather than liberal ones. Realist theory does not attribute great importance to international organization, but allows it a possible role. The "first UN" is the UN concerned directly with security from threats or actuality violent conflict. It chiefly comprises the Security Council, and to some degree the office of the Secretary General. The realist founders of the UN recognized the difficulties these institutions would have if the great powers were in serious conflict, but nonetheless saw these units as having the potential to make a contribution under the right circumstances.

The Security Council was designed as an agent of collective security and enforcement, in principle to be carried out by forces of the UN itself directed by the Military Staff Committee, as provided for in Chapter VII. Of course the Military Staff Committee was fossilized at the outset of the Cold War, and ideas of a standing UN military force, or even of national military and air forces on call from member states by the UN (Articles 43 and 45), were totally still-born. The Security Council has been able to agree on major collective security/enforcement operations twice during its history (the outset of the Korean War, while the Soviet Union boycotted the Council, and in the Gulf War of 1990). It has embarked on "peace enforcement" actions (as ultimately developed in the newly independent Belgian Congo, and later in Somalia and ultimately Bosnia) with mixed and controversial results. The Security Council has also repeatedly authorized not direct military action, but the enforcement of economic sanctions on actors judged a threat to the peace. The widespread opinion that economic sanctions generally have little effect is exaggerated. They seem to have been important in bringing Serbia to the peace table, and at great civilian cost in preventing Iraq from rebuilding its biological, chemical, and nuclear arsenal.

The concept of peace-keeping, however (by impartial forces, to monitor a ceasefire already agreed by the parties, lightly armed and authorized only to use lethal force in self-defense), developed outside the explicit authorization of the Charter, and has overall been more successful. In recent years the UN has increasingly been drawn into purely or largely internal conflicts of states than into interstate conflicts as its founders anticipated. A further innovation has been the development of post-conflict peacebuilding activities (e.g., Cambodia, Mozambique, Namibia) that has been only partially military, devoted more to creating or strengthening the political and economic institutions deemed essential to achievement of stable peace following civil wars. Because these are not primarily military, and impact more on other corners of the triangle than principally on peace directly, I will discuss them below.

If the Security Council constitutes the most visible realist part of the UN, and the "teeth" to defend whatever liberal world order exists, other parts are devoted to constructing institutions and practices which may directly moderate or mediate conflicts. Such international organization functions generally compatible with modest realist expectations include confidence building (as part of an arms control agreement, or a peace-keeping or peace-building operation perhaps), preventive diplomacy, mediation, arbitration, and abjudication. During the Cold War opportunities to exercise these functions were not frequent, but less uncommon outside the arena of East-West military confrontation. Here are a few examples: Secretary-General Javier Pérez de Cuéllar made a major preventive diplomacy effort, coming rather close to success, to avert the Argentine/British war over the Malvinas/Falklands. (For such purposes it is essential as a general principle that the Secretary General always retain a position of impartiality, "out of the loop" of, and above, enforcement actions that inevitably cast him as a partisan.) One of the great achievements of his tenure was to mediate an end to the Iran/Iraq war in 1988. Former US President Jimmy Carter is virtually a one-man INGO devoted to such good works. Another relevant INGO is the Papacy, increasingly trusted, especially by predominantly Catholic states, since it has been shorn of its secular power. Argentina and Chile trusted John Paul II to arbitrate their dispute over the Beagle Islands.

The International Court of Justice rarely gets the chance to adjudicate major security disputes, but this does happen. The ICJ arbitration of fishing rights in the Georges Bank off Canada and the United States illustrates the established generalization that democratic states are more likely to accept third-party settlement efforts, even up to formal arbitration;[23] when Chad and Libya accepted its decision on allocation of the Ouazou Strip between them it illustrated that such willingness is not limited to democracies. On the theme of interactions between democracy and international law and organization note also the finding that interdependent democracies are more likely to recognize and enforce each other's law in their own states than are other types of regimes.[24]

International organizations and interdependence

A "second UN" is that attempting to build the economic and institutional foundations on which the liberal vision of peace rests. Established alongside the realist institutions, it owes its origin to elements of the tradition of Kant, Richard Cobden, and Woodrow Wilson. It is perhaps in symbiosis with the realist parts of the UN, able to operate only where realist considerations initially inhibit the outbreak of violent conflict, yet where these foundations deepen they increasingly make realist calculations tangential or irrelevant. Conditions of "dependable expectations of peaceful change" diminish the fear of losing out in relative terms, and hence facilitate the pursuit of absolute gains through commerce.[25]

The importance of interdependence is variously implied in Deutsch et al.'s specification of several other conditions for integration: superior economic growth, expectation of economic gains, strong economic ties.

Major institutions here include the United Nations Development Programme (UNDP), the Bretton Woods institutions (World Bank and IMF), the World Trade Organization, as well as regional trade and development institutions. These institutions are devoted to the economic development of poor countries, financial stability, and the freer flow of international capital and goods. Their activities apply both to establishing norms and rules for international exchange, and, increasingly with the emphasis on "good government" and "transparency" (near-synonyms for democracy) as well as market economics, to constitutive norms within states. Initially, and again recently, they have taken a major role in providing the resources to reconstruct war-shattered societies.[26] Such a role means both building institutions and teaching the relevant norms.

The record of these organizations is mixed and controversial to be sure, diluted not just because of politics in the UN and between its member states, but from the conflicting recommendations of economics professionals. Nonetheless, their achievements – especially in the realm of freeing world trade and capital markets – are often impressive. Recognition of their achievements need not obscure important critiques that they have been too attuned to the interests of international capital, and too inattentive to the needs of the poor and of environmental preservation.[27] But the record of the chief ideological alternative – state ownership and the command economy – is surely not superior. If the prospect, and the experience, of human betterment is necessary to human security, and so too is some expectation of greater economic equality between rich and desperately poor peoples, then the practice of these international organizations needs appreciation as well scrutiny for the faults of their practice or their ideological underpinnings. It too is appropriate to mention the environmental organizations, some of them engaged in serious monitoring and facilitation of norm-development, and the agencies devoted to public health aspects of human security. UNICEF and the World Health Organization deserve the credit for the global eradication of smallpox. A similar operation against malaria was making great progress until member states decided, disastrously, that it was no longer a major concern.

International organizations and democracy

Finally, we come to the "third" UN of democracy and human rights. One can begin with the UN High Commissioner for Refugees, performing massive services for 30 million refugees worldwide. In addition one should include the fragmented, cumbersome, and weak apparatus directly assigned to monitor and promote human rights: among its parts are the UN High Commissioner for Human Rights, the Center and the Committee for Human Rights, and various functional units. Their record is controversial, primarily because of the unwillingness of many member states to permit these organizations the "teeth" to intrude effectively into "sovereign" areas of domestic law and political practice. Nevertheless, they do matter.

Various NGOs and INGOs (Amnesty International and the International League for Human Rights, for example) make governments accept some transparency, and press them to observe standards of human rights explicitly labeled, despite some vigorous resistance, as "universal." The widely ratified (if also widely violated) 1948 Universal Declaration of Human Rights, and many subsequent Conventions (for instance, on the rights of women, and civil and political rights), protocols, and other agreements establish norms which give non-governmental organizations a basis for comparing the performance of states. Increasingly these international agreements have become embedded in the domestic law of states. Important too are the various UN-sponsored Conferences: talk shops, yes; but talk shops with an ability to develop a common narrative and promote constitutive norms by which governments can in some degree be held accountable. They may give rise to customary international law constraining even states which dissent.[28]

A little-appreciated part of the United Nations system is the Division of Electoral Assistance, in the Secretariat. Since its establishment about ten years ago it has assisted and monitored democratic national elections in more than seventy states, typically easing the transition from authoritarian rule or to independence. Success stories for the election process include such widely recognized cases as El Salvador, Nicaragua, Cambodia, Ethiopia, Mozambique, and Namibia. Its services (and those of many NGOs) include far more than just observing elections, such as advice on building political parties, constitutions, electoral laws, and press freedom.[29] Democratically-elected governments do not always stay democratic, but free and competitive elections are the prerequisite for democracy. It would have been unthinkable for the UN to have taken on this task a decade ago, but with the recent shift toward democratic practice and democratic ideology it is an accepted function. The governments of many autocratic member states resist the norm-setting elements of this effort, but former Secretary-General Boutros-Ghali determinedly (and bravely) pushed it as a normative constituent of what it means to be a "modern" civilized state. It is also a task that no state (such as the United States) could perform nearly so credibly as an impartial third party.[30]

Activities of the "three UNs" and their essential INGO partners come together most closely in efforts of post-conflict peacebuilding. These efforts involve the domestic affairs of newly independent or "failed" states with little or no history of democratic government, whose economies have been devastated by civil war, hundreds of thousands, or millions, of their people made refugees, and whose social and political infrastructure has been demolished. Again, the execution of all these tasks together by the UN is a recent development, impelled by the political upheavals born of the collapse of one end of the formerly stabilizing bipolar international system. Such efforts require, in addition to some variant of peacekeeping, creation of the preconditions to hold free elections and to hope to hold democratic institutions together afterward; massive resettlement of refugees and of discharged soldiers and insurgents; large-scale economic assistance, including support for free markets; and often the creation of new and democratically accountable legal and administrative systems (police, judiciary, military, telecommunications and postal systems). The UNDP carries on many of these activities, addressing both the elites and the general populace.

These efforts are extremely expensive, and difficult to make successful. (Examples include Cambodia, El Salvador, Namibia, and Bosnia). The UN and its INGO associates form an extremely loose system given to administrative overlap and duplication, not to mention working at cross-purposes. Attempts to resettle combatants or create essential administrative structures may compete directly with those to bring a measure of fiscal responsibility and discipline. Peacebuilding necessarily runs into conflict with long-standing principles of impartiality and respect for sovereignty. It cannot succeed without the committed support of UN member states, the will and ability of local actors, and the capacity of local institutions.[31] It may often fail. But without such help it may be quite impossible even to imagine the creation of a security community within such a state, or in its relations with its neighbors.

Authority and legitimacy in international organizations

Most of the activities of international organizations, especially outside of the traditional scope of military security, do not represent the threat or exercise of coercive authority. The United Nations and its family of component or related organizations is hardly tightly coupled; at best it may become a very loosely coupled security community. Such organizations build the institutions of state and civil society with the more or less willing consent of most of the relevant parties within states. While international organizations frequently do intrude on states' sovereignty, typically these instances are the consequence of bargaining (as in the conditionality of development organizations) that leaves both sides better off in the Pareto-optimal sense.[32] Van Wagenen, thirty years ago, judged the consensus-forming result of international organizations as the most important result in building security communities.

In discussing security as well as economic matters, Robert Keohane and Lisa Martin argue, "institutions can provide information, reduce transaction costs, make commitments more credible, establish focal points for coordination, and in general facilitate the operation of reciprocity ... controlling for the effects of power and interest, it matters whether they exist. They also have an interactive effect ... depending on the nature of power and interests."[33] International organizations provide transparency, search for the basis of acceptable compromise or minimum common-denominator agreements, and create preferences for, and expectations of, peaceful settlement. Finally, they engage in norm building – both regulative of the international system and constitutive of its member states.

Some of the most auspicious periods of transnational creativity for changing the international system, limiting the frequency and intensity of war, and creating new international organizations, regimes, and norms to guide behavior tend to follow great wars. The Napoleonic Wars brought the Congress of Vienna and the Concert of Europe; the two great wars of the twentieth century brought the

League of Nations and the United Nations.[34] Outside the realm of military alliances they do not flourish during wartime, but when peace comes policy-makers are often ready to construct new institutional underpinnings. The more stable the peace appears, the readier are states and peoples to trust the new institutional arrangements. Perhaps the end of the Cold War – an intense conflict and quasi-war even if only sporadically overtly violent – offers such an opportunity, maybe a fleeting one. Increasing interdependence, including that of the consequences of violence by state and non-state actors, may create the demand.

No discussion of the role of international organizations in creating, however incompletely and unevenly, conditions for a security community on a global level should avoid questions about the authority structure within the United Nations itself. Those questions are doubly inescapable in an essay which has placed such emphasis on the importance of democratization within states. It has permeated much of the discussion about democracy that has been carried on at the United Nations. The introductory piece in a collection of European essays on *Cosmopolitan Democracy* asks not only whether a "democratic" international organization can thrive when most of its component states do not practice democracy at home, but also whether democratic states can flourish in a world not itself organized on democratic principles.[35] Underlying such questions are appropriate concerns about the implications of hegemony by the global North/West.

A discussion of democracy at the level of global institutions is conceptually difficult because the same principles do not always make sense at both levels. The fundamental democratic principle of "one-person, one vote" runs into special difficulties not just from fears of another source of hegemony (roughly 20 percent of the people on earth live in the Peoples' Republic of China; about 80 percent are in all the developing countries). Where so many states still do not experience free elections in their domestic affairs it is impossible to imagine democratically elected representatives from those states to a global assembly.[36] The alternative principle of "one-state, one vote," as applied to the General Assembly, grossly underrepresents the citizens of great powers at the expense of mini-states. It is probably tolerated there only because the Assembly is such a weak body with so little authority. The entity with the greatest authority, and coercive powers,]blatantly violates both principles. The veto power in the Security

Council is undemocratic in the extreme. By standard measures, virtually all voting power rests in the hands of the five Permanent members; the voting power of any non-permanent member is calibrated in decimals, and of course the 170 states not on the Council at all have zero voting power. The Security Council probably must be undemocratic because of its need to be able to act quickly and efficaciously; it is hard enough to get enough agreement among fifteen states without trying to assemble it among most of 185.

More to the point, if decisions by the Council are to be effective, they must reflect the will and resource commitment of the great powers, the states with the muscle. No action can be taken without the active support of most of them, and none can be taken against the determined resistance of one without destroying the Organization.[37] Therefore the Permanent Five were intended, in 1945, to be those with the greatest military and financial capacity. There was always some fiction in characterizing all Five that way, and there is far less truth in doing so now, especially on the financial side. Yet a "democratic" principle that overtly assigned voting power based on the international distribution of bombers, or of dollars, would be odd indeed. The distribution of voting rights in the IMF and World Bank, for example, is fully recognized as undemocratic, but essential to obtaining the needed resources from the big rich countries.

Thus the discourse on democratization of the UN is typically couched less in terms of voting power than of principles – part of democracy, but not all of it – of "representation," participation, and transparency. To some degree this may be served by increasing permeability of UN bodies to the influence of transnational NGOs.[38] Another element of the discourse is about subsidiarity and delegation to more homogeneous regions (though delegation to regional great powers might be extremely "undemocratic").[39] Much of the effort may have to go to facilitating loosely coupled security communities at the regional level, as well as at the global one. These principles are not irrelevant to states or to peoples. Perhaps they can be applied in ways – differently in different units – that achieve and preserve substantial legitimacy for the Organization as a whole.[40]

The search for acceptable principles of representation and participation, however, cannot come at the expense of effectiveness. Any organization's legitimacy depends as much on its effectiveness as on its principles of governance. A balance must be struck between them. And here is where some potential virtues of hegemony need to be recognized. The new North/West transnational ideological near-hege-mony on democracy and free markets is surely an asset in con-structing many of the necessary conditions of a security community. At the same time, that very ideology (similar to that of a security community) of pluralism and participation militates against the exercise of coercive hegemony.

Moreover, the UN lacks the constitutional machinery to enforce many decisions on its member states. There really is no "hegemonic" state with the will as well as the capacity by itself to impose order on the international system. (The United States *might* in theory be said to have the capacity, but its government certainly does not have the will to do so in most instances.) For many purposes the most that can be expected is for a "core" of powerful states, predominantly but not necessarily only rich ones, to reach agreement and act in some degree as a collective hegemon.

The idea of security community comes to mind less readily for situations of hegemonic imbalance than does that of domination. To be tolerated in any hegemonic role hegemons will have to be "nice" ones who provide collective goods as well as coerce recalcitrants. The Deutsch et al. praise for "strong core areas" needs to be seen in this light, and as cores of identity as well as strength. Moreover, hege-monic groups will have to respect shared norms of the global system when they do act coercively, and be seen as holding themselves to the same norms they enforce. If authoritative rules are to be issued, subordinate states will have to be able to recognize dominant ones as having some right to issue them, derived from shared norms. Some echoes of Gramscian hegemony may be audible.[41]

At heart, global community building is in large part a rationalist enterprise familiar to liberal institutionalists. Yet it is also in part a constructivist enterprise of identity formation, one that has substantial accomplishments among the rich and democratic states of the "West," and discernible if much weaker achievements more globally. It is difficult to see just how all these eventualities will develop, but impossible to imagine a global security community without them. And I mean constructivist very precisely as explicating the Kantian liberal internationalist principles that underlie the concept of security communities. Consistent with those principles, they will have to be grasped and put into practice not just by policy-making elites, but by their peoples. This statement cannot deny the necessity of analyzing the empirical world as dispassionately and objectively as a social scientist ever can. But neither is it ever to deny the possibility of shaping as well as describing reality, and that the description helps the shaping.[42] This latter is not wishful thinking. The kind of world envisaged here is hardly perfect, by any standards of justice or order. Nevertheless it may, considering the alternatives, be the "best" of possible worlds even a pessimist can presently imagine. In some degree, however limited, we continually create the world we desire, and deserve the world we get.

Notes

I am grateful to the Carnegie Corporation of New York, the Center for Global Partnership of the Japan Foundation, the Ford Foundation, the World Society Foundation of Switzerland, and the National Science Foundation for support of various pieces of research that have fed into this overview. I thank the Editors, Stephen Brooks, and Alexander Wendt for comments on earlier drafts. Of course only I am responsible for the results.

1 Of ninety-six armed conflicts during the six years 1989–1994, only five were between two internationally recognized states. Peter Wallensteen and Margareta Sollenberg, "The End of International War: Armed Conflict 1989–95," *Journal of Peace Research* 33, 3 (August 1995), pp. 353–370.

2 For a relatively early but cautiously favorable assessment of the UN as a step toward a global security community essentially as defined in this volume, see Richard Van Wagenen, "The Concept of Community and the Future of the United Nations," *International Organization* 19, 3 (Summer 1965), pp. 812–827. The definition of security community, subsequently adapted by Deutsch, derives from Van Wagenen, *Research in the International Organization Field: Some Notes on a Possible Focus* (Princeton, NJ: Center for Research on World Political Institutions, 1952). Two major reports on UN reform are in many ways implicitly Kantian as I use the term below. See Commission on Global Governance, *Our Global Neighborhood* (New York: Oxford University Press, 1995), and Independent Working Group on the Future of the United Nations, *The United Nations in Its Second Half-Century* (New York: Ford Foundation, 1995); also Bruce Russett, "Ten Balances for Weighing UN Reform Proposals," in Russett, ed., *The Once and Future Security Council* (New York: St. Martin's, 1997).

3 Ann Mason, "The End of Cold War Thinking: Change and Learning in Foreign Policy Belief Systems" (PhD dissertation, Yale University, 1998).

4 By Kenneth Waltz's definition, polarity is determined by the strength of the most powerful state at each pole, not by that of the alliance it leads. See his *Theory of International Politics* (Reading, MA: Addison-Wesley, 1979): 97–99.

5 A detailed historical analysis of political developments in the Soviet

Union is not appropriate here. But the two most-widely used comparative codings judged that substantial movement in the direction of democracy in the Soviet Union took place between 1986 and 1991. Polity III scorings (scale of 0 to 10) assign the USSR a 0 on the institutionalized democracy index in 1986, a 1 in 1989, and an 8 in 1991; on the institutionalized autocracy index a rating of 7 in 1986, 5 in 1989, and 0 in 1991. On the Freedom House indicators the USSR received the least democratic scores (7) on the scales for political rights and civil liberties in 1986, dropped to 6 and 5 respectively for 1988, and to 3 on both scales for 1991. Keith Jaggers and Ted Gurr, "Transitions to Democracy: Tracking the Third Wave with Polity III Indicators," *Journal of Peace Research* 33, 4 (November 1995), pp. 469–482; Raymond D. Gastil, *Freedom in the World: Political Rights and Civil Liberties, 1988–1989* (New York: Freedom House, 1989), and R. Bruce McColm, *Freedom in the World: Political Rights and Civil Liberties, 1991–1992* (New York: Freedom House, 1992). Arguably Russia became less democratic after 1992.

6 See the contribution by Emanuel Adler in this volume. Also John Frye, *The Helsinki Process: Negotiating Security and Cooperation in Europe* (Washington, DC: National Defense University Press, 1993), and Vojtech Mastny, *The Helsinki Process and the Reintegration of Europe* (New York: New York University Press, 1992).

7 Daniele Archibugi rightly points out, in "Immanuel Kant, Cosmopolitan Law and Peace," *European Journal of International Relations* 1, 4 (December 1995), pp. 429–456, that this is not a fully accurate rendition of Kant, chiefly in that Kant thought of peaceful democracies primarily as a monadic phenomenon (peaceful in general) rather than a dyadic one (peaceful with one another). The distinction matters as an item of intellectual history, but it nonetheless seems appropriate to credit Kant for most of the basic insights, recognizing that more than 200 years of experience and scholarship modify them somewhat. Hence I use the term "neo-Kantian." The important consideration is whether the theoretical and empirical evidence for this vision, however one labels it, is sound. The question of whether democracies are relatively more peaceful in general is contested. The most persuasive evidence so far indicates that whereas democracies do not behave more pacifically when they are in crises with nondemocratic states, they are less likely to get into such crises in the first place; see David Rousseau, Christopher Gelpi, Dan Reiter, and Paul Huth, "Assessing the Dyadic Nature of the Democratic Peace, 1918–1988," *American Political Science Review* 89, 3 (September 1996), pp. 512–33.

8 For use of this term, see Commission on Global Governance, *Our Global Neighborhood*; Independent Commission, *The United Nations in Its Next Half-Century*; United Nations Development Programme, *World Development Report 1994* (New York: Oxford University Press, 1994).

9 Michael Barnett, "The New UN Politics of Peace," *Global Governance* 1, 1 (January 1995), 79–98; Mark Zacher, "The Decaying Pillars of the Westpha-

lian System," in James Rosenau and Erst-Otto Czempiel, eds., *Governance without Government: Order and Change in World Politics* (Cambridge: Cambridge University Press, 1992), pp. 58–101. Steven Krasner, however, in an important article, shows that the principles of sovereignty as expressed in the Treaty of Westphalia in 1648 have regularly been violated, by conventions and contracts as well as by coercion and imposition, ever since then. It is also worth noting that Krasner, often considered an arch-realist, makes a critical modification to realist understanding: "At the international level, different rulers can champion different principles not only because their interests vary, but because their normative frames of reference, primarily derived from their domestic experiences, also vary." See his "Compromising Westphalia," *International Security* 20, 3 (Winter 1995/96), 115–151; the quotation is from p. 148.

10 Boutros Boutros-Ghali, *An Agenda for Peace* (New York: United Nations, 1992); *An Agenda for Development* (New York: United Nations, 1995); *An Agenda for Democratization* (New York: United Nations, 1996).

11 Bruce Russett, "Counterfactuals about War and Its Absence," in Philip Tetlock and Aaron Belkin, eds. *Counterfactuals in International Relations* (Princeton, NJ: Princeton University Press, 1996). See also Edward Mansfield and Jack Snyder, "The Effects of Democratization on War," *International Security* 20, 4 (Spring 1996), pp. 196–207, who, referring to their earlier article in that journal, declare (p. 196) they do not contest the consensus that mature stable democracies rarely fight each other. Several critiques are addressed by Zeev Maoz, "The Renewed Controversy over the Democratic Peace Result: Rear-Guard Action or Cracks in the Wall?" *International Security* 22, 1 (Summer 1997), pp. 428–454; also see the exchange initiated by William R. Thompson and Richard Tucker, "A Tale of Two Democratic Peace Critiques," *Journal of Conflict Resolution* 41, 3 (June 1997), pp. 457–477. Good micro-level evidence is in Thomas Risse-Kappen, *Cooperation among Democracies: Norms, Transnational Relations, and the European Influence on US Foreign Policy* (Princeton: Princeton University Press, 1995).

12 Amartya Sen, *Poverty and Famine* (New York: Oxford University Press, 1981); R. J. Rummel, *Death by Government: Genocide and Mass Murder since 1900* (New Brunswick, NJ: Transaction, 1994) and *Power Kills: Democracy as A Method of Nonviolence* (New Brunswick, NJ: Transaction, 1997); Ted Robert Gurr, *Minorities at Risk: A Global View of Ethnopolitical Conflict* (Washington, DC: US Institute of Peace, 1993).

13 David Lake, "Powerful Pacifists; Democratic States and War," *American Political Science Review* 86, 1 (March 1992), pp. 24–37; Bruce Bueno de Mesquita, Randolph Siverson, and Gary Woller, "War and the Fate of Regimes," *American Political Science Review* 86, 3 (September 1992), 638–646; Alan Stam, *Win, Lose, or Draw: Domestic Politics and the Crucible of War* (Ann Arbor: University of Michigan Press, 1996).

14 Charles Tilly, *Coercion, Capital, and European States, A.D. 990–1990* (Oxford:

Basil Blackwell, 1990); Harold D. Lasswell, "The Garrison State," *American Journal of Sociology* 96, 4 (1941), pp. 455–468; Ted Robert Gurr, "War, Revolution, and the Growth of the Coercive State," *Comparative Political Studies* 21, 1 (1988), pp. 45–65. John MacMillan, "A Kantian Protest against the Peculiar Discourse of the Inter-Liberal State Peace," *Millennium* 24, 3 (Winter 1995), pp. 549–562, notes both the necessity to consider peace as a condition for democracy and the need to embed a democratic peace perspective in the wider Kantian emphasis on international law.

15 For early micro-level evidence, see Bruce Russett, *Community and Contention: Britain and America in the Twentieth Century* (Cambridge, MA: MIT Press, 1963). A good review of liberal hypotheses linking interdependence to peace is Arthur Stein, "Governments, Economies, Interdependence, and International Cooperation," in Philip Tetlock et al., eds., *Behavior, Society, and International Conflict*, vol. 3 (Oxford; Oxford University Press, 1989), pp. 244–254. Because of the possibility, cogently presented by Jonathan Mercer, "Anarchy and Identity," *International Organization* 49, 2 (Spring 1995), pp. 229–252, that a sense of mutual identity may well entail characterizing others as "outgroup," it is essential to recognize links of mutual self-interest that do not depend on shared social identity.

16 John Oneal and Bruce Russett, "The Classical Liberals Were Right: Democracy, Interdependence, and Conflict, 1950–85," *International Studies Quarterly* 41, 2 (June 1997), pp. 267–293; Soo Yeon Kim, "Ties that Bind: The Role of Trade in International Conflict Processes, 1950–1992" (PhD dissertation, Yale University, 1988). The importance of *inter*dependence is illustrated in the *dependencia* literature, and dates back to Albert Hirschmann, *National Power and the Structure of Foreign Trade* (Berkeley: University of California Press, 1945). Also note that rich countries are unlikely to fight each other. As a realist would probably recognize, the costs of fighting another rich country with a modern, highly destructive military capability now outweigh any possible economic gain in an era when national wealth depends far more on physical capital (skill, technological capacity, organization) than on land or natural resources. See John Mueller, *Retreat from Doomsday: The Obsolesence of Major War* (New York: Basic Books, 1988), and Carl Kaysen, "Is War Obsolete?" *International Security* 14, 4 (Spring 1990), pp. 42–64.

17 Lisa Martin, "Democratic Commitments: Legislatures and International Cooperation" (manuscript, Harvard University). For evidence that democracies are able to enter into longer-term commitments with each other, see Kurt Taylor Gaubatz, "Democratic States and Commitment in International Relations, *International Organization* 50, 1 (Winter 1996), pp. 109–139. Other versions of the link from democracy and free trade to peace include Daniel Verdier, *Democracy and International Trade: Britain, France, and the United States, 1860–1990* (Princeton, NJ: Princeton University Press, 1994); Erich Weede, "Economic Policy and International Security: Rent-Seeking, Free Trade, and Democratic Peace," *European*

Journal of International Relations 1, 4 (December 1995), pp. 519–537; Robert Putnam, "Diplomacy and Domestic Politics: The Logic of Two-Level Games," *International Organization* 42, 3 (Summer 1988), pp. 427–462.

18 See Harry Bliss and Bruce Russett, "Democratic Trading Partners: The Liberal Connection," *Journal of Politics*, 58, 4 forthcoming November 1998, for strong evidence of this, with a data base and method similar to that of Oneal and Russett, "The Classical Liberals Were Right," and Kim, "Ties that Bind."

19 See especially Alberto Alesina and Roberto Perotti, "The Political Economy of Growth: A Critical Survey of the Recent Literature," *World Bank Economic Review* 8, 3 (September 1994), pp. 355–371; Ross Burkhart and Michael Lewis-Beck, "Comparative Democracy: The Economic Development Thesis," *American Political Science Review* 88, 4 (December 1994), pp. 903–910; Adam Przeworski and Fernando Limongi, "Political Regimes and Economic Growth, *Journal of Economic Perspectives* 7, 3 (Summer 1993), pp. 51–70; John F. Helliwell, "Empirical Linkages between Democracy and Economic Growth," *British Journal of Political Science* 24, 2 (April 1994), pp. 225–248; Zara Arat, *Democracy and Human Rights in Developing Countries* (Boulder, CO: Rienner, 1991); Edward Muller, "Economic Determinants of Democracy," *American Sociological Review* 60, 6 (December 1995), pp. 965–982, and the subsequent exchange (983–96) among Kenneth Bollen, Robert Jackman, and Mueller.

20 Adam Przeworski, Michael Alvarez, Jose Antonio Cheibub, and Fernando Limongi, "What Makes Democracies Endure?" *Journal of Democracy* 7, 1 (January 1996), pp. 39–55; the quotation is from p. 41.

21 Bruce Russett, John R. Oneal, and David R. Davis, "The Third Leg of the Kantian Tripod for Peace: Organizations and Militarized Disputes, 1950–1985," forthcoming *International Organization* 52, 3 (Summer 1998). Note that all the neo-Kantian influences (democracy, interdependence, international organization) operate independently of such realist influences on conflict behavior as relative power, wealth, and alliance patterns. In relations among states where the neo-Kantian influences are weak, the realist ones remain very important.

22 See Martha Finnemore, "International Organizations as Teachers of Norms: The United Nations Educational, Scientific, and Cultural Organization and Science Policy," *International Organization* 47, 4 (Autumn 1993), pp. 565–597.

23 Jacob Bercovitch, "International Mediation and Dispute Settlement: Evaluating the Conditions for Successful Mediation," *Negotiation Journal* 7 (1991), pp. 17–30; Michael Brecher, *Crises in World Politics: Theory and Reality* (Oxford: Pergamon, 1993); William Dixon, "Democracy and the Peaceful Settlement of International Conflict," *American Political Science Review* 84, 1 (March 1994), pp. 14–32; Gregory Raymond, "Democracies, Disputes, and Third-Party Intermediaries, *Journal of Conflict Resolution* 38, 1 (March 1994), pp. 24–42. The process, however, may not result in more durable settlements by democracies; see Raymond, "Demosthenes and

Democracies: Regime-Types and Arbitration Outcomes," *International Interactions* 22, 1 (1996), pp. 1–20.

24 Ann-Marie Slaughter (formerly Burley), "Law among Liberal States: Liberal Institutionalism and the Act of State Doctrine," *Columbia Law Review* 82 (1992), pp. 1907–1996; "International Law in a World of Liberal States," *European Journal of International Law* 6 (1995), pp. 503–538.

25 Robert Powell, "Absolute and Relative Gains in International Relations Theory," *American Political Science Review* 85, 1 (December 1991), pp. 1303–1320.

26 Alexander Wendt (*Social Theory of International Politics* [Cambridge; Cambridge University Press, 1999], ch. 8) argues that the creation of transnational capitalist institutions in the late twentieth century creates conditions of a rule of law regime making interdependence a force for peace that did not exist in earlier periods. Also see Craig Murphy, *International Organizations and Industrial Change: Global Governance since 1850* (New York: Oxford University Press, 1994), and John Gerard Ruggie, *Winning the Peace: America and World Order in the New Era* (New York: Columbia University Press, 1996), chs. 5–6. Katherine Barbieri, "Economic Interdependence: A Path to Peace or Source of Interstate Conflict? *Journal of Peace Research* 33, 1 (February 1996), pp. 29–49, reports that in the 1870–1939 period economic interdependence was positively associated with conflict. The different results seem rooted in differences in the studies' spatial rather than temporal domains. Her analysis includes many very distant pairs of states, while Oneal and Russett limit analysis to major powers and contiguous pairs, where the great majority (75 percent or more) of disputes arise. Without an explicit control for contiguity or distance, trade produces a spurious association between interdependence and conflict: nearby states trade more, and nearby states have a high incidence of disputes because of both opportunities to fight and issues to fight about. See Oneal and Russett, "The Classical Liberals Were Right," p. 272.

27 Andrew Hurrell and Ngaire Woods, "Globalisation and Inequality," *Millennium* 24, 3 (Winter 1995), pp. 447–470; Bruce Rich, *Mortgaging the Earth: The World Bank, Environmental Impoverishment, and the Crisis of Development* (Boston, MA: Beacon, 1994).

28 Jonathan I. Charney, "Universal International Law," *American Journal of International Law* 87 (1993), pp. 529–551.

29 The spatial and functional scope of these efforts is evident in Boutros-Ghali, *An Agenda for Democratization*.

30 For a view of this as the latest manifestation of international organizations' promotion of Western cultural prescriptions for citizenship and statebuilding, see George M. Thomas et al., *Institutional Structure: Constituting State, Society, and the Individual* (Newbury Park, CA: Sage, 1987); Connie McNeely, *Constructing the Nation-State: International Organization and Prescriptive Action* (Westport, CT: Greenwood, 1995).

31 Alvaro DeSoto and Graciana del Castillo, "Obstacles to Peacebuilding," *Foreign Policy* 94 (Spring 1994), pp. 69–83; Eva Bertram, Reinventing Governments: The Promise and Perils of United Nations Peacebuilding," *Journal of Conflict Resolution* 39, 3 (September 1995), pp. 387–418; Steven Ratner, *The New UN Peacekeeping; Building Peace in Lands of Conflict after the Cold War* (New York: St. Martin's, 1995); I. William Zartman, ed., *Collapsed States: The Disintegration and Restoration of Legitimate Authority* (Boulder, Co: Lynne Reinner, 1995); Bruce Russett and David Yoon, "The United Nations as Peacekeeper and Democratizer: A Strategy for Civil Peace," forthcoming 1999.

32 Krasner, "Compromising Westphalia."

33 Van Wagenen, "The Concept of Community," p. 818; Robert O. Keohane and Lisa Martin, "The Promise of Institutionalist Theory," *International Security* 20, 2 (Summer 1995), pp. 39–51; the quotation is from p. 42. Also see the basically rationalist argument of Andrew Moravcsik, "Preference and Power in the European Community: A Liberal Intergovernmental Approach," in *Journal of Common Market Studies* 31, 4 (June 1993), pp. 473–524.

34 Peter Wallensteen, "Universalism vs. Particularism: On the Limits of Major Power Order," *Journal of Peace Research* 21, 3 (1984), pp. 243–257, and John Vasquez, *The War Puzzle* (Cambridge: Cambridge University Press, 1993), ch. 8. On the Concert of Europe, see Paul Schroeder, *The Transformation of European Politics, 1763–1848* (Oxford: Oxford University Press, 1994); G. John Ikenberry, "The Myth of Post-Cold War Chaos," *Foreign Affairs* 75, 3 (May-June 1996), pp. 79–91, contends that the liberal founders of the UN system overtly held a concept of peace deriving from democracy, interdependence, and international organization, and that whereas this concept could not be applied to the whole world before the end of the Cold War, it did substantially govern relations within the western alliance. Spencer Weart, *Never at War: Why Democracies Will Not Fight One Another* (New Haven, CT: Yale University Press, 1998) asserts that only republics form stable leagues which help to maintain peace among themselves.

35 Norberto Bobbio, "Democracy and the International System," in Daniele Archibugi and David Held, eds., *Cosmopolitan Democracy: An Agenda for a New World Order* (Cambridge: Polity Press, 1995), pp. 17–41. Daniel Deudney, "The Philadelphian System: Sovereignty, Arms Control, and Balance of Power in the American States-Union, circa 1787–1861," *International Organization* 49, 2 (Spring 1995), pp. 191–228, contends that geographically or transactionally close states need to modify their anarchy, and that republican states need to modify that anarchy on republican rather than hierarchical principles.

36 Thus David Held, *Democracy and the Global Order: From the Modern State to Cosmopolitan Governance* (Cambridge: Polity Press, 1995), p. 273 recognizes

that such an assembly would have to be limited to representatives from democratic states.

37 Russett, ed., *The Once and Future Security Council.*

38 See, for example, Thomas G. Weiss and Leon Gordenker, eds., *Non-Governmental Organizations, the United Nations, and Global Governance* (Boulder, CO: Lynne Reinner, 1996); Peter Willets, ed., *The Conscience of the World: The Influence of Non-Governmental Organizations in the U.N. System* (Washington, DC: Brookings, 1996).

39 See Michael Barnett, "Partners in Peace? The UN, Regional Organizations, and Peace-keeping," *Review of International Studies* 21, 4 (October 1995), pp. 411–33.

40 See the effort by Daniele Archibugi to begin sorting out some of these difficulties, "From the United Nations to Cosmopolitan Democracy," in Archibugi and Held, eds., *Cosmopolitan Democracy*, pp. 121–162.

41 Duncan Snidal, "The Limits of Hegemonic Stability Theory," *International Organization* 39, 4 (Autumn 1985), pp. 579–614; Bruce Russett, "The Mysterious Case of Vanishing Hegemony," *International Organization* 39, 2 (Summer 1985), pp. 207–231; Lea Brilmayer, *American Hegemony: Political Morality in a One-Superpower World* (New Haven, CT: Yale University Press 1994); W. Michael Reisman, "The Constitutional Crisis in the United Nations," *American Journal of International Law* 87, 1 (January 1993), pp. 83–100.

42 In commenting ("On the Democratic Peace," *International Security* 19, 4 (Spring 1995), pp. 175–177), on my reply to his article, Christopher Layne seized on one sentence to claim I was practicing post-modernism. I found that hilarious. But some elements of constructivism I accept. See also Ole Wæver's contribution in this volume, referring to the phenomenon that if states act as if there is a community, there will be one. And recall the experiments by Robert Axelrod, *The Evolution of Cooperation* (New York: Basic Books, 1984; see ch. 2), in which all the social scientists played more competitively than would have served their best interests.

Part III
Conclusions

12 International communities, secure or otherwise

Charles Tilly

Nineteenth-century analysts of large-scale social change enshrined the word "community" as a votive object.[1] On the left, critics of capitalist expansion dreamed of revolution, demanding an end to alienation and exploitation in the name of socialist, anarchist, or otherwise utopian communities. On the right, enemies of popular movements, nurturing vindictive visions of the dangerous classes, longed for the peaceful, hierarchical little communities they supposed their grandparents to have inhabited. In the middle, liberals hoped that rational dialogue would install harmony among classes who arrayed angrily against each other as a result of sweeping economic transformations.

Right, left, and center shared the same causal theory: that rapid social change injures solidarities and commitments, which only heal through slow, painful adaptation, through charismatic renewal, or through forceful imposition of new controls. The same theory postulated fragmentation of once-coherent identities into a bewildering, unsatisfying, and ultimately threatening variety of fragmented selves. Sweeping dichotomies – Status vs. Contract, Mechanistic vs. Organic Solidarity, *Gemeinschaft* vs. *Gesellschaft* – summed up the century's history as a loss of community, and as a search for its reconstitution.

A haze of Paradigm Lost still surrounds the word "community" in popular parlance, the social sciences, philosophy, and history. Calling up idealized images of solidarity and coherent identity in compact settlements before the advent of today's complexity, the term almost inevitably evokes a mixture of description, sentiment, and moral principle. Users of the term with respect to international relations are usually hoping to create or restore solidarity among nations. This volume, with its quest not merely to identify but also to promote security communities, manifests just such a hope. I share the hope for peaceful interaction among states, but raise questions here about the means Emanuel Adler and Michael Barnett propose for its realization.

Analysts of international communities (including the special variety Adler and Barnett, following Karl Deutsch, call "security communities") ordinarily pursue one or more of these questions:

1. How might we usefully recognize communities at an international scale?
2. What produces such communities?
3. Under what conditions, and how, do such communities secure peace and/or international cooperation?

Analysts often conflate the three questions, to their detriment. Identifying security communities – or any sorts of international communities – and showing how they form simply does not explain how they produce their effects, if any, on international relations. To merge the three questions leaves us without a plausible causal theory.

Such conflation makes it almost impossible to identify and explain the international processes in question; we must separate the three questions. In this coda, I aim to make their distinction and separate pursuit easier. In so doing, I draw on a line of thought (stemming from such great nineteenth-century thinkers as Georg Simmel and now typified by Harrison White's *Identity and Control*) that takes social interactions rather than individuals, societies, or social systems as building blocks of social analysis and conceives of culture not as an autonomous realm but as a crucial component of social interaction. Culture, in this view, consists of shared understandings and their representations. If the view attributes great importance to social constructions, it also insists that processes of social construction themselves require explanation.

In order to identify and explain the phenomena to which the word "community" – international or otherwise – refers, a conceptual journey will help. Social network analysis provides important signposts. The whole path leads through relational territory, through the sort of analysis that offers our most promising alternatives to the holisms and individualisms that have dominated social science for half a century. Relational thinking rejects both social systems and autonomous individuals as starting points of explanation, turning instead to social interactions as its elementary particles.

Social network analysis employs the most explicit relational formulations and most precise models in this vein, but a wide variety of other inquiries labeled "institutional" or "structural" begin with the transaction or relation among actors or social sites instead of the choice-making individual or the self-sustaining social system. A community, in this perspective, is a particular but spectacularly potent combination within a small set of network configurations that have reappeared millions of times at different scales, in different settings, throughout human history.

An excursion into conceptualization will locate communities in a more general terrain of social structures. Here is a set of conceptual milestones for the trip:

> *Social Site*: any connected set of social relations producing coherent, detectable effects on other social relations
>
> *Actor*: any site consisting of living bodies (including a single individual) to which human observers attribute coherent consciousness and intention
>
> *Category*: set of sites distinguished by a single criterion, simple or complex
>
> *Transaction*: bounded communication between one site and another
>
> *Tie*: continuing series of transactions to which participants attach shared understandings, memories, forecasts, rights, and obligations
>
> *Role*: bundle of ties attached to a single site
>
> *Network*: more or less homogeneous set of ties among three or more sites
>
> *Group*: coincidence of a category and a network
>
> *Identity*: actor's experience of a category, tie, role, network, or group, coupled with a public representation of that experience; the public representation often takes the form of a shared story, a narrative

My discussion of communities – international or not – will eventually draw chiefly on the concepts of category, network, tie, and identity, neglecting the rest. I offer the other concepts here because most of them (notably actor, transaction, and group) recur elsewhere in this volume without clear specifications of their meanings. Readers who want to do their own theorizing and operationalizing can use the whole conceptual tool kit as they relate propositions concerning communities to knowledge drawn from other kinds of social structures.

Identity requires special attention. In the Adler–Barnett account of security communities, identity fluctuates uncertainly between *causing* community and *constituting* community. In either case, identity takes a chiefly subjective form. Although Adler and Barnett sometimes speak of "external identities," their main causal story concerns alterations of consciousness, especially consciousness of shared fate with others previously considered as irrelevant, alien, or even hostile. Most definitions of identity, as they say, "begin with the understanding of oneself in relation to others," then move on to transformations of self-understanding. Adler and Barnett reinforce that stress on subjectivity by centering their definition of security communities on "dependable expectations of peaceful change" and by positing social learning as the central causal mechanism in the creation of security communities. In their formulation, the crucial events occur somewhere in consciousness.

Despite remarking that "In this volume transnational identities are generally an elite-centered phenomenon," Adler and Barnett leave unclear whose consciousness undergoes the transformations that generate security-supporting collective identities: individual citizens, powerful elites, agents of states, or the mysterious conscious, collective actor they call a "government." If they insist on their subjective conception of identity, they must eventually solve a series of problems this volume does not address directly: specifying in whose minds the relevant consciousness resides; saying how that consciousness aggregates, diffuses, or otherwise becomes a collective property; and tracing how collectively-experienced consciousness creates its effects on interactions among states.

Since (a) consciousness characterizes individual minds and no other entities and (b) at best we can recognize shared understandings among individual minds, I regard those problems as utterly intractable. Instead of seeking to solve them, let me lay out a relational alternative that seems quite compatible with this volume's superb empirical observations of security communities in the making. A relational view shifts the emphasis from consciousness to conversation, from action to interaction, from selves to sociabilities.

The ubiquitous concept "identity" has remained blurred in political analysis for three reasons. First, identity is in fact not private and individual but public and relational. Secondly, it spans the whole range of relational structures from category to group. Thirdly, any actor deploys multiple identities, at least one per tie, role, network, and group to which the actor is attached. That others often typify and respond to an actor by singling out one of those multiple identities – race, gender, class, job, religious affiliation, national origin, or something else – by no means establishes the unity, or even the tight connectedness, of those identities. That sickness or zealotry occasionally elevates one identity to overwhelming dominance of an actor's consciousness and behavior, furthermore, does not gainsay the prevalence of multiple identities among people who are neither sick nor zealots. It actually takes sustained effort to endow actors with unitary identities. That effort, furthermore, more often impoverishes social life than enriches it. We often call it brainwashing.

The widespread adoption of phenomenological individualism, however, makes these homely truths hard to grasp. Phenomenological individualism is the doctrine that personal consciousness constitutes the foundation, or even the sole reality, of social life. At its despairing extreme, phenomenological individualism becomes solipsism, the claim that no individual consciousness can have access to any other individual consciousness, hence that each individual remains inescapably caged within her own awareness.[2]

Phenomenological individualists have often confused themselves with respect to identities by assuming that language entraps individuals, that preexisting presumptions and categories of language provide filters through which all social experience passes, hence that reliable knowledge of social relations is impossible. Such a view disregards the deeply interactive character of language itself, its location in constantly negotiated conversations rather than individual minds. Indeed, language provides a medium for establishment and renegotiation of identities, seen as an actor's experience of a category, tie, network, or group, coupled with a public representation of that experience. The narrative offered in such a public representation ordinarily stresses interplays of social relations and individual traits: we are Xs by virtue of experiences we share with other Xs in relation to all those (very different) Ys.

Political identities (including the identity of community member, to which this conceptual excursion will eventually take us) are simply those identities to which at least one of the parties is a government. For all their enormous variation in form and content:

- political identities are always, everywhere relational and collective;

- they therefore alter as political networks, opportunities, and strategies shift;
- the validation of political identities depends on contingent performances to which other parties' acceptance or rejection of the asserted relation is crucial;
- that validation both constrains and facilitates collective action by those who share the identity;
-]deep differences separate political identities embedded in routine social life from those that appear chiefly in public life.

Political identities embed in social ties that accumulate their own shared understandings. Thus to assert identity as a Chechnian or a Croat is not to summon up primeval consciousness but to draw a boundary separating oneself from specific others (in the instance, most often Russian, Serb, or Muslim), to claim solidarity with others on the same side of the boundary, and to invoke a certain sort of relationship to those on the opposite side.[3] Similar relational constructions of identity occur repeatedly in social movements, racial conflicts, and interactions of trade diasporas with local communities.

These propositions break with two very different but common ways of understanding political identities: (1) as straightforward activation of durable personal traits, whether individual or collective, (2) as malleable features of individual consciousness. The first view appears incessantly in interest-based accounts of political participation, which generally depend on some version of methodological individualism. The second view recurs in analyses of political commitment as a process of self-realization, and correlates closely with an assumption of phenomenological individualism. My view denies neither personal traits nor individual psyches, but places relations among actors at the core of social processes.

What does "relational and collective" mean? A *political identity* is an actor's experience of a shared social relation in which at least one of the parties – including third parties – is an individual or organization controlling concentrated means of coercion. (If the coercion-controlling organization in question enjoys some routine jurisdiction over all persons within a delimited territory, we call it a *government*; to the extent that it lacks rivals and superiors within its territory, we call it a *state*.) Political identities usually double with shared public *representations* of both relation and experience.

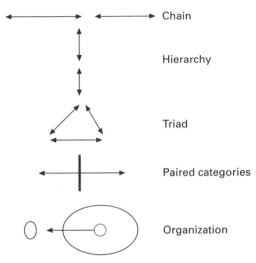

Figure 12.1   Basic social configurations

Behind identities lies a recurrent set of network configurations: distinctive and recognizable arrangements of ties that people create and employ repeatedly as they pursue their social lives. No one has codified our knowledge of these configurations. Provisional nominees for the basic set include the *chain*, the *hierarchy*, the *triad*, the *categorical pair*, and the *organization*:

1. The chain consists of two or more similar and connected ties between social sites – persons, groups, identities, networks, or something else.
2. Hierarchies are those sorts of chains in which the connections are asymmetrical and the sites systematically unequal.
3. Triads consist of three sites having similar ties to each other.
4. A categorical pair consists of a socially significant boundary and at least one tie between sites on either side of it.
5. Organizations are well-bounded sets of ties in which at least one site has the right to establish ties across the boundary that bind members of internal ties.

(We might actually reduce the basic set to three, since a hierarchy is simply a special type of chain and an organization is an overgrown categorical pair; for present purposes, however, it helps to distinguish all five.) Figure 12.1 schematizes the five elementary forms.

I think of these network configurations as social inventions: perhaps developed incrementally by trial and error, no doubt reinvented independently many times, but when recognized more or less deliberately installed as means of coordinating social life. I may be wrong: An alternative line of thought, well represented by Fredrik Barth, regards all existing social structures not as fundamental elements of social life but as emergents, variable by-products of generative principles.[4] Fortunately, it matters little for present purposes whether we are dealing with inventions or emergents; once they are in place people employ them for a wide variety of relational work.

Configurations multiply beyond their elementary forms: chains proliferate into long chains, two-step hierarchies into ten-step hierarchies, triads into dense networks of interconnection, categorical pairs proliferate into triplets, and so on. Anyone who works in a civil service, for example, becomes familiar not just with the relation between her rank and adjacent ranks but with a whole ladder consisting of asymmetrical connections. She learns the concatenation of multiple links into long chains.

Configurations also compound. Hierarchies combine with paired categories to create the classic forms of categorical inequality: male-female, black-white, citizen-foreigner, and so on. An organization emerges when members of a network extend a categorical boundary into a complete perimeter and install at least the minimum hierarchy that endows one position with power to regulate transactions across the boundary. Triads often appear as local clusters within larger structures – trading systems, military hierarchies, job-finding networks – having chains as their larger-scale connectors. Communities, in my view, are just such compounds. They include *all categorically bounded networks in which a substantial proportion of relations fall into triads*. Some communities form organizations in which occupants of certain positions exert control over transactions crossing the boundary. Some concentrate territorially, as in the classic local community. Some incorporate extensive hierarchies and/or internal divisions within their perimeters. Some maintain elaborate beliefs concerning common origin and common fate. Although definitions of community have often insisted on one or another of these additional features, none is analytically essential. Networks qualify as communities to the extent that :

1. they have well-defined and complete perimeters;
2. those perimeters correspond to or define categorical differences: us vs. them, insiders vs. outsiders, members vs. nonmembers, and so on;
3. a substantial proportion of all ties within their perimeters fall into triads, in the sense if A has a given relation to C and B has a similar relation to C, A and B also have such a relation.
4. all sites within them connect, however indirectly.

Such perimeters single out bounded networks from all others. Categorical differences select those in which visible markers appear at the perimeter. Triads identify social relations in which mutual monitoring, pooling of information, and creation of shared understandings generally occurs. Connectedness produces flows of information and structural bases for coordination.

These stipulations establish a minimum definition. They identify the broad class of social structures within which almost all users of the term "community" have located their phenomena.[5] Like Adler and Barnett in this volume, most analysts have then added stipulations for *genuine* communities: mutual dependence, solidarity, strong sense of identity, internal controls, capacity for collective action, and so on. These stipulations generally identify special cases, including intensity thresholds, of the four defining conditions: perimeters, categories, triads, and connectedness. Even the basic definition I propose adopts implicit intensity thresholds: completeness and definition of perimeters, sharpness of categorical differences, proportion of all ties that fall into triads, degree of connection. But for present purposes we need not fret about measurement. Suffice it to say that by such criteria the totality of subscribers to a national telephone service fails to qualify as a community, long-term residents of a named hamlet usually qualify, and most interesting cases lie somewhere between these limits.

To identify large-scale communities, then, look for social loci featuring triadic relations, not only among states, but also among nonstate parties to relations among states; the thicker such relations on the ground, the more communitarian the locus. By now a large sociological literature documents qualitative differences between dyads and triads.[6] Frequent triads do not guarantee solidarity, since they lend themselves to two-against-one coalitions. (In Bosnia, note the frequency with which two of the three parties – Muslim, Serb, and

Croatian – gang up on the third.) But they do mean that third parties frequently have interests, and some power to intervene, in a given paired relation. They also promote the homogenization of shared understandings across whole networks.

Despite implications of evolutionary game theory, by and large trust does not emerge from repeated two-party interactions, but from interactions cemented by their connections with third parties who serve as monitors, guarantors, and sources of support. On a large scale, concatenated stable triads may well be necessary conditions for generalized trust. Triads facilitate the "spillover" from one form of cooperation to another that figures so importantly in this volume's accounts of particular security communities. Although the long-peaceful US–Canadian border seems at first glance to deny this assertion, Sean Shore's analysis actually underlines the significance of triads. At the smaller scale they commonly consist of pairs of non-governmental agents plus a government or pairs of governments plus a non-governmental agent; Shore's examples of international unions and trans-national firms illustrate the latter sort of triad. At a larger scale, the US, Canada, and Great Britain formed a crucial triad, each government strongly interested in relations between the other two. The label "Canada," furthermore, hides a good deal of complexity: of the present Canadian provinces, only New Brunswick, Nova Scotia, Québec, and Ontario formed the confederation of 1867, Newfoundland and Labrador did not join until 1949, the French possessions of St. Pierre and Miquelon still lie between Newfoundland and Nova Scotia, while the large regions of Northwest Territories and Nunavut fall under Canadian jurisdiction without forming part of the confederation. Plenty of interactions across a border containing such a complex organization involved not dyads, but triads and their compounds. That the "United States" also describes a plethora of interdependent actors only strengthens the reasons for rejecting US–Canada interactions as simply bilateral.

Transnational communities did not form for the first time in the recent past. If we scan world history before our own era, we will find plenty of large-scale communities, some of them continental or even transcontinental in scale. The four most influential types were: (1) *trade diasporas* such as Gujarati merchants; (2) *trading federations* such as the Hanseatic League; (3) *religious communities* such as Muslims; and (4) *composite empires* such as the Mongols.[7] Some, but by no means all, qualified as *organizations* in the sense of having central positions whose occupants governed transactions crossing their boundaries. All conducted risky transactions over impressive distances and periods, all established elaborate markers of membership, all resolved acute problems of agency through some combination of triadic monitoring and high – even fatal – costs to members they excluded for violations of trust. They did so in the absence of external powers (states or others) capable of enforcing contracts through their own coercive means.

International communities have thus existed for thousands of years. At times they have dominated the world's large-scale structures. However we define "nation" or "state", full-fledged communities have crossed boundaries of nations and states since the rise of trade diasporas, nonstate religions, and composite empires four millennia ago or more. Indeed the idea of "international community" commits oxymoron to the extent that it assigns priority to the territorially contiguous, centralized, and ostensibly national states that have acquired hegemony in the word since 1750. In the near-absence of anything like national states anywhere before 1600 the term "international" applies oddly to the many large-scale communities that existed in the sixteenth century and earlier.

Over the roughly 10,000 years for which we have evidence archeological or textual – for the presence of coercion-wielding non-kinship organizations exercising priority in important respects over all other organizations within well-delimited territories (such is a viable definition of a "state"), five things are true:

1. only during the last two centuries have organizations qualifying as anything like nation-states held sway anywhere in the world;
2. most states have worked as composites, through indirect rule;
3. creation of what the world came to know as nation-states depended enormously on the interaction of transnational forces;
4. the fitting of the Western national-state pattern to the rest of the world has generally failed;
5. despite strenuous efforts, no state anywhere has succeeded in maintaining or creating a truly homogeneous national culture.

Hence two common suppositions collapse: (a) that the world divides naturally and eternally into autonomous, well-bounded states; (b) that current creation of large-scale non-state structures therefore threatens a natural order. A more accurate rendering of world history would run like this: for a century or so Western states managed a remarkable degree of circumscription and central control over crucial resources, territories, and populations, but in recent decades the world has been returning to its more usual condition: extensive cross-cutting of jurisdictions and powers.

Over the long historical run, cross-cutting jurisdictions and powers have often included entities we can properly call interstate or trans-state communities, and with a bit less accuracy call international communities. Such communities form through the creation of monitored contracts that cross state boundaries and involve at least one of the states in question. Monitored, hence at least triadic, if not more complex. Settlements of wars often bring such contracts into existence, as third parties organize relations between a given state and its neighbors. So, however, do trade, migration, and ethnic solidarity across state boundaries.

Under what conditions do such communities secure peace? The mention of ethnic solidarity makes it clear that not all triadic connections involving states create peaceful relations; Kurds in Iran, Iraq, and Turkey exacerbate relations among the three, as shared relations to Pathans have fomented recurrent warfare along the frontiers of Afghanistan, Pakistan, and adjacent powers. To simplify radically:

1. unfavorable triads include at least one relation organized around a valued activity that war will favor, while
2. favorable triads include at least one relation organized around a valued activity that war will inhibit.

In this view, both transnational ethnic irredentism and smuggling of high value-for-bulk commodities provide examples of war-promoting circumstances. International religious observances and cross-frontier road transport of low value-for-bulk commodities stand as examples of the second, war-inhibiting, circumstances.

In that connection, mainland South America's military actions between 1945 and 1990 provide food for thought; as Andrew Hurrell indicates elsewhere in this volume, they suggest that without formal organization South America operated one or more security communities during the postwar period. Excluding interventions by Great Britain in Guyana and the Falklands, mainland military actions between 1945 and 1990 consisted of four border struggles between Ecuador and Peru, others between Argentina and Chile, Guyana and

Surinam, and Venezuela and Guyana, plus 1962 incidents between Argentina and Paraguay precipitated by the flight into Argentina of dissidents from Alfredo Stroessner's regime.[8]

In the Caribbean, the only events other than colony-empire struggles that might arguably qualify consist of Cuba's Bay of Pigs adventure and US interventions in the Dominican Republic and Grenada. In Central America, El Salvador and Honduras waged the lethal Football War of 1969, and externally-supported civil wars raged repeatedly, but otherwise border skirmishes and fishing disputes constituted all the region's interstate armed conflicts between 1945 and 1990.[9]

While plenty of collective violence, much of it state-incited, was occurring in central regions of South American states, these interstate conflicts not only produced few casualties but also took place almost entirely away from major flows of persons and trade. After a bellicose nineteenth century, Latin American states turned away from interstate war early in the twentieth century without in the least stilling civil violence or inhibiting their militaries from playing prominent parts in national politics; on the contrary, organized violence turned inward. No doubt the looming third-party presence of the United States inhibited the region's interstate warfare, but we can reasonably hypothesize that weakness of cross-border antistate alliances and presence of state-sanctioned cross-border economic interdependence promoted the formation of security communities within the region.

Remarkably, sub-Saharan Africa has undergone a similar transformation from frequent interstate warfare during the nineteenth century toward the abandonment of interstate conflict in favor of civil wars, coups, and a wide variety of state-incited violence during the twentieth. Postwar sub-Saharan Africa gives the impression of having established one or more tacit security communities without benefit of formal organization. The turbulence of postwar struggles against European control disguises the near-absence of war among African states.

Aside from covert interventions and struggles with European colonial powers, sub-Saharan Africa's interstate military actions between 1945 and 1990 consisted of mutual incursions by Senegal and Gambia, intervention of Guinean forces in a Sierra Leone coup, border incidents between Mali and (then) Upper Volta, international intervention in the Belgian Congo's civil war from 1959 to 1965, border battles between Zaire and its neighbors, Libyan and Nigerian interventions in Chad, territorial disputes between Somalia and Ethiopia, movements of Hutu and Tutsi forces across the porous Rwanda–Burundi frontier, attacks on Sudan by rebels (or bandits, depending on your perspective) based in Uganda and Zaire, raids on Uganda by rebels based in Tanzania followed by Ugandan retaliation, cattle raids on the Uganda–Kenya border, Israeli commandos' 1976 raid on hijackers at Uganda's Entebbe airport, multiple African interventions in Angola and Mozambique, sustained war between Rhodesia and adjacent states, and repeated South African interventions against neighbors.[10] Once European colonies dissolved and European control of Rhodesia and South Africa collapsed, sub-Saharan Africa again avoided large-scale interstate war.

We can, of course, invoke special circumstances, notably the European presence, as explanations of sub-Saharan Africa's twentieth-century approximation to a security community. Yet Africa, too, challenges us to look for favorable triads creating not only communities, but security communities: communities whose members eschew war among themselves. If, on the other hand, the unhappy performance of African states in so many other regards disqualifies relations among them as security communities, we should wonder whether (like earlier models of development) the term smuggles in an implicit comparison with rich western countries.

How, then, can we recognize *security* communities without tautology or teleology? We look for networks of relations among multiple states and powerful nonstate actors in which (a) interaction flows intensely and reciprocally, (b) triads appear frequently, and (c) agents of states rarely and/or inconsequentially use concentrated force against agents of other states. We do *not* insert the presence or absence of warlike thoughts – presumably part of security's explanation rather than its definition – into the criteria for security communities. Although we might well impose some threshold period (say twenty years, or fifty) for the admission of a set of states to the category of security communities, we do not rescind membership retroactively if members of the set war with each other beyond that threshold.

Most international communities that thrived before 1750 or so worked as something like security communities, significantly limiting the use of lethal force among community members except as authorized by the communities' central authorities. If autonomous, sovereign, nationally defined states lose the hegemony they have held since the eighteenth century, we can reasonably expect that international security communities will assume some of the powers monopolized by states over the last two centuries. Such communities will not greatly resemble the trade diasporas, trading federations, religious networks, and composite empires that constituted the phenomenon's prime examples before 1750, but they will rely on some of the same principles of triadic connection, pooled fate, and high-cost exclusion that characterized their ancient predecessors. Just as deliberate human action brought most earlier international communities into operation, we can even imagine designing international security communities that incorporate age-old assurances of trust, reciprocity, and mutual identity.

Notes

1 I have adapted a few passages in this chapter from my "Citizenship, Identity, and Social History," in Charles Tilly, ed., *Citizenship, Identity, and Social History* (Cambridge: Cambridge University Press, 1995) and Charles Tilly, *Durable Inequality* (Berkeley: University of California Press, 1998).

2 Charles Tilly, "Softcore Solipsism," *Labour/Le Travail* 34 (1994), 259 268

3 Charles Tilly, "States and Nationalism in Europe 1492–1992," *Theory and Society* 23 (1994), 131-146, "Stein Rokkan et les Identités Politiques," *Revue Internationale de Politique Comparée* 2 (1995), 27–45, "The State of Nationalism," *Critical Review* 10 (1996), 299–306.

4 Fredrik Barth, *Process and Form in Social Life. Selected Essays of Fredrik Barth: Volume I* (London: Routledge and Kegan Paul, 1981), 1–118.

5 George A. Hillery, *Communal Organizations. A Study of Local Societies* (Chicago: University of Chicago Press, 1968), Charles Tilly, "Do Communities Act?" *Sociological Inquiry* 43 (1973), 209–240, Charles Tilly, *An Urban World* (Boston: Little, Brown, 1974).

6 Ronald S. Burt, *Structural Holes. The Social Structure of Competition* (Cambridge: Harvard University Press, 1992), Mark Granovetter, *Getting a Job. A Study of Contacts and Careers* (Chicago: University of Chicago Press, 1995; 2d edn.), John Scott, *Social Network Analysis. A Handbook* (London: Sage, 1991), Stanley Wasserman and Katherine Faust *Social Network Analysis. Methods and Applications* (Cambridge: Cambridge University Press, 1994), Barry Wellman and S. D. Berkowitz, eds., *Social Structures: A Network Approach.* (Cambridge: Cambridge University Press, 1988), Harrison White, *Identity and Control. A Structural Theory of Social Action* (Princeton: Princeton University Press, 1992).

7 Janet Abu-Lughod, *Before European Hegemony* (New York: Oxford University Press, 1989), Kenneth R. Andrews, *Trade, Plunder and Settlement. Maritime Enterprise and the Genesis of the British Empire, 1480–1630* (Cambridge: Cambridge University Press, 1984), Thomas J. Barfield, *The Perilous Frontier. Nomadic Empires and China* (New York: Blackwell, 1989), Terry

Boswell, "Colonial Empires and the Capitalist World-Economy: A Time Series Analysis of Colonization, 1640–1960," *American Sociological Review* 54 (1989), 180–196, Christopher Chase-Dunn and Thomas D. Hall, eds., *Core/Periphery Relations in Precapitalist Worlds* (Boulder, CO: Westview, 1991), K. N. Chaudhuri, *Asia before Europe. Economy and Civilisation of the Indian Ocean from the Rise of Islam to 1750* (Cambridge: Cambridge University Press, 1990), Alfred W. Crosby, *Ecological Imperialism. The Biological Expansion of Europe, 900–1900* (Cambridge: Cambridge University Press, 1986), Philip D. Curtin, *Cross-Cultural Trade in World History* (Cambridge: Cambridge University Press, 1984), Avner Greif, "Reputation and Coalitions in Medieval Trade: Evidence on the Maghribi Traders," *Journal of Economic History* 49 (1989), 857–882, Avner Greif, Paul Milgrom and Barry R. Weingast, "Coordination, Commitment, and Enforcement: The Case of the Merchant Guild," *Journal of Political Economy* 102 (1994), 745–775, Anatoly M. Khazanov, "Muhammad and Jenghiz Khan Compared: The Religious Factor in World Empire Building," *Comparative Studies in Society and History* 35 (1993), 461–479, William H. McNeill, *Plagues and Peoples* (Garden City: Anchor/Doubleday, 1976), Susan Reynolds, *Kingdoms and Communities in Western Europe, 900–1300* (Oxford: Clarendon Press, 1984), G. V. Scammell, *The World Encompassed. The First European Maritime Empires c. 800–1650* (London: Methuen, 1981), Alan K. Smith, *Creating a World Economy. Merchant Capital, Colonialism, and World Trade, 1400–1825* (Boulder, CO: Westview, 1991), Sanjay Subrahmanyam, "Of *Imârat* and *Tijârat*: Asian Merchants and State Power in the Western Indian Ocean, 1400 to 1750," *Comparative Studies in Society and History* 37 (1995), 750–780, James D. Tracy, ed., *The Rise of Merchant Empires. Long-Distance Trade in the Early Modern World, 1350–1750* (Cambridge: Cambridge University Press, 1990), James D. Tracy, ed., *The Political Economy of Merchant Empires* (Cambridge: Cambridge University Press, 1991), Immanuel Wallerstein, *The Modern World System* (New York: Academic Press, 1974–1989, 3 vols. to date), Immanuel Wallerstein, *Geopolitics and Geoculture. Essays on the Changing World-Systems* (Cambridge: Cambridge University Press, 1991).

8 Herbert K. Tillema, *International Armed Conflict since 1945. A Bibliographic Handbook of Wars and Military Interventions* (Boulder, CO: Westview, 1991), 35–44.

9 Ibid., pp. 15–44.

10 Ibid., pp. 61–129.

13 Studying security communities in theory, comparison, and history

Michael Barnett and Emanuel Adler

Karl Deutsch and his colleagues introduced the concept of security communities in 1957, but it sat in relative theoretical anonymity and spawned few empirical studies for the next several decades. The studies that informed the seminal volume went unpublished,[1] and few scholars found the concept of security communities particularly inviting against the backdrop of the Cold War, nuclear politics, and the hyperstatism and systemic theorizing that would come to define the discipline. This volume has offered the first sustained and systematic – but by no means definitive – effort to plow the twin fields of theory and history in order to dramatize the promise of the concept of security communities, and to examine regional developments through its gaze. Our goal, therefore, has been as much exploratory as exculpatory; we have been as interested in identifying the conditions under which security communities might come into existence as in providing greater empirical weight behind a revised conceptual apparatus that might prove better able to generate a rich historical and theoretical lineage.

In this concluding chapter we weave the conceptual framework with the various contributions to tease out some general propositions concerning the study of security community, to identify some shortcomings, and to consider some future avenues of research. In the first section we extend our framework by revisiting the tiers we presented in chapter 2 and refocusing energies on the concept of trust as it marks the development of a security community. To review, we were concerned with precipitating conditions, and with the dynamic relationship between process and structure: the "process" categories include transactions, organizations and institutions, and social learning; the "structure" categories are power and cores of strength, and knowledge. The positive and dynamic interaction between these

413

tiers undergirds the process of collective identity formation and furthers the development of trust, which, in turn, drives dependable expectation of peaceful change. These tiers also have a historical dimension as they are related to a three-phase model of the development of a security community: nascent, ascendant, and mature. In the second section, therefore, we revisit this model, not to identify a single pathway – which was never our intent – but rather to speculate about some of the conditions that might shift one phase to the next and to offer some thoughts on how the change in the underlying normative structure imprints certain facets of security practices. We conclude by reflecting on how the recognition that security communities are socially constructed offers some guidance for thinking about global and security politics in theory and practice.

Trust and its consequences

The concept of trust and its absence appears and reappears in various guises throughout the volume.[2] Recall that trust always involves an element of risk because of the inability to monitor others' behavior or to have complete knowledge about other people's motivations; because of the very contingency of social reality. Dependable expectations of peaceful change, the confidence that disputes will be settled without war, is unarguably the deepest expression of trust possible in the international arena (particularly so if one assumes that states exist in a formal anarchy and thus in the brooding shadow of violence). Trust does not develop overnight but rather is accomplished after a lifetime of common experiences and through sustained interactions and reciprocal exchanges, leaps of faith that are braced by the verification offered by organizations, trial-and-error, and a historical legacy of actions and encounters that deposit an environment of certitude notwithstanding the uncertainty that accompanies social life. As we revisit the tiers of process (transactions, organizations, social learning) and structure (power and knowledge), we focus on how the quality of these interactions and dynamics deposit a reservoir of trust that can be detected in the development of a security community.

Catalysts of change

Our theoretical framework and the empirical evidence suggest that security communities develop from fairly humble beginnings and are frequently far from the minds or the intentions of policymakers at the outset. Instead, governments have various reasons to orient themselves toward each other and to consider ways to address their mutual security and economic concerns and interests. Sometimes the language of identity and references to a shared community are uttered during these first moments of cooperation. But there is no reason to presume that such language and references are anything more than instrumental constructs and contrived conveniences. As David Laitin notes, peoples' choice of an identity "is often guided by instrumental reasoning, based on the potential resources available for identifying yourself."[3] For example, after the fall of the Wall, many Eastern European leaders used "widely shared symbols for their instrumental ends" and attempted to manipulate "these symbols in order to mobilize others on behalf of their political goals."[4] Governments frequently paint a grand and glorious future as they aspire to achieve more secular and short-term goals.

The various contributions describe how security communities are made from small and modest steps. Nearly all the chapters opened by sketching an environment in which interstate violence had recently erupted, informed the expectations for the future, and provided an important backdrop for the initial rounds of cooperation. For a variety of reasons states found it in their mutual interest to contemplate coordination if only to avoid unwanted outcomes or to further their individual security and economic interests. At this initial phase, security cooperation born of a shared security threat is virtually indistinguishable from an alliance; Wæver argues that while NATO might have developed into a pillar of the security community, at the outset it was little more than a strategic alliance. The search for security cooperation, however, can be driven by domestic rather than systemic threats. The ASEAN and the GCC states constructed their own regional arrangements because of their desire for regime survival and to coordinate their policies to confront (or at least to avoid actions that exacerbated) domestic instabilities. Not surprisingly, economic interests also triggered the search for cooperation. The US–Mexican and South American cases demonstrate how the desire to deepen economic exchange led to the development of institutional arrangements in order to reduce transaction costs and to adjudicate anticipated disputes.

Notwithstanding our earlier warning that references to a shared identity at these initial moments should be treated skeptically, the

415

search for cooperation can be driven not only by interests but also by identity. This was most evident following a major systemic change when loyalties and allegiances were in flux and states considered anew with whom they want to associate and according to what principles. Charles Tilly writes that the decline of empires, and we would add other systemic changes, cause populations to reconsider who they are and with whom they want to associate.[5] The two great moments of regional experimentation in this second-half century came after World War II and the Cold War, major systemic shifts that unleashed a reconsideration of state identities and parallel associations. States and regional associations have an incentive to try and contain the aftershocks, and one strategy is to form new associations based not only on shared interests but also on new (and sometimes slightly contrived) identities.

Transactions

The emphasis on economic and political transactions as a source of trust at this early stage underscores interactions as a unit of analysis. Deutsch pointed to the importance of transactions; in this volume Charles Tilly identifies the related network literature, and the chapters themselves document in various ways how transactions are the basis for transnationalism. Interactions and transactions are a longstanding focus of sociology and is closely identified with the foundational work of George Simmel. Simmel claimed that the dominant form of relationship – indeed, a defining property of society – is the exchange. But exchange is more than a "sacrifice in return for a gain." Through exchange, actors learn the relative value of things, establish new bonds, convey the centrality of reciprocity; exchanges are a constitutive factor in all social relationships and provide the foundation for trust. Without a modicum of trust there would be no reciprocity since there is almost always a gap between moments of exchange, without reciprocity all forms of society would disintegrate, and we are more likely to trust those we know.[6] Political and economic transactions, then, are more than simply an exchange of goods and services but also potentially the cornerstone for trust and a sense of community.

Furthermore, during their interaction political actors bargain not only over the issues on the table but also over the concepts and norms that constitute their social reality. The idea that communication, and even communication that is motivated by prior interests, can be the basis for new bonds and understandings is consistent with Deutsch's views of social communication and Jürgen Habermas's theory of "communicative action," according to which, communication and action are different sides of the same enterprise. "In communicative action participants negotiate definitions, values, and mutual understandings as they join in discourse around a task. They bring to this not only formal knowledge but also practical experience and interests."[7] The process of community-building through transactions, then, encourages processes of joint learning where "doing things together" becomes an important component of "knowing together." There is more to exchange than meets the (political scientists') eye.

These observations are supported by the empirical cases, which suggest that states were interested in cooperating not on a single issue area but rather across a range of issue areas in the hope of generating both peace and prosperity. This raises the concept of spillover. Karl Deutsch conceptualized spillover in terms of trust; the trust that developed from cooperation in, for instance, economic cooperation would cascade into security affairs. Ernst Haas's understanding was based on the functional linkages that exist between different issue areas; to cooperate, for instance, in economic affairs implicated environmental matters. The Gonzalez and Haggard chapter finds support for the Haasian version; there is evidence of the Deutschian version in several of the other chapters, including those by Shore, Hurrell, and Wæver. But both versions of spillover share a common concern with how interactions and learning generate trust. Most of the papers were implicitly attentive to the question of issue linkage and spillover; for instance, Shore identifies its existence in the US–Canadian case, Hurrell notes how South American leaders were using accomplishments in one area to inspire cooperation in another, and Barnett and Gause note how scant is the evidence of spillover in the GCC.

The contributions, however, hinted of spillover that transcends even neo-functionalists' and transactionalists' most optimist expectations, but is quite consistent with our emphasis on the relationship between transactions, social learning, and social construction. Policymakers are linking previously discrete issue areas because of new understandings of how to build a better security system. Regardless of whether they are called social epistimes, cognitive structures, or ideas, some policymakers are making new causal connections between previously isolated domains.[8] For example, progressively since 1945, and dramatically so since the end of the Cold War, more economic agreements and economic integration efforts are linked to the question of security and peace, and more security agreements are framed as enabling new forms of commercial interaction. Simply put, we are impressed by the fact that most of the post-1945 studies – and particularly so the post-Cold War statements – that we have examined have policymakers articulating a new set of understandings about the causal relationship between economics, politics, and peace.[9]

International organizations and institutions

International organizations and institutions played an important role in encouraging more intensive and extensive interactions between states through their trust-building properties. This had several dimensions. First, most intuitive, and consistent with the observations of neo-liberal institutionalism, international organizations gave states the confidence to cooperate because they were able to monitor their agreements. Various agreements and fledgling organizations might be akin to a "canary in a coal mine" as they are intended to detect the possibility of extending cooperation to more sensitive areas without suffering the consequences associated with plunging into untrampled terrain. International organizations, in this respect, are important third-party mechanisms that encourage states to cooperate and exchange in the absence of trust, and do so by producing transparency, exchanging information, and monitoring agreements. Secondly, organizations enabled states to discover new areas of mutual interests. A corollary here is that many organizations bundle issues in distinct ways that draw attention to the linkage between different areas and thus have policy implications. Non-security organizations, therefore, can have a security-enhancing function. Wæver argues that the European Union is an important security institution because it has encouraged Europeans to equate their security with integration and their insecurity with disintegration; in this respect, it profoundly shapes whether security or insecurity lies in Europe's future.

Thirdly, international organizations also can shape state practices by establishing, articulating, and transmitting norms that define what constitutes acceptable and legitimate state behavior. State actors abide by these norms not only because of coercive power but also because of the desire to be viewed as operating legitimately; that is, they need to justify and bring their policies in line with accepted practices of state action. This is an important function, as argued by Russett, of the United Nations.[10] At times, and perhaps more so during the nascent stage, the quest for legitimacy may be instrumentally tied to the state's economic and security interests; in later stages, however, the desire for legitimacy can be linked to the states identity.

These three points underline our fourth observation: the truly impressive increase in the number of international organizations that now have a multilateral profile. This suggests something akin to institutional isomorphism.[11] There are various reasons for the ascendance of the multilateral form. Perhaps part of the explanation is organizational emulation as policymakers in one region are drawing from the lessons from other regions in order to build a sense of community. The OSCE's activities and confidence and trust-building practices were genuinely path-breaking in this respect, as various regional organizations have been adopting its multilateral model of community-building to promote a regional identity and mutual trust. But it also is possible that multilateral organizations have obtained a degree of symbolic legitimacy in the contemporary period. Multilateral organizations are increasingly perceived as the proper enactment of regional security and confer legitimacy beyond its expressly functional attributes. Therefore, even in those regions where war is still quite thinkable, new multilateral forms are becoming an important part of the overall security architecture and political landscape. Although the very existence of these multilateral forms does not guarantee that their members are card-carrying multilateralists, it arguably enhances the prospect of peaceful change.

Fifthly, international organizations encourage states and societies to imagine themselves as part of a region. In some cases, such as NAFTA's depiction of a North American region, this role may be a collateral outcome of functional activities. In other cases, such as the OSCE, the GCC, and ASEAN, international organizations deliberately encouraged their members to imagine themselves in a new social space bound by some common characteristics. As the Soviet Union was crumbling at the close of the 1980s, the OSCE strove to instill confidence in the Soviet leadership that would retain a "place" in a common European house from Vancouver to Vladivostok.

This suggests, sixthly, that organizations also can shape the identities of their members. Organizations are not only instruments that enable states to further their already given interests but also can be a site of interest and identity formation. Particularly striking are those cases in which regional organizations have been established for instrumental reasons and then subsequently and unexpectedly come to have an identity component by virtue of their becoming a new site for interaction and source of imagination. The GCC has promoted, however unintentionally, the semblance of a Gulf identity. The studies suggest several ways in which international organizations can be a site of identity and interest formation. To begin, organizations are talk shops; increasingly, they rely on face-to-face encounters like "seminar diplomacy" to instill in the participants a sense of common purpose and community.[12] While it is easy to dismiss these forums as talk and little else, nearly all the chapters provide compelling evidence that from such dialogues come new self-understandings. Moreover, some organizations are designed to spread and reinforce the values of their (core) members, thus operating as a socializing mechanism. In this regard, international organizations that are not specifically created for strategic purposes can have a strong security hue: to transform former members not only into allies but also into members of a security community. This was an important function of many of the Western-based institutions in which Germany and Japan were placed after World War II. The Partnership for Peace operates on the founding principle that bringing the former Eastern Bloc armies into the Western military institutions will transmit new norms from the latter to the former, thus helping to transform the "Eastern" European states into European states. International organizations can perform several trust-building functions.

International organizations are not only sites of interactions but also actors in their own right. Of particular importance here is the attempt of their officials to spread the values of the community in order to reinforce trust. Indeed, these officials may be characterized as the "new missionaries." Armed with a notion of progress, an idea of how to create the better life, and some understanding of the conversion process, many organizational elites wish to expand the values of their community. Officials in the United Nations and the OSCE proudly proclaim that they are carriers of values, attempting to convert actors from their old way of life and to bring them into the fold. To this extent they see themselves not only as social engineers but also as peddlers of trust. To be sure, their success is dependent on more than their persuasive capacities, for their rhetoric must be supported by state power, but to overlook how state power and organizational missionaries work in tandem is to disregard a fundamental feature of value diffusion.

Two conclusions on organizations follow from these previous observations. First, multilateralism essentially describes two types of activities. On the one hand, there is a weak version of multilateralism – for example, the international trade, monetary, and nuclear non-proliferation regimes – that responds to the instrumental logic of self-interested states that coordinate their policies on the basis of consensual principles of conduct. On the other hand, there is a "strong" type of multilateralism, of which this volume gives ample evidence, that refers to the social construction and institutionalization of security communities by means of multilateral community-building dialogue and practices.[13] An important avenue of future research will be to determine when, how, and why "weak" multilateralism becomes "strong" multilateral institutions, and when, how, and why strong multilateralism has the effects that we have outlined.

Secondly, we are struck by the tremendous growth in the number of regional organizations that have as their stated mission the development of something akin to a security community, and how much region-building and acts of cooperation are offered as trust-building and trust-testing mechanisms.[14] Deutsch downplayed what most studies in this volume have clearly demonstrated: the extent to which social communication becomes institutionalized and embedded in international organizations, and, in turn, how these organizations express an intent to develop trust and mutual identification. International organizations are an important part of the equation in the development of the security community.[15] The US–Canadian, the US–Mexican, and Nordic cases suggest that security communities can develop outside a highly institutionalized environment. But given the proliferation of international organizations in the contemporary period, it is difficult to imagine those conditions existing again.

Social learning

The way interactions and institutions and organizations affect processes of mutual trust and collective identity formation also hints to the role that learning plays in these processes. Even if Deutsch did not explicate in detail how and why learning is important to the development of security communities, he tied learning to the development of mutual responsiveness, and was categorical in insisting that "peaceful change does not seem assured without a continuous learning process."[16] In our study, however, we have interpreted learning in a more demanding fashion than Deutsch did. To recall, we defined learning as an active process of redefinition or reinterpretation of reality on the basis of new causal and normative knowledge. Our notion of learning means that the very act of learning can have not only a technical but also a social dimension to it because it can promote mutual trust and shape the identities of actors.

Many of the studies in this volume support our reading of learning and suggest, some more explicitly than others, that learning was necessary for the development of mutual trust and collective identities. Below, we briefly consider the role played by learning as part of the diffusion of norms between countries, and in promoting new definitions of security, the development of collective identities, and even a redefinition of regions. First, the spread of norms has facilitated learning processes that enlarge the area where mutual trust and collective identities can emerge. For example, although a collective identity between the US and Canada, on the one hand, and Mexico, on the other, is still very weak and perhaps nonexistent, NAFTA has encouraged the strengthening of democracy and the rule of law in Mexico – as evidenced by the latest elections – and, therefore, created a more fertile ground for the development of an overall North American collective identity (to the extent that democracy is part of the North American identity). Moreover, the workings of international organizations, such as the United Nations, NATO, and the OSCE attest to the importance of the teaching of norms in expanding the space within which states approach their security needs with cooperative measures. The activities of these institutions also show that seminar diplomacy has become a premium forum for collective learning and, thus, for building mutual trust and, eventually, collective identities.

Secondly, learning enabled the redefinition of regional security in ways that promoted the building of trust and the social construction of collective identities. Wæver, for example, describes how once economic integration became defined as a security problem, Western Europeans laid the ground not only for the development of a collective identity but also for the definition of their prevailing source of threat: disintegration. More broadly, by designing and helping to institutionalize the concept of "cooperative security" in the area stretching from Vancouver to Vladivostok, the OSCE played an important role in changing the way security is understood there, namely, as reassurance and trust-building. The role of learning in collectively redefining security occurred not only in the European continent, however. Higgott and Nossal showed that during the 1980s and 1990s Australians redefined their understanding of security with greater emphasis on economic issues, and that this learning process took place, in part, because of an epistemic community of scholars and practitioners working on questions of alternative security.

Thirdly, learning played a direct role in collective identity formation. For example, a revision of previously existing images and the generation of new understandings of their mutual relationships was critical for the development of a collective identity among Americans and Canadians. According to Shore, learning encouraged Americans and Canadians to begin understanding each other in more pacific terms; for example, demilitarization was something of a "cognitive punch" that forced both countries to reevaluate their prior beliefs. The case of ASEAN, on the other hand, shows that learning led to the creation of shared norms, symbols, and habits, which, in turn, promoted the development of collective identities. It also shows that learning can occur take place in illiberal settings and can proceed in the absence of cultural similarities. In fact, the ASEAN case demonstrates that learning may help create or discover previously non-existent or unrecognized cultural similarities among different states. In turn, Hurrell hinted to a learning process in the discovery by Argentina and Brazil of the importance that regional and sub-regional economic liberalization has for their own well being and security. Although he did not find strong evidence that a collective identity between these two countries has become fully developed, economic liberalization and integration has already helped enhance mutual trust – as evidenced by these countries close cooperation in the nuclear field – and may serve as a foundation for the future development of a collective identity.

Finally, learning led to the social construction or redefinition of regions themselves. Adler notes how the OSCE contributed to creating not only a security regime but also the boundaries of a region where adherence to shared liberal norms and cooperative security practices enhances the security of member states. Acharya, in turn, observes how the painstakingly developed ASEAN Way, with its particularistic symbols and processes of socialization, led to the notion that ASEAN constitutes a distinctive region. And Higgott and Nossal highlight that a learning process helped to bring about Australia's structural redefinition of itself as part of Asia and, thus, its liminal status.

Power and knowledge

This volume supports Deutsch's observation that security communities develop around cores of strength. But we go beyond Deutsch and differentiate between two distinct but arguably necessary ways in which state power and cores of strength facilitate the development of a security community. The first, which is consistent with neo-liberal institutionalism, is that cores of strength distribute the carrots and sticks that are frequently necessary to form and maintain the group and accomplish collective action.

The second, which is consistent with constructivist approaches, is the ability to project a sense of purpose that has a magnetic pull; in other words, the core power is not someone to be feared but rather someone to be emulated. The contrast between the US–Canadian and the US–Mexican cases is instructive here. Gonzalez and Haggard argue that asymmetries in US–Mexican relations has been a consistent brake on cooperation. Yet Shore demonstrates that similar power differentials were not an obstacle to a high level of mutual trust and cooperation in US–Canadian relations. There is greater need to examine how asymmetries play themselves out, but these North American cases suggest that power may work as a core of strength only when accompanied by cultural affinities between greater and lesser powers.

But the concept of power as projecting a sense of purpose also suggests a subtler form of power – the ability to create meanings and categories of legitimate action. In this reading the ability to create the underlying rules of the game, to define what constitutes acceptable play, and to be able to get other actors to commit to these rules because they are now part of their self-understandings is perhaps the most subtle and most effective form of power.[17] There is a fine line here between learning and socialization, between consent and coercion. We have a healthy respect for the claim that there is a relationship between knowledge and power; knowledge is rarely value-neutral and frequently plays into the creation and reproduction of a particular social order that benefits some at the expense of others.[18] The disciplining effects of "legitimate" meanings in the case of NATO places former communist states on "probation" until they have demonstrated a commitment to Western political and economic practices. Is this part of a Western hegemonic project? If so, how do we account for the fact that this is "hegemony by invitation" and that the populations of these states have demonstrated a greater interest in entering into the West than the West has in admitting them? Australia's attempt to convince its neighbors of the virtues of open regionalism, multilateralism, and market-led integration may also be considered as a case of attempted (though not quite successful) redefinition of the parameters of politics that are designed to make Asia safe for Australia.

We are now in the terrain of shared knowledge. The question is: are certain cognitive structures more prone toward trust-building and better able to advance a security community? More to the point, is liberalism a necessary condition for the development of a security community? For many, the mere fact that First World states are liberal states and Third World states are illiberal states goes a long way toward explaining their distinct records on the issue of war and peace. One objective of this volume was to break out of such stereotyping, to stop modelling the concept of security communities as if it were owned and operated by Europe, and to explore the possible existence of security communities in non-European settings. To this end, the chapters on the non-Western regions raised questions regarding whether liberalism was a necessary condition. Acharya was most explicit here, arguing that there is a "ASEAN way" that might enable its members to continue down the road of a security community without necessarily swallowing a dose of liberalism. Barnett and Gause note that Saudi Arabia is rumored to have intervened to halt democratizing trends in Kuwait for fear of similar demands in Saudi Arabia, only deepening mistrust in the GCC.

Yet other studies in this volume hinted that political instability in general and the absence of democracy in particular might be an obstacle to the development of a security community. Gonzalez and Haggard observe that the most fundamental factor determining the weakness of US–Mexican institutionalized cooperation have been the former's perceptions of the latter's underlying political instability and lack of democracy. And the South American case arguably comes closest to observing that an important precondition for the development of a security community is liberalism. Thus, while liberalism might not be alone in enabling trust, it might be better able to encourage this outcome. That said, the issue might not be liberalism *per se* but rather a willingness to allow myriad transactions between societies among leaders who are generally secure in their domestic rule, and agree on general standards of conduct in domestic and international affairs. Clearly there is a need for better specification and identification of the role of cognitive structures in the development of trust and a security community.

Identity

The chapters in this volume provide indirect and sometimes direct support for the claim that interstate interactions can foster a collective or transnational identity. Acharya, Adler, Barnett and Gause, Higgott and Nossal, and Shore all provide evidence of how the quality and duration of transactions can shape collective identities. We attempted to, first, identify some of the mechanisms and processes that led to a collective identity, and, secondly, draw a tentative link between the emerging collective identity and new security practices. Below we identify several themes for future consideration as it pertains to the relationship between the emergence of a transnational identity and security practices.[19]

In this volume transnational identities are generally an elite-centered phenomenon. Most of the studies focused on political elites, intellectuals, state officials, and international bureaucrats and civil servants, who were part of or who had immediate access to state power. These studies, moreover, offered evidence of growing transnational identities among elites. One indirect indicator of such a transnational identity was the self-conscious attempt by policymakers to promote regional ties and identities among their populations. Such efforts, as suggested by the cases of Australia and South America, are driven by liberal-minded political and economic elites who believe that their material and political interests are at stake. By imagining a new geographic space, policymakers are attempting to encourage new forms of interactions that are ultimately grounded in material interests; but, so goes the expectation, the change in interaction patterns will also produce a shift in identity and conceptions of place. To that end, policymakers and public intellectuals have attempted to create a transnational identity through the construction and maintenance of symbols.[20] Acharya, for example, noted that symbols are bound up with the formation of an ASEAN identity. From Western Europe to Australia, from the Persian Gulf to North America, intellectuals have played an epistemic role in the development of myths, norms, symbols, institutions, and practices that are the building blocks of a security community.[21]

426

Not all will welcome this attempt to extend the boundaries of politics and identity. This elite-sponsored transnationalism, specifically, is likely to be resisted by societal groups who perceive that they are being asked to transfer their loyalties and to make political and economic sacrifices. Such resistance, if the European case is representative, can be destabilizing for the security community.[22] Said otherwise, during the early phases of the security community, the adjustment costs shouldered by societal groups are likely to be minimal compared to the adjustment costs of later developments; as the costs rise, so too should the resistance. In general, there is expected variation in attachment to the transnational identity among the members of the region. Although transnational affinities might develop first at the grassroots level and then drag along reluctant policymakers, the history of state-building and the contributions in this volume suggest that transnational identities first emerge and become politically consequential among the political and economic elites.

Many of the articles suggest how narratives provide a useful way to trace the movement toward a transnational region, and how that narrative might be linked to security practices. In chapter 2 we noted how a narrative analysis can include an interpretive dimension as it examines how actors locate themselves within a storyline. By locating themselves within a storyline, actors provide evidence for how they locate themselves and others in a historical space. Some of the articles explicitly employed a narrative analysis to this end. Wæver argued that the individual European states maintain a national narrative that is tied to the European identity, which reflects and helps to reproduce the European security community. Shore observed that after the construction of the myth of the undefended border Canadian and American intellectuals and policymakers began to articulate a "North American" identity, to link Canada and the US in fundamentally new and consequential ways. In other words, there is nothing like a good myth to instill a sense of confidence and forge a shared identity. Russett relates how there is a particular narrative coming from the UN headquarters concerning the path of progress, the anticipated shape of human history, and how states locate themselves in relationship to that wider narrative. Acharya noted how members of ASEAN now articulate an "ASEAN way" and in so doing are identifying with each other in some novel ways.

Finally, conflict prevention practices can become constitutive of

427

transnational identities. ASEAN and Australia, and to some extent the OSCE, suggest that cooperative security has become, or is becoming, part of the states' collective identity. The proposition is partly sustained by the USA and Canada, where shared democratic norms and arbitration practices helped to create a sense of North America "as a political unity, distinct from Europe, with its pacific style of politics."[23] Hurrell identified a distinctive South American diplomatic culture that induces the peaceful resolution of disputes, and suggests that in the last few years South America has been forging a collective identity around liberal economic values and democratic ideals. Indeed, since the 1991 Santiago Declaration, the OAS has begun transforming democracy into a constitutive norm and the basis for regime legitimation.[24] In turn, Acharya suggests that the practice of multilateralism has become one of the most important constitutive elements of ASEAN's collective identity.

Security communities

This volume was concerned more with tracing the development of a security community and less with identifying their practices and mechanisms of reproduction after they came into existence. We want to identify four themes for future research that follow on this latter issue. The first concerns the sanctioned use of power among those who are members of a security community. While states in a security community no longer employ military power as a tool of statecraft within the community, they can be expected to try and influence others in the security community through nondiplomatic means. Gonzalez and Haggard observed that while the USA and Mexico handled their disputes through non-militarized means, the USA does police its border to combat nonmilitarized threats. Such policing, of course, is less visible and prevalent at the US–Canadian border.[25] A security community does not eliminate the exercise of power – just its most coercive form.

A second theme concerns the relationship between the state's identity and that of the security community. To participate and to be counted as a member of a community requires that the state must proclaim itself as a member of the community, and express and uphold those values and norms that constitute it. The community becomes an important source of state identity, and those states within the community frequently express similar historical roots, a common heritage, and shared future. But not all members will be able to maintain a stable identity that is consistent with the narrative of the security community, or be viewed by others of the community as a full fledged member.[26]

When confronting a rapidly changing international and domestic context, many states may find it particularly challenging to maintain a stable identity that is consistent with a larger community. At the international level, a change in systemic patterns can trigger widescale societal debates concerning the collective identity and the state's relationship to the wider community and the purpose of the state's foreign policy. This is best exemplified by the vivid debate over the national identity in the Eastern European states and in Russia since the end of the Cold War. As evidenced by the case of Australia, at the domestic level, changes in territorial boundaries, political economy, and demography, can also enliven the debate over the national identity. "Where is Australia?" Is it part of the West or Asia? Because of Australia's contradictory locations and its frontier status, Higgott and Nossal suggest that Australians are presently involved in the highly contested debate over Australia's identity and geographic location. In general, the state may have a difficult time keeping a particular narrative going, and, accordingly, maintaining an identity that sustains it as part of the security community.

Such matters highlight the ongoing contestation over the national identities and the practices that are associated with it. Sometimes the national identity is consistent with the transnational community, but at other times it might be inconsistent.[27] This presents one way of thinking about the relationship between identity and a stable order: that the domestic and international narratives that shape the state's identity are congruent. In other words, the more congruent are the norms and behavioral expectations generated by domestic and international actors, the more stable will be the system. Wæver similarly argues that by incorporating a different conception of "Europe" into their national identities, European states are threatening the future of the security community in Western Europe. Yet this process also includes the effort by Europeans to ensure the community's endurance through discursive and material means. By adding the security argument to European integration, a particular meaning of Europe helps to determine whether Europe will fragment or "be."

A third consideration is how the boundaries of the community expand. We have already suggested how organizations and learning processes can play a role in this regard. Since the end of the Cold War, the OSCE, NATO, the EU, and other European organizations have been hard at work to expand the Euro-Atlantic community boundaries eastward, by a combination of economic and security incentives and socialization techniques. The issue of expansion and its conditions has also been a defining concern for ASEAN. Acharya chronicles how ASEAN's highly contested decision to extend membership to Myanmar was shaped by strategic considerations alongside a calculation that bringing it into the fold would increase regional stability. As the contemporary cases of NATO and ASEAN suggest, such expansion carries opportunities as well as risks – with the latter including perhaps the very vibrance and definition of the group.

A final issue concerns the distinction between tightly-coupled and loosely-coupled security communities. Distinguishing between loose and tight security communities enabled us to transcend the Deutschian dichotomy of amalgamated and pluralistic security communities and to become more discriminating when describing the latter category. This, of course, expanded the range of relevant cases of pluralistic security communities. But we did not address the key issue concerning the factors that are likely to promote one form over another. That said, the studies suggest that a tight variant is likely to emerge when, in the context of large-scale changes in technology, communication, and the global economy, an external threat arises that encourages states to entertain new forms of governance, coordination, security relations, and even harmonization of national laws.[28]

Our conceptual edifice furthered the goal of considering the array of relationships that exists between the relevant variables, their relationships, and their synchronic quality. As expected, however, the contributions identified more nuanced, complex, and multifaceted ways that were unanticipated by the original framework that was organized around three tiers of precipitating, intervening, and proximate conditions of dependable expectations of peaceful change. The theoretical and empirical efforts, then, combined to suggest various ways that states can become involved in a process that begins with modest proposals for developing their relations, later includes closer identification and mutual trust, and ends with dependable expectations of peaceful change.

Phases revisited

The tiers also had a temporal dimension as they are related to a three-phase model of the development of a security community – nascent, ascendant, and mature. We never intended to identify a single pathway, or, as Stephen Jay Gould once put it, to "shoehorn history."[29] We are well aware that efforts to compartmentalize historical change into phases conjures up teleology at its worst. Rather, we offered them as a heuristic device to further comparison and to aid research. And true to form, nearly all the contributors found that their case deviated in significant ways from the model.[30] But this model served its purpose to the extent that the essays were able to make some explicit observations based on it. We now want to speculate about some of the conditions that might underwrite a shift from one phase to the next and to offer some thoughts on how a change may occur in the underlying normative structure that defines the distinction between the phases and imprints certain facets of interstate security practices.

A defining property of the development of a security community was path dependence, that is, how initial choices persist because individuals and social groups come to identify and benefit from past decisions, and because the cost of change become more significant over time. Path dependence is closely associated with the concept of "punctuated equilibrium," moments that are points of transformation that restructure social relations. Therefore, in contrast to the tendency of social scientists to view history as a data field in which events are independent and discrete, a path dependent view demands a greater sensitivity to the structured and causal relationship that exist between these events that shape the trajectory of historical development.[31]

Such matters rivet our attention on those periods that are particularly instrumental in encouraging or discouraging the development of a security community, that is, moments when the security community moves from one phase to the next.[32] Ann Swidler refers to such moments as "unsettled periods," when normative consensus is particularly important because of the necessity of collective accomplishments and the need to answer "who are we and how should we live."[33] These moments can be seen as "tests:" whether the group is able to rise to the challenge and follow through on past commitments or expressions of obligation and support. In this intimate way, these transitional moments are trust-building or trust-eroding exercises.

Such moments can come in various guises: disputes within the group that might have become militarized but did not because of a collective awareness that disputes were not handled in this manner; or disputes between the group and outside party that provides the members of the group an opportunity to contribute (or not) to the collective cause. Nearly all of the essays link challenges presented by unsettled periods to community-building and maintenance. But even those regions that met the challenge continue to face new tests and crises. Wæver warns that Europe is now passing through such a period and may stumble. South America's current economic difficulties, together with the fact that blame is laid at liberalism's doorstep, augurs poorly for the unsettled period there. In general, adopting a historically contingent approach to the concept of security communities elevates unsettled events that are trust-building and trust-breaking exercises.

The normative structure that exists within each of these different phases can be expected to contain different security dynamics because the group's social fabric will imprint the form of their conflict, competition, and conflict regulation.[34] Several themes emerged in this regard. The first was the tendency to supplement or, in some cases, even to replace the norm of non-intervention with the norm of "mutual accountability" at some point after the nascent phase.[35] States are widely observed to be highly protective of their autonomy and independence in a variety of spheres, perhaps most so over who has the authority to regulate the behavior of their citizens. During the ascendant phase states tend to skirt those issues that potentially increase interdependence in areas that might unleash domestic instability or opposition. One of the interesting characteristics of the development of a security community is that as states moved from one phase to the next they were more willing to become mutually accountable to one another in a host of areas, including how they treat their citizens. There are many reasons why states might become more willing to submit themselves to oversight and reduce their autonomy in once highly sensitive spheres, but one possibility is that the growth of transnational identification and linkages encourages citizens and groups to become mutually accountable on particular issues.

Secondly, the declining security threats from others in the security community produces a shift in the discourse and practice of security. Wæver suggests that security communities develop *because* traditional military security issues become "desecuritized, that is, "a progressive marginalization of mutual security concerns in favor of other issues."

Once formed, however, security communities may go through a process that he calls "resecuritization"; in the case of Western Europe, resecuritization has been largely due to the fact that Europeans are now identifying disintegration as the gravest threat to their security. Resecuritization processes in Europe highlight that while mature security communities do not expect war they still experience non-military security dilemmas. This is a critical observation for, as Wæver further argues, such non-military security dynamics are indicators of the stability of the relationship, are likely sources of the security community's (dis)integration, and identify how security is being conceptualized.[36] Relatedly, a movement toward forms of "cooperative security" may also indicate that states are entering a higher phase of a security community. For example, the chapters on the OSCE and ASEAN regions demonstrate how a transition from classic balance of power politics to cooperative security reflects structural changes that are consistent with an ascendant phase of security community.

A significant way that a change in the practice of security will be felt is with the elimination of traditional security dilemmas. Once traditional security threats have been eliminated, what security dilemmas remain are likely to derive from economic or environmental sources of insecurity. This is so because: once war between states becomes unimaginable, the system is "inoculated" against the psychological anxieties that are characteristic of security dilemmas; these "new" security issues are less amendable to military solutions. Security dynamics, particularly the pernicious variety that have captured the imagination of international relations scholars, are likely to undergo significant change as there is a change in the security environment in which states dwell.

Thirdly, the declining salience of external threats is likely to affect the role of the military in security affairs. This does not mean that militaries are unnecessary or quaint and archaic; rather, it suggests that the military is likely to take on new roles. In the contemporary period, for instance, the military has become more actively involved in channeling military activities to community-building measures and peacekeeping operations. And when external threats have receded from view, the military becomes more active in "out-of-theatre" operations and involved in quelling internal security threats that are increasingly identified as sources of international disorder. Furthermore, the development of a security community can encourage a more stable and successful civil–military relationship to the extent

433

that the military plays an "apolitical" role. Hurrell claims that in South America regional integration has deprived a highly nationalistic military of the traditional mobilizing issues, thus preventing a nationalist military from promoting military adventures in the region. Relatedly, the ability of the East European states to become members of the European security community is dependent on various civil–military reforms that suggest an apolitical profile.

Fourthly, as the security community develops from one phase to the next the source of compliance with the norms of the group will shift from material to ideational factors. For instance, if during the early phase of a security community there are confidence-building and verification measures designed to quell any fear of war or being placed in the sucker position, over time such measures should become less important as policymakers cease to consider waging war against other members of the community because such actions would potentially threaten their own identity and self-understanding. In general, we expect that norm compliance is less dependent on overt sanctions, enforcement mechanisms, and the like with the move from one phase to the next.

In sum, we included the phases in this volume's methodological quest as an effort to construct indicators that reflected not only the accomplishment of a security community but also its path and development. These indicators attempted to tap into the phase of development as defined by the extent of a transnational region and the semblance of dependable expectations of peaceful change. There are several problems with such linear thinking, including the fact that dependable expectations of peaceful change may emerge for reasons other than the growth of a transnational region. This was a principal reason why nearly all the contributors identified ways in which their pathway differed from our heuristic model, and, accordingly, that the indicators gave either a false positive or a false negative. The insufficiency of the indicators does not jettison their utility per se but rather questions their validity.

Moreover, the finding that security communities evolve toward maturity in distinct ways, and exhibit variation of indicators relevant at each phase of development, is consistent with the notion that security communities are socially constructed. Because the contextual socio-cognitive and material conditions that give birth to security communities vary from case to case, security communities will exhibit different path dependence "tracks," and therefore researchers are unlikely to identify a "master variable." This places a premium on tracing historically the material and cognitive conditions that shape the evolution and institutionalization of the security community.

Security as social construction: security communities and the study of international security

Are security communities a fashionable feature of the post-Cold War era, likely to disappear as have had all great idealist moments after the end of wars? Each geopolitical shift of this century has produced a comparable intellectual shift; with each shift in the distribution of power has seemingly come a shift in the balance between "idealism" and "realism." Is the study of security communities likely to succumb to the inevitable darkening of the security horizon? It should be obvious by now that we answer in the negative. To this end we want to close with some final thoughts on the question of security communities in theory and practice.

To begin, we hardly envision that the world is heading toward a security community "moment." There is no inevitable march of security communities. We have pointed to developments in global politics that make security communities less of an oddity and perhaps more expected, but we have also identified the vagaries that must conjoin, and sometimes the occasional historical accident, that propels their development. We are not sanguine about the possibility that more security communities will dot the global landscape, would not react in complete disbelief if some of those that are currently in place crumbled suddenly (though we would invite others to imagine with us the unlikely conditions under which that might happen). These are not qualifiers but rather appraisals from seasoned appreciations for how rare are security communities in practice and how varied are the forms of political association and the organization of security.

But in order to contemplate the very existence of security communities, scholars of international politics must take two moves. The first is that international relations theorists must be willing to recognize that the "problem of order" is defined not by anarchy and controlled by force alone. Sociologists have long recognized that the question of order is never solved but rather is accomplished for various lengths of time by a combination of force, exchange produced by self-interested actors, and normative integration. Different political orders entertain different weights of these three dimensions, but few political orders have ever been sustained on one pillar alone. This study hopefully contributes to the growing understanding that different groups of actors can stabilize normative expectations and can create a stable peace according to different dynamics. Nearly all of the studies began with the assumption of anarchy and force as principal mechanisms in the production of security, shifted toward a recognition that patterned exchanges produce new and stabilized relationships, and then contemplated how something akin to normative integration produced a parallel shift in the production of and prospect for a stable peace. There is variation over regions and history regarding how a stable peace is produced, but the only way to understand how states get there is to move away from the materialism and rationalism that currently defines much of international relations theory.

The problem of order, of course, is directly related to governance structures. The post-Cold War research agenda of globalization, transnationalism, regionalism, and multilateralism invites us to rethink not simply that state sovereignty is under threat or that states must establish new international organizations to protect their power but rather that there are new forms of international governance that cannot be easily packaged with the categories that have defined the discipline over the last several decades. Sometimes these forms of state and transnational associations might be contemplated as an instance of community, perhaps more often not. But this volume will have accomplished one of its principal goals if it convinces other scholars of international relations that it is worth thinking the unthinkable – the possibility of international community.

The second move is a recognition that the field of international relations and the study of international security have been unnecessarily encumbered by the stale, dichotomous, categories of idealism versus realism. Realism, the language of statecraft, high politics, and "true" strategic thinking, dominates the language of security politics and demands that we conceptualize managed security by working within the limits of some ontologically privileged anarchy and thus imagining security as accomplished only through alliances, balances of power, hegemonies and the like. This is how the study of international security has proceeded through the Cold War, and those who continue to inhabit its halls insist that the end of the Cold

War has not changed the structure of interstate politics or the means by which states secure their existence. In contrast to this world of realism is that of idealism. Long discredited because of its supposed errors and excesses during the interwar period and blamed for the intellectual climate that permitted the onset of World War II, few international relations scholars dared labelled themselves idealists and fewer still were welcomed by those who studied security politics.

Realism and idealism, however, share similar roots, and, not surprisingly, share more traits than some of their interpreters have been willing to recognize. Many of the classic realist statements had "idealist" currents and recognized that different communities operated according to different principles and constructed alternative security orders. Some of the classic idealist statements were quite aware of the realities of power politics but were willing to entertain that under certain conditions states might discover a role for international organizations in helping them overcome their worst fears. Neither idealists nor realists sought to divide the world into rarified material and social elements but rather exhibited a willingness to examine how their combination worked themselves out in theory and practice.

This volume demonstrates that idealism – the recognition that social life is *social* – and realism – the acceptance that states are concerned with the production of security – need not be artificially divided but rather can be fused in some interesting and provocative ways as political communities fuse, merge, and divide. Our belief is that constructivism enables scholars to overcome the realist-idealist divide and to contemplate the relationship between structures, defined in material and normative terms, the practices that are made possible and imaginable by those structures, the security orders that are rendered reachable within that field, and how those security orders regulate or extinguish the use of force.

More to the point, we hope that this volume encourages students of global politics to consider how constructivism can inform some of the most topical and important debates that currently exist in international politics. Prior to the end of the Cold War came a series of challenges that invited a reimagining of global space and asked that we recognize that global politics – like all human endeavors – are socially constructed. The end of the Cold War provided greater opportunities for those working within the emerging tradition, frequently labelled as constructivism, to interrogate security politics and practices. It is worth reiterating that constructivism shares with Karl Deutsch a recognition that social communication, identity, and "half-baked" integration between peoples and states helps us to understand whether material power capabilities are threatening or not. In other words, the sources of state insecurity are not limited to anarchy and the distribution of power but also extend to the distribution of knowledge. The notion that security and insecurity are social constructs means that the development of security communities has states "co-binding"[37] not only their military capabilities but also their identities and their destiny.

To understand security requires the fundamental recognition that policymakers have the ability to act upon the world with new knowledge and new understandings about how to organize security. These new understandings can emerge through coercion or dialogue, sometimes occurring at the same moment. Security communities, then, do not portray an ideal world of international security. On the contrary, they show that international security changes with time, and that such changes are a result of mixtures of anarchy and hierarchy, and coercion and communication. In the last instance, security communities are not part of a speculative and elusive dream but rather are as imaginable as the wars they are designed to overcome.

Notes

1 See Karl Deutsch, ed., "Backgrounds for Community: Case Studies in Large-Scale Political Unification," mimeo, 1963.
2 Although a range of cooperative activities may trigger the development of trust, cooperation also is a by-product of trust. Those who cooperate because of trust, rather than merely to build it or in its absence, are able to overcome the uncertainty of the situation and therefore engage in diffuse reciprocity and exhibit some degree of mutual obligations.
3 As quoted in Sidney Tarrow, "Mentalities, Political Cultures, and Collective Action Frames," in Aldon D. Morris and Carol Mueller, eds., *Frontiers in Social Movement Theory* (New Haven: Yale University Press, 1992), p. 185.
4 Ibid., p. 186.
5 "States and Nationalism in Europe, 1492–1992," *Theory and Society* 23 (1995), pp. 131–146.
6 Georg Simmel, "Exchange," in his *On Individuality and Social Forms*, ed. Donald Levine (Chicago: University of Chicago Press, 1971), p. 51.
7 Judith E. Innis, *Knowledge and Public Policy*, 2nd edn (New Brunswick: Transaction Publishers, 1990), p. 34.
8 John G. Ruggie, "Territoriality and Beyond: Problematizing Modernity in

International Relations," *International Organization* 47 (Winter 1993), pp. 139–174; Emanuel Adler, "Cognitive Evolution," in Emanuel Adler and Beverly Crawford, eds., *Progress in Postwar International Relations* (New York: Columbia University Press, 1991), pp. 43–88.

9 It is important to note the case of the early United States where its architects were self-consciously attempting to fashion an political organization that was somewhere between anarchy and hierarchy. See Daniel Deudney, "The Philadelphian System: Sovereignty, Arms Control and Balance of Power in the American States-Union, ca. 1787–1861," *International Organization* 49 (Spring 1995), pp. 191– 228.

10 Also see Inis Claude, "Collective Legitimization as a Political Function of the United Nations," *International Organization* 20 (Summer 1966), p. 373.

11 See Walter Dimaggio and Paul Powell, eds., *The New Institutionalism in Organizational Analysis* (Chicago: University of Chicago Press, 1991); W. Richard Scott, *Institutions and Organizations* (Thousand Oaks: Sage Press, 1995); and W. Richard Scott and Soren Christensen, eds., *The Institutional Construction of Organizations: International and Longitudinal Studies* (Thousand Oaks: Sage Publications, 1995).

12 See Adler in this volume.

13 Ibid.

14 See James Rosenau, "Organizational Proliferation in a Changing World," in Commission on Global Governance, *Issues in Global Governance* (Boston: Kluwer Law International, 1995), pp. 371–405, for a historical and numerical survey of the explosion of international organizations in global politics over the last century.

15 Parenthetically, international organizations are not the only non-state actors that are involved in building of trust, spreading new norms, instilling new categories of action, or offering to monitor prior agreements. NGOs and transnational movements have functioned to this end and thus can play an important role in the development of security communities. This is particularly so in the realm of promoting specific norms and monitoring their compliance. In the ASEAN case, for example, various private strategic centers promoted the development of ASEAN and its security forum; in the European case there have emerged a proliferation of NGOs and transnational organizations that have as their sole function the promotion and monitoring of certain values that they take to be constitutive of the community. Similarly, diplomatic, business, and intellectual elites endowed with common diplomatic, commercial, and intellectual cultures have been at the forefront of imagining new possibilities and creating new organizational forms to that end. We thank Keith Krause for this point. See John Boli and George Thomas, "The World Polity in Formation: A Century of International Non-Governmental Organization," *American Sociological Review* 62, 2 (March, 1997), pp. 171–190.

16 Deutsch, *Political Community*, p. 30.

17 See Michael Williams, "Hobbes and International Relations: A Reconsideration," *International Organization* 50 (Spring, 1996), pp. 213–237.

18 See, for instance, Michel Foucault, *Power/Knowledge: Selected Interviews and Other Writings, 1972–1977*, ed. Colin Gordon (New York: Pantheon, 1980).

19 Also see the similar concept of interactive capacity, Barry Buzan, "From International System to International Society: Structural Realism and Regime Theory meet the English School," *International Organization* 47 (Summer, 1993), pp. 327–352.

20 Anthony P. Cohen, *The Symbolic Construction of Community* (New York: Tavistock, 1985); Harold Lasswell, "Future Systems of Identity in the World Community," in C. Black and R. Falk, eds., *The Future of the International Legal Order*, vol. 4 (Princeton: Princeton University Press, 1972), p. 6; and S. N. Eisenstadt and Bernhard Giesen, "The Construction of Collective Identity," *Archives European Sociologie* 36 (1995), pp. 72–102.

21 Iver Neumann, "A Region-Building Approach to Northern Europe," *Review of International Studies* 20 (1994), pp. 53–74.

22 Ole Wæver, "Securitization and Desecuritization," in Ronnie D. Lipschutz, ed., *On Security* (New York: Columbia University Press, 1995). Oskar Niedermayer records that there has been a steady increase in trust among the members of the European Union alongside significant variation in terms of which states are viewed as most and least trustworthy. "Trust and Sense of Community," in Oskar Niedermayer and Richard Sinnott, eds., *Public Opinion and International Governance* (New York: Oxford University Press, 1995).

23 Shore in this volume.

24 Also see the collection of essays in Tom Farer, ed., *Beyond Sovereignty: Collectively Defending Democracy in the Americas* (Baltimore: Johns Hopkins University Press, 1996).

25 Thomas Risse-Kappen's study of the Western alliance provides a compelling argument for how the deployment of power is channeled into methods short of war. *Cooperation Among Democracies: The European Influence on U.S. Foreign Policy* (Princeton: Princeton University Press, 1995).

26 See Michael Barnett, "Identity and Alliances in the Middle-East," in Peter Katzenstein, ed., *The Culture of National Security: Norms and Identity in World Politics* (New York: Columbia University Press, 1996), pp. 400–447.

27 Buzan's concept of concentric circles of commitment similarly claims that some states are better able and more willing to adhere to the norms of the community than are others because of their "proximity" to certain core identities. Barry Buzan, "From International System," p. 145.

28 Alan S. Milward, with George Brennan and Federico Romero, *The European Rescue of the Nation-State* (Berkeley: University of California Press, 1992).

29 Stephen Jay Gould, *Wonderful Life: The Burgess Shale and the Nature of History* (New York: W. W. Norton, 1989).

30 There are obvious comparisons to the state formation literature. The early foundations of this literature was teleological and envisioned a set of stages toward an endpoint. Recent formulations, however, have been more interested in establishing an understanding of the variety of different paths and different types of states that exist across time and space. See Charles Tilly, "Entanglements of European Cities and States," in Charles Tilly and Wi. Blackmans, eds., *Cities and the Rise of States in Europe: AD 1000 to 1800* (Boulder, CO: Westview Press, 1994), pp. 1–27.

31 See William Sewell, "Three Temporalities: Toward an Eventful Sociology," in Terrence McDonald, ed., *The Historic Turn in the Human Sciences* (Ann Arbor: University of Michigan Press, 1996), pp. 245–81; Ronald Aminzade, "Historical Sociology and Time," *Sociological Methods and Research* 20 (May, 1992), pp. 456–80; and Andrew Abbott, "Sequences of Social Events: Concepts and Methods for the Analysis of Order in Social Processes," *Historical Methods* 16, 4 (Fall, 1983), pp. 129–146.

32 Alexander L. George, "Case Studies and Theory Development: The Method of Structured, Focused Comparison," in Paul Gordon Lauren, ed., *Diplomacy: New Approaches in History, Theory, and Policy* (New York: Free Press, 1979).

33 "Culture in Action: Symbols in Strategies," *American Sociological Review* 51, 2 (1986), pp. 273–286.

34 For general sociological and anthropological statements on this view, see, respectively, Georg Simmel, *Conflict and the Web of Group Affiliations* (New York: Free Press, 1964), ch. 2; and Marc Howard Ross, *The Culture of Conflict* (New Haven: Yale University Press, 1993). These claims are generally accepted in the English School but less accepted in the American school. See, for instance, Richard Little, "Neorealism and English School: A Methodological, Ontological, and Theoretical Assessment," *European Journal of International Relations* 1, 1 (1995), pp. 9–34; and Chris Brown, "International Theory and International Society: The Viability of the Middle Way?" *Review of International Studies* 21, 2 (April, 1995), pp. 183–196.

35 The normative concept of "mutual accountability" acquired formal recognition in the context of the OSCE. See Adler in this volume.

36 Wæver in this volume.

37 Deudney, "The Philadelphian System."

Index

CAMBRIDGE STUDIES IN INTERNATIONAL RELATIONS